SOCIAL INTERACTION AND PERSONAL RELATIONSHIPS

EDITED BY DOROTHY MIELL AND RUDI DALLOS

SOCIAL INTERACTION AND PERSONAL RELATIONSHIPS

EDITED BY DOROTHY MIELL AND RUDI DALLOS

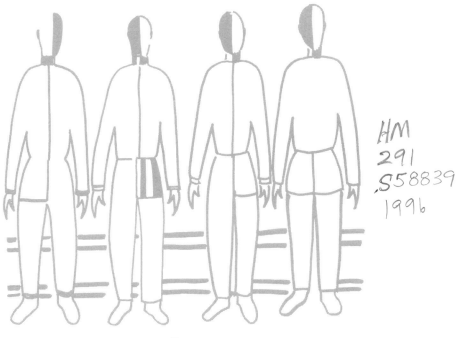

SAGE Publications
London • Thousand Oaks • New Delhi
In association with

The Open University

Cover illustration: Kasimir Malevich, *Sportsmen*, *c*. 1928–32, oil on canvas, 142×164 cm., State Russian Museum, St Petersburg.

The Open University, Walton Hall, Milton Keynes MK7 6AA

© The Open University 1996

First published in 1996

SAGE Publications Ltd
6 Bonhill Street
London EC2A 4PU

SAGE Publications Inc
2455 Teller Road
Thousand Oaks
California 91320

Sage Publications India Pvt Ltd
32, M-Block Market
Greater Kailash - I
New Delhi 110 048

British Library Cataloguing in Publication data

A catalogue record for this book is available from the British Library

ISBN 0 7619 5035 4

ISBN 0 7619 5036 2 (pbk)

Library of Congress catalog record available

Edited, designed and typeset by the Open University.

Printed in Great Britain by Butler and Tanner Ltd, Frome.

This text forms part of an Open University course D317 *Social Psychology: Personal Lives, Social Worlds*. Details of this and other Open University courses can be obtained from the Central Enquiry Service, PO Box 200, The Open University, Milton Keynes MK7 6YZ. For availability of other course components, contact Open University Educational Enterprises Ltd, 12 Cofferidge Close, Stony Stratford, Milton Keynes MK11 1BY.

Contents

Social Psychology: Personal Lives, Social Worlds Course Team

Open University Staff

Dr Dorothy Miell (Course Team Chair, Senior Lecturer in Psychology)

Penny Bennett (Editor, Social Sciences)

Pam Berry (Compositor)

David Calderwood (Project Control)

Lene Connolly (Print Buying Controller)

Dr Troy Cooper (Staff Tutor)

Dr Rose Croghan (Research Fellow in Psychology)

Sarah Crompton (Graphic Designer)

Dr Rudi Dallos (Staff Tutor)

Jonathan Davies (Graphic Design Co-ordinator)

Margaret Dickins (Print Buying Co-ordinator)

Jane Elliott (Producer, BBC)

Janis Gilbert (Graphic Artist)

Dr Sue Gregory (Senior Lecturer in Psychology)

Jonathan Hunt (Book Trade Department)

Tom Hunter (Editor, Social Sciences)

Carole Kershaw (Course Secretary)

Vic Lockwood (Senior Producer, BBC)

Dr Janet Maybin (Lecturer, School of Education)

Jeannette Murphy (Senior Lecturer in Health Informatics, University College London Medical School, co-opted on to team during course production)

Lynda Preston (Psychology Secretary)

Dr Roger Sapsford (Senior Lecturer in Research Methods)

Varrie Scott (Course Manager)

Brenda Smith (Staff Tutor)

Paul Smith (Media Librarian)

Richard Stevens (Senior Lecturer in Psychology)

Dr Kerry Thomas (Senior Lecturer in Psychology)

Dr Frederick Toates (Senior Lecturer in Biology)

Pat Vasiliou (Psychology Discipline Secretary)

Dr Diane Watson (Staff Tutor)

Dr Margaret Wetherell (Senior Lecturer in Psychology)

Kathy Wilson (Production Assistant, BBC)

Chris Wooldridge (Editor, Social Sciences)

External authors and tutor consultants

Dr Michael Argyle (Emeritus Reader in Social Psychology, University of Oxford)

Hedy Brown (Retired, Senior Lecturer in Social Psychology, Open University)

Dr David Devalle (OU Social Psychology Tutor)

Professor Robert Hinde (Retired, St John's College, Cambridge)

Dr Mansur Lalljee (University Lecturer in Social Psychology and Fellow of Jesus College), University of Oxford

Jackie Malone (OU Social Psychology Tutor)

Dr Patrick McGhee (Head of Psychology and School Director Teaching and Learning, University of Derby, OU Tutor Consultant)

Helen Morgan (Psychotherapist and Consultant)

Dr Jonathan Potter (Reader in Discourse Analysis, Loughborough University)

Dr Alan Radley (Reader in Health and Social Relations, Loughborough University)

Dr Arthur Still (Part-time Senior Lecturer in Psychology, University of Durham, OU Social Psychology Tutor)

Dr Arlene Vetere (Lecturer in Family Psychology, Reading University)

External assessors

Professor Jerome Bruner (Research Professor of Psychology, New York University, Senior Research Fellow in Law, School of Law, New York University)

Professor Michael Billig (Professor of Social Sciences, Loughborough University)

Professor Steve Duck (Daniel and Amy Starch Distinguished Research Professor of Interpersonal Communication, and Adjunct Professor of Psychology, University of Iowa)

Professor Kenneth J. Gergen (Mustin Professor of Psychology, Swarthmore College, Pennsylvania)

Foreword

Studying social psychology and studying history are akin in one particularly interesting way. For either of them to matter much in your own life, you must end up making what you have learned your own. And the only way to do that is to explore different ways of framing or constructing the subject-matter at hand until you have found *your* way of making sense of it. For just as there is no *the* history, say, of the French Revolution, there is no *the* social psychology of the family. Both 'subjects' gain their meanings through the perspective one brings to bear on them. The French Revolution is a struggle for the rights of man, and it is a chapter in the story of mob tyranny. One studies it differently, even chooses one's facts differently, depending upon which of the two perspectives one has chosen as a focus. And so too the social psychology of the family – whether one wishes to look at family life in terms of 'systems theory', or in terms of the working out of the psychoanalytic Oedipus theme, or from the point of view of the phenomenologies of family members and how they are negotiated in dinner-table conversations.

This Open University social psychology course is a radical departure in teaching social psychology. Rather than insisting that there is a 'right and only' way to look at phenomena social psychologically – *the* social psychology of this or that – it takes the truth of perspective as its starting point. Its aim is to present a variety of perspectives on the standard 'topics' of social psychology, not only to give them depth but also to equip the student with the wherewithal for creating her or his *own* perspective. But it does this in such a way as to recognize not only the relativity of social knowledge, but also to honour the canons of good social science. For the relativity of perspective does not mean that 'anything goes'. Rather, it means that whatever perspective one brings to bear carries with it requirements of method. Has one gained sufficient information on the matter at hand, protected oneself against facile presuppositions, looked with sufficient care at the antecedents of the phenomenon one is studying, and so on? The course attempts to give as clear a view as possible of what constitutes good enquiry as conducted from the vantage-points of several crucial perspectives.

After studying the volumes in this series, the student should be prepared to evaluate different perspectives in social psychology and, as noted, to come up with one of his or her own, one that meets the standards of sound social science. In this sense, these books deliberately merge the conventional categories of teaching and research. The authors have succeeded in resisting the usual 'teacherly' approach of giving standard reviews of the existing literature on some narrow topics, and instead have provided abundant opportunities for the student to try his or her hand at creating original syntheses of several related topics that bear on each other. In doing so, they use the tools of research as a means of teaching in a most creative way.

There is one further feature of the series that needs special mention. Its emphasis upon the place of perspective in the legitimizing of 'facts' and the construction of theories inevitably leads to questions about the philosophy of knowledge – to puzzling issues in epistemology. Rather than simply tabling these and leaving them for some other course to discuss, this course tackles them head on. So in a way, it is a course not only about social psychology, but also, if I may use an odd term, about social epistemology. At times, then, the student will find himself or herself in a dialogue whose other members are not only psychologists and sociologists, but also philosophers and even literary theorists (for in a very deep sense, the 'data' of social psychology are texts of what people said about what they thought or felt, narrative texts at that).

The series crosses many disciplinary boundaries that are often regarded as either taboo or as too forbidding for students to cross. For social psychology is a field of study that grew out of two traditions that have often been regarded as antithetical – even at war with each other. One tradition is primarily societal or cultural, and looks at social interaction from the point of view of the roles and statuses that people occupy within a social structure, specifying the obligations and rights that activate and constrain those who fill these roles and statuses. This is 'sociological' social psychology – and a good part of social psychology as a disciplinary study is situated in sociology departments of universities. The other tradition is psychological, its emphasis squarely on the individual – his or her attitudes, values, reactions, and the like. And as psychological social psychology, this side of the discipline takes its methods from the different approaches that psychology has adopted over the century since its founding. It may emphasize a more strictly experimental approach, a more humanistic one, or one based on what has come to be called 'social constructionism' that sees the data and theories of psychology as situated in or deriving from the discourse of human beings in interaction. The volumes try to make a place for all of these approaches, treating them not as antagonistic to each other, but as complementary.

In tackling social psychology in so multifaceted a way, these books manage something that is rarely tried in the teaching of this subject. They bridge two traditions that rarely meet in the theatre of university instruction – a principally North American 'scientific' tradition based on the positivist ideal of objectivity, and a European tradition that is much more strongly interpretivist in spirit. And they manage to make as good a case as possible for both of them. Some critics of the books will doubtless say, I'm sure, that they give too much credence to one side, some to the other. And this is as it should be.

It is impossible to teach an honest course in social psychology in our times without taking into account the diversity of modern society. There is no such thing as a standard family or a standard work-place about which to make generalizations – whether they be statistical generalizations or interpretative ones. There are indeed families in Britain, for example, that meet the traditional criterion of being 'standard'. They are White, Anglo-Saxon, Protestant, Middle-class. They may fare better on the job market, but they are hardly 'standard' save in some possibly hegemonic sense. What holds for them does not hold for Jamaican families in Spitalfields, for immigrant Pakistani families in Bradford whose children are struggling to find an identity, and so on. So, again almost inevitably, social psychology needs to be sensitive not so much to 'society in general' but to the changing social patterns of our times. And I believe that this series achieves such sensitivity.

During the long preparation of these volumes, I have served in the role of what is called, in Open University terminology, the Course Assessor.

The Course Assessor quickly becomes a partner in dialogue with the course team. I have been such a partner 'from a distance' – geographically if not psychologically. We have been engaged for more than a year in a constant and busy exchange of chapter drafts, memoranda, and conversation – me in New York or in my writing hideaway in West County Cork, they in Milton Keynes. We have used every imaginable form of telecommunication – post, fax, e-mail, telephone. I have found it enormously rewarding, both psychologically and intellectually. For this series has been an adventure for those of us involved in constructing it, not only a scholarly one but, indeed, a moral one. For this is a series designed to teach people not just *about* social psychology, but how to *think* social psychology. And as with any such undertaking, it forced all of us to think hard about what a social psychologist *ought* to be. So I must close this foreword by thanking my friends at the Open University for what I can only describe as a 'consciousness raising trip'. And I rather suspect that the readers of this series will do the same when they're done with it.

Jerome Bruner, New York University

Preface

Social Interaction and Personal Relationships is one of three books which form the core of the Open University course D317 *Social Psychology: Personal Lives, Social Worlds*. The others are *Understanding the Self* (edited by Richard Stevens) and *Identity, Groups and Social Issues* (edited by M. Wetherell). Students of the Open University course receive supplementary material, including an opening 'trigger unit' which uses discussion of health and disease to introduce the topics with which the course will be concerned. There is also a book on philosophical and methodological issues in social psychology, a set of projects, four television and eight radio programmes, and three audiocassettes which feature debates around key issues. The three volumes published in this series have been designed to be read independently of this supplementary material.

We recognize that social psychology comes in many forms. Our own particular approach has been developed from the previous social psychology courses which we have offered, and as a result of intensive discussions among members of the course team. We have adopted what might be called a multiple-perspective approach, in that we have included a number of different perspectives on social psychology from social constructionism to experimental social psychology and from psychodynamics to experiential psychology. We believe the essential subject-matter of social psychology to be the meanings through which each of us makes sense of the social world and acts within it. Such meanings are personal and social constructions which need to be understood in the context of both individuals and the interactions and social practices in which they engage. Likewise, any way of investigating or theorizing in social psychology is a construction and needs to be recognized as such. Thus a feature of the course is the explicit attempt to comment on the different perspectives and to discuss the kinds of understanding they represent and the implications of these.

While we have not set out to be fully representative, the three volumes in this series contain a wide range of material, including much of the seminal research and theorizing in social psychology; however, this has been reworked in the context of the overall philosophy of the course. We hope the reader/student will take from the books a broad understanding of the different forms that social psychology takes and develop the ability to work in a structured and coherent way with a diversity of ideas and approaches; also that they will stimulate both critical thinking and awareness of some of the wider issues which arise out of studying social psychology. What kind of knowledge, for example, is possible and appropriate in this area? At the same time, each of the books is intended to heighten the reader's capacity for reflection on his or her own life in the light of the concepts and theories presented. We want you to be able to relate the ideas here to your own experience and through this to understand more clearly the social behaviour of yourself and others. Thus, the many activities provided are oriented towards both pedagogic and personal development.

The study of relationships occupied a relatively minor part in the evolving drama of social psychology until the 1980s when the situation began to change radically. This book attempts to capture the diversity, depth and vibrancy of this rapidly expanding area of social psychology. Like many other developments in psychology the impetus comes from theoretically based research as well as from clinical practice. Though initially separate activities these two areas are developing interesting integrations which this book seeks to embrace.

The book considers critically contributions to the study of relationships from a range of different sources – academic social psychology, sociology, and communication, and also clinical practice. In doing so, an exposition is offered of the relative contribution of different theoretical orientations and methodologies. The book also integrates qualitative and quantitative approaches. It does so by continually moving between and reflecting on the different perspectives offered from the 'outside' – observable, objective aspects of relationships and interactions (such as non-verbal behaviour) and from the 'inside' – the personal, mutually constructed meanings that participants create and which evolve and change over time. Ample use is made of examples; from clinical case study material and personal accounts. Personal position papers by influential authors and researchers make up the concluding section of the book, in which each puts forward their reasons for espousing a particular approach to the study of interactions and relationships.

We have found the stimulating and wide ranging contributions and suggestions of the academic members of the course team invaluable in developing this book, and are particularly grateful for the patient involvement of the authors and assessors from outside the Open University who threw themselves into the intensive course team environment in a very creative partnership. We are also grateful for the assured support throughout production of Varrie Scott as Course Manager and Tom Hunter as editor, and the highly effective secretarial team of Carole Kershaw, Lynda Preston and Pat Vasiliou.

Dorothy Miell and Rudi Dallos
for the Course Team

CHAPTER 1
INTRODUCTION – EXPLORING INTERACTIONS AND RELATIONSHIPS

by Dorothy Miell and Rudi Dallos

Contents

1 Studying interactions and relationships

Arguably, interactions and relationships are central to most people's everyday lives. At the simplest level we interact with people when we bump into a neighbour, visit the bank, or go shopping – even these basic activities involve some interaction with others which can provide interest, stimulation or, at times, some difficulties. Most of us are also engaged in a range of important relationships; with colleagues at work, members of our family, our children's teachers, our friends and partners. These interactions and relationships are important not only for our physical survival but also for our emotional well-being. There is evidence to suggest that people who are excessively isolated and lonely may be more prone to negative feelings, such as sadness and depression, and may also deteriorate physically and intellectually.

Without physical interaction, we can still interact with others through letters or even electronic mail and, in a different way, we can engage with unknown readers, viewers or listeners through published writing or the mass media. We also spend a considerable amount of our time thinking about our own relationships, mulling over previous interactions – what was said (or left unsaid), how one of us behaved. We are also much concerned with thinking (and talking) about the state and development of relationships between other people we know.

The central importance of relationships in our lives is also reflected in the extent to which they form the subject matter of so much of the world's art and literature. What is fascinating is how the stories, plays and poetry focusing on relationships have struck chords with people from diverse cultures and, in many cases, from across the centuries. More recently, there has also been the phenomenon of the immense popularity of the television 'soaps' or serials, which display people struggling with ordinary relationship problems and dilemmas, and successfully invite millions of people to identify with them each week.

Given the centrality of interactions and relationships in people's lives, we can ask why social psychology has until relatively recently paid so little direct attention to them. Since the early 1980s, a burgeoning interdisciplinary research effort has developed which focuses on personal relationships, but for many years studies were fragmented into explorations of behaviours which comprise some aspect of relationships, such as initial attraction, altruism, interpersonal aggression or social skills. It was not that such research simply studied individuals in isolation, but it did not have the relationship itself as its focus. Though resulting in many findings of some considerable interest (some of which will be discussed later in the book), this type of research has been criticized for largely ignoring three central aspects of relationships:

1   *Joint Construction.* From the earliest interactions between infants and their carers to relationships between adults, joint or shared activity is evident. A large part of our lives is about doing things with others, playing games which have shared rules, working together on shared goals, engaging in mutually pleasurable activities with others, and so on. All these involve the development of joint activities wherein people have constructed shared or mutual patterns of actions, shared understandings and feelings. Embracing these patterns of joint activity is a sense of shared identity, an 'us' which contains ideas about how the participants view the relationships that they have built – 'we get on well', 'we like a laugh', and so on. These joint constructions emerge from the continual flow of daily interactions, conversations, home or work routines, and patterns of contact with other people.

2   *Time and development.* Many of our interactions and relationships, such as those with friends, other family members and work mates, extend over time. Relationships evolve, they develop and change over time, sometimes appearing to progress, at others to deteriorate or remain stable. Previously, in much of the research, the tendency had been to focus on isolated slices of relationships such as initial meetings, rather than on the more typical continuing everyday relationship experiences. Studies of such interactions (predominantly between strangers in laboratory experimental situations) tell us very little about important long-term relationships.

3   *The diverse functions of relationships.* Varieties of relationships, for example a friendship as opposed to an intimate sexual relationship or a parent-child relationship, are fundamentally different, and meet quite different needs (Weiss, 1974). Various types of relationships are therefore not just interchangeable, since the overall *amount* of social contact is less important than the *nature* and *quality* of that contact. As a result, in-depth exploration of what different types of relationships mean to people, what they gain from them, what expectations are embedded in them and so on suggests that people experience them as fundamentally different.

In short, much of the research has neglected the developmental, evolving and ecological context of relationships. Much of it was also conducted in laboratory situations and was rather contrived, for example employing college students as subjects to make judgements of attractiveness from photographs of people unknown to them. Social psychologists and clinicians attempting to deal with people's problems and difficulties started to realize that in fact we knew very little about how people conduct their diverse, complex and intricate webs of interactions: the real, everyday relationships. A clinician and one of the founders of the family therapy movement, Jay Haley, stated this gap in our knowledge forcefully, '...we know less about the courtship behaviour of American adolescents than we do about ... the courtship behaviour of the graylag goose' (Haley, 1981, p. 46).

In this volume we will be attempting to cover some of the developments in the now burgeoning field of the study of human relationships. A good deal of interdisciplinary research has emerged which does attempt to look in detail at the networks of everyday relationships, the functions they serve, the complex processes of communication involved in interaction, at development and change over time, and at the underlying emotional dynamics. This range is reflected in the material discussed later in this volume, as are the variety of research techniques which have evolved away from their original focus on the laboratory towards exploring relationships and their meanings in natural settings.

This growth of interest in studying relationships within the disciplines of social psychology, communications, sociology and family studies has accompanied developments in the fields of marital and family therapy. Clinicians working in these areas have been observing, assessing and treating couples and families involved in long-term relationships since before the 1950s. A rich source of knowledge and theory about interactions and relationships has as a result been generated within these therapeutic traditions. Since therapy normally continues over some considerable time, it is possible to note changes in the internal dynamics, beliefs and emotions of family members and other relationships. The advent of video recording facilities and their use in therapy has also meant that the interactional processes and dynamics can be captured and systematically analysed. Attempts at facilitating therapeutic change have also produced further information about relationships which has prompted the development of interactional models and stimulated further specific research. Curiosity was also activated about why problems develop and whether it is useful to develop models of 'normal' progress and change in relationships.

We will return to discuss the key developments in the area of relationship research later, but first we would like to invite you to examine the following three extracts from accounts of relationships which exemplify something of the diversity and range of relationships that exist, and also help us to draw out some of the common themes that this volume will explore.

2   Three relationships: friends, siblings and colleagues

The three extracts we have chosen exemplify different types of relationships and interactions within them. Hopefully, they capture some of the variety, richness and vibrancy of everyday relationships. Though different, the three types of relationships illustrated by these accounts also contain some common themes that will form the bases of the discussions of interactions and relationships in the following chapters in the book. You might find that some aspects trigger memories of your own relationships, or that you feel more empathy with some of the accounts than others. Each account is followed by a brief commentary suggesting some of the themes that we feel emerge from each of the extracts which will be taken up later in the book. We will suggest a number of areas or themes for you to focus on as you read each of the three extracts. Following your own analysis we will offer some of our own ideas on each of these as well as introducing several further themes. As you proceed through the extracts these will build up to form a conceptual map – an outline of the themes running through the various chapters to follow.

2.1   Friendship

The following are two accounts given by young people discussing their relationships with a close friend. The first is Jenny (aged 13) who describes her friendship with a classmate and the second is Alex (aged 21) a post-graduate student who likewise describes a current friendship with someone who he met through school and with whom he has continued to keep in contact. Through describing their relationship with a 'good friend' they both also explain their ideas about the importance of friendship generally.

---

1   Read through this first extract quickly to gain a 'feel' for the type of   ACTIVITY 1.1
relationship that is being described.

2   Now read the extract again and make brief notes on the following:

(a)   What do Jenny and Alex appear to derive from their friendships? What benefits do they say they gain and what would they miss if they did not have such friendships?

(b)   How do Jenny and Alex view their friendship? How do these views appear to shape the kind of friendships they have?

(c)   What changes do they describe in their relationships? How have things altered over time?

Extract 1.1 *Friendships*

Jenny – aged 13 (discussing her friendship with Anna, also 13, a classmate and a 'good friend').

Interviewer: Can you tell me what is important about having a good friend?

Jenny: Someone to share feelings with and talk to, go out with, have a good time with and laugh with ... You do things with a good friend and share secrets with a good friend.

Int: When did you first become friends with Anna?

Jenny: We became friends in my old school because she was friends with some of my friends and then when we went on to high school we became good friends because she was the only person I knew.

Int: What first attracted you to her?

Jenny: She had a good sense of humour, always laughing at something and lots of energy

Int: In what ways do you think Anna is similar or different to you?

Jenny: Well ... we're both quiet, we don't work that hard and we both find the same things funny, ... and we both like doing the same things, we both like the same people and we both dislike the same people and the main difference is that we, she's quite a bit more intelligent than me or works a bit harder than me ... and uhm ... she's more stubborn than me, and she's more butch than me, bit of a tomboy...

Int: Have there been any times when there were doubts that you might not become friends or don't want to be any more?

Jenny: We've had arguments, yes ... but never anything big...

Int: What do you think is the most important thing that people get from friendships and how would they feel if they didn't have friends?

Jenny: Most important thing is that they have someone to talk to and express their feelings to and trust. [If they didn't have friends] they would probably feel that uhm, they were worthless and lonely and feel that they were never going to get any friends because they are different.

Source: Interview conducted for this chapter by R. Dallos

Alex – aged 21 (discussing Rusty, a current 'good friend' from school days).

Interviewer: What makes Rusty a 'good friend'?

Alex: Ahm ... although we don't see each other very often, every time that we do see each other, we pick it up almost straight away and also we talk about things that I don't usually talk about with other people. Ahm ... he's very intelligent as well and is sort of more logical than me so we sort of balance each other out ... I respect him and admire him because of his background, the sort of trouble that he's known and come through ... we tend to sort of go to the pub or the movies, we don't do anything majorly special ... we just sort of hang around in coffee bars ... we do have conversations that are quite sort of serious and quite intense but that is OK as long as we don't see each other more than two or three times a year ... we don't actually agree on many things, because my ideas change quite rapidly and I'm a lot more politically sensitive than he is, or think I am. He is much more philosophical, an abstract kind of person ahm ... also I'm kind of the arty one I'm always reading or inventing stories or buying new records, whereas he doesn't really have much time for that. He likes that but he won't really go out of his way to read stories and stuff. So it's, we kind of serve as foils for each other ... balancing,

Int: Could you just think back right to the beginning, the first bit of contact you had with Rusty and the kind of feelings or thoughts that you might have had. Who made the first approaches, how did it happen?

Alex: We met at school ... He was from Montreal and he still had the accent and he was quite a shocking looking bloke ... bright red hair ... and there was a of sort of danger about him ... we did share common interests in the beginning, e.g. science fiction fantasy novels ... I just sort of bumped into him through the playground ... a sort of space established on the playground where a larger group of us would hang out and we would always congregate in that space and then there was a group of us who would bunk off lessons and go to a Kentucky or something. I think it was within that nexus of a larger group of people that we were able to establish a sort of common interest. My parents were very worried that he would lead me astray. We used to just do stupid things like ... one time he was trying to buy some whisky and his step-father caught him, Rusty was only about 14, and he wasn't allowed out and he stole some Baileys from his mother. So we walked along the street drinking this Baileys and we ended up at his place watching a sort of porno movie. It was a real sort of teenage activity ... There was him and Gareth and myself, and we really didn't like each other but we were kind of like the odd balls.

Int: What about low points in your friendship. How did you come out of those?

Alex: I think they were just resolved by us taking a break from the person I think and re-establishing the conditions of the friendship but more tentatively. The only major times I can remember ... once he insulted my brother ... I think he knew he was out of order and other people in the group knew he was out of order ... I think I stormed off and told him to get lost ... and then when we moved back to being friends it was kind of silent, it was never approached ... it just sort of came up and through the process of it coming up it just sort of worked itself out.

Source: Interview conducted for this chapter by R. Dallos

Commentary on Extract 1.1

As you can see there is a richness and complexity to these extracts and there are many aspects of the relationships that we could discuss. However, the extracts include a number of themes that we want to pick out here as they will be developed throughout this volume.

Functions: Both Jenny and Alex discuss the important functions served by relationships, particularly for their own identity: Jenny talks about how she thinks she can 'share secrets', and that you would feel 'worthless' if you didn't have friends. Alex suggests that with Rusty they engaged in 'teenage activities', and as a result developed the identity of 'oddballs'. Part of the function of the friendships can be seen to be a validation of each other, although they value both the similarities and the differences between each other. There is also quite a lot of talk from both Jenny and Alex about what they and their friend put into and get out of their relationship – in considering what functions the relationship serves they appear to weigh up the relative rewards and costs of the relationship for each of them.

Meanings and definitions: Both of them have ideas about what constitutes a 'good friendship'. These include ideas about doing things together, sharing a sense of humour, being able to talk about feelings and so on. Each of them also has their own ideas or 'theories' about why or how the relationship works – Jenny sees her friend Anna as similar but a bit different 'more intelligent, stubborn and butch' and Alex emphasizes difference and complementarity 'we don't actually agree on many things ... we serve as foils for each other'.

Change and development: Their relationships have existed over a period of time during which they have changed and evolved. Jenny talks about how her relationship with Anna changed from 'friends' to 'good friends' when they moved from junior to high school. Likewise, Alex discusses how his friendship with Rusty has altered from being one of a crowd, to friends, to rebels together, and reports handling conflicts by 'taking a break', re-establishing the relationship and being long-term friends who, despite now rarely seeing each other, can still talk about intimate matters.

Conflicts: Though largely enjoyable, both friendships also appear to involve at least some conflict. Jenny suggests that Anna is 'more stubborn' and that sometimes they have arguments, and likewise Alex talks about how Rusty once 'insulted his brother' and he 'stormed off'. These conflicts are resolved in various ways, such as by changing the subject, or taking time off from the relationship.

Networks: Both of them stress how they are part of a group, Jenny says Anna was a 'friend of friends' and Alex talks about a space in the playground where 'a larger group of us would hang out'. Alex also discusses how his friendship with Rusty involved important incidents with their respective families, for example his parents being worried that Rusty would lead him astray. The relationships exist as part of a nexus' or web of other relationships, each influencing and being influenced by the others.

2.2   Siblings

ACTIVITY 1.2

1   Again read through the extract quickly to start with.

2   Now read the extract again and make notes on the following:

   (a)   What appear to be some of the struggles over power that Mrs V recounts in her family?

   (b)   What are some of the ways in which relationships can be seen to exist over time? How do memories of previous events still appear to influence current events and experiences?

   (c)   What ideas can you detect about societally shared expectations or 'norms' of relationships which have influenced Mrs V's experiences? In what ways does she consider that these have altered since her youth?

Extract 1.2   *Siblings*

In this extract Mrs V, who is eighty years old, is recounting aspects of her relationship with her brothers and sisters when she was a young woman.

Mrs V: I can remember my mother buying blue velvet dresses ... and she dyed them black, all the same, three black velvet dresses.

Interviewer: That for the funeral? [father's funeral, when Mrs V was about 12 years old].

Mrs V: For the funeral, and she dyed them black ... Oh they were pretty, I can remember ... with little lace ... I don't know where the hell she got them from. And little white ... black, black patent shoes. I can remember, that's the only pair of shoes I ever had! She always used to make me wear boots – hobnail boots, for the boys, yeah, true! My sister [Gloria] wouldn't believe it, but she [other sister, Ann] knew that, she remembered that. Well, I was arguing the other day with her, well, when she was alive. I said, 'there's no way, you two could wear shoes, I had ... to ... have hobnail boots'. So Glor said, 'no you never, you had the same as me', so Ann said, 'oh yes she did, she...Mum made her wear hobnail boots'. Why me hobnail boots? – do you wonder I retaliated! [laughs] She used to keep us nice, we used to have little dresses with little white pinafores, all goffered, and ribbons through there, and a hat with daisies all round! ...

Int: How did you get on with your brothers?

Mrs V: Oh, I got on all right with my brothers. Now, I had a ... my eldest brother got drowned ... I was very friendly with him...

Int: What was his name?

Mrs V: Fred, Alfred, his name was, but we called him Fred ... As I grew up, I used to mix with anybody, if I liked them that is. And a friend of mine, one day, I said ... oh I was never allowed to stay out late, and I can remember, the old Queen's coronation – not this one that's ninety, I'm talking about the other, before her...

Mrs V: So, um ... on this particular day, it was like a coronation, or ... It might have been a jubilee, and she said to me, 'Don't go home tonight Isobel' she said, 'stay here ... um, stay here' she said, 'and we can sleep in my ... my mum won't mind letting you sleep in our bed'. I said 'all right'. Well I knew that someone had came searching for me, and they knew where I hung out but they didn't actually know where my sis ... where my friend's house was, right. And we were sitting on ... we used to sit on the steps then outside the houses in them days, we ... and we were going to get up early on that, next morning, just to see the procession. And, I was looking down the road and I saw my two brothers coming along, or, foster brother, he was, my elder brother, and I said, 'ooh, it's my brother Fred, let's get in, get in the passage quick', so we got in the passage, had the door open a little bit, and we could see them, and they didn't know which house it was, so of course they couldn't find me, and off they goes home. So I ... clever, I never realized what was in store for me, so I stayed out all night, seeing the show, didn't I? [laughs]

Int: How old were you then?

Mrs V: I must have been about 16!

Int: Oh God! [laughs]

Mrs V: ...And I thought, right, I'm going home now. I said, 'right, Mary' – eh, I'll have to figure out her name now – I said, 'I'm going home now ... Ellen, I'm going home now Ellen' I said, and 'see you tomorrow, or I might see you tonight'. Well I never thought or anything and when I knocked on the door – had to knock on, they wouldn't let you have a key – it was my mother opened the door, so she said, 'And where' – and you've got to remember my mother was big then ... 'and where do you think *you've* been all night?' I said, 'I've been with my mates, went to see the ... the, whatever you call it...

Int: Yeah.

Mrs V: ...the show'. 'Oh have you?' she said 'and very nice too' she said. 'You *don't* stay out all night, you don't stay out' she said, 'until, after ... after 11 o'clock that's your time. You *don't* do as you like here, you do what I tell you'. I said, 'oh, give over mother', I said, 'I'll do as I like'. And with that someone smacked me such a smack round the face! [laughs] 'Don't talk to your mother like that' – it was my brother, my eldest brother, see! I looked at him – I used to knock about with boys, so I said ... I looked at him, so I said, 'I'm bringing all my ma ... my mates up to you, they'll ... give you one for it.' Now, my nose bled! I said, 'You don't do that to me, spiteful old ...' I won't tell you what I did say, so he said, 'Don't use that sort of tone here,

Int: Mm.

Mrs V: you're in your own home, we won't have it. Who you mix with we don't care, because you're going to regret it when you grow up.

Int: Mm.

Mrs V: When your mother says come in ... I had to ... I have to act as a father now I'm grown up' he said, 'and you do what your mother says and what I say' he said, 'because, if we turn you out of this house you know what's going to happen to you, don't you?' You knew in them days ... it was frightening...

Int: Yeah, yeah.

Mrs V: ...So I said, um, 'Well, all right', but I couldn't go out that night, but I went out the next night, that was all forgotten, but I never ever done it again. I knew I was in st ... I knew what I was doing, but I never ever thought I'd get a ... ooh, it didn't half hurt! [laughs] They don't do that today, they let them do as they like.

Source: Interview conducted by C. Holland (unpub.)

Commentary on Extract 1.2

Time: Relationships exist across time, for example Mrs V is recounting incidents that occurred 65 years previously but which are still influential in how she regards her family. Memories of events and shared experiences can frame current feeling and interactions. If Mrs. V's older brother were still alive, the memories of such incidents would to some extent shape their current relationship. This extract also illustrates how meanings are changed over time, for example the punishment was resented at the time but retrospectively Mrs V suggests that it may have been legitimate, even necessary, and she can in any case laugh about it now.

Power: The account also indicates some of the power struggles that pervade family life, for example Mrs V felt that she had a right to go and see the jubilee and stay out. When accused of staying out all night by her mother Mrs V says 'oh, give over mother ... I'll do as I like', indicating a common theme of family life (that is, adolescent rebelliousness). Her mother tells her in no uncertain terms that 'You don't do as you like here, you do what I tell you'. The brother joins mother in a coalition against her in the dead father's place, by striking her and telling her 'not to speak to your mother like that'. Mrs V's reaction to the smack was to threaten her brother with her friends and this in turn met with a threat of being 'turned out' from the home, where a young woman alone would have fared very badly given the role of women in society at the time. The power lines within and outside the family were very clearly drawn.

Relationship norms and roles: Mrs V's account illustrates how ideas about what is appropriate in relationships change and alter. She seems to accept, retrospectively, that in her youth physical punishment was legitimate and also that it was acceptable for an older brother to administer it. However, she also indicates that ideas have changed, 'They don't do that today, they let them do as they like', that is, ways of relating in families have changed and this defines and constrains what is acceptable.

Mrs V's account of being the only one of the three daughters who had to wear boys' hobnailed boots is an example of a family norm – she was singled out and this made her feel odd. In addition, these beliefs within the family are contrasted with wider social norms about gender at that time, that is boys wore hobnailed boots and girls didn't. This definition of her as being odd and singled out is also seen by Mrs V as a potential cause of resentment which justified her later behaviour – 'do you wonder I retaliated?'. There are also some tensions about how roles are defined, for example brothers should not normally act like parents, but in this family the oldest brother was allowed to because he was needed as a surrogate father after their father had died. Though at the time contesting his role as surrogate father, and especially his right to hit her, Mrs V seems, retrospectively, to have accepted it.

Negotiation of events: Mrs V and her sister Gloria disagree about whether Mrs V had to wear hobnailed boots or not. Memory for past events appears to be subject to distortions, even in relation to 'facts' such as whether or not she did have to wear them. What these events are seen to have meant at the time may be even more variable. Mrs V's account suggests that she and her sister Gloria in their reminiscences about past events did not simply recall but re-constructed or negotiated versions of past events.

Interactional patterns and processes: Mrs. V's account contains some examples of the escalating patterns that can occur in relationships. For example, when her mother confronts her about having stayed out all night she replies that, 'I will do as I like' and this is accompanied by a smack administered by her brother. This simple sequence demonstrates not only a power struggle but how one person's actions lead to a response from another (feedback) and how this can escalate, even into physical violence.

2.3 Colleagues

In the last account presented here, you read about Harry and Mary who have worked together for 15 years. A year ago they moved from working in an office with a dozen or so people to working together on their own in a smaller office. They are similar in age (late 40s).

1 As before, skim read the extract to start with.   ACTIVITY 1.3

2 Now read the extract more carefully to make notes on the following:

  (a) To what extent do Mary and Harry consider that their relationship is due to, or results from, their choices? That is, has it developed as they wanted it to be as opposed to developing spontaneously, perhaps even outside their conscious awareness?

  (b) What patterns can you detect in their relationship from the flow of the conversation in the interview, for example who talks most? What kind of an emotional atmosphere can you infer exists between them, who appears to initiate in answering the interviewer's questions, and so on?

  (c) What factors can be seen to become possible only as a relationship arises, for example here in the specific nature or style of the pattern of dominance between Mary and Harry?

Extract 1.3 *Two colleagues Harry (manager) and Mary (secretary/administrator)*

Individual interviews:

Harry: We get along as far as I am concerned extremely well, and we're able to talk as friends about various situations, personal problems. We share quite a lot of ourselves with each other, but it's done in the context of the work environment like friendly colleagues, or colleagues who are friends ... I think the structures of a social relationship [friendship] are essentially equal and unconstrained, and this sits discordantly with the working things which require boundaries, ... Outside the work situation we never contact each other – friendship is within work and does not extend outside work. I think it [our relationship] is a friendly thing which has boundaries which no-one has imposed, but that we are conscious of, kind of instinctively – the proprieties of the relationship are kept as friends and colleagues and both people are sufficiently aware that keeping certain boundaries facilitates ease of work ... The person that has the more senior, more highly remunerable position in an organization usually thinks the way he or she operates (more often he) is tremendously democratic and egalitarian and very friendly. I suspect the more junior, subservient person sees it rather differently, ... I would hope there is not too huge a discrepancy. It [friendly colleague relationship] can only work given a particular mix of professional competence, shared endeavour, equanimity of temperament, recognition of boundaries, sensitivity where people are [concerned]. With some people that would come fairly easily and instinctively, as it has with us, we haven't had to work at it, we just arrived at it. I can think of other secretaries where this would not work at all and one would have to adopt a sort of rigid 'colleagues approach'. Others where the friendship element could become a problem, acquire a kind of life and momentum of its own with unforseeable consequences.

Mary: Harry makes the ultimate decisions, it is only petty things that are left to me without consulting him. Our relationship is very easy going, definitely a case that I am working for Harry but on the other hand he treats me like a fellow colleague not 'I am a boss' ... very easy going work. I suppose if we did socialize outside it would be a friendship ... but we are friends [at work], we certainly discuss things between us that are not work related quite openly ... probably not quite as much as I would a female friend, but its surprising, quite a lot, not great boundaries ... I think ... if you didn't have a sort of friendly relationship with someone you worked for, if there was a separation between the boss and the secretaries it wouldn't feel comfortable at all.

Joint Interview:

Interviewer: You've both said your relationship is based on genuine friendship ... structurally, though, Mary is in a subordinate position and is this more in the back of her mind?

Harry: Yes and no, ... office management, equipment, physical environment – Mary essentially deals with...

Mary: If I wanted to take leave I wouldn't take it without your permission

Harry: No...

Harry: I suppose you respect people's positions as long as they do the work they are supposed to do, mode of social interaction can be whatever they like as long as it doesn't constrain ... I suppose it would be unnatural within our social environment traditions, to have a very formal 'Good morning Mrs ... S', 'Good morning Dr. ... S', well, you might find in some rather formal big offices...

Mary: I think it would be very difficult in this situation...

Int: Do you both see it as – a bit of friendliness is necessary and more is a bonus?

Harry: I can think of some colleagues where the social dimension is a bit out of control and occupies a disproportionate proportion. In general, if people feel relaxed and happy and others treat them as human beings rather than in a mechanistic way then they feel happier.

Int: The shift from the old office to this one – reduced network of other contacts and friends – how has it changed things?

Mary: We did wonder if we would continue [having a good relationship] being shut in here – but you've had a fair number of meetings … [that is, away from the office].

Harry: We did think two people sort of, on top of each other...

Int: So it's been a little bit more like a marriage – under each other's feet?

Mary: Our work relationship hasn't changed.

Harry: If it wasn't a good relationship before, this kind of situation could be a strain, [I] can think of relationships in the old office which broke down despite the network of support, if we didn't get on it would have been dire...

Int: Your previous office had other relationships, sometimes conflictual, for example if one of you had had a row with someone else, did you smooth it out for each other?

Harry: In a sense, but now because other people aren't there, [there's] less potential for irritation.

Mary: Not so much an argument that either of us had had...

Harry: But shared situations we had observed, less talk about other people now...

Int: Those conversations about others – what do you substitute for those now?

Harry: ...there was quite a lot of gossip and back-biting that its quite nice not to be part of now, there were cliques, inside, outside 'the magic circle'...

Source: Interview conducted for this chapter by R. Dallos

Commentary on Extract 1.3

Emergent properties of relationships: Mary and Harry both agree that the relationship 'just happened', that they were not consciously aware of how or why it came to establish this form. Harry says it would not always be like this with other secretaries, who would be less able to fit in – so how did he know Mary would? This may suggest that there is more going on in terms of predicting the other person's views and opinions and attributing causes for behaviour than people remember or consciously reflect on. Some of the inferences about how a relationship will develop appear to be based upon early, and possibly not fully explicit or conscious predictions.

Autonomy/choice: Both Mary and Harry explain the nature of their relationship as being partly due to their own choice – this is the way they prefer to relate and work with each other. They also, however, say that it developed this way as a result of their personalities 'fitting'. This suggests that choices in relationships are 'contingent', that is, both Harry and Mary had ideas about what kind of a relationship they wanted, but whether they could achieve this depended on the wishes and ideas of the other.

Interactional patterns and processes: This is the only extract in which we get a flavour of the actual interaction between the partners, through their participation in the joint interview. Whilst many studies of relationships rely on people's accounts of their relationships, including their accounts of interaction and of past dialogue (such as those provided in Extracts 1.1 and 1.2), what actually goes on between participants as they interact with each other is a very valuable source of information about their relationship. As a result, a large body of research exists which analyses interactions between pairs and groups of people who know each other to a greater or lesser extent, and this will be discussed later in the volume, particularly in Chapter 2. As you will see there, much of this research focuses not only on what the participants *say* to each other (as we can do with the material in Extract 1.3), but also on their non-verbal behaviour. This includes aspects of communication such as gestures, body movements and tone of voice which often convey subtle messages between participants and to onlookers. Part of this communication is 'feedback' or information about what effects a person's verbal and non-verbal actions have had on others.

Specifically, we could suggest that despite Harry's statement that their relations was egalitarian, the extract suggests that he talked much more and tended to initiate answers. However, any possibility of the relationship escalating into an excessive imbalance of power appeared to be avoided in various ways, such as some good humoured banter. Their relationship appeared to have an overall stability or balance.

Meanings and definitions: Harry and Mary both state that they see their relationship as 'friendly colleagues'. This definition involves ideas about what their roles are, colleagues but also friends, and they appear to agree broadly on the mixture and degree of overlap of these roles. There are boundaries to their relationship, so that they do not meet outside work, but that even at work it is legitimate to discuss personal, quite intimate, non-work matters.

Function: There is a balance here between work and friendship. There are obvious set tasks that need to be carried out as part of the job and so they both receive satisfaction in a job well done when the relationship works well, but the relationship itself is also seen to be rewarding, offering some opportunity to talk about personal matters, to 'gossip' about other work colleagues and so on. There are also ideas about what and how much is appropriate, for example Harry comments on the 'disproportionate' time spent on chat by some colleagues.

Power: There appear to be differences in the power held by Harry and Mary. Mary suggests that the responsibilities she holds are 'petty' and yet Harry seems to see her responsibilities as more wide ranging (although he acknowledges that the more senior member of a team often is rather unaware of the way the more junior members perceive their responsibilities and their managers). At one level this power difference is explicit and a structural aspect of their work, however since they see their formal relationship as also a friendly one this difference is not emphasized. The power difference between them is legitimated by the organization they work in, but another important structural difference, their different genders, is not mentioned. Harry does however make a side comment about 'the boss – usually he', which implies a recognition of men and women's typically unequal access to positions of power in society.

Relationship norms: Though this relationship has evolved gradually, through accumulated interactions between Harry and Mary over a number of years, they also appear to have ideas about what is normal or acceptable for the relationship of 'colleagues' more generally, and to draw on these ideas in evaluating their own relationship. The perceptions of commonly held ideas about relationships can be seen in their discussion of how such relationships are perceived from the 'outside' (as Harry said, 'for some colleagues the social dimension is a bit out of control').

3 Common themes

How do the notes you made for Activity 1.1 compare with those in the commentary sections? No doubt you have considered additional points and perhaps felt that the extracts illustrated some points better than others. There are many possible ways that we could explore these rich accounts further and there are no right and wrong analyses. This illustrates one of the core issues to be addressed in this book, which is that in exploring relationships what we see is inevitably coloured by our own experiences and perspectives. In each of the extracts the participants selectively focused on some parts of their relationships, what they could remember most vividly and what sprang to mind as relevant at the time of the interview, and consequently parts were missed out. Likewise, if you think back to the three accounts again now, some parts may stand out more in *your* memory than others. Perhaps this is because you can relate some aspects of these relationships to your own experiences – for example you might be more able to understand the experiences of others of your own gender or of those similar in age to you. We will examine further this influence of our own views and experiences on the perception of other relationships later in this volume.

Another theme emerging from these extracts is the distinction between 'interactions' and 'relationships'. The extracts give examples of people's ideas about relationships and also of incidents or pieces of interaction. By 'interaction' what is usually meant is that two or more people engage in some activity together for a period of time. This can include brief exchanges between two strangers in the street, a transaction between a shopper and salesperson, or a piece of communication between two people who know each other well:

> Examples are many and various; they extend from things like buying a loaf of bread, or joining others in a lift, to being examined by the doctor or kissing one's daughter goodbye at the airport ... people talk to each other, they exchange signs of affection or friendliness and will show greater or lesser degrees of intimacy in their behaviour
>
> *(Radley, Ch 2 of this volume)*

Interactions are 'visible' in the sense that we can observe and record them from the 'outside' – behaviour, patterns of actions, what is spoken and so on. Relationships may be seen not simply in terms of individual factors but also in terms of the processes occurring *between* individuals. This point is further emphasized by the suggestion that in everyday language there are some adjectives available for describing interactional states, such as close, cooperative, democratic, egalitarian, communal, hierarchical and conflictual. These focus on *what is going on* between people, on the dynamics, the patterns of actions and reactions. In contrast, the terms for types of relationships (marriage, friendship, colleagues, doctor-patient) do not tell us specifically about their processes. We might assume that a friendship will be characterized by close, cooperative patterns of interactions but friendships vary widely and not all are primarily characterized in this way. It can be argued further that the English language contains relatively few such interpersonal adjectives compared with the wealth of terms available to describe and differentiate individual states (Kelley, 1994). One consequence may be that we miss or underemphasize important aspects of relationships, for example the powerful influences that the nature of a relationship once established can exert on the experiences of the individuals involved. Furthermore, we may also overestimate the extent to which any one person can exert unilateral control or influence over the pattern and development of a relationship.

A central concept in this volume is that of time, which we have considered repeatedly in our commentaries on the extracts. Relationships are characterized by having a history of interactions over time, so that current interactions are framed by previous ones. Most importantly, we believe that relationships are concerned with the construction of *meanings*. That is, our concern (with Duck, 1994) is with

> the ways that people develop the sense that they are in a personal relationship with someone else, and ... [with] *sharing* meaning, by which I mean the deep processes of understanding someone else's ways of thinking about their experiences in the world. I am concerned not with what it *is* to be in a relationship so much as what it means, and not so much what it is to be a person in a relationship but what it means.
>
> *(Duck, 1994 p. xv).*

People are seen to construct their relationships by the shared meanings that they create, for example to understand a friendship we have to try to understand what it means *to the friends themselves*. Is the friendship based on mutual interests? Is it based on loneliness? Is it based on mutual admiration? Do they see it as temporary or permanent? Do they think it is all right to have the occasional row to clear the air? In talking about a relationship, such as when giving the accounts in Section 2, people are able to 'teach' us what their relationship is about, what it means to them, and how they make sense of it.

Review of section 3

Some of the dominant themes that serve as a conceptual guide throughout this volume and which have been identified in this section are as follows.

- Power.
- Meanings and definitions.
- Time and development.
- Autonomy and choice.
- Interactional patterns and processes.
- Functions of relationships.
- Norms of relationships.
- Emergent nature of relationships.

---

4 Storyline of the book

Though this volume discusses the contribution made to the study of relationships and interactions by different theoretical and methodological perspectives, chapters are based around aspects of relationships rather than being predominantly focused on individual theoretical perspectives. Research on relationships is a relatively new field for psychology and there is a strong interdisciplinary emphasis as well as a degree of eclecticism in the use of methods and theories, as you will see. Early attempts to study relationships by isolating individual components (for example, similarity of attitudes between people and resultant attraction between them) were found to be inadequate and it has become apparent that this field requires a broader approach which frequently combines perspectives. Each chapter has a different point of emphasis and consequently focuses more on some perspectives than on others, but there is also considerable overlap and some of the perspectives appear in more than one chapter.

The final part of the book however is an exception to this. It is made up of a series of position papers written by practitioners and researchers committed to a particular theoretical perspective to studying relationships and interactions. Each author presents his or her personal arguments for the perspective of his or her choice and so each paper gives you a direct account of how each perspective has been applied to a particular topic area.

The other chapters are based, as we have said, on different aspects of interaction and relationships. Chapter 2 begins with the study of interaction, analysing what goes on between people when they meet, the rules of interaction in various public situations and so on. As well as dealing with the verbal and non-verbal components of partners' communication, the chapter also covers material on the norms and rules which might govern the ways in which people interact with each other in social relationships. Chapter 3 extends this discussion by exploring interactions in more personal relationships, such as friendships, intimate or sexual relationships and families. One aspect of this is a consideration of how repeated interactions develop over time into relationships. Chapter 3 also examines cognitive aspects of relationships – the beliefs and cognitions which people have about their relationships and how these can be seen as being interpersonally constructed, even from our earliest days as infants.

Chapter 4 continues to stress the importance of the time dimension, examining how early relationships can affect our feelings, thoughts and behaviour in adulthood. It also explores a rather different aspect of our 'inner world' of relationships – the emotive rather than the cognitive – in examining the psychodynamic notion of transference. Chapter 5 focuses on change and development in relationships – taking three key transition points in personal relationships as examples and exploring the common and distinctive themes in each. These are then considered within the framework of 'family life cycle' models which attempt to capture the evolving and inter-connected nature of such changes. In Chapter 6 the diversity and variety of relationships that people engage in is discussed with reference to the various needs that different types of relationships serve. The wider social issues affecting relationships are also discussed – not only the web or network of other relationships within which any one relationship is located, but also the social structural factors (such as economic power) and the dominant ideologies or beliefs about relationships (such as expectations of gender roles) which can affect our experiences even within the most personal of relationships.

References

Duck, S. (1994) *Meaningful Relationships*, Thousand Oaks, Sage.

Haley, J. (1981) *Uncommon Therapy* (2nd edn.) New York, W.W. Norton

Holland, C. Unpublished PhD Thesis, Milton Keynes, The Open University.

Kelley, H.H. (1994) 'Personal Commentary', *International Society for the Study of Personal Relationships Bulletin,* vol. 11, no. 1, pp. 1–3.

Weiss, R. (1974) 'The provisions of social relationships' in Rubin, Z. (ed) *Doing Unto Others*, New Jersey, Prentice-Hall.

CHAPTER 2

RELATIONSHIPS IN DETAIL: THE STUDY OF SOCIAL INTERACTION

by Alan Radley

Contents

1   Introduction

'Form is no mere formality'

Heinrich Mann, Man of Straw

This chapter will examine the study of everyday interaction as it occurs between people in their face-to-face relationships. It discusses the main ways in which social psychologists have, over the years, studied the form and detail of people's dealings with each other. It will compare some of the different explanations that have been offered, and discuss how useful these have been in accounting for relationships in everyday life. The discussion will also make the point encapsulated in the quotation at the head of the chapter: form and detail can make important differences to the course of relationships. *How* something is said and done, as well as *what* is said and done, affects people's expectations and understanding of each other.

By reviewing what social psychologists have tried to establish about interactions in general, we shall be in a position to see how well their explanations fit over topics that will be discussed more in the chapters to follow. As will be seen, some of these interactions are minor things, like buying a loaf of bread, or joining other people in a room. Others are more significant, or potentially so, such as kissing one's daughter goodbye at the airport or being examined by the doctor for the presence of a serious disease. All of these things involve some sort of interaction between those concerned; people talk to one another, they exchange signs of affection or friendliness and will show greater or lesser degrees of intimacy in their behaviour. However, although these happenings are there to be seen by the interested onlooker, they can form only a starting point for a study of social relationships. The stranger cannot see what these individuals are thinking, nor can this person know from observation alone about the wider background of their relationship.

There are two reasons for discussing the detail of interaction at this point in the book. First, it raises the question of what should be studied under the umbrella term 'relationships'. Should we be examining people's feelings; their thoughts expressed in words; their actions; their facial expressions? This raises a more significant question: can relationships be 'explained' in terms of the detail of what passes between the individuals concerned?

The answer to this latter question depends partly upon which kinds of relationship are chosen for study, for example, whether husband-wife, teacher-student, friend-friend, or waiter-diner. There are important assumptions in each of these relationships that limit the kinds of interaction that can take place. One of these assumptions concerns the degree to which people know each other personally. There are things that family members or friends might say (or be expected to say) to one another that would be surprising or even unacceptable between strangers or those whose dealings are restricted to impersonal matters. For that reason, we can distinguish between *personal relationships* on the one hand, and *social relationships* on the other. Because so much research into social interaction has focused upon strangers and impersonal situations, much of what is discussed in this chapter will bear more directly upon social relationships, as this term has just been used.

Having said that, it is important to emphasize that both kinds of relationship involve interaction. More important, this distinction is not a hard and fast one. Whilst people do get to know one another better over time, they sometimes lose touch, so that what was once a personal relationship becomes merely a social one. It is also possible for one's doctor to be friendly, one's husband to be a work colleague and one's friend to become a lover. This suggests that how relationships are fashioned -- and how they change – involves, in part, the detail of what people say and do.

There is another reason for discussing interaction at this point in the book; it provides a historical overview of research into how people form and conduct their everyday life. This will show that ideas which social psychologists use to talk about social relationships draw upon assumptions that these researchers make about how thought, action and speech are organized. By taking a historical perspective, we shall be able to see how different theorists have, successively, tried to pin-point what is essential to 'social relationships'. The course of the discussion will take us from (1) attempts to specify what is general to all interactions, via (2) what have been held to be crucial differences between major groupings, to (3) more recent ideas about how relationships are made to work. This will show that what social psychologists have thought about relationships is not immune from what they think individuals in society do, and are capable of.

Aims of the chapter

1   To show the different ways in which social psychologists have studied interaction;

2   To describe some of the detail of interaction, including verbal and non-verbal behaviour;

3   To compare the main explanations that have been put forward by social psychologists and others concerning interaction in social life;

4   To show how a knowledge of social interaction can illuminate our understanding of everyday relationships.

2   Early research: the study of norms and roles

2.1   Norms – expected ways of behaving

In this first part of our review, we shall concentrate upon some general features of social life that appeared, at least to earlier social psychologists, to govern all social relationships. This approach, focusing as it did upon norms and roles, owed much to the belief that social psychology's contribution (as opposed to that of individualistic psychology) must be grounded in the influence of the social context itself.

There are two reasons for including this work at this point. First, it raises issues that are still under discussion, though more often by sociologists than social psychologists. Graham Allan, in *Reading E* at the end of the book, makes the point that apparently 'free-floating relationships are not just personal, are not just a matter of preference'. We do have choice in our dealings with each other, but these are 'boxed in by underlying elements of our social experience and our social circumstances'. The second reason for discussing work on norms and roles is that it shows just how these things depend upon the social interaction of participants.

Social psychology has always been concerned with the relationship of the individual to the group and wider society. In the 1930s, one important question was how individuals come to share a common frame of reference, or way of seeing, that allows them to act as a group. In a study where groups of individuals were asked to make perceptual judgements, Sherif (1936) showed that, once established for an individual, shared frames of reference will 'determine or modify his reactions to situations'. This, however, must follow the formation of norms as 'a product of the contact of individuals'. That is, norms cannot be taken simply as the cause or reason for why people act as they do: social interaction is also the *basis* of norm formation, not just the *product* of it.

From this perspective, social norms were thought of as shared ways of seeing things, and also as shared ways of acting. This point of view emphasized the commonality of social norms because it took an outsider's perspective. On reflection, it soon becomes apparent that not all norms are shared, and that people see different norms as requiring different degrees of adherence. Another way of putting this is to say that some norms *prescribe* what should be done, while others merely *describe* what people 'generally do' in given situations.

Taking the normative approach, social interaction appears to be guided by perspectives, or frames of reference, that are somehow 'kept in mind' by each of us in the course of everyday life. For example, the way that family members conduct themselves at dinner is then explained in terms of the norms that, as a family, they share together. The way that a group of young people act in a McDonald's restaurant is (amongst other things) guided by the norms of their group, and of their youth culture.

Because the concept of norms emphasizes the 'sharedness' of social life, it leads us to look at relationships in terms of what people have in common. However, it is quite possible for family members to differ about what is expected, and also to make exceptions for each other (or the family as a whole) under particular or exceptional circumstances. That is, in the cause of maintaining 'good relationships' people may bend the very rules which are assumed to govern their behaviour.

Which norms are operating at a particular time is not an easy thing to specify. Take the example of the young people in the McDonald's restaurant. Is it the norms about eating that they share with family, the norms applying to their particular friendship group, or the norms of the wider youth culture that guide their interactions with one another? Seen in this way, social interaction is something that the concept of norm seems easily to embrace, but not really able to explain completely.

ACTIVITY 2.1   You might like to replace the example given above with one concerning your own mealtime arrangements involving other people. Write down what you consider to be some of the norms governing these occasions, whether happening in the home or outside. Do these norms apply equally to everyone present? Are they the subject of discussion or dispute among the individuals concerned? What is it that illuminates, say, family relationships at the table — the keeping of norms or their being broken?

Do your notes made for Activity 2.1 support the view that norms, while being expected ways of behaving, are actually guidelines that are often altered? Even if they do show such flexibility, it is possible that, in certain situations, and at certain times, they can have the feeling of being prescriptions. Look at Box 2.1 for an example, from a different period, of a detailed prescription of social behaviour.

We know, however, that unambiguous instructions like those shown in Box 2.1 would today be limited to very special circumstances. Instead of being fixed rules, norms are often things to which we make appeal when needing to explain our actions. That is, in becoming things which people can discuss, norms can become the subject of the interaction. Then it can be said that someone 'had to act as she did given what her family expected of her'; or that 'bringing up that subject at the funeral was disgraceful'. Considered in this way, norms are not mechanisms that influence action in a deterministic way: rather, they are appeals that make social life appear orderly, at the same time attributing motives or reasons to individual actors. If then, there is a claim that this is the 'usual way of doing things', it is not said because life has to be that way. It is said because it makes that situation, what each person did or failed to do, sensible, acceptable and perhaps even forgivable.

BOX 2.1 Concern with social interaction is not new – the world of etiquette

During the last few hundred years in Europe, there was a general concern with manners and deportment that extended to quite detailed prescriptions of how to greet and address others, with special reference to their social position. This is the prescription for the 'Lady's passing curtsy' as carried out in seventeenth-century France:

> If the person, or persons, are on the right-hand side, a quarter turn to the right is made, in order to face them. This is done by simultaneously turning to the right while taking a step sideways on to the left foot, leaving the right leg and foot at the side without the weight on it. The right foot is then drawn in against the left, before sliding it gently forward in front the distance of a short walking step, while at the same time bending both knees slightly. As the knees bend, the body inclines forward a little, and care must be taken to keep the toes and knees turned rather outward. The head must not droop forward. The curtsy is finished as the weight moves smoothly forward on to the front foot, whereupon the body straightens as the legs straighten.
>
> *(Wildeblood, 1973, p.205)*

A distinction can also be drawn between norms that we are aware of and those that seem to be more like habit. Each one of these seems to operate at a different level of social life. On the basis of Sherif's work, it might seem that norms governing ways of looking, or the body in general, might be those that 'control us'. By comparison, expectations to do with social life (for example how to act at parties, in tutorials, or at funerals) are matters of which we are more aware, and over which we have greater control. However, this notion of levels or layers of social interaction is actually misleading. As will be shown later on in this chapter, it is the *detail* of what is said and done that sometimes carries enormous significance in social relationships.

2.2   Roles – group organization and interaction

This section will review the work carried out by Bales (1950) and his associates, who made a special study of how people in groups organize themselves to carry out a given task. The relevance of this work for our discussion of relationships is that it continues the social psychologists' insistence that social life is not reducible to the similarities between individual personalities. When people meet together, in this case in small groups, the relationships that they form are subject to processes that lie, as it were, *between* rather than within people. This implies that, to understand the relationship that two people might form, we need to comprehend the social setting in which they meet. After all, we do not spend all our time meeting together as couples, but often with several people together. When we communicate in such settings, it is the structure of the group that can be important in what is said and done between particular individuals.

Bales's studies of small groups are regarded as examples of seminal social psychological research. The importance of his work for the study of social interaction is twofold. First, it raised new questions about how interaction is organized in relation to roles occupied by different individuals. It was not what they shared, as members of one group, that was important. Instead, it was how they differed within the group that gave their interactions a particular significance. Second, Bales devized a method for studying small groups that made interaction the focus of attention. What individuals said to each other in this context mattered in a way that it had not mattered before.

Bales's studies, carried out in the late 1940s, were an extension of his research into groups such as those run by *Alcoholics Anonymous.* He was interested in the dynamic workings of the group, an idea that owed much to the writings of Sigmund Freud. Along with the sociologist Talcott Parsons, with whom he worked, Bales put forward a theory that stressed the group as a functioning whole. The different interests and actions of its members provoke tensions that are worked out in the course of the effective functioning of the group. Differences in kinds of interactions become apparent, and their significance for the group as a whole become the main subject of study.

What is important to note about Bales's work is that the differentiation of roles (the emergence of the two kinds of leader) is the outcome of what individual members said and did in relation to each other. This means that the relationships which are established in the group *emerge* from the interaction: they do *not simply cause* it. They are not the result of personality characteristics that are brought, fully fledged, into the group. This should not imply that what individuals bring to the group counts for nothing, or even for little. What it suggests, instead, is that the claims that individuals make to play particular roles are subject to certain collective assumptions and to specific reactions from other group members.

It can happen that the kind of processes that Bales described do not happen at all when people meet together as a group. In cases where group members had little or no consensus about what they should be doing, then this kind of group organization simply did not happen. The lesson to be drawn is that, while these roles may come to guide and shape action in later group meetings, they are created out of what individuals say and do in the earlier ones. In particular, Bales suggested that it was the attempts of the task leader to organize his fellows, that led to negative feelings being directed at him by the others.

BOX 2.2   Bales's Method for studying small group interaction: Interaction Process Analysis

Bales conducted a series of studies using five-man groups, each group meeting several times and being asked to solve a range of problems. A typical problem would be to ask the group to read an imaginary case study of an organizational issue, and then to make recommendations to the manager concerned. The subjects did not know each other, so that the early meetings involved the men in working out how they should solve the problems set them. How they did this was central to Bales's inquiries into the style of organization that each small group would eventually adopt.

From the point of view of a study into social interaction, Bales's choice of methodology was most significant. He drew up a schedule of different kinds of things that could be said or done by group members as they communicated with each other. These categories included the content of the message, its presumed intent, and whether it was asked for or communicated. For example, a person saying 'I think we should tackle the question of the map first', might be checked as 'giving suggestion'. Should another group member say nothing to this, but sneer and look out of the window, then he might be checked as 'showing antagonism'. What each member said or did was allocated to one (or more) of twelve such categories. The main data for Bales's studies were, therefore, the categorization of all communications made by each individual in the course of all of the groups' meetings.

In addition to this, at the end of each session every man was asked to say whom he thought had had the best ideas for solving the problem in the meeting, and which of his fellow group members he personally liked or disliked. This introduced into the study a measure of difference in what Bales termed the task or socio-emotional focus of the group. By analysing changes in these preferences, and by relating them to different patterns of communication defined by the category system, Bales was able to say something about interaction and the development of group structure.

It was found that men who had the best ideas were *not* those most liked. They were the ones most likely to initiate attempts at solving the problem supplied to the group, making suggestions and giving opinions. By comparison, the men who were most liked were those who had often shown solidarity with others, released tension by making jokes, or defused potential arguments. Bales suggested that these individuals were occupying two different roles that gradually emerged in the course of the group discussion. He called the first of these the *'task specialist'*, and the second the *'social specialist'*. Where these two roles were each occupied by particular individuals, then one can speak of the group having two leaders – the 'task leader' and the 'socio-emotional leader'.

The detailed findings of Bales's experiments are not of further concern to us in this chapter (but see Radley, 1991). It should be said that Bales's work had considerable influence on social psychology over the quarter-century following the publication of his main findings. As a result of this work, it became possible to ask questions about the conditions under which different kinds of role-relationship emerged in the course of group meetings. This has relevance for a study of social relationships because it widens the inquiry from laboratory groups, in particular, to groups of people in everyday settings. Of course we are part of various established groups, and of course we leave and join new ones. The question can then be asked, 'to what extent are group processes responsible for shaping the relationships between the individuals concerned'?

Bales's results suggest that relationships in groups are shaped by a process of role differentiation, rather than by pre-existing norms. Does this square with your own experience? Think of groups to which you belong. When someone else takes the lead, directing others, do you respond favourably to this initiative? Do others? Does it matter who takes the lead (for example, man or woman, friend or stranger)? Or is it the matter at hand that is the decisive factor?

Thinking about these things will be good preparation for reading the next section, where we review some findings about just these kinds of variations in group life.

2.3   Legitimation and diversity in group interaction

In this section we shall take a critical look at the finding that people's relationships are, in the group setting at least, to be explained in terms of roles. More precisely, we shall examine the notion that whether we are respectful toward someone, or find him or her a friendly character, is explicable in terms of the dynamics of the group we are in at the time. This raises, once more, the distinction between *social* and *personal* relationships, as we distinguished between these terms earlier on. Some group situations involve individuals who know each other well; but many do not, and as with Bales's groups of students, consist of people who have perhaps met each other once only or not at all.

It matters whether the members of a group are strangers or are known to one another. When, as with Bales's original study, members are strangers, and when the requirement is to work out a *modus vivendi* for the group, then a struggle for (task) leadership is likely to follow (Burke, 1967). When, on the other hand, the members know their relative standing and responsibilities, and do not see the need to work out a different social order, then this will not occur. An example of the latter might be a company board meeting in which the chair sets out the business to be followed. Objections might be raised as to detail, but the chair's right to run the meeting is not in question. That is to say, his or her claim to defining the task does not generate the negative sentiment crucial to the evolution of the role of socio-emotional leader. This is not to say that these dynamics will never occur in some board meetings. What it says is that how people interact in the group (effectively, whether a Bales-type scenario ensues) depends upon group members' perceptions of two kinds of legitimacy. The first is the legitimacy of the task (what should we be doing here?); the second is the legitimacy of the leader (do we accept X as being in charge?).

This shows that, while occupying a role is important, it is not sufficient as the basis upon which to know how one is to deal with people and they with you. What Bales recognized as a necessary consensus among group members, has been defined here as a perception of the legitimacy of the task. People do not interact out of single role sets (for example as a mother, as a student, as a manager), but as multiples of these brought together in different, and sometimes new situations (for example as a woman deciding whether or not to miss her MBA class because her son is ill that evening). In this example, there are questions concerning her simultaneous membership of several groups that bear upon how she will act in any one situation. The woman has various social identities, which will be implicated in her decision about whether she ought to attend the class or stay home and look after her son.

There is one final, and important point that this overview of early research underlines; *interactions are not the same as relationships*. The different findings implied in the use of strangers or people who know each other is evidence of this. What has been called 'the legitimacy of the leader' refers to this feature. Strangers in a group have to work out their dealings with one another; directors and employees, husbands and wives, tutors and students are already in a relationship. (As indeed was clearly illustrated in the extract in Chapter 1 where Mary and Harry discussed their relationship and working practices.) This does not mean that we should not compare ways of interacting in this and that relationship, looking at the amount of talk here or styles of bodily conduct there. It does mean, however, that we should be cautious about explaining the relationship simply in terms of the detailed interactions that pass between the individuals concerned. Also, we must be cautious not to generalize from studies of social relationships to what happens in personal relationships (and vice-versa). Being a stranger has its own psychological reality, just as does being a friend, confidant or lover.

The extent to which a study of social interaction can illuminate distinctions such as those mentioned above will be discussed in the sections to follow. In doing this we shall be making a change of course, away from a concern with psychological processes in general to an analysis of differences between groups. Because these differences have taken up much of the attention of those studying social interaction, we shall give space to them under separate headings. In particular, we shall examine what

social psychologists have had to say about the effects of group membership on language use in interaction, as well as upon communication of a
non-verbal kind.

This shift in emphasis will continue in the direction that has already
been set in the analysis of norms and roles. We have seen that these can
be understood as things that follow from what people do: they are not
just structures that bind people into relationships of definite forms.
Individuals not only follow norms, they make appeal to them as justifications for what they do, or for what others should not do. People do
not just fill roles, but they lay claim to them, contest them or perhaps
attempt to extricate themselves from their grasp. This way of thinking
suggests that people are more active in their relationships than norm/
role explanations would allow. However, to explore this idea in any
detail, we need to address some of the questions raised explicitly in
relation to problems of first language, and then bodily conduct.

Review of section 2

- The study of social relationships has its roots in social
  psychology's concern with the individual in society. Early
  studies of norms emphasized what people come to *share*
  in social relationships.

- The assumption that norms are shared by all, or that
  they are unbending prescriptions has been shown to be
  wanting. Some norms prescribe what should be done;
  others only describe what most people do.

- Bales's work on group organization explored interactions
  in terms of the role differentiation of members.
  Interaction gives rise to task and socio-emotional leaders,
  whose emergence shapes later interactions within the
  group.

- The idea that interaction in groups invariably leads to
  this form of role differentiation has been questioned. It
  relates, instead, to certain special conditions of group
  setting, namely legitimacy of the task, and legitimacy of
  the leader.

- There is a need to be aware that interactions established
  on the basis of social relationships, where people hardly
  know one another, cannot be generalized to personal
  relationships which exist over time.

3   The social context of interaction: language

3.1   Language and context

When we think of individuals in social relationships, we often imagine them speaking to one another. It is taken for granted that much of what passes for social interaction will go on in terms of language. There is a mundane reason for this – that much of what people do involves speech. There is also the reason that language is the medium through which we make sense of the world for each other, establishing 'how things are'. This taken-for-granted aspect is reflected in the fact that we are largely unaware of how we speak, and how we understand. Ordinary exchanges illustrate this in the way that those concerned apparently comprehend so easily what is being said. For example:

Wife: 'Do you think it will matter about the coat?'

Husband: 'Doubt it – where's my watch gone?'

Wife: 'It's over there. I said, do you think it matters?'

Husband: 'Of course not. Hell, how should I know, hurry up will you?'

This episode illustrates a number of things. Some of these can be appreciated once we are told that it takes place in the bedroom of a couple getting ready to go out for the evening. Without knowing that, we might be uncertain as to what is going on. In everyday life, because people normally know the context and background of what is said to them, things 'make sense'. The fact that these two people are going to a party, that they both might wish to make a good impression on their hosts and the other guests, are crucial to understanding what is said. Not only is there an immediate context in which the interaction takes place, but there is a wider world of socializing that makes the exchange sensible. It is because we have knowledge of that world – even if it is only second hand – that we can appreciate the meaning of what is said.

This point is also applicable to something which might be thought quite unproblematic; that the action takes place in the bedroom of a man and woman who are married to one another. The activity of getting changed, of taking off and putting on, of choosing and discarding, presumes a physical world of clothes, possessions, and jointly owned furnishings. What language does in any specific exchange is to make some of those features matter in relation to the intentions of the people concerned. The wife's coat and the husband's watch take on a significance that they might not ordinarily be seen to have. Therefore, language does not just reflect context, it also shapes it.

ACTIVITY 2.2   Consider for one moment the power of assumed context in understanding what words mean. What if the exchange did not involve a married couple in their bedroom, but a man (married to another woman) and a woman (married to another man) talking in a hotel bedroom? Read the above exchange once more, and compare the resulting interpretation to the one suggested initially.

These points underline the argument that language supports context. However, it also shapes it, in the sense that the words chosen can make something seem positive, neutral or negative (Giles and Coupland, 1991). In the extract given above, the husband might have said, 'We musn't be late', rather than 'hurry up will you'. The words chosen not only do the work of conveying information about the matter at hand (the time the couple have available). They also indicate something about the couple's relationship, concerning that particular moment and, per-haps, their habitual manner of dealing with each other.

3.2 Language and social background

What is it that determines which words are chosen? This is a very broad question, but it suggests that individuals do not have a completely open choice in the matter. Being born into a particular gender, ethnic group or neighbourhood will affect the way that the person speaks and is spoken to by others. Various social groups have different verbal repertoires on which they draw, employing not only different words, but distinct forms of expression. In Britain, first impressions are still often formed on the basis of regional accent; the prospect of the kind of relationship one might have with another person is shaped by what we 'have in common to talk about'.

An early example of research that explored this difference was carried out by Basil Bernstein (1971), who compared the language use of young peo-ple in middle-class and working-class Britain. Developed in the 1950s, his argument rested upon assumptions about social class that would be chal-lenged if they were put forward in this way today. Bernstein argued that working-class speech relied heavily upon the maintenance of a way of life in which role positions were traditionally ordered. This meant that individuals would fall back upon these traditional structures as shared knowledge. Rather than be encouraged to search out new forms of expression, they would often use what Bernstein called a 'restricted speech code'. By comparison, the middle-classes were concerned to spell out ideas in relation to personal experience, so that, in addition to the 'restricted code', they also had access to what he called an 'elaborated code' in their dealings with each other.

Bernstein's theory tried to deal with both the context dependency and context shaping functions of language. However, it met with criticism for suggesting that restricted code was a limitation to wider social interaction for the educationally disadvantaged. In particular, it seemed to suggest that people's social background could lock them into certain kinds of relationship, so that they could only relate in ways that their speech community allowed. It did not address sufficiently the question of what might happen when individuals meet others outside of their home setting.

This issue was taken up in a study of New Yorkers from different backgrounds. The findings showed that people's language increased in its use of 'prestigious forms' as the topic of conversation moved from being less to being more formal (Labov, 1966). That is to say, individuals do not simply interact within a speech code typical of their group. They are more or less aware of how others speak, and will adopt the appropriate form when they think it useful to do so.

The adoption of the manner of speaking typical of one group, by a member of another, has been called *speech accommodation*. For example, in relation to accent, it has been shown that speakers who adapt their own speech to that of the listener are more positively evaluated by that person (Giles and Coupland, 1991). Specifically, this is an example of 'speech convergence', in which interpersonal differences are reduced by one party to facilitate communication with the other. The complementary situation, 'speech divergence', was shown to occur in exchanges where one of the speakers acts so as to distinguish (and presumably strengthen) his or her identity. Bourhis and Giles (1977), for example, had a confederate challenge Welsh speakers about the value of the Welsh language, and noted the subsequent broadening of their Welsh accent in the English in which the interview was conducted.

This accommodative movement does not just work in the direction of progressing 'upwards' to more elaborated, formal or prestigious forms of speech. In a study of the health beliefs of working-class families in East London, Jocelyn Cornwell (1984) found that her respondents (most were women) began by using what she termed the 'public' language of medicine. This is the language, if not of doctors, then of educated people. Later on, as she got to know them better, they told her stories of their own illness experiences and those of their families. These were couched in terms more typical of how they would speak to friends in their neighbourhood. Such stories Cornwell called 'private accounts' of illness, which not only described different kinds of experience, but also signalled a different relationship between interviewer and interviewee. This change in story-form was not some switch of role, given that it was sometimes tentative and not always complete. Rather, it was the result of these women being able to treat the investigator (or trying to treat her) as if she was 'one of them'. It seemed that 'public accounts' were those required where the women felt it necessary to justify their position, both as adults responsible for their own health, and as mothers responsible for the health of their children.

In summary, we can say that while linguistic differences between people from different parts of society are important, they should not be seen as features that wholly limit or define what can be said or done. Individuals would seem to have a good idea (some better than others) about how others speak, and about the advantages to be gained from adopting a different style or accent to one's own. In Chapter 3 we shall look more closely at the ways in which people can 'manage their impressions', so as to strike a more favourable chord with others. At this juncture, the point to be taken is that linguistic styles do differ, but how those differences are *made* to matter is something beyond mere group distinctions.

3.3 Language and gender

As well as looking at language use in a single context, it is possible to examine its role in communication by individuals from different groups. Perhaps the most actively researched area of this kind in recent years has been the place of language in the relationship between the sexes (for reviews see Eckert and McConnell-Ginet, 1992; Graddol and Swann, 1989). Much of this research was stimulated by Lakoff's (1975) claim that, compared to men, women use 'powerless' language, and that men interrupt women more than women interrupt men. (The latter issue relates to turn-taking in conversation, and will be considered further in section 5.1.)

Because they are socialized into using different modes of expression, women (and men), it is claimed, replicate the existing power structures in society that favour men. The generality and stability of these research findings have subsequently been questioned, because they suggest that linguistic forms are attached to gender groups as fixed properties. They do not take account of variations in women's and men's social situations, or even in their varied personal scope for communication.

In spite of this, a number of grammatical formations have been identified as characteristic of women's talk. These, it is claimed, underline their relative powerlessness in relation to men. Women have been shown to use what are called back-channel noises like 'mmm...' or 'yeah' to indicate that they are still listening, and they use fewer commands in their speech (Poynton, 1989). The last point can be illustrated as follows. Where a man might say 'Close the door', a woman is more likely to choose a different phrasing, modulating what is formed as an order. So she might say instead, 'Would you mind just closing the door, please?'.

This talk is not limited to mixed sex situations, but is also observed in places where women meet alone together. One that has received much attention (owing to Lackoff, 1975) is the use of 'tag questions'. An example of this might be, 'We'll come here again sometime, *won't we*?' The italicized words turn what might have been a statement ('I'd like us to come here again sometime') into an appeal. Other grammatical forms supposed to be typical of women's speech include what are called 'hedges', which soften or otherwise modify a direct statement or request. So, instead of saying, 'Please take this to the post office', the request becomes, 'I was wondering if you could possibly do me a favour – if you wouldn't mind?'.

Research has shown, however, that tags and hedges are not restricted to women's speech, but appear in that of men too (Poynton, 1989). They are, as claimed, often taken to be signs of powerlessness, but this is not necessarily the user's intention. Using tags like 'what do you think?' or 'shall we?' are ways of trying to exert some control in situations where it might be felt to be lacking. One study of couple's talk showed that tags are used by women in an attempt to elicit a response. This occurs at points in the conversation where they are getting inadequate responses from men (Fishman, 1979). That is, these linguistic forms are strategic devices which become signs of powerlessness where they fail to gain their desired effect, or must be used repeatedly.

Just as important as the presence of these grammatical structures may be the ways in which men and women interpret them, perhaps as requests for help. Where women share experience and offer reassurance, men are more likely to respond by giving advice, or acting as experts (Maltz and Borker, 1982). What matters is what each sex perceives its role to be, and how each individual acts so as to be consistent with that gender behaviour pattern. That there is a broad consensus in the population about how men and women speak was shown in a study of children drawn from sequential school grades (Edelsky, 1977). Children in the sixth grade (11–12-year-olds) were found to show greater sex-typing in this matter than adults, for example 'adorable' was seen as peculiarly a woman's expression while 'I'll be damned' was seen as a man's. However, it should be borne in mind that being asked to make judgements about tag questions is not the same as interpreting them in the course of conversation.

This commentary suggests that styles of speaking are more like ways of *portraying* ourselves as men or women, not just giving voice to prescribed features of social roles. If this is the case, then we should expect that there will be situations in which women attempt to escape these gender role expectations by deliberately using the language of men. Examples of this would include those situations where women deliberately resist using 'powerless' language in men's company, or where they take on the language of men, in order to be accepted. Recent evidence suggests that, in any case, it is a mistake to consider men and women as homogeneous populations, because language styles differ across contexts and between social domains (Cameron, 1988; Giles and Coupland, 1991).

BOX 2.3   Tag questions re-visited – a study by Cameron, McAlinden and O'Leary (1988)

These researchers began by questioning whether tag questions must signal tentativeness (on the part of women or men). They suggest that these utterances might be fulfilling several possible functions in speech, and that to declare all of them 'tag questions' (with relevant overtones) might be an analytical mistake. One possibility is that, for women, talk of this kind can be a suggesting move, not a communication of weakness. That is, what is distinctive in women's speech style might possess virtues of its own, rather than be just the result of male dominance.

To test this they first distinguished between what have been called 'modal tags' and 'affective tags'. Modal tags are those where the speaker is requesting information or confirmation of information (for example 'you weren't here last week, were you?'). Affective tags, on the other hand, signal concern for the addressee ('quite a nice room to sit in, isn't it?').

The researchers used conversations and interviews recorded from radio and television broadcasts, and analysed them according to gender, whether speakers were powerful or powerless, and the kinds of tags used. The results are shown in Table 2.1.

Table 2.1   Tag questions in unequal encounters

	Women		Men	
	Powerful	Powerless	Powerful	Powerless
Modal	3	9	10	16
	(5%)	(15%)	(18%)	(29%)
Affective	49	0	29	0
	(80%)	–	(52%)	–
Total	61		55	

(Adapted from Cameron et al., 1988, p.89)

Cameron et al. drew attention to the fact that men have more modal tags, while women have more affective ones. This supports the idea that women are more concerned for the other speaker. The most striking difference, however, is that between powerful and powerless speakers. Powerless speakers of either sex use modal tags, but no affective ones. This suggests that such linguistic devices are not just sex-specific but are also to do with the rights and responsibilities of the speakers concerned.

If you can, videotape part of a studio discussion programme shown on television, or record one broadcast on radio. Identify the tag questions used by the participants. Do you notice any difference between the numbers used by men and by women? Can you identify the different contexts in which these tag questions occur?

ACTIVITY 2.3

What the discussion in this and the previous sections suggests is that language may be context *dependent* but it is not context *determined*. As individuals born into a particular social class, a specific ethnic culture, and as members of a given sex, certain linguistic repertoires will give form to our experience. Language is therefore a *medium* of communication. However, it is also a *means* for communicating, and its different forms can be adopted or discarded depending upon the relationship and the situation. These forms of speaking into which we are socialized guide our expressions, at the same time offering to others clues as to our social identity.

However, language is not the sole means of communication that we have at our disposal. Before we can take a more critical view of its place in social interaction, we need to look first at other ways in which social life is conducted. Foremost among these is the use of the face and body in communication, which social psychologists identify as the field of non-verbal behaviour.

Review of section 3

- Because language is a shared medium of communication, it affects how we conceptualize social life, including our social and personal relationships.

- This sharing is not universal, in that social groups may differ in their language use. Men and women have been shown to use language in gender-linked ways, although the claim that certain forms (for example tag questions) are gender-specific has been undermined by recent research.

- It has been shown that individuals can use different language-codes (or styles) depending upon whom they are with, and according to their purposes at the time. The scope of this use is affected by a person's position of power relative to others.

- Where individuals can articulate their experience (literally, 'have their say'), then that use of language is a means for them to shape their social and personal worlds.

4   The social context of interaction: non-verbal behaviour

4.1   The background to the study of body movement

By definition, face-to-face interaction involves more than words, because individuals have bodies. We see each other's expressions, movements and postures, not to speak of our physical shape, size and clothing. This section will examine some of the research that has been undertaken into non-verbal behaviour as it takes place during interaction. It was pointed out in Chapter 1 that while accounts of relationships are important, so too is 'what actually goes on between participants as they interact with each other'. We shall see, in this section, that what 'actually' happens is often a matter for debate if not argument between social psychologists and others. To see how and why this comes about, it is useful to make oneself more aware of some of the differences in how individuals typically behave, or think they behave, when with others they know either more or less intimately.

ACTIVITY 2.4   *General dimensions of communication associated with relationship development*

As a way of beginning to think about the role of non-verbal behaviour in social relationships, try the following. Look at the seven dimensions set out in Table 2.2, which have been proposed as ways in which our communications change as we get to know another person better. As a relationship becomes more intimate, it is suggested that the terms in the right-hand column describe how people act. Conversely, as the relationship becomes more formal (or impersonal) the terms in the left-hand column describe the participants' behaviours. For each one, note down some of the *non-verbal behaviours* that you think might signal a change to greater intimacy on each dimension.

Table 2.2   **The seven dimensions of communication**

More Formal	More Intimate
Narrow, precise	General, diffuse
Stylized	Unique
Rigid	Flexible
Awkward	Smooth
Public	Personal
Hesitant	Spontaneous
Taken for granted	Explicit, spelled out

(Adapted from Knapp, 1983)

Reflect upon the behaviours you have noted down. Do the same communications appear on every dimension? What does this suggest to you about how non-verbal behaviour is used to communicate greater or lesser intimacy?

The term 'non-verbal behaviour' covers a very wide range of movement. This includes facial expressions, voice intonation, gestures and the kinds of postures that people variously adopt (for a review, see Knapp and Hall, 1992). Judging from the number of popular books available, there would seem to be wide public interest in what is often called 'body language' or 'body codes'. The underlying reason for this is the premise that one can read bodily conduct so as to know the other person's motives or feelings. From that point of view, non-verbal behaviour is assumed to have some kind of communicating function, though it requires a knowledge of the code to understand what is being 'said'.

On the other hand, non-verbal behaviour also appears in a very public way in the customs and traditions that are part of everyday culture. People meet in the street, they stop, shake hands, talk and then take their leave with a smile and wave of the hand. In the workplace, they knock at the manager's door, stand while given instructions and then exit when the boss makes it clear that the meeting is over.

These two examples are deliberately chosen because they reflect both the informal and the formal poles of our daily cultural experience. Unlike the facial expressions and hand movements of the individual under scrutiny from the 'body language' guide, these episodes are easily recognizable by anyone in the relevant culture. If it is to be understood, non-verbal behaviour need not be expressive of individual intentions, because it is patterned in ways that derive from social forms. This distinction – between individual intentions on the one hand, and social patterns on the other – provides the basis for our discussion of research into non-verbal behaviour in the following sections.

4.2 Non-verbal behaviour in natural contexts

The study of non-verbal behaviour within social psychology has drawn upon a number of sources, but none more than the work of social anthropologists (see Kendon, 1990 for a review). People like Raymond Firth, Margaret Mead and Gregory Bateson had been studying pre-industrial societies during the 1930s. As part of this work, they had developed a number of techniques for recording their observations. Among these was the use of film to capture the detail of everyday life.

This focused attention upon specific gestures, inviting analysis of a kind not possible beforehand.

The relevance of these ideas for the study of relationships is the suggestion that non-verbal behaviour is conducted within a shared set of cultural rules. We have already seen that there are limitations to the proposal that people share anything (language, gesture) in its entirety, or across all social groups. Nevertheless, it seems that sometimes, in some relationships, we must draw upon prescriptions that, we believe, specify how one should act in that context. This might be because we simply do not have any experience of how to act in that situation, or because we draw upon our understanding of how 'members of our group' normally act in that kind of setting. Here are two examples (described below and in Box 2.4.) of how non-verbal behaviour has been studied in two real-life situations. One concerns a more formal relationship, in that the people concerned are a therapist and patient. The other involves a couple who were filmed, in documentary style, kissing on a park bench.

Scheflen's (1964) methodology, sometimes called *context analysis* is based upon the assumption that any given act – a smile, a hand movement – has no intrinsic meaning. Such acts can only be understood when taken in relation to each other. Scheflen made studies of body movement employed by therapists and patients during consultations (see Figure 2.1). He made particular note of the sequencing and patterning of the movement of both parties, relating these to events in the course of the therapy session. Scheflen used the analogy of the linguistic system to specify smaller and larger changes in posture as occurring at different levels of communication. For instance, small movements like head tilts were called 'points'; shifts in body posture, such as straightening oneself in the chair, were called 'positions'; finally, larger and more extended postural changes (for example getting up and pacing the room) he called 'presentations'.

What Scheflen aimed to show was that changes in body movement at these different levels were associated with developments of a similar degree in the course of the conversation. For example, stages in an argument would be indicated by shifts in position; moves to a different phase of the meeting, such as when the formal business has been completed, might be marked by a change in presentation. Taken together, this means that more complex events constitute the context of other events that occur within them.

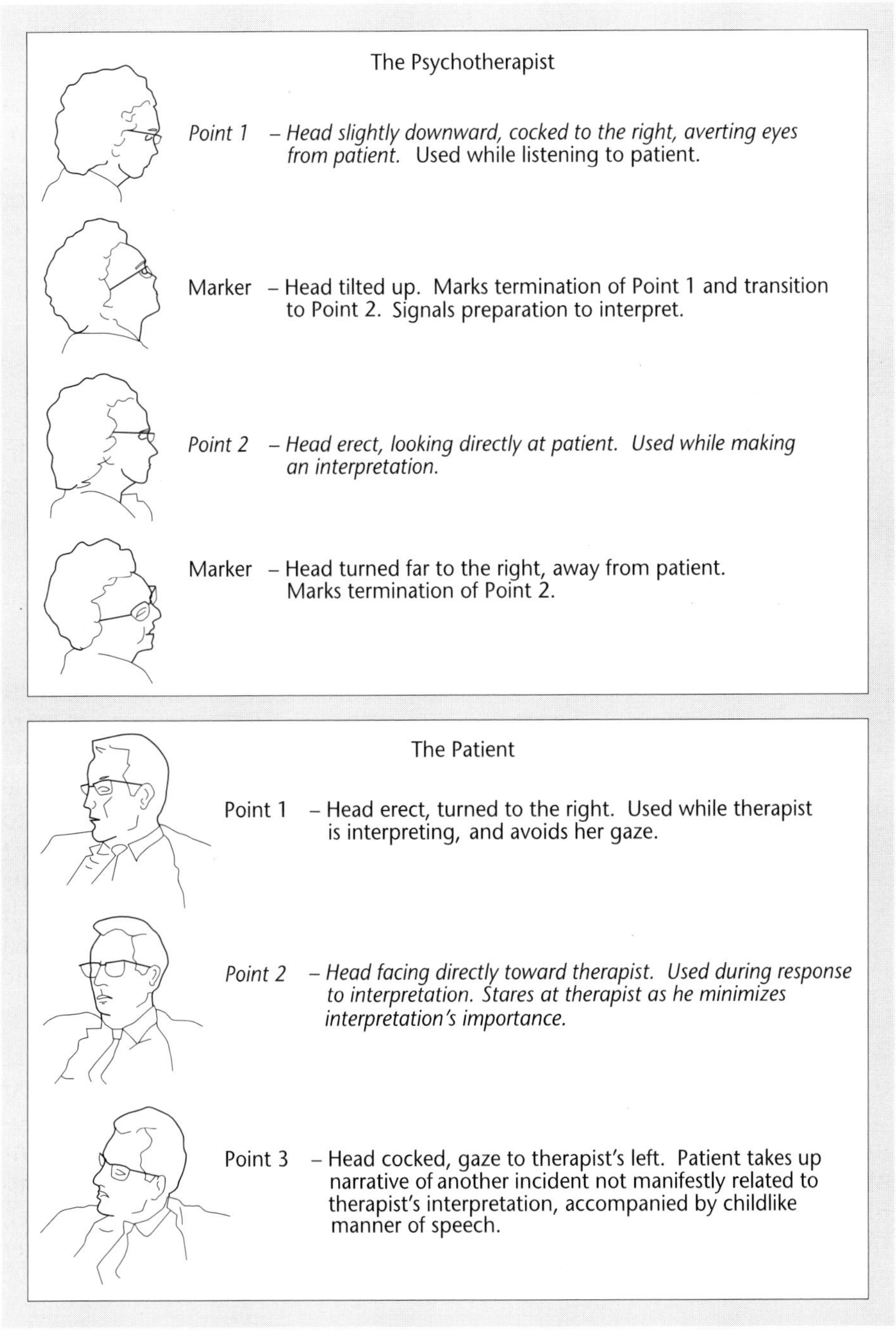

The Psychotherapist

Point 1 – *Head slightly downward, cocked to the right, averting eyes from patient.* Used while listening to patient.

Marker – Head tilted up. Marks termination of Point 1 and transition to Point 2. Signals preparation to interpret.

Point 2 – *Head erect, looking directly at patient.* Used while making an interpretation.

Marker – Head turned far to the right, away from patient. Marks termination of Point 2.

The Patient

Point 1 – Head erect, turned to the right. Used while therapist is interpreting, and avoids her gaze.

Point 2 – *Head facing directly toward therapist. Used during response to interpretation. Stares at therapist as he minimizes interpretation's importance.*

Point 3 – Head cocked, gaze to therapist's left. Patient takes up narrative of another incident not manifestly related to therapist's interpretation, accompanied by childlike manner of speech.

Figure 2.1 *Head placements and markers of points in a psychotherapist and patient*

Source: Scheflen, A. (1964) 'The significance of posture in communication systems', *Psychiatry,* 27, pp. 316–31

> **BOX 2.4** The study of interaction during a 'kissing-round'
>
> Another example of this approach has been provided by Kendon (1975) who analysed a film, made for television, of a couple kissing on a park bench. While it was found that the man's face was relatively stable during the course of the observation, the woman's face showed nine different expressions. These were:
>
> A Base face   B Closed smile   C Teeth smile
>
> D Kiss face 1   E Kiss face 2   F Dreamy face
>
> G Lip forward   H Wide face   I Frown face
>
> These different 'faces' were obtained by analysing the patterns of movement observed on the film. Kendon then examined these patterns, for the man and woman separately, in relation to their movements toward and away from each other. One of the study's main findings was that the man initiated kissing, while the woman regulated the different directions and degrees in which the episode should proceed. This, Kendon concluded, was why the woman's facial displays were more highly differentiated than those of her partner.

Whether the findings described in Box 2.4 hold for all acts of kissing is another matter, though a more recent study of heterosexual couples observed in bars in the USA has supported Kendon's argument, at least for the early stage of courtship behaviour. Women were seen to exercise more influence in the beginning of a flirtatious relationship, but allowed the men to take the initiative later on (McCormick and Jones, 1989). Nevertheless, these studies deal only with courtship within white heterosexual couples. It is questionable whether their findings can be generalized to all couples. There are complex issues here involving relationships between social, cultural and biological ways of thinking.

ACTIVITY 2.5   Now read *Reading A*: 'Gender differences in close relationships' by Robert Hinde, at the end of the book, which deals specifically with this issue. Note Hinde's conclusion that neither biology nor experience alone can account for gender differences in social behaviour. When you have finished, try using his idea of an interaction between the two to reflect back upon the 'kissing round' described in Box 2.4.

What do these examples tell us about non-verbal behaviour in social life? They suggest that the body acts as a medium for communicating things about the interaction itself. Gesture need not refer to something beyond itself, either in the personalities of the individuals concerned or in the wider society. Non-verbal behaviour becomes a way of indicating something about the kind of relationship in which people are engaged. For the couple kissing on the park bench, the pattern, the passion and the length of their kisses communicates, in a way stronger than words alone, what kind of situation this is. Like language, non-verbal behaviour does not just support context: it is an important way in which the ongoing episode is defined.

Bearing upon this last point, the anthropologist Mary Douglas (1973) has argued that societies vary in the degree to which they exert tighter or looser control over bodily expression. For example, when the pygmies of the Kalahari laugh, they lie on the ground and kick their legs in the air. She suggests that laughter (in any culture) is not signalled by specific gestures or facial expressions, but by the deportment of the whole body. In effect, what any one gesture means depends upon the scope that people have for using their whole body to convey information. In cultures setting 'high' thresholds of bodily control, like that of the Kalahari pygmies, a free use of the body is not just allowed, but is often required if individuals are to convey meaning. In a country such as Britain, that sets a 'low' threshold on the body's use (that is, it is more constrained), raising one's voice or making expansive gestures runs the risk of the person being labelled 'emotional' or 'unruly'. This is what is meant by saying that the meaning of any particular gesture derives from the potential scope for expression *in general*.

It might be argued that Douglas's view holds good for small, pre-literate cultures, but not for complex industrial societies. In the latter case, we expect a large variation in the rules of deportment, in part because of the wide range of situations and groups that exist. For example, attending a funeral requires that the mourners conduct themselves 'with dignity', defined in terms of the limits of bodily display. In contrast, at a party, the people concerned are expected to behave, if not with abandon, then with a freedom of movement and expression that conveys that they are enjoying themselves. The point remains, however, that it is not the specific gestures that matter, as much as the difference in scope and style of bodily conduct that the situation allows.

How, then, should we think of this cultural inheritance in relation to particular episodes of social interaction? Once more, we can affirm that it is a mistake to say that we are entirely subject to rules of behaviour; if effective, these would lock us into our respective cultural groups. There is evidence, however, that some facial expressions are universally recognized, dealing as they do with 'basic' human emotions, such as happiness, disgust or fear. Reviewing a number of studies in this field, Ekman et al. (1982) concluded that, in general, people are able to make accurate judgements of emotion from facial behaviour.

However, this argument cannot hold for the whole range of gestures which, we have already established, are learned and are culturally specific. Just as there is scope for people to accommodate their speech in the company, say, of someone whom they want to impress, so it is possible to do the same with their bodily conduct. It has been shown that mutual influence, the way in which one person adjusts to the other, happens in a wide variety of interactions (Cappella, 1984). The posture adopted when talking, amounts of looking, and the degree of proximity are some examples of ways in which this can occur.

While we may be unaware of the detailed movements involved in gesture, we are yet conscious of what we are doing as we make them. An awareness of, and a sensitivity to context are the basis of 'good manners' and social decorum. There are many occasions where to show one's feelings would be to risk disapproval or perhaps loss of status. Disappointment when losing a contest is one example; the contestant who comes second in a beauty contest masks her sadness with a smile. By comparison, the businesswoman who gains promotion over her colleague minimizes her joy (at least in the other's presence), while the other neutralizes her disappointment with a 'warm' congratulation.

This important feature of non-verbal behaviour was investigated by Ekman and Friesen in a study comparing the reactions of Americans and Japanese to a film containing stress-inducing sequences (Ekman, 1971). They found that there were similar facial responses among the two groups, but that the Japanese subjects modified their expressions in the presence of an observer. They interpreted this as the operation of a cultural convention that discourages the direct expression of emotion in public. Ekman and Friesen called such conventions *display rules,* arguing that they operate widely as guides to how we should appear in front of others. It is important to note that display rules are not just devices for hiding feelings that are imminent in the body's physical attitude. They are, if anything, more appropriate when we anticipate how we wish to be seen. An example, in Western culture, might be the widow attending her husband's funeral. She is allowed to grieve, indeed is expected to be upset: but she is also expected to bear her loss with dignity and fortitude. Nobody, seeing her walking steadily and with composed features, would mistake this attitude for a lack of feeling on her part. By operating under these display rules the widow brings about two positive conditions, one public and one private. On the one hand, she endorses the ritual aspect of the funeral, allowing others to play their parts. On the other, by making this public presentation, she preserves her feelings 'as her own', averting the gaze of others from the special conditions of her grief.

With the growth of the mass media, display rules have become less transparent, more open to scrutiny. Think of the nominees at award ceremonies, who are being televized while the envelope is torn open to reveal the winner's name. Anticipation of winning, and the readiness to suppress disappointment should one fail, are there to be read in their faces. However, the fact that people in such circumstances may be more aware of the requirements of 'putting on a good face' does not relieve them of the felt obligation that they should do so.

4.3   Gesture in everyday interaction

The point made earlier about language can also be made for non-verbal behaviour; it provides a resource for communication and a way of formulating ideas. As a resource, ways of using the body as a whole, and making specific gestures in particular, are behaviours into which people are socialized. We normally use them as we do words – in the course of thinking, not as the objects of our thought. It might even be said that we 'think through them', in as much as gesture is part of the flow of communication exchanges between the individuals concerned. One study, conducted in New York in the 1940s, compared Jewish and Italian immigrants with older generation Americans (Efron, 1972). It found that, where the Italians used conversational gesture in a declamatory way (that is, one at a time), Jewish speakers used gestures plentifully, and together. One tactic that was noted, during arguments between the latter group of individuals, was holding one's opponent's arm, thus preventing them from gesticulating and effectively stopping them speaking altogether.

Within Western culture, there is a good deal of common knowledge about different kinds of gesture. Everyone is (more or less) acquainted with such things as V-signs, shrugs, or signals to stop. Similarly, there are gestures that express mood during conversation, such as excitability or determination; and there are movements taken to be indications of anxiety or embarrassment that involve foot shuffling or covering one's face with one's hands. Gestures are commonly used in social life, so that we should understand their place in the give and take of relationships, both personal and between strangers.

Gesture can be divided into three classes, as shown in Box 2.5. This, however, requires a cautionary comment. First, the identification of what is an emblem, an illustrator or a body manipulator in actual interaction is not that easy. Because the status of these gestures is context dependent, there is no way that one can allocate a particular movement to any one category in a universal fashion. Even within a sub-culture, a wink can accompany speech (to illustrate a knowing attitude) or be a special signal of greeting.

Also, the study of emblems, illustrators, and regulators is limited if it only tells us about what happens in general, or between strangers, or in one 'snapshot' of an exchange between people. If you refer back to Activity 2.4, you can reflect on some of the changes to non-verbal behaviour that you thought might occur as people get to know one another. Knapp (1983) himself suggested that less intimate relationships would be those to exhibit the most common emblems, or the most stereotyped facial expressions. For example, the handshake that begins as a stylized action between strangers becomes something accompanied by a hug, or even may disappear completely between friends.

BOX 2.5   Classifying gestures

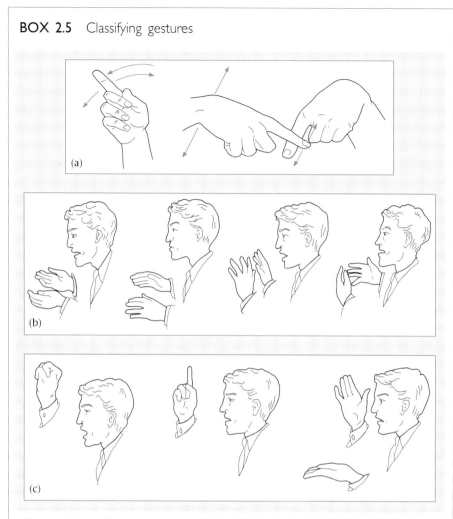

Figure 2.2 (a) Finger emblems (United States) for 'no' (left) and 'shame on you' (right). (b) Palm gestures. (c) Punctuation gestures.

One scheme for categorizing non-verbal behaviour was put forward by Ekman and Friesen (1969). They suggested three main classes of gesture:

1   *Emblems* are symbolic actions where the gesture has a specific verbal meaning shared by the people of a culture or sub-culture. Common examples in British society are nods of the head, holding up the hand to stop a car, or giving someone a V-sign. Sometimes, emblems are used instead of speech, because they can effectively act as a substitute. (Note that they are to be distinguished from sign language for the deaf. Because this makes use of words [the signs] organized into larger structural units such as phrases and sentences, it is classed as verbal communication [Brien, 1992]). At other times, emblems express precisely what a sentence or two might say in a roundabout

fashion; a shrug or a raising of the eyes conveys just what is intended. Because they are symbolic, emblems are not universal, though every society would appear to have some emblem for greeting and departure, for directing locomotion and for referring to physical states of the person. However, they are not context free. Their exact meaning depends upon who makes the gesture, to whom and in what setting.

2   *Body manipulators* are movements in which one part of the body does something to another part. Examples include scratching the head, biting the lips or playing with one's hair. Unlike emblems, body manipulators are things of which the actor is often unaware. For that reason, the observer does not usually see them as being deliberately communicative. This does not mean, of course, that the observer can make nothing of them. Interviewees who fiddle with their clothing, repeatedly smooth their hair or keep winding a pencil around their fingers are likely to be seen as nervous. As Ekman (1977) puts it, where the message provided by the emblem is 'given', the information gained from body manipulation is 'stolen'. Body manipulators do not tie in with changes in the flow of speech, although they might appear or disappear with a change in topic.

3   In contrast to the above, *illustrators* are movements intimately tied to the content and the flow of conversation. They include any act that substitutes, fills out, or otherwise modifies what is being said. The British, who are comparatively quiet in this mode, are always fascinated by the use of hands and arms that accompany speech in the rest of Europe. Illustrators both give messages and provide a display that conveys more than each gesture's specific meaning. Unlike emblems, however, they do not have a clear symbolic meaning, but are much more context dependent. Take, for example, the pointing of the finger. As an emblem it means 'you' ('come here', 'go over there', 'now you're for it') depending upon the situation and the people involved. During conversation, it could carry any of these meanings, but also serve to underline a point being made, where the referent is something or someone else. Ekman and Friesen have suggested five functions of illustrators, including substituting for a word that cannot be thought of; explaining through pictographic display ('you go straight on, and turn right'); punctuating speech by underlining or marking off clauses; and indicating the speaker's enthusiasm for the topic under discussion.

This brief overview of non-verbal behaviours shows the danger of trying to employ guides or ready-made classifications of gesture in everyday life, tempting as this might be. It is possible to look at a picture of someone and read into their behaviour the meaning suggested by the text. However, this turns everything that people do into emblems, which clearly cannot be the case. In our face-to-face relation-ships our actions and expressions are of varying importance, some behaviours being more significant than others. When one thinks of arguments and misunderstandings that seemed to turn upon inflections of the voice, or upon a shrug or a frown, then it appears that, even when not emblematic, non-verbal behaviour clearly matters in relation-ships.

The question remains as to *how* it matters, and how we communicate by means of the face and body. In the next section we shall look more closely at this issue of non-verbal behaviour as a means of communi-cation, and see how we can distinguish more precisely between what is and is not intended in our bodily conduct.

4.4 Non-verbal behaviour: communication, code or sign?

Early investigations into non-verbal behaviour were influenced by advances that had been made in research into the structure of grammar. For that reason, the idea that body movement could be explained in a similar fashion remained a guiding principle in much of the social psychological research that followed (Kendon, 1990). This assumed that non-verbal *behaviour* is, essentially, non-verbal *communication*. Terms bor-rowed from linguistics underlined this view, in which the sender ('encoder') transmitted meaning through patterned behaviour (a 'code') so that it could be read by an observer ('decoder'). From what we have said already about non-verbal behaviour, this seems a narrow view of events. It was limited further by the fact that nearly all of the studies in this field concentrated upon the interpretation of the behaviour (the decoder). Because the intentions of the sender were not always clear, and in some cases absent (that is, the individual did not intend that particu-lar posture, or facial expression), the problem of encoding was largely left to one side.

ACTIVITY 2.6   It is said by some social psychologists that 'all behaviour is communication'. Look out of your window (or step outside) and watch some people going by. Choose a person. Look at the way s/he walks. What is that walk communicating? Now think of walking in the street yourself. What are you communicating in doing this?

On the basis of the observations made during Activity 2.6 you will have formed some opinions about the extent to which 'all behaviour is com-munication'. If it means *all behaviour is intended* communication, this seems unlikely.

At the level of everyday experience, we know this already. Well-worn examples of whether a woman asked for the attentions of a man because of the way she looked at him, or moved, or selected which clothes to wear that evening are testimony to this fact. If there is a universal code or body-language, it seems that not everyone understands it, even if we all claim to be fluent speakers.

However, as far as many social psychologists were concerned, the assumption that body movement is, by definition, communication effectively remained unchallenged. The problem was eventually confronted directly in a paper which argued that all non-verbal behaviour is *not* communication (Wiener et al., 1972), in spite of it being made to appear so in much of the early research. Wiener et al.'s case was based upon two features: (1) the concentration upon decoders, which suggests that all signs are communications, and (2) the assumption that non-verbal behaviour is subject to a code from which it takes its meaning.

This critique centred upon the confusion of the idea of 'sign' with 'communication'. In essence, it argued that some non-verbal behaviour consists of signs that are spontaneously 'given off', without any deliberate intention on the part of the person concerned. For example, think of someone blushing (or walking, as in Activity 2.6). The idea that blushing is an intended act, designed to communicate one's confusion and embarrassment, is the *opposite* of what one wishes. Of course, *some* gestures and expressions are intended, though among these are deliberate body movements which are designed *not* to be seen as such. Standing, holding in one's (otherwise protruding) stomach, is a posture that is deliberately taken up to convey a particular physique. The fact that this is achieved through muscular effort is precisely what must *not* be seen by others if the effect is to be successful.

What is at issue here is the presence or absence of a code, that might or might not be shared by the individuals concerned. Having just said that there is no single language-like code for body movement, this does not mean that there are not any limited codes applying to certain groups in specific situations. See Box 2.6 for an explanation of how these differences can be explained.

The three forms of non-verbal behaviour set out in Box 2.6 do not occur separately but, more often than not, together. In new situations, or with strangers, individuals try to make a particular impression but, in so doing, they reveal more of themselves than they might wish. (They might also reveal less: for example, being so concerned to make a good impression, one 'seizes up' and does not communicate one's 'spontaneity'.) However, in these situations, and especially in relationships where people know each other well, there will also be communication, in the sense that the participants rightly perceive each other as intending the messages they give. Whether this involves the use of widely shared, cultural codes is another matter.

In summary, it can be said that non-verbal behaviour is not language-like, if by that we mean that it has a grammatical structure. Having said this, there are codes which allow us to interpret (accurately or mistakenly) the behaviour of others, just as there are some gestures that are

---

BOX 2.6   Non-verbal behaviour: when is it communication?

Posner (1989) has defined three kinds of non-verbal behaviour – (1) communication; (2) signification; and (3) indication. He also suggested that any complete interaction involves a sender, a code, a sign, a context and a recipient. In the case of *communication*, the sender and the recipient share a code and a sign system for sending messages. Language is of this kind. Sometimes, particularly in the case of emblems, non-verbal behaviour can be like this also. Then, the sender intends to send a message that the recipient can interpret (for example the V-sign).

However, even though an individual does *not* intend to send a message in the course of behaving, the other person can make an interpretation on the basis of it. Just by appearing, an individual makes available information that others use to form a judgement. We could say that the sender's intention is absent, but signs are made, and a code is available for interpreting that behaviour. These signs can be made with the body, or they can be made upon it. In the latter case, aspects of physique or facial appearance are signs that have been given particular cultural meanings. So, indolence, intellectual ability, or strength of character can be inferred from posture; sexual passion or weakness can be read from a person's face. These are examples of *signification*, where a code is used to interpret signs that are 'given off' in movement or expression. (A formal use of signification is the diagnosis by the doctor of measles on the basis of the appearance of spots on the skin. In this case, the patient does not intend the spots, nor does s/he necessarily share the code.)

The third sign process is one that involves no code at all. *Indication* occurs when a gesture or expression is made that is not recognizable within a code system. There are many body movements and facial expressions that people fail to recognize as meaning anything in particular. This does not imply that they are unintended, nor that they do not call out any response. Various glances, postures and expressions might be made deliberately as part of a person wishing to fashion a particular impression. This does not guarantee (nor even require) that there be a cultural code for making those particular signs. Posner (1989) gives the example of a young man who, in the presence of a woman who happens to look at him, imitates one of her involuntary movements in order to express his sympathy for her. In this example, this action might have an effect upon the woman or it might not. In either case, the sign is outside of a code that would give it a meaning that could be understood in any 'culturally accepted' sense.

symbolic, in the sense that they can communicate particular meanings. In addition, there is a range of behaviours that are indicative, which fall outside of codes. These actions can intimate desired change in the relationship (for example 'come closer') or they can maintain the interaction by regulating the exchange (for example who speaks when in the conversation). In order to be able to say more about these actions, we need a different theory about the place of the body in social life. This must be one that allows for non-verbal behaviour to play a more central role in defining social relationships, not just be a vehicle for conveying particular ideas from one individual to another.

This section has placed a question mark over the idea that there is a 'language of gesture' which individuals employ in the course of everyday life. The idea that conducting a relationship is an elaborate exchange of semaphore signals is an oversimplification of what occurs. The body is not just a complex system for the communication of ideas and feelings that emerge ready-made. As we shall see in section 6.1, this is a parallel to the situation regarding language. Words, as the Russian psychologist Vygotsky (1962) once said, are not merely the clothing for pre-fashioned thoughts. Taken together, these points suggest that social interaction is not a blow by blow exchange of individual meaning and intention. Radley (1995) has suggested that something altogether more subtle is involved, which involves us in being able to use our bodies to portray, intimate and allude, as well as to define, specify and determine. Before seeing how this is done in the course of conversation, we need to review what is known about the ways in which different groups of people use non-verbal behaviour. Such differences between cultures, or between men and women, will have implications for how individuals from different backgrounds overcome (or exploit) these variations in the course of forging relationships together.

4.5 Gender differences in non-verbal behaviour

We have already looked at gender differences in verbal behaviour, and shown that relationships between men and women may reflect differences in how they speak with one another. Having now introduced the basis of the study of non-verbal behaviour, we turn again to questions of gender difference. There are good reasons why we should take notice of these. Relationships between the sexes involve matters of appearance. This does not just mean facial attraction, but the whole range of signals that are used in courtship and, equally important, in the communication of exchanges that are 'not courtship'.

With this as background, it is not surprising to be told that a key topic in the study of non-verbal behaviour has been how men and women differ in the way they communicate with their bodies. A number of everyday observations suggest that this is true, and that this difference is sometimes used as a marker of gender identification. At the simplest level, a person in the distance can sometimes be identified by their walk. The point is not just that men and women have different styles of walking, but that these styles are recognized as being gender typical. So, it is possible to say of a woman that 'she walks like a man', or of a man that 'he has a "camp" way of walking'. Such labels are, more often than not, used in a derogatory fashion. This being the case, it is not surprising that there are normative pressures upon individuals to adopt, and maintain, the appropriate physical bearing of their respective gender. To 'be a woman' or to 'be a man' involves appearing as such, exemplifying and asserting one's gender-being in the small as well as in the large things that one does.

Anecdotal, but worthy of note, is the observation made by the French sociologist Marcel Mauss (1972) in the 1930s, concerning cinema usherettes in Paris. He noted how they walked differently from other French women, because they appeared to have adopted the walk of the American actresses whom they had seen on the screen. Mauss's point was that walking is a culturally learned behaviour, not just a functional derivative of biological endowment. However, we not only make gestures but we observe them, and we observe in what context and in what company they are appropriately made. Let us reflect for a moment upon who is doing the looking here and who is doing the walking. It is Mauss, the man, who watches; it is the usherettes, the women, who do the walking. This distinction is itself an example of the kind of work that has since been carried out into gender and non-verbal behaviour.

More often than not, research has underlined differences in looking which suggest that the sexes differ in who looks at whom, and under what circumstances. It has been shown that male pedestrians on a college campus maintained a more direct gaze at an approaching person than did females. Whereas the women tended to avert their eyes when stared at, the men were more likely to stare back if looked at in the street (Cary, 1978). This has been interpreted as being the result of men exerting more power than women in public, resulting in women feeling threatened in contexts such as these. There is a social expectation that women will be the object of men's attention, so that the looking behaviour of men and women in public reflects this fact. Furthermore, the observation has been made that, while men expand into social space, women remain more restrained. Where a man might sprawl across a park bench, a women is more likely to sit with her arms and legs close to her body. It has been argued that men take up more relaxed postures than women, in any situation, and when with members of either sex.

These views have been offered by Nancy Henley (1977), who adopted a broadly feminist approach to the study of social interaction. Henley's particular contribution was to show that such behaviours can be read as signifiers of power differences between the sexes. A look or a touch does not so much signal a specific personal intent, as it carries a meaning that defines group membership, for men and women, in their relative social positions. This perspective offers a different view to that of experimental psychology, which treats non-verbal behaviours as neutral acts, varying only in frequency or degree. This difference in approach shows that the 'facts' we obtain in social psychological research are dependent upon both the methods used, and upon the theoretical framework in which they are interpreted.

Now read *Reading B:* 'A gender sensitive perspective on personal relationships and therapy' by Arlene Vetere at the end of the book. Note how she raises the issue of power differences between men and women. She also discusses the implications of this for their relationships with one another, particularly within the family. You might think about other relationship settings in which gender remains, in her words, a 'hidden dimension', and how this is communicated non-verbally.

ACTIVITY 2.7

Perhaps it is not surprising, therefore, that several studies have been carried out to determine whether women and men differ in their ways of communicating non-verbally, and particularly in the accuracy with which they interpret other people's non-verbal messages. It has been found that, on average, women are better judges than men at interpreting non-verbal cues, particularly those expressed with the face (Knapp and Hall, 1992). Where this finding applies, it has implications for the way that men and women form relationships, and perhaps for the ways in which misunderstandings might occur.

Do you think that women are better than men at reading other people's expressions and moods? Think of one or two men and women whom you know very well, and recall a time when they misread your 'mood'. Also consider how you show your mood to different people. Do you think the misreading was a failure on their part alone? Do we read mood like we read books?

ACTIVITY 2.8

The above Activity might have raised a number of questions for you about how men and women interpret each other's non-verbal signals. Among these is the issue of the specific relationship between the people concerned. One researcher who has examined this question in detail is the Australian psychologist Patricia Noller. Instead of just asking subjects to make judgements about posed pictures, she videotaped interactions between husbands and wives, allowing an analysis of non-verbal communication in the context of the relationship itself. Box 2.7 describes one of her studies.

Within social psychology, the explanation for findings such as this has been that young girls are taught, from an early age, to be sensitive to the moods of others. In the context of a society where men have more power (the argument goes), women must learn to watch out for signs of displeasure among their menfolk. In the home, the mother tells the children not to disturb their father because 'he's had a hard day at work'; in the office, the secretary tells a subordinate that 'the boss is in a terrible mood today'. This hypothesis proposes that women are more accurate because they are more watchful; and they are more watchful because they are less powerful, and hence need to protect their interests.

BOX 2.7   Non-verbal communication between husbands and wives

In one of her experiments Noller (1980) examined the communications of husbands and wives, asking them to read out statements to each other. Each statement was accompanied by a description of the imaginary situation that formed its context, together with an intention that the speaker had to try to get across to the spouse. For example, a wife might be given the following:

Situation: 'You and your husband are sitting alone on a winter evening. You feel cold.'

Intention: You wonder if it is only you who are cold or if he is cold too.

Her husband would be given a card describing the same situation, but showing three alternative meanings, one of which is correct for the message his wife will send. These would include:

1   You wonder if it is only you who are cold or if he is cold too.
2   You want him to warm you with physical affection.
3   You are feeling that he is being inconsiderate in not having turned up the heat by now and you want him to turn it up straight away.

By videotaping the interactions as well as recording the judgements of each partner, independent ratings were obtained of the quality of each performance, that is how well that person conveyed the intention in what was said. It was found that, for all subjects, negative messages were more clearly sent than positive ones. That is, negative statements are clearer, or stand out more than positive ones. However, the most interesting results emerged from the comparison of wives' and husbands' messages. The women had significantly more of their communications rated as being clearly sent than did the men. The wives appeared to be better at communicating their intentions non-verbally; they were also better than their husbands at sending positive messages.

When it came to accuracy of interpretation, the men made more incorrect judgements of their wives' neutral messages, than vice-versa. In a group of couples designated as having 'poor marital adjustment', this effect was found even for messages judged (by raters) as being clear. Where couples were judged as being high in marital adjustment, the men were relatively good at sending clear messages to their wives.

An elaborated form of this explanation carries the label the *accommodation hypothesis* (Rosenthal and DePaulo, 1979). This suggests that women's 'politeness' towards men extends beyond looking, to a whole range of non-verbal behaviours. Women smile more, laugh at jokes rather than make them, listen more and interrupt less, and are more revealing of their personal feelings. Therefore, the accommodation hypothesis has two sides to it; a tendency to comply and a tendency not to intrude on the other's (men's) personal space. In their own studies asking subjects to make snap judgements about non-verbal behaviour, Rosenthal and DePaulo found that this tendency to 'politeness' in some women also resulted in their focusing upon what was 'good' in the cues given off by others. In situations where the cues were fleeting and ambiguous (as in deception), some women perceived these incorrectly. That is, they were more likely to be deceived about the other person's meanings and motives.

The picture one obtains is of women being generally more accurate in their interpretations of non-verbal behaviour, and yet more accommodating to the conversational demands of men. On the one hand, women are shown as being passive and coerced in relationships with men; on the other, they are believed to have a better working understanding of the social rules appropriate to various social situations (Noller, 1986). From a feminist perspective, these differences in the non-verbal behaviour of men and women are the outcome of power relations in society: they are products *within*, not determinants *of* social interaction.

One further point is worth drawing from this work on gender differences in accuracy of perception. It is interesting that a man from a marriage described as 'low in adjustment', who is particularly poor at decoding his wife's communications, can nevertheless make relatively accurate judgements of a stranger's non-verbal signals (Noller, 1984). This implies that the quality of judgement men and women make *within* relationships may not be the same as that which they make *outside* of them. Whether people understand one another is not only a matter of accuracy, because what is at issue in their dealings may be something about which they disagree, or in which they have quite different investments. Many spouses and partners know that what is openly acknowledged depends in part upon what one wishes, or is prepared, to see. Perceiving non-verbal communications is not a neutral process that goes on untouched by passion and interest: it is, to a significant degree, part of how the individuals concerned define their relationship to one another.

The distinction that was made earlier between *social* and *personal* relationships is relevant here. Specifically, we need to be aware that conclusions drawn about the role of non-verbal behaviours in formal encounters, might not apply (at least, not directly) to more personal and intimate relationships. Having made this point, it might be thought that in *social* relationships men's non-verbal behaviour controls the actions of women by underlining differences in status (for example the boss patting his secretary's back); in *personal* relationships (for example the couple kissing on a park bench), non-verbal behaviour between the sexes communicates something quite different. This is not the case. In the example of the kissing couple, the individuals remain a man and a woman, each subject to the rights and obligations attaching to their gender roles. What can, ought, or may be done to and by each partner is defined with respect to such expectations. This means that, even when mutual trust has been built up, appeals may be made to the rights and obligations concerning how men and women in general should treat one another. For example, an adolescent boy might try to persuade his girlfriend, of some months standing, that she should allow sexual intercourse because 'his friends would think him silly if they hadn't done it after this amount of time going out together'.

By comparison, situations of apparent formality also contain many regulatory features usually associated with more personal relationships. Male bosses relate to their female secretaries in ways that promote their superior status; they call them by their first name, may dictate what clothes they should wear, and may touch them (not necessarily sexually) in the course of their work. That is, behaviours can be status controlling that are usually associated with informal, personal relationships.

Sometimes, however, there can be a reversal of the *status quo*, even if only temporarily. Should the boss cut his finger, his secretary might bandage it for him while telling him to be brave. In this case, a set of caring behaviours from the domestic sphere are brought to bear in a way that, even if only fleetingly, allows the secretary to appear the dominant partner in the relationship (Walkerdine, 1981).

This discussion of gender differences in non-verbal behaviour has raised some important issues. Men and women are socialized into using different repertoires of behaviour, though they should not be thought of as being trapped within these. Also, a consideration of gender relationships has pointed up the issue of whether non-verbal behaviours are primarily status difference definitions. While actions do signal intentions and claims, and while they mark power relationships, they also do more than this. They intimate, or invite new directions that the relationship might take. When a boss invites a subordinate to have a drink, this can be read as his exercising an initiative that would be seen as inappropriate for the latter to take. However, it can also signal a change in the boss's willingness to take the subordinate into his confidence. Quite what the boss's invitation means, in terms of the balance of these two possibilities, must probably await the subordinate's response to the invitation. This signals the fact that there is an incompleteness in much of our non-verbal communication. We shall be taking up this issue in some detail in later sections of the chapter. The point to be taken here is that what specific non-verbal behaviours mean is difficult if not impossible to decide by taking a single, 'outside' view on the matter.

4.6 A comparison of structural and functional approaches to non-verbal behaviour

This discussion of non-verbal behaviour highlights a distinction between the methods adopted by researchers using different approaches. In particular, our survey shows a difference between those (often anthropologists) who have attempted to describe behaviours in natural settings, and others (mainly social psychologists) who have adopted the experimental method as a way of trying to establish causes and effects of non-verbal behaviour. (Yet another approach to examining non-verbal behaviour is described in Chapter 4 of this book.)

The former perspective, which attempted to describe patterned movements and sounds, has been labelled the *structural approach* (Scheflen, 1979). It was influenced by work in social linguistics, which regarded speech as having a number of levels, some influenced more by culture, others by the individual. Using this as a model, the aim was to describe body movement and posture by use of a scheme similar to that used to identify grammatical structures. Just as sounds (phonemes) are used to build up words (morphemes) that are strung into sentences (syntax), so it might be possible to see body movement as having a similar hierarchic form (Birdwhistell, 1971). Broadly speaking, researchers tried to analyse movement in terms of units which, once given a notation, could be recorded in different combinations recognized as 'internally meaningful material'.

In contrast, some social psychologists have been keen to relate changes in these behaviours to specific features of the situation (or the participants), as a way of finding out their particular place (or function) in the course of interaction exchange. This attempt to relate specific non-verbal behaviours to contextual features, usually through the use of experimental methods, is called the *functional approach* (Cappella and Street, 1985).

For an example of work adopting the functionalist position, especially its reliance upon the experimental method, see *Reading C*: 'The experimental study of relationships' by Michael Argyle (especially the section on Method).

ACTIVITY 2.9

An early example of this approach was Argyle and Dean's (1965) 'equilibrium theory', which examined the mutual effects of different 'channels' of communication. In experimental investigations, it was found that moving people closer together had the effect of their avoiding looking at each other's faces, rather like people crammed together in a bus or underground train. Argyle and Dean's idea of equilibrium was meant to account for the fact that, in any specified relationship, there would be a comfortable condition applying to the various channels. This meant that if these equilibria were disturbed (as in finding oneself cheek-by-jowl with others on the bus), then compensatory action would be taken to adjust for this by, for instance, staring at the advertisements or out of the window.

Argyle and Dean's original formulation was added to by Patterson (1985) as part of a broader 'functional model'. He saw the informational and regulatory functions as being related to relatively brief and minor acts, such as inclinations of the head or changes in gaze. Compared to these 'molecular' acts, the expressive function and a further two – the social control and the service-task functions – are more 'molar' or extended in time. By social control, Patterson means actions that are made to influence another person. From the functionalist point of view, it refers to behaviours that are deliberately managed to create a specific impression. In this way it is different to the expressive or intimacy function, which is more likely to involve spontaneous behaviour.

The functional model takes an 'outsider's view' of what happens. It is based upon the experimental approach, traditional in social psychology, which assumes that behaviours must have causal antecedents in the person's background, and (or) in the situation of the moment. From this perspective, non-verbal behaviour is for achieving control, either between individuals, or of one person by another. To study this, it is argued, requires the investigation of quite detailed movements, as might be observed in a laboratory.

The strength of the functional perspective is that it encourages researchers to specify possible relationships between different features of individuals and their relationships. A good example of this is the study by Noller (Box 2.7), in which features of the marital relationship were shown to relate to variations in the non-verbal communications between husband and wife. Also, by using controlled conditions and attempting to randomize chance happenings (a key part of scientific experimentation), the investigator can generalize findings to other contexts.

Set against this, the functional approach necessarily divides behaviour and experience into separate 'things', which are then treated as discrete variables. This objective view makes the perspectives of the people concerned difficult to grasp. It also deflects attention from the possibility that non-verbal behaviours do not always have functional aims or specifiable antecedents. This raises the question of whether non-verbal behaviours, acting as regulators, are necessarily brief acts, 'molecular' in form. This relates to what was said in an earlier section, where it was suggested that the regulation of an exchange, such as who should speak and when, might well be an extended feature of the relationship.

Structuralists like Douglas or Scheflen argue that non-verbal behaviour needs to be appreciated in a total way, not examined in terms of the functions of each of its channels taken separately. Rather than see the body as a kind of static signal box, emitting and receiving coded signals, they propose that it is a medium through which social controls can operate. By comparison, the structural perspective makes bodily conduct into something more like a means for reflecting people's definition of the social world. This does not mean that the body is determined by social rules, though it is interpreted in terms of it. For example, situations in which constraint is the norm (for example being in church) are those in which a raised voice becomes more meaningful, not less.

The structural approach is different from the functional perspective because it employs descriptive techniques rather than experimental ones. It also sees behaviour as part of culture, rather than as something abstracted from it. As a result, where the functionalists consider specific channels, structuralists view the body as a whole. In Douglas's scheme, what a person does specifically is expressive of the wider social order in which he or she lives. This is not the same as saying that the behaviour is 'caused' or even 'influenced by' the situation or relationship. Rather, the body is a medium or vehicle through which people can endorse or deny what is expected in that situation. A loud guffaw from someone during a church service might be coded within one of several of Patterson's functional categories. In contrast, from Douglas's perspective, to pick out the laugh as an example for discussion depends upon a shared cultural understanding (the problem of dividing 'molecular' from 'molar' once again). That is, the laugh does not exist, separately and for ever, as a piece of behaviour. It comes into existence only in the context of a social framework that gives it its significance. This means that any classification of non-verbal behaviours – functional or otherwise – must be understood to be culture-specific.

The distinctions between these two approaches are important for a study of what goes on in the course of social relationships. This section has raised issues to do with theory and with methodology, and shown how social psychologists (and others) have come to very different conclusions about what happens when people communicate their ideas and feelings. In particular, the study of non-verbal behaviour has highlighted questions about the role of the body in social relationships. This role is not always going to be important (say, when communicating by computer link, or even by telephone), but there are many contexts where it is both medium and focus. The study of the 'kissing-round' is one example, but there are many others. (You might like to jot down a list of your own.) One might add, here, the situation of people for whom disability, chronic illness or infirmity present special problems. In these cases, limitations in ability to 'signal and receive' (for example through blindness) are compounded by other people's expectations of disability. The 'Does he take sugar...?' syndrome, whereby the disabled are selectively ignored by the able-bodied, is just one example of the vital role that the body plays in our assumptions of what it means to be a 'player' in the social world.

Review of section 4

- In the broader context of everyday life, how people use their bodies is subject to cultural patterns that are learned over time.

- Some expressions are recognized universally, but most gestures are culture specific. Amongst these, the gestures that accompany or replace speech (*emblems*, and *illustrators*) are most readily seen as conveying particular meanings.

- There have been attempts to unravel what are assumed to be the language-like forms of non-verbal communication. Distinguishing between *communication*, *signification* and *indication* shows that non-verbal behaviour is not structured in a similar way to the grammar of spoken language.

- There is evidence that women and men are different in their use of non-verbal behaviours. In particular, women have been shown to be better than men at decoding non-verbal cues. Explanations for this difference have centred upon the relative position of men and women in society, with attention being drawn to status and power differences.

- Two distinct approaches to the study of non-verbal behaviour have been noted: the *structural* and the *functional*. This difference is reflected in the way that bodily conduct appears, on the one hand, to be culturally based (concerning social relationships), and on the other to be expressive of personal wishes, or of intentions directed towards another individual. In the course of social interaction, it seems that non-verbal behaviour can convey both of these kinds of information simultaneously.

5   Verbal and non-verbal behaviour: the problem of interaction control

5.1   Taking turns in conversations

Having a conversation involves individuals taking turns at speaking, avoiding interruptions and long silences where these would disrupt the exchange, and linking the content of their speech in a coherent way. In this section we shall look at some different ways in which this is achieved, and at some of the consequences when it is not. One aim is to show how verbal and non-verbal behaviours operate together in every-day conversation, rather than as separate systems in the way set out above.

The idea that there might be different patterns of looking in a conversation was confirmed some time ago. By matching the patterns of gaze to the course of speech in the conversation, Kendon (1967) was able to show that people tend to look up when they are about to finish speaking, and to look towards the other when they wish to, or are about to talk.

Does this mean that there are two different spheres of control – the verbal and the non-verbal – as these research findings seem to imply? Claims have been made for the greater importance of non-verbal over verbal clues, suggesting that how one says something is more important than what is said (Argyle et al., 1970). Recent experimental evidence, which attempted to utilize more natural situations, has provided support for the opposite point of view, that is that visual information is less important than either verbal or vocal information (Howe, 1989). The conclusion to be drawn is that it is probably a mistake to separate entirely the verbal from the non-verbal channels when considering social interaction. We have already seen that some gestures are symbolic, while others are closely involved in the act of speaking. Also, the choice of words used can convey a great deal about the relationship and how it is to be defined. For example, even if said in the same tone of voice,

1   'Good morning!'

2   'Good afternoon!'

convey quite different things when addressed to a colleague entering the office at ten o' clock in the morning.

Given that these two mediums of communication need to be treated alongside one another, this prompts the question, what role do they play in the control of conversational turn-taking?

BOX 2.8   Some cues used in signaling 'It's your turn to speak....'

Duncan (1972) proposed the following series of cues that are used by speakers to signal a change of turn:

1   Intonation – rising or falling pattern.

2   Drawl – often on the final syllable.

3   Sociocentric sequence – the presence of such things as tag questions.

4   Pitch/loudness – letting the voice 'fall away' at the end of a sentence.

5   Syntax – the completion of a grammatical clause.

6   Gesture – change in the hand position used while speaking.

Duncan's work showed that a smooth turn (no interruption or cross-talking) in the conversation is more likely if these cues occur together. This suggests that several of these might combine to signal that the speaker is about to relinquish the floor.

However, in a study of students in tutorials, Beattie (1983) found that often only three of Duncan's cues were implicated, and that over 13 per cent of all smooth speaker-switches occurred in the absence of any turn-yielding cues. In fact, the cue most frequently associated with smooth turns was 'syntactic clause completion'. That is, these people knew when to start speaking because of the grammatical structure of the other's speech.

Do the findings set out in Box 2.8 suggest that non-verbal cues are unimportant for the regulation of conversation? If we follow Beattie's argument, these cues will be more or less important depending upon the context and upon the relationship. He noted that, where previous studies had used subjects who did not know one another, his experiments involved supervisors and students who knew each other quite well, at least in the tutorial setting. This meant that, in this latter situation, the people involved did look at each other because, we might conjecture, they knew each other and so were relaxed in each other's presence. Therefore, looking within a context where looking is already high, is *less* likely to act as a cue. Looking in a context where looking is relatively low, is *more* likely to be attended to for its possible meaning.

The conduct of the conversation, the ordering of who speaks first, and the carefulness with which one person rather than another will wait for his or her turn to speak, all depend upon the relationship in which this occurs. Think of a patient attending a first psychiatric consultation; of a daughter arriving home with news of an examination result; of two people who have decided, seemingly independently, to break off their relationship. Given the range of relationships involved, where matters of age, sex and status apply in different measures, it would be surprising if there was one fixed pattern of cues that held for all of them. There are likely to be different conventions about speaking that will vary across cultures and groups.

ACTIVITY 2.10   Conversational turn-taking is readily seen as if governed by rules. One rule, which applies to telephone conversations, is that 'the answerer speaks first' (Schegloff, 1968).

You might note down the different ways in which people answer the phone, either at home or at work. Think of your own reactions if, when calling someone up, nothing is heard from the other end. What happens if both parties begin to speak at once? Who gives way, or waits for the other to speak?

Your experience can be compared with Schegloff's findings. He argued that when nothing is heard, the caller will say 'hello, hello!' as a prompt to the other to speak. That is, the caller is drawing the other's attention to the need to identify his or herself. On occasions when both parties speak together, it is the caller who withdraws to allow the other to speak.

The approach called *conversation analysis* uses the method of recording talk from real-life situations and examines it for patterned structures. An example of this is given in Box 2.9 below.

BOX 2.9   Analysing turn-taking in conversation

In the course of conversation, turns are indicated by the use of 'turn-constructional' and 'turn-allocational' components (Sacks et al., 1974). The first refers to syntactic features that allow us to guess what follows. If the other says, 'So there it is, and I just wanted to know what you...' one might expect the next word to be 'think', and that an answer is now expected. The allocation of speakers is done either by the person speaking designating the next ('Bob, what do you say?'), or else by the other beginning to speak ('Well, I think that...'), or the present speaker starting to talk again.

One important feature is that conversation is seen to unfold, so that what happens next depends upon the meaning inferred from the previous statement. This is more than saying that what B says depends on what A said first. Take this example presented by Wooffitt (1992), based upon an extract from Schegloff (1968).

Mother: Do you know who's going to that meeting?

Russ: Who?

Mother: I don't know.

Russ: Oh, prob'ly Missiz McOwen en prob'ly Missiz Cadry and some of the teachers and the counsellors.

The mother's opening words can be interpreted in two ways: either as a direct question (requesting information) or as a pre-announcement of some news concerning who might be attending the meeting. Russ makes the second interpretation, because he returns the floor to Mother in order that she can tell him who will attend. Only when she makes it clear that her question was just that – a question – does he proceed to give her the information.

Wooffitt underlines the following point: the way turns are taken is tied up with tacit interpretations made about the 'work' that each utterance is doing. Individuals do not respond to the previous speaker in a 'cause and effect' fashion, but by unfolding the meanings and intentions that are implicit in the statements made.

The points illustrated in Box 2.9 are relevant to questions of the role of gender differences in conversational turn-taking. Early work (setting off a long line of similar research) showed that, in a university community, interruptions and overlaps in speech were made by men at the expense of women. However, a recent review of the evidence suggests that no clear conclusions can be drawn as to whether males' interruptions are, compared to those of women, 'attempts to seize the floor' (James and Clarke, 1993). One of the major problems is that there is no simple, objective criterion to determine exactly what someone is intending when he or she makes an interruption.

This can be illustrated by a study that found that men initiate topic changes more than women do (West and Garcia, 1988). However, most changes of topic were collaboratively closed by the women and men together (that is, they were agreed upon). On these occasions, women then initiated just as many topic changes as did men. It was only in the minority of cases, where there remained ambiguity about 'what to do next', that men took the initiative and changed the subject of conversation unilaterally. The distinction between the 'single floor' and the 'collaborative floor' is between conversations where one speaker is attempting to define what is to be discussed, and those where a number of speakers contribute to the definition of what is at hand.

Extract 2.1

In this extract, Edelsky describes in more detail what happens as people take turns and develop 'floors' in their talk together. The work described here shows women to build 'collaborative floors' by joking, arguing and directing more than men. It also shows that turn-taking is not a mechanical nor even a rule-bound process: who speaks first, who hesitates, how many incidents of cross-talking occur, are not merely dependent upon the relationship but help to define it.

Turn and floor defined

by C. Edelsky

Turn

I define turn as *an on-record 'speaking'* (which may include nonverbal activities) *behind which lies an intention to convey a message that is both referential and functional.*

As others have emphasized, just any talk does not count as a turn. A turn is taken among particular participants. Therefore, what is truly off-record and is said to one or a few persons rather than to all, usually in a subdued voice, is considered *a side comment* since the participant makeup of the group which is addressed has now changed. Example (10) shows Len, Rafe, and Sally making side comment ... (Len is jokingly asking for sympathy for a broken university-issued pen; Rafe teases that his works; Sally asks Carole to pass her a cookie.) Note especially that chairperson Rafe also takes a turn, shifting voice tone and topic as he moves from side commenting to taking a turn. He even marks this with a preface, *uh, in this lab,* to his on-record topic-shifting turn.

(10)

(the topic has been scheduling)

Rafe: other than that
it stays where it is

Sally: Awright

Len:	Is there a doctor here?
Marion:	(laugh)
Rafe:	(to Len) It's OK I've tried mine It works well =
Sally (to Carole):	I need one of those cookies

Rafe: Uh in this lab, this lab is
going to be named the
Hudson Room.

Floor. The *floor* is defined as *the acknowledged what's-going-on within a psychological time/space.* What's going on can be the development of a topic or a function (teasing, soliciting a response, etc.) or an interaction of the two. It can be developed or controlled by one person at a time or by several simultaneously or in quick succession. It is official or acknowledged in that, if questioned, participants could describe what's going on as 'he's taking about grades' or 'she's making a suggestion' or ' we're all answering her.'

There can thus be messages which are meant for public hearing (on record, not side comments), have both propositional and functional content (not merely encouragers) and are therefore turns, but which do not constitute the official what's-going-on. Such *non-floor-holding turns* can be seen in (13) with my question of clarification as Rafe describes a party as a bad situation, in (14) with Len's wisecrack as Rafe introduces a new topic, and in (15) with Sally's addition of a detail to Len's report on how to fund Young Author Days. (These are examples taken from single floor episodes.)

(13)

Rafe: any y'know Fran's just a very
nice person and to her it is in
terrible shape and

Carole: Fran's the blonde?

Rafe: No, dark hair and uh, oh my, god it
was just bad

(14)

Rafe: Uh y'know there's uh
something that uh
Bud wanted brought up
(chuckle) is uh a

Len: Dinner

Schedule about   Anne: (laugh) Carole: laugh
scheduling

(15)

Len: Well, they're gonna offer,
because we need we need the money,
they're gonna offer to do workshops

Sally: But you have to
pay for it

for a fee, for a fee and what they
want the school district to do.   Sally: Right

In other words, it is possible to take a turn without having the floor. [...]

Turns that jointly build one floor can be separated in real time by another turn as Sally's is from Len's and Marion's in (17) around the start of the meeting.

(17)

| Len: But I certainly wish we'd call this meeting together | Rafe: Oh there are some things |
| | Marion: C'mon Rafe |

Rafe: The meeting is called together

| Sally: I have to go |

Here, Sally, Len and Marion are heard as collaborating in producing what's going on: directing/prodding Rafe to hurry.

Source: Edelsky (1993) pp. 207–11

In order to see how this definition (see p.68) might take place, let us return to the sequencing of statements within a conversation. Important to any relationship are occasions of agreement and disagreement between the parties concerned. Disagreements, in particular, can cause problems, and work is often done within the conversation to minimize their disruptive effects. In their analytic study of discourse, Potter and Wetherell (1987) examined how responses to questions or invitations can often be split into preferred and dispreferred parts. For example:

Tony: Do you think you'll be coming on Wednesday evening?

Bill: Well, um, not sure. I will if I can get away...

The preferred response to what is more of an invitation than a question is 'yes I'll be there'. The dispreferred part is the refusal. (This distinction holds no matter how the individuals feels; he or she might not want to go to a wedding, but the preferred [socially normative] response to the invitation is still 'yes'.) In their analysis of conversations, Potter and Wetherell (1987) point to the way in which responses containing a dispreferred element often involve some small delay, and include pausing features such as 'um' or 'well'. In making a rather weak refusal, the question is also treated as if it were a request for information rather than an invitation. However, the tacit recognition of it as an invitation is shown in the way in which the response contains a justification of the refusal. Rather than simply refusing or disagreeing in the example above, Bill actually accounts for his response with the words 'I will if I can get away...'.

The way in which conversation unfolds is a matter of individuals setting out (that is, constructing) their position in the light of their understanding of what the other person intends. This, the perspective of *discourse analysis* does not see interaction as an exchange of ready-made views (or feelings), nor as the playing out of role expectations. Instead, it gives language a central role as the medium through which each person can make and share their version of the world. An important part of the world is, for the individuals concerned 'our world', our relationship. Taking this view, the process of how people share ideas and feelings becomes significant in understanding how relationships are forged. This approach, studying how relationships are put together, gives us the opportunity to take an 'insider's' rather than an 'outsider's' view of social interaction.

Review of section 5

- Relationships are conducted through conversation, in which both verbal and non-verbal features play their parts.

- When two (or more) people hold a conversation, they use a number of cues to determine when each should speak and listen (conversational turn-taking).

- The ordering of the interaction does not follow pre-set rules, and people do not follow these turn-yielding cues automatically. Instead, disagreements and interruptions form points at which work is often done by those involved to minimize disruptive effects.

- Studies of conversations show that they unfold, allowing sharing of ideas and feelings. This revelation of feelings and intentions, together with mutual definition of the interaction, are crucial to the development of personal relationships.

6 A shift in perspective: interaction and the making of impressions

6.1 Ways of knowing: three models of interaction description

At this point, it is necessary to review what we have covered so far, and to anticipate the direction of the remainder of the chapter. The reason for this is that we shall be taking a perspective that, to some extent, embraces the ones to which you have been introduced so far. The purpose of this section is to make explicit these different perspectives and to show their relationship to the various ways of describing social interaction. Having done that, it will be possible to appreciate how ideas about social interaction have changed in recent years, and what this implies for future studies by social psychologists.

So far in this chapter, we have examined interaction in terms of the repertoires of verbal and non-verbal behaviours available to people in social life. By focusing upon the patterning of what is said and done, it has been possible to explain relationships in terms of how groups typically act, attaching particular behaviours to individuals in different positions. From this perspective, social interaction can appear largely pre-determined, as if the language and behaviour of one's culture and sub-culture makes certain kinds of exchanges, if not inevitable, then certainly likely.

It is against this background that we turn to a closer examination of the concept of 'rule', because it encapsulates many of the issues that we shall touch upon in the sections to follow. For a start, rules can be thought of as prescriptions, saying what must or ought to be done in certain situations. An example of this might be the rules that cover games, allowing and disallowing particular moves or choices at certain points. These rules are often explicit, written down for people to refer to, as things to which they can appeal. Social interaction is not like this, except in certain limited situations like ceremonies, which we shall consider in more detail below. More often, the rules believed to guide our actions are implicit, in the sense that, only if challenged need we give an account of what we are doing. Sometimes it is only when rules are broken, as when people do the unexpected, that we become aware of what is usual, and taken-for-granted. (This was developed quite deliberately into a research technique by Harold Garfinkel [1967], who would do things like invade people's personal space and then ask them to say why they were annoyed or surprised.)

The idea that social interaction is guided by rules that are implicit, allows for the fact that we do things without consciously having to make decisions about them. It also allows for the idea that, while there are general rules that can be applied, exactly how they will be employed is a matter for the individuals concerned.

This is the position set out in the *Reading E:* 'A sociological perspective' by   ACTIVITY 2.11
Graham Allan, which you should now read. In particular, note the section on
'The social organization of friendship', in which he discusses the idea of 'rules
of relevance'. Look at this now, prior to continuing with this discussion of rules.

In the Reading, Allan emphasizes that, while the application of rules in a relationship is not pre-determined, the fact that they can be applied depends upon 'general knowledge and common understandings'. Whether one makes friends with someone is not rule-bound, but neither is it wholly at the whim of the individuals concerned. The pattern and structure that we observe in friendship results from the application of these implicit understandings of what constitutes a friendship and what does not. For example, someone might feel that not sharing some delicate information shows a 'lack of trust' that implies a shortfall in 'what is expected' of a friend.

While the concept of rules in this second interpretation allows for greater variability in what people do, we can still ask what 'work' this idea is doing. Why do we need it? In part, it provides a link between all kinds of 'friendship', making that term into a social idea rather than an individual one. By that is meant that 'rules of relationship' are in society, not just in the heads, so to speak, of individual people.

The third position on this is one that we shall be exploring in the last part of the chapter. It holds that people do not interact in terms of rules that pre-exist, either in social structures or in individual minds. Instead, the working out of 'what to do' is altogether more precarious and uncertain. This is because people negotiate together what they expect, demand and will accept from each other. This is not meant to imply that they always agree, or are concerned only to share. What it means is that what comes to be regarded as a rule is itself the subject, the outcome, of what people do together. In the context of friendship, Duck (1994) makes the point that relationships do not just have a 'bright' side and a 'dark side'. Rather, the way that people manage the 'dark' in the context of the 'light' is what distinguishes some relationships from others.

This way of thinking about rules can be seen as a progression in social scientific thought, and has been set out as such in relation to language. It is worth our while to examine this more closely, because we have seen that ideas about language have been very important in social psychologists' explanations of interaction. For example, the way that researchers have studied non-verbal behaviour has depended upon assumptions about what language 'is' and what language 'does'. As you read Box 2.10, bear in mind what was said earlier about the search for codes of non-verbal communication; about the need to understand action in a cultural context; and about social groups as distinct 'speech communities'.

BOX 2.10   Three models for describing social interaction

David Graddol (1994) has described how social scientists' views of language can be seen to have followed three basic models. We can use his classification to cover matters of social interaction in general. This puts into perspective the material that we have covered so far in the chapter, and signals the kind of issues that we shall be addressing in later sections.

Model I

This perspective, developed in the early part of this century, assumes that human communication works by transferring ideas from the mind of the speaker into the mind of the listener. For this to happen, language must be shared in terms of a rule-system that guides the construction of sentences. Language is studied as an autonomous system, access to which allows speakers/listeners to 'encode' and 'decode' messages appropriately.

From this viewpoint, social interaction is subject to systems of norms and roles. People participate in relationships because they know what to do (say) and can understand others because they know what the rules governing those exchanges require. Relationships are structures to be explained in terms of pattern and regularity. (Look back over sections 2.1 to 2.3. Also see the assumptions underlying work on non-verbal codes.)

Model 2

This model assumes that language does not exist apart from society and culture. Instead, meaning depends upon the social context in which words are used. This gave rise to the research approach called sociolinguistics, which focused upon how speech varied according to the social identity of the speaker and the situation. (See the reference to the work of Labov on non-standard English in section 3.2.) Meaning is not just different because social context makes it so, but speakers may be aware of a variety of codes or speech forms that they can employ to make their meaning. People 'read out' meaning on the basis of their understanding of the situation and the speaker concerned. Individuals act in terms of rules, or else invoke them so as to achieve their intentions.

There is diversity in interaction because people can take up different roles, or adapt situations in the light of their wishes to appear a 'this' rather than a 'that' kind of person. This model underlies much of the work set out so far in this chapter. (See particularly the research on differences in language and in non-verbal behaviour.)

Model 3

In this model (which Graddol calls the 'post-modern'), the study of language is not restricted to speech but embraces fields of sign use, including music, pictures, and material culture. These are all considered as 'texts'. The authorship of 'texts' (including a conversation) is multiple, so that meaning cannot be allocated to one individual alone, or to the social context. Communication is altogether more precarious and uncertain, because speakers not only adopt different standpoints but, within their talk, employ internally contradictory positions. In a conversation, what is said depends upon responses to messages that are themselves often incomplete or ambiguous. Language, therefore, is not explained in terms of pre-set or pre-existing structures, whether they be internal (the cognitive/ linguistic system) or external (the speaker's social group membership).

Model 3 sees interaction as basically incomplete and ambiguous. It is the special focus of the next section, and will be outlined in detail overleaf.

Having distinguished these three models, it is important to note that much research overlaps the boundaries separating them. This is because they can be considered as a historical progression, so that particular studies are grounded in one set of assumptions, but then challenges to these have been made in the light of subsequent analysis. Something of this overlap is discernible in the discussion to follow, where the work of Goffman employs ideas about rules (Model 2) but goes on to question how these are formed and used (Model 3).

It should also be said that most research in social psychology adheres to a position somewhere between Model 1 and Model 2. The postmodern position (Model 3) is not accepted by the majority of social psychologists working in Europe and the USA, and many critically reject it. The reasons for this are varied, but include the fact that this approach relies almost exclusively upon qualitative analyses, which are aimed at questioning the assumption of causal links between variables, upon which scientific (Models 1 and 2) investigations crucially depend.

6.2 Incompleteness and ambiguity in social life

The approach that we shall explore in this section questions whether social interaction might not be more open and ambiguous than earlier ideas suggested. It assumes that relationships and interactions are not clear-cut events which have a ready-made structure that we can inspect and describe. The reason that social psychologists have taken this approach has been proposed to be the result of a particular 'fallacy' in their thinking (Shotter, 1987). This accusation of 'fallacy' is a direct criticism of the assumptions underlying Model 1, set out above. It argues that the tendency to see all action as bounded by clear-cut motives or functions misses the possibility that much of what we do is open-ended and incomplete.

Extract 2.2

The second extract is an article by John Shotter which concerns the essential 'vagueness' of human action.

The unaccountable outcomes of joint action
by John Shotter

But this is not the only, nor the major reason why such behaviour is so difficult to account for. Another reason — and this is a difficulty people themselves face in accounting for their own behaviour from *within* transitional relationships — is that they are involved in a creative or developmental process *still in progress*, rather than in an outcome or product of such a process. In other words, whatever has been so far achieved, practically, in the relationships is still *incomplete*. As such, it is still open to, or able to take on, or be 'lent' further specification. And this is exactly what happens in our attempts to describe it: we describe incomplete processes by their supposed final product...

The consequences of such a state of affairs are profound: it means, as we shall see, that even the attempt to describe the making of relationships in terms of narratives, stories and plot structures runs into trouble. Witness the making of sexual approaches. 'I'm just off to the cinema', says a woman in the vicinity of a man she is attracted to, in the hope that he will respond as she desires. The significance of her utterance is not yet complete, however. If he says, 'Oh, can I come too?' then he has completed its significance as an 'invitation', and she is of course happy to accept it as having been as such. If he just says, however, 'Oh, I hope you enjoy the film', then he completes it simply as an 'informative statement'. Embarrassment has been avoided by her not having to issue a direct invitation, which might risk a direct refusal. The real indeterminacy of utterances often allows for their significance to be determined retrospectively.

But if he did turn her down, was it because to go to a film at that time was truly impossible for him, or because he truly did not want to be with her? Clearly, the significance of the situation between them is still somewhat vague, and thus requires further practical investigation between them if they are to clarify it further. Let us imagine that he did accept her invitation, and as they walk out of the cinema after the film, she then says, 'Would you like to come back for a coffee?'. He says, 'Oh, yes please!' and goes to put his arm around her. But she draws back and says, 'Whatever gave you that idea?' He is taken aback. He knows what gave him the idea, it was the whole way she offered the original 'invitation': it seemed to imply an invitation to greater intimacy — but at the same time, as both she and he were aware, it did not explicitly request it. The character so far of the relationship they are in is 'open' to such reversals as these; while perhaps unexpected they are not unintelligible.

Relevant here too is Sartre's (1958, pp. 55–6) analysis of 'bad faith', in which he discusses the example of a woman who, in conversation with a man she knows cherishes certain sexual intentions regarding her, allows him to take her hand, but leaves it limp within his, 'neither consenting nor resisting — a thing' (p. 56). Her 'bad faith' as he sees it, is in not treating the event with its proper significance. For, by allowing him to take her hand, she lets him risk requesting a greater physical intimacy:

> To leave the hand there is to consent in herself to flirt, to engage herself. To withdraw it is to break the troubled and unstable harmony which gives the hour its charm. The aim is to postpone the moment of decision as long as possible.

Sartre does not say how the relationship went on, but perhaps she shortly afterwards broke it off. But isn't that what she intended to do all along? Not necessarily, perhaps originally she had intended it to flourish. While that is what it later resulted in, that is not what it began as; its significance later was not the same as at the time of its origin.

Reference

Sartre, J.P. (1958) *Being and Nothingness: an essay on phenomenological ontology*, trans. Hazel Barnes. London, Methuen.

Source: Shotter, J. (1987) pp.227–229.

Shotter argues that people's actions do not simply follow from their intentions: instead, some of what they do is unintended, either in its execution or in its consequences. At the same time, because social exchanges are jointly carried out, there is also a sense in which what unfolds is not wholly attributable to either participant, or even to the sum of their individual intentions. When this happens we speak of people being 'in relationships', that appear to contain and to guide what they do. From this position, one can question the idea that there is, in fact, an objective relationship to be described. Instead, it might make sense to consider whether each of the parties describes a different relationship. Duck and Sants (1983) point out that, from Jack's point of view, there is a 'Jack-Jill' relationship; but from Jill's point of view there is a 'Jill-Jack' relationship.

Shotter also makes the point that, because action unfolds (rather as we saw conversation unfold), it is incomplete. For example, holding out one's hand to another might be met with a firm handshake in return, or even a refusal. It might be 'refused' because the other person gives you a hug instead. The point is that the proffered hand is an anticipation of certain possibilities that are only realized through the other person's action. For example, if I hold out my hand in a tentative fashion and it is not taken, I can perhaps withdraw it without it appearing (or even my believing) that the offer was 'really' made in the first place. If the hand is grasped, then the response makes my gesture into a 'warm greeting' *by completing it*. The point is, in being completed in this way, the 'warm greeting' makes my initial offer of my hand into something that it had only the potential to be in the first place.

This point of Shotter's is crucial for an understanding of social relationships. Its value, amongst other things, is that it puts in question the assumption that coherence and clarity, being the aims of psychological research, should also be the guiding principles of social life. Unfortunately, the steady focus upon what individuals intend, or have in mind, often turns questions of incompleteness into issues of mixed messages and misunderstanding.

Rather than incompleteness being an exceptional case (perhaps something that only happens early on in relationships), there is good reason for seeing this element of ambiguity as running throughout all of social life. Already, in this chapter, we have seen a number of things that would support this way of thinking. When reviewing Bales's work, it was pointed out that a key ingredient of the experimental situation is that someone makes a claim to organize the group. This person might – but only might – come to be accepted by the others as the 'task specialist'. There is no certainty about this, although within a role or 'group as system' theory, there was no way for Bales to investigate how and when this would occur. In terms of personal relationships, the idea that action is incomplete means that we have to shift our focus of inquiry. We need, as Duck has put it, 'to discuss the ways in which persons deal with uncertainty, segment experience, make choices between alternative expectations for the future, are affected by life's continually unfinished feel, and express their conclusions, hypotheses, and expectations to other people' (1994, p. 41).

A second, more specific, reason for needing to be sensitive to the issue of ambiguity is the fact that, both in verbal and non-verbal communication, there is considerable scope for misinterpretation and for its remedy. The previous section showed that, in the context of gesture, it is possible for unintended actions to be taken up and imbued with a significance that they never had for the person carrying them out. More to the point, this knowledge is not restricted to social psychologists: we know it in everyday life. That is, we act in the knowledge of the possibility that we might be misunderstood, or that our actions might be given greater weight than we might want to put on them ourselves. Sometimes it is better not to be too generous ('I wouldn't want him to think I'm always available'); or too accepting of another's overtures ('I said I couldn't possibly accept such an expensive gift – you know, I didn't want to encourage him').

There are two points to be drawn from this. First, people have intentions about how to act in their social relationships. These might be clear, cloudy or conflicting, but they need to be taken into account when explaining interaction. Second, what matters to the individuals concerned is what they believe to be the state of affairs, which is (for them) the reality of the situation. It is the impressions which they form of others that matter, and the impressions which others form of them. Like their intentions, there is no guarantee that people's perceptions are true in a scientific sense. These can be the source of considerable confusion and dispute, but they must also be (in the absence of anything else) the basis for how we treat each other as friends, enemies or lovers – or a mixture of all three.

This approach differs in two important respects from views about language and non-verbal behaviour that emphasize either structure or function (Model 1 and 2 type explanations). First, it places a question mark against behaviour denoting objective social categories, like 'women', 'student' or 'task leader' (that is, what we do does not just follow from our membership of particular social groups). Second, it focuses attention upon the potential for altering the visibility of behaviour (and the audibility of speech). By disclosing or keeping hidden certain aspects (saying or doing certain things), we can foster or deny particular impressions of ourselves. From this perspective, social interaction becomes something that individuals actively fashion, even though they will continue to draw upon language and behaviour made available by their culture and group. More than this, these cultural and social differences have a double significance in the power they give to individuals at various situations in society. For example, people in lesser positions have more limited scope to manage their impressions; for example they have fewer material and personal resources. One can consider the unemployed, the poor and the elderly as examples of groups whose 'power to signify' in this way is diminished relative to others.

6.3   Social interaction as ritual and ceremony: the theory of Erving Goffman

Erving Goffman has been one of the most original, and certainly the most influential writers on social interaction since the publication of his first book, *The Presentation of Self in Everyday Life* in 1959. His work is a major development of the position briefly outlined at the end of the preceding section. Goffman was a Canadian sociologist, who spent most of his professional life in the USA. As an undergraduate at the University of Toronto he was taught by Birdwhistell, who made him aware of the potential of anthropological methods for sociology. (For a review of Goffman's life and work, see Burns [1992]. See also Chapter 3 in this volume for a discussion showing Goffman's legacy to cognitive and humanistic social psychology.)

Extract 2.3

Goffman's theory is set out in publications that explore, often through example and illustration, the subtleties of social life. To get a flavour of his style, the third extract is from an article which sums up his view of ritual in everyday interaction.

The nature of the ritual order

by E. Goffman

The ritual order seems to be organised basically on accommodative lines, so that the imagery used in thinking about other types of social order is not quite suitable for it. For the other types of social order a kind of schoolboy model seems to be employed: if a person wishes to sustain a particular image of himself and trust his feelings to it, he must work hard for the credits that will buy this self-enhancement for him; should he try to obtain ends by improper means, by cheating or theft, he will be punished, disqualified from the race, or at least made to start all over again from the beginning. This is the imagery of a hard, dull game. In fact, society and the individual join in one that is easier on both of them, yet one that has dangers of its own.

Whatever his position in society, the person insulates himself by blindnesses, half-truths, illusions, and rationalizations. He makes an 'adjustment' by convincing himself, with the tactful support of his intimate circle, that he is what he wants to be and that he would not do to gain his ends what the others have done to gain theirs. And as for society, if the person is willing to be subject to informal social control — if he is willing to find out from hints and glances and tactful cues what his place is, and keep it — then there will be no objection to his furnishing this place at his own discretion, with all the comfort, elegance, and nobility that his wit can muster for him. To protect this shelter he does not have to work hard, or join a group, or compete with anybody; he need only be careful about the expressed judgments he places himself in a position to witness. Some situations and acts and persons will have to be avoided; others, less threatening, must not be pressed too far. Social life is an uncluttered, orderly thing because the person voluntarily stays away from the places and topics and times where he is not wanted and where he might be disparaged for going. He cooperates to save his face, finding that there is much to be gained from venturing nothing.

Facts are of the schoolboy's world — they can be altered by diligent effort but they cannot be avoided. But what the person protects and defends and invests his feelings in is an idea about himself, and ideas are vulnerable not to facts and things but to communications. Communications belong to a less punitive scheme than do facts, for communications can be by-passed, withdrawn from, disbelieved, conveniently misunderstood, and tactfully conveyed. And even should the person misbehave and break the truce he has made with society, punishment need not be the consequence. If the offence is one that the offended persons can let go by without losing too much face, then they are likely to act forbearantly, telling themselves that they will get even with the offender in another way at another time, even though such an occasion may never arise and might not be exploited if it did. If the offence is great, the offended persons may withdraw from the encounter, or from future similar ones, allowing their withdrawal to be reinforced by the awe they may feel toward someone who breaks the ritual code. Or they may have the offender withdrawn, so that no further communication can occur. But since the offender can salvage a good deal of face from such operations, withdrawal is often not so much an informal punishment for an offence as it is merely a means of terminating it. Perhaps the main principle of the ritual order is not justice but face, and what any offender receives is not what he deserves but what will sustain for the moment the line to which he has committed himself, and through this the line to which he has committed the interaction.

Source: Goffman (1955), p.228

From the Extract it is possible to see one of Goffman's main concerns: that is, what makes interaction possible in the first place? In this he was unlike most social psychologists in the interactionist tradition. They tended to select some aspect of interaction to focus upon, relating it to matters of group structure, interpersonal valuation or failure of mutual understanding.

Goffman proposed that, in any relationship, *individuals have an obligation to maintain face*. Social encounters involve those concerned in acting out a line, a pattern of verbal and non-verbal acts through which each person expresses his or her definition of the situation. This definition includes a valuation of the other person as well as of the individual concerned. So, for example, a parent who has made an appointment to visit her child's teacher has expectations of how she will be treated that are expressed in her behaviour. How she acts, what she says on entering the room, even the clothes she has chosen to wear for the occasion, are expressive of the stand she takes. The same conditions apply to the teacher too. She adopts a manner that expresses her definition of the situation, a vital part of which is her professional standing in relation to the mother. These definitions may or may not be in accord; either way, they form the basis of both parties' expectations of what they believe the encounter to be about, and their respective roles within it.

Having taken a particular line (defined the situation in a certain way), each of the participants in the example has made claims to be a certain kind of person. On the one hand, perhaps, a responsible and caring parent; on the other, a knowledgeable and experienced teacher. In doing this, says Goffman, their behaviour has a *promissory character*, in that it holds out a tacit claim that each is, indeed, that kind of person. In the course of their discussion, should evidence come to light that undermines these claims, then the appropriate person might find herself to be 'in wrong face'. For example, the teacher might reveal that she knows the child has been allowed to play truant; or the parent might produce a letter from the teacher containing misspelled words.

While it might appear from this that a primary aim of social interaction is to put the other 'in wrong face', Goffman is, in fact, making quite the opposite point. His argument is that social interaction can only proceed if the participants ensure that a particular *expressive order* is maintained. This refers to the regulation of the flow of events that bear upon the maintenance of face of both parties. Successfully carried out, this means that the participants can achieve other ends within the episode concerned: '...ordinarily maintenance of face is a condition of interaction, not its objective' (Goffman, 1972, p.12). In the example suggested above, while the parent will want to underline her responsible attitude, discussing her child's education might not be furthered by undermining the teacher's claim to professionalism. By treating each other 'with respect', and their different points of view 'with due consideration', a discussion of sorts can take place and other ends be pursued.

Goffman called the study of the ways in which people maintain face (for self and others) *face-work*. It includes a whole range of practices that are well-known, once they are pointed out. These include poise, through which potentially embarrassing incidents are controlled; avoidance, as when one does not notice that the other's stomach is rumbling; and the use of tact. An example of the last mentioned is when someone holds out their hand when a handshake is not appropriate; then 'the hand-shake that should not have been extended becomes one that cannot be declined' (Goffman, 1972, p.28). This might also account for the obli-gation upon those of high status not to embarrass those lower down in the social hierarchy; and the obligation upon the handicapped to accept offers of help that they could actually do without.

Goffman's term for the sphere of social interaction is the *interaction order*. For him, to study what happens in exchanges such as face-saving is 'to study the traffic rules of interaction' (ibid, p.12). What this reveals are the codes employed in social life: not the motives for following or break-ing them, but their form. One example of this is the corrective process that is brought into play when something occurs to threaten the face of one (or more) of the participants. As yet another example of face-saving, it is disclosed in the small 'excuse me-s' and 'sorry-s' that pepper every-day talk. Writ large, the corrective process involves full-blown accu-sations and apologies. The sequences involved in a typical face-saving exchange are shown in Box 2.11.

The stages shown in Box 2.11 reflect a 'ritual process' made up of sym-bolic acts that refer to the status of the individuals concerned. To show that we are dealing with a *symbolic* order, note that the significance of the incident does not lie only in the physical disarrangement produced. Of course, should the tray be knocked to the ground, then the challenge will be greater, as will likely be the offering. The point, however, is that the incident matters because the 'face' (the social standing) of the offended party is brought into question. And this being the case, the expressive order that governs the episode we call queueing is itself disrupted. What the ritual does is to repair this breach to the expressive order, allowing those concerned to proceed with their interaction, mini-mal even though it might be.

BOX 2.11   An analysis of 'sorry's' and 'excuse me's'

The sequence of acts involved form an interchange. Imagine the provoking incident to be as follows. You are standing in the queue in a cafeteria, when the young man behind you reaches for a paper cup, spilling your tea onto the tray. This constitutes a breach of the expressive order, requiring some apology on his part if he is to maintain his claim (face) to be a responsible individual in this setting. The corrective sequence might be:

You: 'Oh, ...er'

Young man: 'Damn. Sorry about that.'

You: 'That's O.K.' (Replacing cup)

Young man: 'Right, right.'

The words 'Oh,...er' constitute a *challenge*, which calls attention to the incident as something that will need to be brought into line. (By implication, the line that you adopt as a worthy individual is one that is going to be held.)

Following this, there is an *offering* by the young man in the form of an acknowledgment of responsibility and an apology. In effect, this is an expiation of his guilt, signalling that he is still a responsible individual in spite of the breach of rules. The response 'That's O.K.' is the *acceptance* of the offering, in the sense that it confirms that the challenger's face has been effectively saved and no further expiation is necessary. In cases where a major insult is claimed, more than one offering may be necessary because substantial as well as symbolic repair will have to be made. In this example, 'you' might have said, 'It's all spilled. What are you going to do about it?'. The subsequent offering might then be, 'Let me buy you another one'.

The final words 'Right, right' indicate a terminal phase signifying gratitude on the part of the offender towards the challenger, for accepting his offering.

The happenings surrounding the 'spilled tea' illustration are examples of what Goffman called *avoidance rituals*, in that their guiding principle is deference, the avoidance of 'treading upon the other's toes'. (Note how these commonplace terms to do with the rules of interaction often concern the use of the body.) Since Goffman wrote, there have been empirical studies looking at the kinds of problem that he defined. It has been found that there are five strategies that individuals typically use when reproaching another for some failure or insult, and seeking repair of the situation (Cody and McLaughlin, 1985). These include (1) projected concession (I'm sure you didn't mean to...); (2) projected excuse (Were you held up in the traffic?); (3) projected justification (You might have been pushed, but...); (4) projected refusal (Don't say you didn't see me standing here); and (5) silence (for example fixing the perpetrator with a stare of reproval).

In their research, Cody and McLaughlin examined what kinds of outcome followed the use of different types of account strategies. Outcome is considered from the point of view of the reproacher, so that if the other's account is *honoured*, the reproacher might laugh, agree or show other signs that the account is acceptable as repairing the damage. *Retreating* occurs when the account is partially accepted, so that the person, though remaining 'morally wounded', accepts the reason why it occurred. *Rejection* of the account happens when the offended person does not accept the account, and re-states the original charge, perhaps more forcibly. It was found that honouring occurred more frequently when accounters used excuses. Retreating occurred more frequently when they used either justifications or concessions; and rejection was more likely when the perpetrators failed to give any account at all, or made poor justifications.

It is important not to see these findings as suggesting that one kind of outcome *inevitably* follows a particular form of accounting. From what has been said previously about the unfolding of action sequences, these are better seen as alternative moves in episodes that people understand as having greater or lesser scope for them to claim or to reinforce their social identities. Such accounts can be seen as involving 'alignment moves', that seek to remedy disruptions to relationships by promoting comprehension and fostering understanding (Poole, 1985). Statements like, 'I was in such a hurry to get this work finished...', create an impression of someone who, though having committed some breach of social etiquette, did so in the course of trying to be a responsible and worthy person.

In addition to avoidance rituals, there are *presentational rituals*. These concern the specific things that someone does to show how the other person is regarded and will be treated in the exchange to follow. Examples are access rituals, through which people begin and end interaction episodes. Greetings and farewells provide a way of linking together past and future meetings in a way that re-affirms the respect in which the other is held.

Many of the small access rituals that Goffman discussed are recognizable in everyday life. When friends or acquaintances meet in the street, they will often greet each other with a 'hello' or 'how are you?'. The latter question is, except under special circumstances, not a request for information. It has a symbolic value, shown by the speaker rarely pressing the other when a cursory 'OK, and yourself?' comes back in return. In many brief meetings of this kind, the last thing the questioner wants is a long tale of illness, or a blow by blow account of the person's experiences at the hands of medical practitioners.

The strength or enthusiasm of greetings and farewells also reflects the relative period of absence of the parties concerned. Rather, we should say that people are given (and expect) the greeting that they feel is due to them. When someone has been away for a long time, the other person will stop to chat for a while, enquiring where they have been and what they have been doing. Of course, it is possible that the other simply hails them and passes by, or (worse still) regales them with an account of his or her doings, ignoring the fact that they have been away at all. This latter possibility, with the resulting pique felt by the returning individual, underlines once more that these are symbolic exchanges, not just substantive ones. These conventions are the stuff of social status and personal worth, matters whose proper negotiation is vital to the smooth running of everyday interactions.

By proposing avoidance rituals (deference) on the one hand, and presentational rituals (demeanour) on the other, Goffman pointed up a conflict inherent in social life. We must depict our appreciation of other people, but at the same time we must not invade their personal reserve. It is a sign of sympathetic concern to ask after a person's health, and that of his or her family, but only if it is appropriate for you to ask it of that person, at that time. People whom one does not know, who are of much higher social status, or whose family might be discredited, are among those of whom one might not ask this question. Among all of our friends, colleagues and acquaintances, steering adroitly between avoidance and prying is a task requiring, if not conscious attention, then at least our constant sensitivity.

Goffman's contribution to the study of social interaction is to show how we can understand, not just what happens, but how it is made to happen. Compared to previous work that emphasized roles or norms, or even patterns of exchange, his work provides insights into how relationships are built up by ritual forms, and how they are made to matter. Of this he said:

> Routinely, the question is that of whose opinion is voiced most frequently and most forcibly, who makes the minor ongoing decisions apparently required for the co-ordination of any joint activity, and whose passing concerns are given the most weight. And however trivial some of these little gains and losses may appear to be, by summing them all up across all the social situations in which they occur, one can see that their total effect is enormous. The expression of subordination and domination through this swarm of situational means is more than a mere tracing or symbol or ritualistic affirmation of the social hierarchy. These expressions considerably constitute the hierarchy; they are the shadow *and* the substance.

> (Goffman, 1976, p.74)

At this point, it is necessary to explore Goffman's contribution to our understanding of larger episodes, where the focus is widened from the detail of the interaction itself.

6.4   Social episodes as ceremonial occasions

The kind of rituals that have been mentioned so far in relation to Goffman's work are those that are part of the flow of everyday interaction. It is possible to make ritual a focus of interest by concentrating upon those episodes that have a ceremonial form. Alternatively, one can look for the ceremonial aspects of any given social exchange. In this section we shall look at examples of studies that have done one or other of these things.

By ceremony is meant any episode 'in which a certain sequence of actions are conventionally held to constitute the performance of an act' (Harré and Secord, 1972). Like minor rituals, it is in the doing of the actions that the meaning of the episode resides; it is symbolic rather than substantive. To illustrate this, we can examine an example given by Harré and Secord – the wedding ceremony. They point out that a wedding is composed of roles such as bride, groom, priest, best man etc. It is also made up of rules concerning what must be said and done by the various participants, to whom and at what point in the proceedings. There are constraints upon which categories of people can fill particular roles (for example who can officiate). There are also conventions about the application of the rules, so that (in certain cultures) it is expected the groom will place the ring on the third finger of the bride's left hand.

The point about ceremonies is that their completion is dependent upon a satisfactory enactment of the rules by those in appropriate role positions. There might be expectations about the states of mind of those taking part, and about the desirable level of their blood alcohol, but these need not necessarily be fulfilled for the act to be completed. Just as long as the bride and groom say the right words at the right time (accepting no other invalidating intrusions), then they will be declared married.

The use of the term 'rule' was extended by Harré and Secord to cover social episodes in general. (This is an example of a Model 2 explanation, as set out in section 6.1.) They envisaged that one might understand some of the more enigmatic exchanges between people by treating them as if they were rule-governed. The face-restoring moves discussed in the previous section are of this kind. To discover the rules, one would need to ask people about what they do, and hence gain an idea of the grounds of action and of what is expected. So, if we want to know about shopping, we would (amongst other things) ask the person behind the counter about what he or she does in relation to different kinds of customer, the various goods requested, and so on. In this way one might build up a picture of the rule-set that governs the role of the shop assistant.

One of the problems with this view is that it makes rules appear as separate things that underlie, or oversee what people do, as described under

Graddol's Model 2. Either they are 'out there' in the situation, or they are 'in here' in the minds of the actors concerned. In fact, Harré and Secord realized that rules were not really like this, for they appear in the accounts that people give of their action. Harré and Secord had, however, subscribed to the views of Goffman, whose own position on rules has since been shown to be ambiguous (Burns, 1992). However, in an invited article written some twenty years later, Harré took the opportunity to revoke the idea that rules are the causes of orderly behaviour. Instead, he endorsed the view that they '...express and help us determine whether what we have done is warrantable and intelligible' (Harré, 1993, p.26). For example, when someone says, 'What are you doing that for?' we are quite likely to reply something like, 'I'm just clearing the dirt away from the valve, so that I can screw back the outer ring'; or else, if asked, 'Why did you say that to her?', we might respond, 'I thought that I ought to explain what she might have to do when...'. In each of these cases, there is an element of 'in this situation you should do this before (or after)...', thus expressing some rule about how to act under the given circum-stances.

The point to notice is that the reply is itself a justificatory account. In saying this, one is not merely invoking the rule, but setting it out afresh in order to give a reason for one's action. At the same time, this justifi-cation makes a claim about one's own position in relation to the other ('I know what I'm about, thank you very much!').

BOX 2.12 Rules as 'exhibiting' relationships

A study that bears upon this was conducted by Wieder (1974), who carried out a participant observation of a half-way hostel for ex-convicts. He noted the way some members of the hostel would respond to his questions about its workings with the remark that they 'would not snitch' on their fellows. Wieder concentrated on understanding this 'telling the code' (that is, rule), and came to the conclusion that it achieved several things. It justified the inmate in not having to answer the question (which was simultaneously rendered illegitimate), and it defined the exchange as one going on between an 'insider' and an 'outsider'. Seen as discourse, spelling out the rule provided a version of what was going on in the particular circumstances of the interview (Potter and Wetherell, 1987). It defined the interaction as well as being a report of how members of the hostel conducted themselves. Wieder put it as follows:

> Thus, 'telling the code', and any particular instance of formulating the code, *exhibits*, rather than describes or explains, the order that members achieve through their practices of showing and telling each other that particular encountered features are typical, regular, orderly...[etc].

> *(Wieder, 1974, p.171)*

Clearly, the kind of analysis which Harré and Secord thought suitable for formal episodes does not apply to the many and varied informal exchanges that we call 'social interaction'. One of the problems of focusing upon ceremonies, like weddings, is that one may underestimate just how special they are. As Goffman (1983) himself pointed out, ceremonies are relatively insulated from everyday life. The people who take part in them (for example, relatives who seem only to turn out for weddings and funerals) might never meet together again. In situations like celebratory meals between friends, who see each other only rarely, the celebration can become the very substance of the relationship, rather than its expression.

In another important respect, ceremonies, as social relationships, are different from personal relationships in precisely the way that makes the latter crucial. In a personal relationship it is the other person, as a particular individual, who matters. So, for the bride and groom the occupancy of their respective positions is vital – it matters absolutely to whom one is getting married! However, this also shows that, while one cannot understand personal relationships on the basis of a study of ceremonies, these two kinds of relationship cannot be kept strictly apart: they are actually entwined in many everyday situations.

One way to demonstrate this is to show the lengths to which we must sometimes go to separate the personal from the social. Instances of this occur, for example, in the course of patients undergoing physical examinations by medical staff, for example a female nurse giving a male patient a body-wash prior to surgery, or a woman receiving a gynaecological examination from a male doctor. On these occasions there are particular strategies that doctors and nurses use to avoid mentioning, or bringing to attention, aspects of the patient's sexuality (that is, 'personal' matters), which could provoke embarrassment for all parties involved. These include speaking about parts of the body in a neutral, objective way, and talking in a tone that says 'this is as much a "matter of fact" situation for you as it is for me'.

In conclusion, the view of 'rules' as being justifications made within discourse is consistent with Graddol's Model 3, the postmodern position. Rules are not structures that have an existence either 'outside', in the social context, or 'inside' individuals, as attitudes or fixed frames of reference. This does not mean, of course, that individuals do not feel rules to be either of these things, or will not refer to them along these lines if asked to justify their own actions (see Box 2.12 above). However, those taking the Model 3 position criticize the assumption that people's talk is a reflection (an effect) of other, underlying, structures. Instead, discourse is the action through which people together fashion the relationship, as, simultaneously, they make sense of it.

Review of section 6

- This section has presented a view of rules as matters of claim, justification and explanation.

- A comparison of three 'models' was presented to show the way that thinking about interaction in relationships has changed in recent years. Model 1 defined interaction in terms of rule-structures governing behaviour; Model 2 allowed for individuals to take up different roles, or to utilize rules according to situation; Model 3 saw interaction as open and ambiguous, allowing multiple meanings of what is said and done.

- The idea that social interaction is rule-guided has been explored, mainly through the work of Erving Goffman. His analysis of the interaction order showed how individuals engage in avoidance and presentational rituals as ways of maintaining social relationships.

- The idea of social relationships as forms of ceremony is limited in its application to personal relationships, where matters of identity are of paramount importance.

- Rather than think of rules as ready-made guidelines for action, telling us how we should conduct ourselves in social life, they may be seen as the product of interaction. This has implications for explanations of informal relationships. It suggests that these are not essentially like games, having strategies and fixed outcomes, but involve a far more complex weave of claim, counterclaim and accommodation.

7 Making the difference: relationships and the study of interaction

This concluding part examines what a study of social interaction can tell us about social and personal relationships. Previous sections have shown that what people say and do is interpreted in the light of what we, as investigators, know of the wider context of 'the relationship'. One dimension of this context is the way that it touches other aspects of people's lives, something about which more will be said below. Another important dimension is that relationships are extended in time; you might say that you have a relationship of a kind with the lady at the corner shop, where you go several times a week, but not with the milkman whom you only see when you pay him once every so often.

This brings us back to the distinction, made at the beginning of the chapter, between social and personal relationships. There it was acknowledged that what is said and done between people who are engaged in a passing exchange, compared with those who are long-term friends, will be different. We now turn to an examination of what this difference might be, or rather, how it is brought about.

The possibility that relationships provide a wider context for interactions, is similar to the idea that communications constitute the 'building blocks' of personal relationships. With respect to the latter point, a number of reservations have been made about whether detailed studies of verbal and non-verbal interchanges alone could ever explain significant features of relationships. Specifically, individuals are not only concerned with what is said and done, but also with what is *not* said and *not* done. The absence of formalities can mean a more intimate and relaxed exchange will follow; alternatively, if anticipated endearments are not forthcoming, the romantic interlude that might have developed no longer takes place.

More generally, however, two aspects of *personal* relationships have been poorly dealt with by research into *social* interactions. On the one hand, the focus upon what is done rather than how it was achieved, means that there has been a rather static view of relationships. This concerns the important fact that relationships are extended in time. This means that subsequent meetings will take up, and perhaps alter, things that happened in previous exchanges. In between times, those concerned will think about, go over, anticipate and otherwise do what might be called 'imaginative work' to do with the relationship. And second, personal relationships are more than isolated exchanges because they often have a public existence. Other people know who is friendly with whom, or who has 'broken off' with whom. The individuals concerned can also represent themselves publicly through their relationships, which can be a special cachet for the young adolescent or, indeed, for those who want to be known for knowing the famous.

These points suggest that the study of social interaction must take account of both the kind of relationship that is involved, as well as the depth and extension of the link between the individuals concerned. One reason for thinking that social psychologists might not always do this, is that their methods have often tended to make them focus down on detail. This means either that (as in the case of the structuralists) important features of the relationship become part of the background context; or else (as with the functionalists/experimentalists) the variables selected are treated as universal, and are therefore believed to operate in that way within every relationship.

To adopt the 'universal variable' point of view makes the relationship into something separate from, but enclosing what is said and done in the interaction. As a result, there is a resulting problem with this position. It misses the opportunity to see how the detail of the interaction is used by the individuals concerned to make sense of, and to lay claim to the exchange as being a 'this' or a 'that' kind of relationship. Within the experimental approach, the two terms – interaction and relationship – connect only in statistical associations made possible by assumptions 'in the mind' of the investigators.

Making a similar point, Goffman (1975) selected the example of kissing. He argued that it is the way kissing is carried out, by whom, and with what intention, that makes the act into what it is. Compare the kiss of a husband saying goodbye to his wife at the airport, with a kiss from John being careful not to smudge Mary's makeup. The relationship is somehow *expressed* in the kiss; counting the number or frequency of a specific behaviour called 'kissing' could not convey the distinction being made between these acts.

The problem is to say how the elements of social interaction 'connect' with the idea of relationship. Knowing someone well enough to say 'hello' to them, perhaps using their name, is a relationship of the simplest kind. It might well not go beyond the ritual greeting that follows when one meets accidentally in the street or in other public places. In a sense, the obligation to make and to receive this greeting is both evidence *of* the relationship, and the relationship *itself* (Goffman, 1983). Perhaps that is why, in everyday terminology, we would not normally speak of this as a relationship, because it is not 'deep' enough.

There is a clue here as to how we might think of interaction and relationships in social life. It is through interaction that we are able to express or invite extensions or changes to the relationship as it stands. For example, flirtation involves the intimation of a change in relationship, by the use of signs (verbal and non-verbal) that are, in a sense, elusive. What this means is that the elements of social interaction (gaze, speech, posture, gesture) are employed so as to express more than they literally say. Whether the other person will recognize these signs for what they are, respond positively, or feign ignorance of their implied meaning, are not predictable outcomes. This is because the exchange is not an isolated event, but is influenced by the history and context of that particular relationship (Duck, 1981). One would expect that increasing intimacy in romantic relationships is accompanied by an increase in what both individuals can 'take for granted'. If there are rules of flirtation, they are rules of performance (of flirting well, with skill), not of what the outcome must be.

In the case of relationships that are breaking down, or are being brought to an end, the details of the interaction might well be used to convey this, where a direct statement would offend. To declare to somebody, out of the blue, 'I don't want to meet you again', is not only to be seen as rude on this particular occasion, but to detract from the social value of personal relationships in everyday life. The ceremonies and rituals that surround the breaking-off of relationships are there to preserve both the social order and, it must be emphasized, the 'good name' of the perpetrator.

Therefore, social interaction is not just what goes on 'inside' relationships; it is the means by which specific messages are communicated and the medium for endorsing (or undermining) the context itself. In his early writings, Goffman (1959) conveyed this idea by distinguishing between what is 'given' and what is 'given off'. In any exchange there will be things communicated explicitly, and things conveyed elliptically. Often, what is given off in this way concerns matters to do with the kind of relationship itself; how people speak, the grammatical forms used, how enthusiastic they appear, all give clues to their general attitude to the situation and their role within it.

From this perspective, the elements of social interaction are not so much the building blocks of relationships, as the brushstrokes on the canvas of social life. The notion of building blocks goes back to the idea of roles and rules that structure relationships, so that in describing these we get a picture of what the relationship is 'made up of'. This chapter has shown that, except in formal situations, what is done involves something more akin to making claims, or offering invitations. Goffman called these *displays*, in the sense that:

> Displays don't communicate in the narrow sense of the term; they don't enunciate something through a language of symbols openly established and used solely for that purpose. They provide evidence of the actor's alignment in the situation. And displays are important insofar as alignments are.

> *(Goffman, 1976, p. 69)*

To take an example, when men and women interact (say, in flirtation) they do not express some inner 'masculinity' or 'femininity'; nor do they follow a set of external rules about how to act the role of man or woman. What Goffman suggested is that, together, they portray *the idea of these roles:* they do not just fill them (as men or women). By aligning their performances with the generally understood schedule for such roles, individuals can appear more or less manly or feminine, aggressive or yielding, dangerous or complicitous.

Making this shift in perspective shows how, in being employed as the medium of interaction, words and gestures carry meaning for the relationships of which they are a part. The interaction order is not merely a means for communicating particular messages, for creating particular impressions or for controlling the other's behaviour. It is also the way in which individuals can show how social relationships matter, both to them personally and to the groups and culture to which they belong.

Therefore, while we may study the detail of social interaction, what that detail means for the relationship in question cannot be understood from its study alone. There is more to relationships than what is said or done at the time, although the communication 'this is what this relationship is for me' will be carried by just those specific actions. Knowing the typical pattern (for example of greeting, of courtship, of psychotherapy) is a key part of understanding the schedule with which people work. That is, the rituals and ceremonies of social interaction do comprise important features of social life, but not merely because they are the 'normal' thing to do. If that were simply the case, then, to borrow from Mann's quotation at the head of the chapter, 'form would be mere formality': but, it is not. Although ideas of what is 'good form' vary, being gauche or having poise, for example, are what they are because they reflect upon the relationships in which they take place.

What makes relationships good, or bad, what makes them intimate or distant is, in each case, irreducible to the sum of the 'formalities' of interaction. To appreciate how words and blows become (or are made) significant for the individuals concerned, we need to look at a broader range of relationships than has been possible in this chapter. The following chapters will do just this, illuminating questions of change over time, points of transition, and the variety of relationships that take place in the wider social context.

Review of section 7

- This section has argued that interactions should not be considered as merely the building bricks of relationships. Personal relationships extend over time, and also have a public existence; they impinge upon other aspects of life.

- Social interaction not only defines or endorses our current engagements with others; it is also the means for opening up new relationships and for changing existing ones.

- Using Goffman's concept of display, it is possible to view interaction as a series of claims and invitations. Taking this view, what is said and done are not just explicit communications that can be studied in isolation.

- Interactions allude to matters concerning the definition and scope of relationships, their past or their possible futures. This bears upon questions of variety of and change in relationships, to be addressed in the chapters to follow.

Further Reading

Beattie, G. (1983) *Talk: an Analysis of Speech and Non-verbal Behaviour in Conversation*, Buckingham, Open University Press.

This book describes a number of studies examining the verbal and non-verbal features of conversation. It gives a useful insight into the way such studies are carried out, showing how turn-taking occurs between tutors and students. For readers with a feel for history, it also analyses why Mrs Thatcher was so often interrupted during interviews.

Coates, J. and Cameron, D. (eds) (1988) *Women in their Speech Communities: New Perspectives on Language and Sex,* London, Longman.

This book takes a critical look at quantitative approaches to gender differences in speech. It contains some interesting chapters showing how women from different communities in Britain use speech, and what this diversity means for our understanding of language in general.

Duck, S. (1994) *Meaningful Relationships: Talking, Sense, and Relating,* Thousand Oaks, Sage.

A re-appraisal of the field of personal relationship research, this book shows the influence of recent thinking about discourse on the social psychology of interpersonal interaction.

Goffman, E. (1971) *The Presentation of Self in Everyday Life,* Harmondsworth, Penguin.

This is Goffman's first book, and the one which introduced social psychologists to the 'dramaturgical approach'. Written in Goffman's open style, it is packed with examples and observations that make this rewarding reading.

Goffman, E. (1982) *Interaction Ritual: Essays on Face-to-Face Behaviour,* New York, Pantheon.

Here are the essays that form the basis of Goffman's work on what he called 'the traffic rules of interaction'. It includes most of his writing on deference and demeanour.

Harré, R. (1993) 'Rules, roles and rhetoric', *The Psychologist,* 6, pp. 24-8.

This short paper is very useful as a statement of how ideas about social interaction have changed from being based upon the assumption of pre-existing rules, to ideas of conversational negotiation.

Kendon, A. (1990) *Conducting Interaction: Patterns of Behaviour in Focused Encounters,* Cambridge, Cambridge University Press.

This book shows the historical background of the structural approach to non-verbal behaviour and gives detailed examples of how this methodology is applied.

Patterson, M.L. (1985) 'The evolution of a functional model of nonverbal exchange: a personal perspective' in R.L. Street and J.N. Cappella (eds) *Sequence and Pattern in Communicative Behaviour,* London, Edward Arnold.

Here is a summary of the functional perspective showing the methodological concerns of researchers who approach the study of non-verbal behaviour through the experimental method.

Potter, J. and Wetherell, M. (1987) *Discourse and Social Psychology: Beyond Attitudes and Behaviour,* London, Sage.

This highly influential book has been many social psychologists' introduction to what was called in the chapter 'Model 3 explanation'. It provides a critique of structural theories based upon attitudes and groups, and shows how discourse can be analysed to understand conversational exchange.

Radley, A. (1991) *In Social Relationships: an Introduction to the Social Psychology of Membership and Intimacy,* Buckingham, Open University Press.

A precursor, in many ways, to the present chapter. This is an introductory book that uses the idea of ambiguity in interaction to review the field of social relationships. It draws heavily upon example to make its points, rather than upon descriptions of method.

References

Argyle, M. and Dean, J. (1965) 'Eye-contact, distance and affiliation', *Sociometry,* vol. 28, pp. 289–304.

Argyle, M., Salter, V., Nicholson, H., Williams, M. and Burgess, P. (1970) 'The communication of inferior and superior attitudes by verbal and non-verbal signals', *British Journal of Social and Clinical Psychology,* vol. 9, pp. 222–31.

Bales, R.F. (1950) 'The analysis of small group interaction', *American Sociological Review,* vol. 15, pp. 257–64.

Beattie, G. (1983) *Talk: an Analysis of Speech and Non-verbal Behaviour in Conversation,* Buckingham, Open University Press.

Bernstein, B. (1971) *Class, Codes and Control: Theoretical Studies Towards a Sociology of Language,* Volume 1, London, Routledge and Kegan Paul.

Birdwhistell, R. (1971) *Kinesics and Context: Essays on Body-motion Communication,* London, Allen Lane.

Bourhis, R.Y. and Giles, H. (1977) 'The language of intergroup distinctiveness' in Giles, H. (ed) *Language, Ethnicity and Intergroup Relations*, London, Academic Press.

Brien, D. (1992) *The Dictionary of British Sign Language/English,* London, Faber and Faber.

Burke, P.J. (1967) 'The development of task and social-emotional role differentiation', *Sociometry,* vol. 30, pp. 379–92.

Burns, T. (1992) *Erving Goffman*, London, Routledge.

Cameron, D. (1988) 'Introduction' in Coates, J. and Cameron, D. (eds).

Cameron, D., McAlinden, F. and O'Leary, K. (1988) 'Lakoff in context: the social and linguistic functions of tag questions' in Coates, J. and Cameron, D. (eds).

Cappella, J.N. (1984) 'The relevance of the microstructure of interaction to relationship change', *Journal of Social and Personal Relationships,* vol. 1, pp. 239–64.

Cappella, J,N. and Street, R.L. (1985) 'Introduction: a functional approach to the structure of communicative behaviour' in Street, R.L. and Capella, J.N. (eds).

Cary, M.S. (1978) 'Does civil inattention exist in pedestrian passing?', *Journal of Personality and Social Psychology,* vol. 36, pp. 1185–93.

Coates, J. and Cameron, D. (eds) (1988) *Women in their Speech Communities: New Perspectives on Language and Sex,* London, Longman.

Cody, M.J. and McLaughlin, M.L. (1985) 'Models for the sequential construction of accounting episodes: situational and interactional constraints on message selection and evaluation' in Street, R.L. and Cappella, J.N. (eds).

Cornwell, J. (1984) *Hard-Earned Lives: Accounts of Health and Illness from East London,* London, Tavistock.

Douglas, M. (1973) *Natural Symbols: Explorations in Cosmology,* Harmondsworth, Penguin.

Duck, S.W. (1981) 'Toward a research map for the study of relationship break-down' in Duck, S.W. and Gilmour, R. (eds) *Personal Relationships 3: Personal Relationships in Disorder,* London, Academic Press.

Duck, S.W. (1994) *Meaningful Relationships: Talking, Sense, and Relating,* Thousand Oaks, Sage.

Duck, S.W. and Sants, H.K.A. (1983) 'On the origin of the specious: are personal relationships really interpersonal states?', *Journal of Social and Clinical Psychology,* vol. 1, pp. 27–41.

Duncan, S. (1972) 'Some signals and rules for taking speaker turns in conversations', *Journal of Personality and Social Psychology,* vol. 23, pp. 283–92.

Eckert, P. and McConnell-Ginet, S. (1992) 'Think practically and look locally: language and gender as community-based practice', *Annual Review of Anthropology,* vol. 21, pp.461–90.

Edelsky, C.(1977) 'Acquisition of an aspect of communicative competence: learning what it means to talk like a lady' in Ervin-Tripp, S. and Mitchell-Kernan, C. (eds) *Child Discourse,* New York, Academic Press.

Edelsky, C. (1993) 'Who's got the floor?' in Tannen, D. (ed).

Efron, D. (1972) *Gesture, Race and Culture,* The Hague, Mouton.

Ekman, P. (1971) 'Universals and cultural differences in facial expressions of emotion' in Cole, J.K. (ed) *Nebraska Symposium on Motivation,* Lincoln, University of Nebraska Press.

Ekman, P. (1977) 'Biological and cultural contributions to body and facial movement', in Blacking, J. (ed) *The Anthropology of the Body,* London, Academic Press.

Ekman, P. and Friesen, W.V. (1969) 'The repertoire of nonverbal behavior: categories, origins, usage and coding', *Semiotica,* vol. 1, pp. 49–98.

Ekman, P., Friesen, W.V. and Ellsworth, P. (1982) 'What are the relative contributions of facial behaviour and contextual information to the judgment of emotion?' in Ekman, P. (ed) Emotion in the Human Face, Second Edition, Cambridge, Cambridge University Press.

Fishman, P. (1979) 'What do couples talk about when they are alone?', in Bultorf, D. and Epstein, E. (eds) *Women's Language and Style,* Akron, University of Akron Press.

Garfinkel, H. (1967) *Studies in Ethnomethodology,* New Jersey, Prentice-Hall.

Giles, H. and Coupland, N. (1991) *Language: Contexts and Consequences,* Buckingham, Open University Press.

Goffman, E. (1959) *The Presentation of Self in Everyday Life,* New York, Doubleday Anchor.

Goffman, E. (1972) *Interaction Ritual: Essays on Face-to-Face Behaviour,* Harmondsworth, Penguin.

Goffman, E. (1975) *Frame Analysis: an Essay on the Organization of Experience*, New York, Harper and Row.

Goffman, E. (1976) 'Gender advertizements', *Studies in the Anthropology of Visual Communication*, vol. 3, whole no. 2.

Goffman, E. (1983) 'The interaction order', *American Sociological Review*, 48, pp. 1–17.

Graddol, D. (1994) 'Three models of language description' in Graddol, D. and Boyd Barrett, O. (eds) *Media Texts: Authors and Readers*, Clevedon, Multilingual Matters.

Graddol, D. and Swann, J. (1989) *Gender Voices*, Oxford, Blackwell.

Hall, J. A. (1978) 'Gender effects in decoding nonverbal cues', *Psychological Bulletin*, vol. 85, pp. 845–57.

Harré, R. (1993) 'Rules, roles and rhetoric', *The Psychologist*, vol. 6, pp. 24–8.

Harré, R. and Secord, P.F. (1972) *The Explanation of Social Behaviour*, Oxford, Blackwell.

Henley, N.M. (1977) *Body Politics: Power, Sex and Nonverbal Communication*, Cambridge, Cambridge University Press.

Howe, C.J. (1989) 'Visual primacy in social attitude judgement: a qualification', *British Journal of Social Psychology*, vol. 28, pp. 263–72.

James, D. and Clarke, S. (1993) 'Women, men and interruptions: a critical review' in Tannen, D. (ed).

Kendon, A. (1967) 'Some functions of gaze in social interaction', *Acta Psychologica*, vol. 26, pp. 1–47.

Kendon, A. (1975) 'Some functions of the face in a kissing round', *Semiotica*, vol. 15, pp. 299–334.

Kendon, A. (1990) *Conducting Interaction: Patterns of Behaviour in Focused Encounters*, Cambridge, Cambridge University Press.

Knapp, M.L. (1983) 'Dyadic relationship development' in Wiemann, J.M. and Harrison, R.P. (eds) *Nonverbal Interaction*, Beverly Hills, Sage.

Knapp, M.L. and Hall, J.A. (1992) *Nonverbal Communication in Human Interaction*, Third Edition, Fort Worth, Harcourt Brace Jovanovich.

Labov, W. (1966) *The Social Stratification of English in New York City*, Washington, DC, Center for Applied Linguistics.

Lakoff, R. (1975) *Language and Woman's Place*, New York, Harper and Row.

Maltz, D.N. and Borker, R. (1982) 'A cultural approach to male-female communication' in Gumperz, J.J. (ed) *Language and Social Identity*, Cambridge, Cambridge University Press.

Mauss, M. (1972) 'Techniques of the body', *Economy and Society*, vol. 2, pp. 70–88.

McCormick, N. B. and Jones, A.J. (1989) 'Gender differences in nonverbal flirtation', *Journal of Sex Education and Therapy*, vol. 15, pp. 271–82.

Noller, P. (1980) 'Misunderstandings in marital communication: a study of couples' nonverbal communication', *Journal of Personality and Social Psychology*, vol. 39, pp. 1135–48.

Noller, P. (1984) *Nonverbal Communication and Marital Interaction*, Oxford, Pergamon Press.

Noller, P. (1986) 'Sex differences in nonverbal communication: advantage lost or supremacy regained?', *Australian Journal of Psychology*, vol. 38, pp. 23–32.

Patterson, M.L. (1985) 'The evolution of a functional model of nonverbal exchange: a personal perspective' in Street, R.L. and Cappella, J.N. (eds).

Poole, M.S. (1985) 'The "task" function. Tasks and interaction sequences: a theory of coherence in group decision-making interaction' in Street, R.L. and Cappella, J.N. (eds).

Posner, R. (1989) 'What is culture?: toward a semiotic explication of anthropological concepts' in Koch, W.A. (ed) *The Nature of Culture*, Bochum, Brockmeyer.

Potter, J. and Wetherell, M. (1987) *Discourse and Social Psychology: Beyond Attitudes and Behaviour*, London, Sage.

Poynton, C. (1989) *Language and gender: Making the Difference*, 2nd edition, Oxford, Oxford University Press.

Radley, A. (1991) *In Social Relationships: an introduction to the social psychology of membership and intimacy*, Buckingham, Open University Press.

Radley, A. (1995) 'The elusory body and social constructionist theory', *Body & Society*, vol. 1, (2) pp. 3–24.

Rosenthal, R. and DePaulo, B.M. (1979) 'Sex differences in accommodation in nonverbal communication' in Rosenthal, R. (ed) *Skill in Nonverbal Communication: Individual Differences*, Cambridge, Mass., Oelgeschlager, Gunn and Hain.

Sacks, H., Schegloff, E.A. and Jefferson, G.A. (1974) 'A simplest systematics for the organization of turn-taking in conversation', *Language*, vol. 50, pp. 697–735.

Scheflen, A.E. (1964) 'The significance of posture in communication systems', *Psychiatry*, vol. 27, pp. 316–31.

Scheflen, A.E. (1979) 'On communicational processes' in Wolfgang, A. (ed) *Nonverbal Behavior: Applications and Cultural Implications*, London, Academic Press.

Schegloff, E. A. (1968) 'Sequencing in conversational openings', *American Anthropologist*, vol. 70, pp. 1075--95.

Sherif, M. (1936) *The Psychology of Social Norms*, New York, Harper and Row.

Shotter, J. (1987) 'The social construction of an "us": problems of accountability and narratology' in Burnett, R., McGhee, P. and Clarke, D. (eds) *Accounting for Relationships: Explanation, Representation and Knowledge*, London, Metheun.

Street, R.L. and Cappella, J.N. (eds) (1985) *Sequence and Pattern in Communicative Behaviour*, London, Edward Arnold.

Tannen, D. (ed) (1993) *Gender and Conversational Interaction*, New York, Oxford University Press.

Vygotsky, L.S. (1962) *Thought and Language*, Cambridge, Mass., MIT Press.

Walkerdine, V. (1981) 'Sex, power and pedagogy', *Screen Education*, vol. 38, pp. 14–24.

West, C. and Garcia, A. (1988) 'Conversational shift work: a study of topical transitions between women and men', *Social Problems*, vol. 35, pp. 551–73.

Wieder, D.L. (1974) 'Telling the code' in Turner, R. (ed) *Ethnomethodology: Selected Readings*, Harmondsworth, Penguin.

Wiener, M., Devoe, S., Rubinow, S. and Geller, J. (1972) 'Nonverbal behavior and nonverbal communication', *Psychological Review*, vol. 79, pp. 185–214.

Wildeblood, J. (1973) *The Polite World: a Guide to the Deportment of the English in Former Times*, London, Davis-Poynter.

Wooffitt, R. (1992) *Telling Tales of the Unexpected: the Organization of Factual Discourse*, Hemel Hempstead, Harvester Wheatsheaf.

CHAPTER 3

CREATING RELATIONSHIPS: PATTERNS OF ACTIONS AND BELIEFS

by Rudi Dallos

Contents

1 Introduction

A good deal of our lives is taken up with our being in a variety of social and personal relationships; with friends, with intimate partners, with colleagues and with relatives. Even when we are alone, the chances are that we will spend a considerable amount of time mulling over relationships we have been involved in recently, or in anticipating new relationships. Chapter 2 looked at how interactions and relationships evolve from both intentional and unintentional communications. We will now explore further the meanings which underlie relationships; the participants' intentions, beliefs and understandings, and how these shape their actions. In this chapter we will examine the idea that relationships can usefully be regarded as patterns of shared actions and meanings jointly created by the participants over time. Relationships involve predictable sequences of actions such as: shared activities, ways of making decisions, mutual demands and emotional expression. Relationships also evolve through predictable patterns of conversations and it is primarily through these that people come to be able to anticipate each other's perceptions and understandings. An analysis is offered of how the patterning of relationships evolves from the interweaving of the individual partners' beliefs and their unique interactional dynamics.

We will start by exploring the nature of early relationships between infants and adults (predominantly mothers). Apart from being of interest in their own right, these relationships are a useful starting point because they help to identify the developmental bases of later adult interactions and relationships. Also, since the infant does not initially possess language, this also allows us to consider further the discussion of non-verbal behaviour developed in Chapter 2. On one level these early interactions can be seen as less complex since language is absent, but on another level they may be *more* complex because of the consequent difficulties posed for communication and for developing and sharing understandings. Much of social psychology attempts to make inferences about adult actions from childhood development, for example psychodynamic theory (see Chapter 4). This study of childhood relationships may begin to illuminate how early processes of relating with others and the dynamics which emerge as a result lay the groundwork for subsequent adult relationships.

The initial section, therefore, will focus on inter-subjectivity – the sense of connectedness, similarity of experience, understanding of and empathy with another person. This section will end with an exploration of the influence of beliefs and expectations, particularly on the mother's part, and how these serve to shape the relationship. Section 3 will then develop an analysis of individual cognitions and beliefs and their role in the development of relationships. Two approaches will be outlined: Personal Construct Theory and Attribution Theory. The section will consider how relationships involve participants forming inferences not only about each other's actions but also about each other's understandings.

Section 4 combines these ideas of patterned actions and personal and shared meanings. A central theme of this section is that the patterning of actions can be seen to be mutually shaped by and in turn create interlocking systems of beliefs. This section also considers relationships between three or more people and how each person's experiences may be shaped by relationships between the others. Finally, the chapter considers some aspects of the wider societal context, especially beliefs relating to gender, which shape and constrain relationships.

Aims of the chapter

1   To outline a view of relationships as displaying patterns of actions, meanings and emotions.

2   To discuss the view of relationships as emerging from a continual process of mutual influence over time.

3   To outline the effects on relationships of differences and inequalities of power between the participants.

4   To demonstrate the interdependence of relationship participants' beliefs and actions.

5   To discuss some of the ways in which wider societal contexts shape the patterning of relationships.

2   First relationships

Infants are not merely adapted to elicit care of their vital functions. They also possess rudimentary personal powers that affect their caretakers intimately so that within a short time of birth a subtle infant-caretaker relationship is established.

(Trevarthen, 1980, p. 336)

In the mid-1970s there was a significant challenge to common-sense assumptions that infants contribute little to interactions with significant people in their lives. Social and developmental psychologists began to suggest that infants, even those of only a few days old, had remarkable capacities for engaging in relationships. The spur for this came from detailed analyses of films of mothers interacting with their babies. These analyses indicated that from birth babies appear to be predisposed to be social. For example, within two weeks of birth, infants' crying is arrested more effectively by a human voice than by a rattle or mechanical sound (Wolff, 1969). Babies also demonstrate finely tuned patterns of coordinated interactions with their mothers such as patterns of mutual eye-contact, smiling and hand-movements. Trevarthen has gone on to suggest that simple forms of relating occur even before the baby is born:

Communication by sound can begin even earlier in development ... A foetus inside the mother is capable of detecting, reacting to and learn-ing features of her vocal expression. Hence, a baby may, within hours of birth, demonstrate a preference for the mother's speech or voicing over that of another woman. Distinctive features of her voice were learned *in utero*. Evidently the affective attachment between infant and mother can start to form *before* birth.

(Trevarthen, 1992, p. 4)

2.1   Patterning of actions

Studies of interactions between babies and their mothers arose from an interest in the causes of problems, such as infants who appeared to be withdrawn or distressed and parents' neglect and abuse of babies. A pae-diatrician, Berry Brazelton, and some colleagues (1974, 1991) had become interested to discover whether it was possible to trace the initial causes of problems of 'why things had gone wrong' to the very earliest days of the relationships. The question he asked was whether, and how, the early interactions between infants and mothers led to the develop-ment of 'problematic' relationships. He had observed that interactions between mothers and babies seemed to have rhythmic qualities, such as bursts of attention followed by withdrawal. At times he noted that they seemed to be engaged in a sort of harmonious joint 'dance' but at other times were 'out of tune' and tense. Prompted by these observations he embarked on a study of mothers and babies to try to explore the nature of these early interactions in detail and in order to generate some guide-lines for the diagnosis of vulnerable relationships.

Initially attempts were made to code the behaviours of the mothers and babies by scoring the number of vocalizations, smiles, exchange of looks, movements and gestures in one-minute episodes of interaction between them. However, Brazelton found that this presented a stilted series of snapshots which did not capture the true flow of the interactions over time. Rather than simply counting behaviours, an attempt was made to explore the behaviours as exchanges and in terms of a narrative docu-menting changes in these over time. An example of the kinds of patterns detected is shown below (see Figure 3.2).

BOX 3.1   Brazelton's study of mother-infant interaction

One of Brazelton's early influential studies examined five 'normal' (that is, non-clinical), white, middle-class mother-infant pairs (babies aged from 2 to 20 weeks). The studies took place in a laboratory setting with the baby placed in an adjustable reclining seat with a head support. The baby was free to move its arms and legs and to turn its head. The mother was seated in front of the baby, her face at a distance of about 18 inches (which is an infant's focal distance) and she was free to lean forward, touch or hold on to the baby. Two mirrors were located around them so that an image of each of them was registered simultaneously on film (see Figure 3.1).

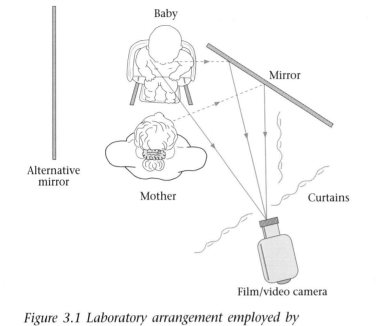

Figure 3.1 Laboratory arrangement employed by Brazelton and his colleagues

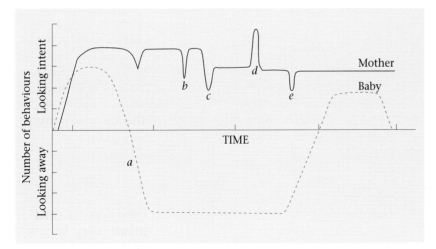

Figure 3.2 Number of behaviours added in a five-second period of interaction

Source: Brazelton, T.B. et al. (1975) Early Mother-Infant Reciprocity, Amsterdam, Elsevier, pp. 50–3

ACTIVITY 3.1   Look at Figure 3.2 and try to describe what appears to be happening. Can you detect a pattern that describes this sequence?

The graph consists of time shown along the horizontal line. The curves drawn above the horizontal line indicate that the mother or baby was looking at the other, and curves below indicate that they were looking away. Solid lines represent the mother's behaviour and broken ones the baby's. So, for example, a high unbroken line above the horizontal line indicates that the mother was looking at the baby and emitting several behaviours. An unbroken line below the horizontal indicates that the baby was looking away from her while engaged in several behaviours

Brazelton summarized the interaction depicted in Figure 3.2 as follows:

[It] shows a baby starting a cycle by looking at his mother. She follows by looking at him and adding four more behaviours in rapid succession – touching him, smiling, talking and nodding her head. He watches her, vocalizes, smiles back, cycles briefly, and then begins to decrease his responses and turns away at (a). She stops smiling as he begins to turn away but rapidly adds facial gestures to try to recapture his interest. She continues to talk, touch him, nod her head, and make facial gestures until (b). At this point she stops the gestures but begins to pat him. At (c) she stops talking briefly and stops nodding at him. At (d) she makes hand gestures in addition to her facial grimaces but stops them thereafter. At (e) she stops vocalizing and he begins to look at her. He vocalizes briefly and then looks away again when her activity continues…

The kind of sensitivity to each other's needs for attention and non-attention that a couple might exhibit is represented by these cycles. Examples (a) and (d) seem to represent real sensitivity. The kind of insensitivity of the mother to the baby's turning away represented by Figure 3.2 seems to prolong the period of looking away. In Figure 3.2 reducing her activity acts as a stimulus to bringing him back to respond to her after a long period of withdrawal.

(Brazelton et al., 974, pp. 62–3)

In order to make sense of the mother-child behaviour over time Brazelton looked at it in terms of sequences of *joint action* (an idea introduced in Chapter 2). This notion of sequences of mutually created actions is an important one not only for this chapter but for this volume as a whole, and in particular for Chapter 5. We can, of course, think of many instances of joint actions, for example how two young friends play together, how colleagues reach a decision, how a family prepare and consume a meal or how a couple make love. This concept of joint action involves regarding the behaviours of the part-

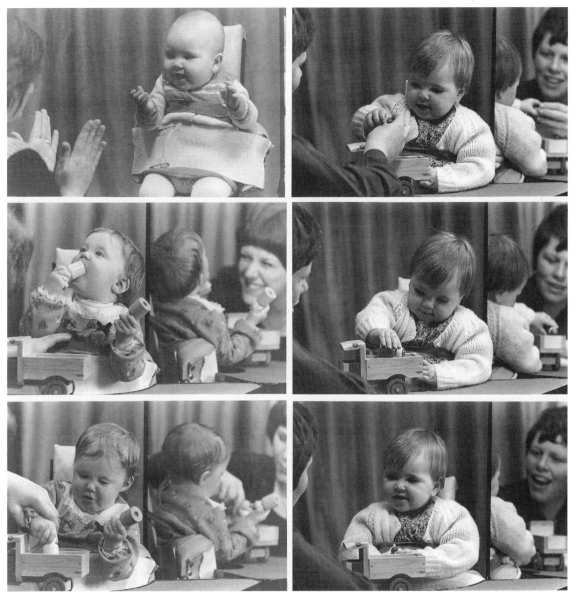

Left: Emma, at six months, has learned the clapping song 'clappa clappa handies'. Esme, at nine months, plays with wooden dolls and a truck, usually ignoring her mother, and she has to be 'persuaded' to follow the instruction, 'Put the man in the truck'. Right: At one year Basilie is willing to cooperate in a joint tasle. Her mother says, 'Put the man in the truck'. Basilie takes the offered doll, carries out the instruction, then looks up and grins while her mother congratulates her. She is clearly enjoying their share motives with respect to the toys.

ners as contingent and reciprocal, so rather than simply asking who started a sequence or who controlled it the focus is on how each *continually influences* the other, for example, 'as she increases her activity he turns away ... She begins to nod at him ... and he begins to look at the curtain'. It is also apparent in Brazelton's analysis that he is attempting to interpret how the mother and the child are understanding each other's behaviour, for example when the mother '...rapidly adds facial gestures to *try* to recapture his interest'. This raises methodological questions about how valid such inferences by researchers about the mother and child's intentions might be, in the case of the mother we could obviously ask her, but for a young infant lacking language we have to rely predominantly on inferences based on observation. Brazelton and other researchers, such as Trevarthen (1974, 1977, 1980), predominantly base such inferences about intentions upon changes in the babies' actions within the interactional context and also upon their evident signs of emotions, such as pleasure, frustration, interest and distress.

Biology and arousal

Brazelton and his colleagues emphasized biological elements in the relationships between mother and baby and argued that the mother-infant relationship functioned in such a way as to regulate or maintain the baby at an optimal level of arousal. The relationship appeared to incorporate as one of its functions that the baby did not become over or under-stimulated and aroused. So, if the mother was looking away and not stimulating the baby he might start to wriggle or cry to get her attention, likewise if he was getting too excited he might turn away and/or the mother might look away or offer less stimulation. Limitation of gaze would be a means of regulating stimulation to manageable proportions (Stern, 1985). However, Sylvester-Bradley (1981) suggests instead that it is not simply the *quantity* of stimulation which is crucial but its *quality*. He quoted evidence to suggest that infants do indeed reduce visual stimulation by turning away, but that this response is related more to the nature of the stimulation, for example whether it captures the baby's interest, its novelty and complexity and so on. Turning away is therefore seen more as a 'choice' or a 'wilful' response. Thus emotions such as pleasure and frustration are seen as playing a central role in the establishment of early relationships.

Inter-subjectivity

The detailed studies of mothers and their babies suggest that from birth the infant is not only able to respond to its mother's voice, movements, gaze, smiles and so on but is also able to actively influence her behaviour. Trevarthan (1980, 1992) has argued that infants are biologically provided with a 'readiness to know another human' and that they respond differently to people than to inanimate objects. This is not to suggest that the mother does not have more power to shape the relationship, as we will discuss later, but to emphasize that mutual influence is fundamental. The early exchanges between babies and mothers have been termed *proto-conversations* (Bateson, 1972). As this term suggests, the patterns of turn-taking, mutual attention, changes in movement, smiling and so on observed in these early interactions have been regarded as embodying the fundamentals of the verbal conversations of older children and adults.

In the following extract, Trevarthen (1980) quotes some of the evidence he has collected on the various aspects of the early relationships between mothers and babies. Trevarthen supports Brazelton's findings that infants have the capacity to influence the mother and not simply respond to her. He adds that infants also imitate the mother who likewise may mimic the baby's actions.

ACTIVITY 3.2

As you read through the account try to visualize what the early exchanges between mothers and babies may look like, or if possible you might like to observe an infant interacting with her or his mother. At the same time, consider the following two issues:

1   What evidence is there that babies are actively involved in influencing the mothers rather than simply responding to them?

2   What part do emotions, such as expressions of pleasure through smiling, appear to play in these early relationships ?

> ...An infant of this age has forms of motor expression by which considerable control is obtained over joint activity with the mother. These include apparently purposeful orientations of eyes, ears, mouth, or hands. Attentional focalizing and outline patterns of hand and arm extension move as if to grasp, leg and foot extend as if to step out in a particular direction. The movements have sufficient regularity of form and of temporospatial adjustment to environmental events for an observer, such as the mother, to have some grounds for imputing intentions to them. The babies also exhibit clear patterns of excitement, catching of interest, avoidance, and so on that are triggered by events they perceive. They seem, even as neonates, to have begun to have motives and feelings, to be aware, and to do things in adjustment to the world. But there are also purely communicative movements that can never have effect on the physical world except by influencing a human mind: remarkably rich facial expressions for changes in emotional state, gesturelike hand movements, and lip and tongue movements that are evidently precursors of verbal expression.
>
> *(Trevarthen, 1980, p. 318)*

Emotions as interpersonal

Trevarthen is suggesting that emotions are a central ingredient of early relationships, in that mother and baby are continually reacting and adjusting to each other at an emotional level. However, he adds that emotions are not simply *in* the mother or the baby but are essentially a part of the process *between* them:

> All human emotions are capable of changing another person's feelings and motives. Whatever its other functions in defending vital processes, or regulating action on the world and cognitive operations inside a subject, including self-awareness, every emotion that is expressed can directly and immediately affect emotions in another person. The nature of these transmitted affects will depend not only on the clarity of their expression, but also on the state of emotional equilibrium within the other. Emotions resonate between subjects, coupling and mutually 'inter-animating' their motives and consciousness.
>
> *(Trevarthen, 1992, p. 2)*

Chapter 4 of this book will take up a discussion of the role of emotions in relationships further, but Trevarthen's point is important to underline here. He is arguing that emotions are fundamentally inter-personal. (They are part of, and cannot be separated from, the process of relating.) Their function, certainly in early relationships, is to produce an effect in others. More contentiously he is also arguing that emotions have a 'direct' and unmediated biological effect on experience.

In Toates (1996) it is suggested that emotional experiences are at least partly socially constructed and shaped, apart perhaps from the most primitive, 'fight or flight', self-preservation responses. A considerable amount of energy in childhood and adult life seems to be taken up with trying to bring even these reactions under conscious control, for example engaging in 'risky' or dangerous activities in order to overcome or 'master' our fears. The psychodynamic perspective (discussed in Chapter 4) also stresses that energy is expended in building up defenses against unwanted thoughts and feelings. You might consider the extent to which you feel Trevarthen's position gives emotions too much of a 'biological primacy'.

Trevarthen also argues that there is a fundamental link between emotions and a sense of control or influence in the relationship. Not only does he see mothers and babies as mutually influencing each other, but as having an emotional need to do so:

> In addition to his [the infant's] basic articulation with reality, the strong orientation to movements of the face, voice, and hands of the mother and the production by the infant of forms of facial expression, oral movement, hand displacement, postural change – which we take to signify human feelings of enjoyment, curiosity, puzzlement, annoyance, sadness, fear, and an effort to 'say' or to 'show' something – offers evidence of a specialized set of motives aimed to get the attentions of a human partner.
>
> *(Trevarthen, 1980, p. 325)*

Emotions such as pleasure and excitement are seen as resulting from relating and also as providing the vital motivational 'glue' to maintain interaction. In addition, Trevarthen has observed that an inability to exert influence or to establish mutual, synchronized interaction generates negative emotions such as frustration and anxiety. This link between emotional experiences and the ability to exert some influence was investigated in a series of experiments in which the moment-to-moment processes of mutual influence were deliberately disrupted (see Box 3.2).

BOX 3.2 Disrupting interactions

Trevarthen explored what happened if mothers were requested to act in an irrelevant or non-reactive way with their babies, for example a mother was asked to remain unreactive: still, silent and with a blank face in the middle of an exchange of expressions with her baby (Murray and Trevarthen, 1985). This caused a two-month-old child to cease communicating pleasure and then to make elaborate movements signifying distress, such as: a generally less relaxed facial expression, grimaces, yawns, frowns, finger sucking and the touching of face and clothes. However, when the mother was momentarily distracted by the experimenter speaking to her and she turned away, the baby did not appear to become distressed but made some vocalizations and gestures as if to 'call her back'.

For a second study, a delayed video replay situation was employed. In this, the baby saw its mother on a television screen acting in a happy and lively manner, however since this was merely a replay of a recording of one of their previous interactions, the mother's actions were not synchronized (except by chance) with those of the baby. Again, similar signs of distress were shown by the baby. But compared to the 'blank face' experiment, the baby appeared to be more withdrawn and less inclined to protest.

In another experiment in which mother and baby interacted via a video link between two rooms a replay of the infant's part in a previous interaction was substituted (without the mother being aware). In this situation, the mothers still thought they were interacting 'live' with their babies. Even although the baby appeared to be happy and expressive, the mother could not establish normal contact and influence (synchronized interaction) and tended to see her infant as 'perverse, distracted, unhappy, or withdrawn' in order to explain the disconnection between them.

Autonomy and power

Trevarthen is arguing that an ability to engage with others as persons and specifically to be equipped to engage in mutual influence over others is a fundamental capacity of infants, albeit in a primitive form. Disruption of this capacity to exert some degree of influence over the mother is experienced as distressing. What appears to be crucial is that there is a coordination of emotions over time, so that the mothers' and infants' actions, reactions and emotional expressions must be contingent. Disruption, whereby control cannot be exerted so that these emotions become synchronized, appears to result in states of distress for both participants.

Having argued that in early relationships participants can be seen as mutually influencing each other, the question remains of the extent to which this is an asymmetrical relationship. Mothers have the full capacity of language, more experience of interactions as well as greater physical abilities of movement, strength and so on with which to exert influence and control the relationship. To what extent, then, does the adult control the relationship and in what ways can and does the infant gain control? There are also questions of whether some forms of relating foster the development of autonomy more than others and, returning to Brazelton's interest, whether some forms of relating are associated with the development of 'problems' in the baby or the mother-baby relationship

Scaffolding

Though infants do have the capacity to exert influence it can be argued that, particularly in the early stages of the relationship, the mother can be seen to take charge of the baby's learning and development as well as being responsive to the baby's contribution. Mothers appear to be sensitively tuned to their baby's movements, gaze, gestures and vocalizations. An important ingredient in this relationship is the achievement of joint attention, thus a mother will follow an infant's line of regard and work out what he or she is looking at, she may then touch or manipulate that object, pull it nearer, tempt the child with it, let the child play with it and so on. An example of this is described by Newson and Newson (1977) in the teaching of a four-week-old infant to follow the movement of a dangling ring:

> …the [mother] will carefully attend, not just to the general state of arousal of the infant, but to his precise focus and line of regard. Having 'hooked' the attention of the infant upon the ring, one then begins to gingerly move it across his field of vision in such a way that the infant's eyes continue to hold the object with successive fixations until eventually the head follows the eyes in that coordinated overall movement pattern which denotes successful tracking. If the [ring] is moved too suddenly, or is left static for too long, the visual attention of the infant will flag and the attempt will have to begin all over again from scratch. In this instance what is happening is highly skilled monitoring by the adult and a consequent adjustment of the dangling object moment by moment, depending on the feedback which is being obtained from the spontaneous actions of the infant … The resulting sequence of the infant is therefore a combination of his own activity and an *intelligent manipulation of that activity by the much more sophisticated adult partner.*

The adult, by being contingently responsive to the infant in a way which only another human being could be, manages both to hold the infant's attention and to shape the course of his ongoing activity pattern.

(Newson and Newson, quoted in Oates, 1994, p. 284)

Mothers in this way provide a framework, or 'scaffold' within which the child's abilities can be built. Bruner (1977) and others argue that through these shared learning activities the infant's abilities develop rapidly, and a child of about four months is able to follow its mother's line of regard. It can also start to initiate joint attention to objects by drawing its mother's attention to them by patting or touching them while engaging in eye contact: 'there is present from a surprisingly early pre-linguistic age a mutual system by which joint selective attention between an infant and his caretaker is assured – under the control of the caretaker or of the child' (Bruner, 1977, p. 276).

Fostering or inhibiting autonomy

With very young infants, the question remains of the extent and the manner in which they can exert some influence on an adult. This is a fundamental question for relationships in general – the nature of power differences and how these contribute to the nature of the relationship. One approach to this question is to analyse in detail the interactions between infants and adults to see how they shift in the form of activity and who is predominantly in control or directing it. Fivas-Depeursinge (1991) has suggested that interactions can be seen to fall into *episodes*, such as mutual gaze, and that these contain briefer episodes, such as mutual smiling. The gaze episodes themselves can be seen as 'nested' within larger episodes of holding – the posture and physical support of the adult. To take an example, after a period of an infant wriggling around or a parent 'jiggling' it, they may both settle into a frame of holding where their body posture is stable and apparently 'comfortable'. Within this they may have bursts of mutual gaze and within this bursts of smiling. More broadly, the mother can be seen to have more control over the initiation of episodes, for example she may hold the infant and gaze for longer at her baby who may look away and back again (as Brazelton described). Mother's gaze therefore frames the infant's shorter episodes of gaze.

By examining not only which partner seems to have more control over the initiation of an episode but also how this changes over time, we can gain further insight into how control – the power to direct or influence the relationship – occurs. For example, 'a daughter showed that she no longer liked the sitting position, her father gave in to her and held her standing in front of him, both looking intently at each other. She alternatively danced and paused, in brief episodes nested within long episodes of reciprocal gaze' (Fivas-Depeursinge, 1991, p. 108).

Like Brazelton, Fivas-Depeursinge and her colleagues were interested to discover how early relationships became problematic. They observed that, for some infants and their parents, mutual co-orientations of gaze and attention did not develop. One simple question they asked was whether the parents were holding the infants in a way that made it diffi-cult for the child to make eye-contact and therefore exert any influence through gaze. This is an important means of communication and of exerting influence for the child and if it is blocked this may impede his or her developing sense of control and autonomy.

BOX 3.3   Patterns and problems of early relating

In a study of 16 families (Fivas-Depeursinge, 1991) 8 non-clinical and 8 with clinical problems the patterns of episodes of holding and mutual gaze were explored. The infants were recorded in interactions with their mother, father and a stranger (experimenter's confederate). The observations indicated that interactions could be seen in terms of sequences of offers of different types of engagement, so that how the adult held an infant resulted in a counter offer by the child's type of gaze. Further, the research suggested that the forms of relating could be classified as consensual, conflictual or paradoxical

Consensual engagement – the adult provides a clear frame by holding the child 'appropriately' which allows the child the opportunity to engage easily in eye contact and therefore in a joint episode of mutual gaze.

Conflictual – an initial clear attempt at engagement, for example gaze directed by the adult at the child followed by mutual eye contact. The infant might then follow this by withdrawal, looking away or crying, whereupon the adult might continue to try to engage the child for some time longer and then disengage.

Paradoxical – here the adult makes an ambiguous offer, for example by initiating gazing or vocalizations but holding the child 'inappropriately' too far away or too close, sideways and so on. The infant eventually also 'replies' in an ambiguous manner, for example looking away or in a glazed manner or staring at the parent's forehead rather than making eye contact.

The study suggested that there were significant differences between the patterns of holding and gaze between adults and infants in the clinical and non-clinical families, such that the patterns of paradoxical interaction were more common in the clinical sample. Furthermore, the interactions between the infant and the stranger were more consensual in the clinical sample, suggesting that the infant's paradoxical interactions were a feature of their interactions with their parents.

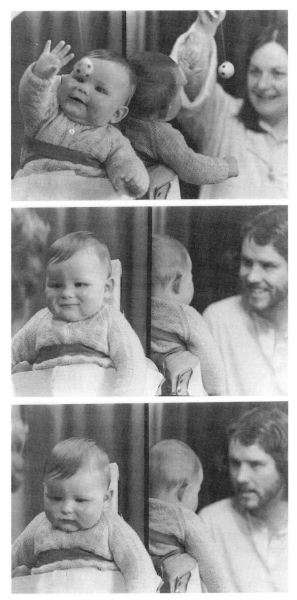

An eight-month-old boy happily plays 'catch the ball' with his mother but is shy and distressed with a friendly stranger.

This study, in conjunction with those described earlier, suggests that although adults have more power to determine the pattern of interactions, the infants can direct or change the episodes, for example a child can maintain eye contact and begin to 'dance' around, thus changing the dominant frame from 'holding' to 'gaze'. Importantly the infant is also able to initiate a change by emotional expression, for example 'insistent crying'. The study by Fivas-Depeursinge (1991) suggested that the parents construct options for the child which can foster or inhibit the development of autonomy. Specifically, the consensual mode was seen to allow most opportunity or options for the infant – to engage or not and to alter which episode is dominant. Moreover, it is possible that these early forms of relating start to set a pattern which may be evident in later relationships, for example the paradoxical form of interaction described resembles the account of a contradictory form of communication which has been seen to characterize 'pathological' forms of relating (Bateson, 1972; Watzlawick, 1963).

An obvious question that arises is, why do parents differ in how they relate to their infants? Psychodynamic approaches (see Chapter 4) consider the mother's emotional state and explore how she may be unconsciously 'projecting' her feelings onto the child. So a paradoxical form of engagement may be related to her feeling frustrated, anxious and unhappy with herself and hence unable to act confidently and clearly with the child. In addition, her actions may also be intimately related to her cognitions, beliefs and understandings: 'I think he is going to be stubborn; if he doesn't want to drink, he won't. He sort of puts his bottom lip in. I was stubborn apparently when I was young' (Brazelton and Cramer, 1991, pp. 133–7).

Such framings or expectations can potentially have a powerful self-fulfilling effect, so that by seeing the baby as 'stubborn' the mother comes to act towards her baby accordingly and a pattern starts to emerge. However, as we have seen, the relationship that develops is at least in part a mutual product – the infant also plays a part in shaping what occurs. As Trevarthen emphasizes, fundamental actions such as smiling, wriggling, crying and so on carry significant emotional features. How these are defined and what meanings are attributed to them, however, may vary widely both between parents and between cultures.

Cross-cultural differences

Some aspects of the findings in this section, especially the suggestion that patterns of mother-baby interaction are fundamental and universal, need to be considered with some caution. There is an attendant danger of generating ideas of what constitutes 'good' parenting which can lead to tendencies to assign blame for childhood problems to mothers. Schieffelin and Ochs (1983) suggest that many cultures contain a 'developmental story', an assumption or image that sees the infant as a social being and the mother's role as being to take the perspective of the child. This contains pervasive ideas of the 'need' for parents, and especially mothers, to be sensitive, responsive and accommodating. One consequence may be to prompt mothers to be continually concerned and vigilant about whether the child is receiving enough stimulation, is not bored and is generally 'happy'.

However, not *all* cultures appear to share this view and some display markedly different ways of interacting with infants (Oates, 1994). From their studies of the Kaluli culture in Papua New Guinea, Schieffelin and Ochs (1983) suggested that in this culture babies are seen as helpless and unable to understand anything that is said to them. Mothers are the primary caregivers and are attentive to their infants' physical needs. They are carried with them almost continually even while the mother may be working. However, infants are never treated as communicational partners and utterances are rarely addressed to them, apart from greeting them by name. Mothers and infants do not gaze into each other's eyes, and rather than facing their babies and speaking to them, the mothers tend to face the babies outward towards the others in a social group. When older children greet or speak to the infant the mothers tend to reply and speak for the baby. This can also be seen as a form of teaching or modelling, whereby the child is shown how to relate to diferent people in the community (an argument which is put forward in a further discussion of this study in Wetherell and Maybin, 1996).

Likewise, Fajardo and Freeman (1981) compared the interactional styles between mothers and infants in three American cultures, white, black and Navajo. Considerable variations were found, for example black mothers provided more intense and continual stimulation until the baby 'switched off'. Black infants also seemed to posess a higher tolerance for stimulation and did not turn away from their mother's intensified displays but instead appeared to find this interesting. However, at the point that the babies did turn away they were left alone. White mothers in contrast seemed more concerned with 'getting the baby to perform'. The researchers suggested that although the black mothers are highly stimulating they did not seem as intrusive as white mothers because the patterns of the black mothers' actions were not so much a response to the infant's non-attentiveness as their own interests and pleasure in performing for the baby. In contrast to both of these groups, the Navajo mothers seemed to have no clear pattern but were passive and silent with their infants who nevertheless spent an equivalent amount of time gazing at their mother's relatively impassive faces. However, the babies in all three cultures were found to be equally alert.

Oates (1994) suggests that such apparent variations between cultures indicate that culturally shared assumptions and expectations do play at least *some* part in shaping the nature of mother-child interactions. The culturally shared discourses help to construct the framings that mothers and other carers apply to their relationships with their infants, and this as well as their personal experiences shape the nature of their relationship with the infant. These early ways of relating and the beliefs guiding them may lay the basis for later forms of relating in adult life.

The next section signals a progression from looking at early relationships to those between adults. In this section we have ended by considering how the influence of mothers' cognitions – understandings, explanations and beliefs, play a vital part in shaping the relationships with their infants. The nature of these cognitions and how they shape actions will be explored in the next section.

Review of section 2

This section has explored the nature of early relationships in order to gain an understanding of them and to help us to gain insights into the fundamentals of adult relationships. One significant aspect of these early relationships is that one partner, the infant, does not posess language. Consequently, this allows us to see more clearly the importance and complex role of non-verbal features of interaction and synchronization of action. Some of the key findings from these studies of early relationships are as follows:

- Infants appear to be pre-disposed to engage in coordinated, joint action from a very early age, this forms the basis of shared understanding and expectations of future relating.

- Relationships can be regarded as to some degree *mutually* constructed rather than simply predominantly shaped by the adult.

- Meanings and emotions emerge from, and are shaped by the continual process of interacting – they do not simply reside inside each partner but continually change and are changed by the interactions.

- The ability to exert some control or influence over the other partner is essential and is linked to and guided by emotions.

- There is evidence that patterns of reciprocal action and mutual influence are fundamental, but the social organization of this appears to vary to some extent between cultures.

3   Developing individual understandings

...a personal relationship ... is about *sharing* meaning, by which I mean the deep processes of understanding someone else's ways of thinking about their experiences in the world. I am concerned not with what it *is* to be in a relationship so much as what it *means*.

(Duck, 1994, p.xv)

At the conclusion of the previous section we saw how mothers make assumptions about or 'frame' the dynamic processes with their infants; conferring 'as if' meanings upon them. Saying, for example, that the baby is not feeding because he is 'bored and wants to play' or because 'he wants

his own way and is stubborn'. We will now examine the nature of cognitions held by participants in adult relationships and will focus on the
extent to which these shape the relationship that each participant
attempts to construct and the ways in which these influence, respond to
or control the actions of the other. The concept of 'framing' briefly raised
at the end of the previous section forms the springboard for this section.
This suggests that at any moment each partner may hold a variety of ways
of 'framing' – of understanding, explaining and predicting both the partner *and* the relationship. These framings may serve as 'theories' or
'hypotheses' which have a central role in shaping the relationship.

This emphasis on developing understandings of our own and our partners' actions forms the basis of two approaches: Attribution Theory and
Personal Construct Theory (PCT). The latter is sometimes referred to as
Kelly's Personal Construct Theory because it was George Kelly who first
articulated it. This theory embodies the reflexive perspective which
emphasizes people's potential to create a variety of meanings and to be
able to reflect on these. Attribution Theory adopts an experimental
approach in attempting to draw out general theories of how people
explain events in their relationships.

3.1   Personal Construct Theory and relationships

George Kelly (1955) suggested that we are all potentially autonomous
and capable of actively making choices about events in our lives, including our relationships. Though believing that there is an objective reality
'out there', he proposed that we can only know this through our personal construct system – our idiosyncratic system of interconnected constructs or beliefs which metaphorically is like a lens through which we
view the world. Each construct in our system represents a personal set of
contrasts – a bipolar division. For example when I use the term 'friendly'
the contrast (for *me*) might be 'pushy'. But for someone else the contrasting pole of the construct 'friendly' might be 'aggressive' or 'sullen'. In
fact the meaning an individual ascribes to a term such as friendly, Kelly
argued, can *only* be guaged if we know its opposite – its contrast – for
that individual.

We do not simply see the world and make decisions in our relationships
based upon isolated constructs, however, instead, Kelly argued that constructs are organized in a hierarchical way and linked together to form
explanations and predictions. Narratives or stories that we may have
about ourselves, and which we offer to others as explanations, may feature a set of constructs connected together. For example, Mary might say,
'I am wary of showing feelings in my relationship because I came from a
rather "reserved" family background'. This statement links together a construct about herself – *wary of showing feelings* with a construct that
explains her childhood background – *reserved family*. Kelly called these
linkages of constructs their 'implications' and regarded people as employ-

ing clusters of constructs to explain events. However, he described some constructs as being more central or 'core' than others, for example to think of onself as 'honest' and 'trustworthy'. In relationships we are concerned that our partners should validate or support our core constructs, and in particular our preferred view of ourselves. Rejection or invalidation of our core views and our preferred view of ourselves is potentially a great source of distress, and a prime reason many people give for terminating a relationship.

Anticipation and replication

ACTIVITY 3.3   Think of a relationship that you are currently involved in. What expectations do you have about how your relationship will proceed – how you will both act the next time you see each other? How are your expectations shaped by the way you construe the other person and the relationship with him or her?

Since the world, especially our social world, is continually changing, so also our understandings must be able to adapt and change. Kelly argued that the choice of action taken on the basis of personal constructs influences the interaction that will follow which in turn affects the constructs held by both partners.

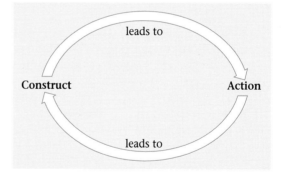

Figure 3.3 *Beliefs and actions are mutually interdependent*

Construct – My parents will be angry that I am using the phone 'all the time'...

Action – Use the phone in a secret and furtive manner and act apologetically, or alternatively act in a rebelious angry manner...

Either of these possible courses of action could then start off a self-fulfilling cycle whereby the parents react to the child's actions, triggering further actions from him or her. For example, if he or she acts furtively and apologetically his or her parents might suspect he or she has something to be secretive and apologetic about and start to 'question' or 'accuse' him or her. Alternatively, if he or she acts rebelliously this might prompt angry counter accusations and criticism.

Kelly suggested that our constructs may not invariably be conscious, so we may have a feeling about somone which is based on construings of which we are not fully aware. He did, however, emphasize our potential for conscious reflexivity – people are seen as able to become aware and to reflect not only on the actions of others but also on their own actions, thoughts and feelings (this aspect of his work is discussed further in Stevens [1996]). Importantly, he also believed that we are capable of reflecting on our relationships, anticipating both the other person's actions and also the outcomes of our own actions. He proposed that gaining insight and awareness of such patterns facilitates change, growth and development in our relationships. This is complicated, however (as we will see in the next section) since such unilateral change may be difficult to achieve, especially since the other's continued actions can have a powerful influence in maintaining our constructs and eroding attempts to change. It is also complicated by the fact, as we will see in Chapter 4, that some of our actions and feelings in relationships are based upon unconscious processes which are not readily accessible to conscious reflection.

Kelly suggested that all of us are like scientists in the sense that we are concerned with anticipating events in the world. Our constructs help us to make decisions about how to act towards others. We can then test our constructs by seeing how well or badly they help us to anticipate the situations that we enter into. We form hypotheses and build theories about the world which are more or less useful to us in anticipating what is likely to happen. In the case of our relationships this process of anticipation and revision becomes even more critical. People do not usually change unpredictably from moment to moment but certainly they do change. Even if we propose that people have stable personalities which change very little we would have to admit that friendships change, people grow older and take up different interests, relationships develop and disintegrate. In relationships, changes in people's beliefs about each other are required, for example due to changing roles such as becoming a parent, the transition from 'child' to 'adult' status in families, changes in status at work or changes in health. At the same time as allowing us to anticipate and cope with change, our constructs also provide us with a sense of continuity and predictability. We predict the future by expecting a measure of replication of past events. For example we probably expect our friends, our partner and our children to stay 'pretty much' the same, at least over relatively short periods of time – days or a few weeks. Probably most of us expect our interactions with others to be predictable in the sense of being 'like' the interactions we had previously. Constructs therefore provide a bridge and continuity between the past, the present and the future. As we will see, it is more fruitful to think about how our beliefs held about past events construct our future and present behaviour, than it is to think about the past events as 'in themselves' determining what happens.

However, relationships would become extremely chaotic if we did not have any resistance to giving up our constructs in the face of limited samples of evidence. For example if we radically re-evaluate a relationship based upon each shift in the other person's mood we might find it extremely stressful (if not impossible) to plan and organize any activities with them. We might also abandon too readily some useful ways of seeing things. Alternatively, there can be a danger that we become too resistant and try to ignore, discredit or even falsify the evidence available to us. In relationships, a particularly pernicious process can occur (Bateson, 1972; Laing, 1969) when participants falsify evidence so that eventually they may have difficulty in distinguishing 'what is really going on'. Such inability to be able to anticipate, predict and have a sense of control over events and relationships has been linked to serious mental illnesses (Bannister, 1960; Watzlawick et al., 1974).

The commonality and sociality corollaries

As we have seen, Kelly saw relationships as consisting of two or more potentially autonomous and reflexive people trying to make sense of each other and to anticipate not only each other's actions but also each other's thoughts and feelings:

> It would be good to identify two levels of construing. The first would be concerned with events and with [persons] treated as events ... a second ... would be concerned with construing the constructions of other [people]. Instead of making our sense of what others did, we would try to understand what sense they made out of what they did.
>
> *(Kelly, 1955, p. 203)*

In order to engage in a relationship it is seen as fundamental that each person has some idea about how the other sees the world, including how the other sees them. Kelly referred to two key processes governing relationships, the first is a recognition of *commonality:* 'To the extent that one person employs a construction of experience which is similar to that employed by another, his psychological processes are similar to those of the other person.' (Kelly, 1955).

Commonality has at least two aspects here. Firstly, two people think about the world, and in particular their relationship, in a similar way. One part of such commonality is that we use similar language, for example, a couple who are vegetarians may use terms which they both find familiar, such as 'organic', 'macrobiotic' or 'vegan'. Secondly, their commonality is reflected in their actions (they do not eat meat) and their ways of describing their feelings and experience.

Sociality is the extent to which each person has an understanding or empathy regarding how the other person sees the world: 'To the extent that one person construes the construction processes of another, they may play a role in a social process involving the other person' (Kelly, 1955).

Sociality involves an ability to predict how the other person uses constructs and this may happen irrespective of the level of commonality. We might understand how someone sees events but totally disagree with them. Likewise, Kelly argues that it is possible to have a high level of commonality with someone but not recognize it, for example if we do not have much communication or discussion with them. The level of sociality, recognition of similarities and differences may fluctuate as a relationship develops.

The idea of commonality suggests that people in relationships evolve some shared ways of construing events, others and each other. Duck (1988, 1994) suggests that in relationships people are continually trying to generate new meanings and explanations and to find more effective ways of understanding each other. An important area of negotiation and potential conflict for any relationship can be the development of a set of understandings and agreements about the relationship itself. A relationship can be seen as a set of ideas or beliefs – a system of meanings. Participants develop a set of constructs about the relationships between each other then establish some agreement or shared way of seeing the relationship; the roles they will play, how they divide up their time, and issues of obligations, rights, intimacy, dominance and so on. Through participation in a variety of joint activities; cooking, discussions, decorating, physical intimacy and so on people develop a shared set of constructs about each other, including ideas about each other's personalities, but also about how they 'get on together'. Procter (1981) has suggested that a key part of such shared understanding is the agreed allocation of 'roles' within a relationship. For example, one partner may be seen as the reliable, practical and unemotional one in contrast to the other who is seen as more emotional, imaginative and spontaneous. In addition to this, there may also be a shared view, accompanied by positive feelings, that this combination 'works well', that they complement each other and so on. Obviously if there is total disagreement about these constructs then the relationship is likely to dissolve into endless arguments, inaction or dissolution. A personal construct theory perspective emphasizes that the important agreement is about the domain of choices seen to be possible, for example, both the roles seen to be necessary and who should fill them. However, both of these may be more or less negotiable – they represent choices seen to be available at any one time in the relationship.

The idea of a shared construct system can be seen in terms of a metaphor of a deck of cards containing an array of options or choices that are seen to be possible by the participants in the relationship. These choices can be presented as bipolar options or constructs. A pair of people may not agree about the choices they should make but there is likely to be more agreement about what choices are possible. Their shared construct system sets out the domain of perceived choices or the 'agenda' for the relationship. The formation of a new relationship can be seen to involve a reshuffling, a synthesis of two decks of options that each partner has brought from their previous experiences. Evolution and changes are possible and prompted by the influences of peers, friends and local community and the wider cultural changes in the attitudes and expectations regarding relationships, for example the implications of changing gender roles within the family.

Emotionality

Relationships are also about sharing emotions, joint experiences of pleasure, joy and sadness. Kelly argued that emotions and constructs were inseparable. We do not simply have emotions but have emotions *based upon* ascribed meanings. Relationships, as we all know, can generate profound and at times intense feelings. From Kelly's perspective these feelings are directly linked to the extent to which we feel a relationship validates our views, and in particular how we would like to be seen, our prefered view of self. Positive emotions: happiness, joy, love, may result from such validation and in contrast negative ones from invalidation. Negative emotions, such as anxiety and anger occur, he suggested, when our constructs are in some way inadequate to help us to predict or exert some influence in a relationship. This may be associated with a sense of inability to be able to influence or persuade another to regard us in a way that we find acceptable or desirable.

ACTIVITY 3.4 Turn back and read again the account of the relationship between emotions and inter-subjectivity offered in section 2. What similarities and differences do you see between Kelly's analysis of the role of emotions in relationships and those of Trevarthen?

Since he or she does not possess language, a young child in contrast to an adult may experience distress or bewilderment in terms of a loss or breaking down of some pleasurable joint activity. The sense of connectedness inherent in the concept of inter-subjectivity may for a young child be related to a sense of being a part of and able to influence the initiation of such episodes of joint activity. For Kelly, emotions appear to be (to some extent) secondary to a sense of validation of our constructs, whereas for Traverthen emotions are fundamentally related to the process of mutual, joint action.

Kelly's definitions emphasize that emotions are fluid and changing as each partner is attempting to deal with the demands and fluctuations of the relationship. He saw problems as associated with an inability to formulate constructs to enable renegotiation and adjustment acording to changing circumstances. In any relationship, agreements are seen as to some extent temporary and open to renegotiation. Since these renegotiations will touch central aspects of ourselves it is expected that they will be accompanied by a variety of emotions which may at times result in a relationship becoming volatile, and in some cases the negative emotions may inhibit each person's thinking processes leading in some cases to forms of constrained or 'pre-emptive' construing, a sort of 'tunnel vision' (see Chapter 4 for a further dicussion of the effects of emotionality in relationships). This is a pattern whereby the constructs operate in a rigid either/or way, revealed by the use of adjectives and adverbs, such as 'every', 'always', 'never' – 'you *always* do that', 'you *never* listen to what I have to say' and so on. In a relationship one person, for example the husband, may see his wife as vindictive and nothing but vindictive, and this feeling may become reciprocated by his wife who may come to see her husband as abusive and nothing but abusive. Typically, the construct will be applied very rigidly to a wide range of actions without any allowance for exceptions or alternative ways of seeing them. Pre-emptive construing has a quality of pushing the other person into a particular role 'whether they like it or not'.

In contrast, the development of relationships, growth, change and more positive emotions seem to be accompanied by a less rigid, propositional style of construing which has a pragmatic quality, rather like a 'working hypothesis' (Kelly, 1955). For example we might see the actions of a work colleague who has been a 'bit short' with us in a number of possible ways, he is tired, is having a hard time at work, is worried about his family etc., rather than just thinking: 'the creep is out to get me, again'. Finally, Kelly also suggested a similar dimension of 'loose versus tight' for describing the person's overall construct system. Overly constricted or tight construing occurs when constructs are used which only cover a very limited range of events, hence the risks of disconfirmation of the constructs are limited. In other words, we can attempt to become more and more certain about fewer and fewer things. In contrast, a construct system can be so loose and vague that it becomes virtually impossible to falsify or test it effectively.

These styles of construing can be seen to be part and parcel of the shared patterns of actions, feelings and beliefs in a relationship. Kelly was keen to emphasize that we are capable of taking a reflexive stance in which we can become aware of our shared experiences, what type of a relationship we are in, how we want to change it and so on, which can be a basis for a discussion and re-negotiation leading to some agreed changes in roles and expectations.

In conclusion, Kelly's PCT offers a view of people in relationships as potentially autonomous, actively making decisions about how to act with others on the basis of their personal systems of meanings. In turn, this system of meanings is seen as fluid, evolving and changing not only in response to changes in a relationship but also simultaneously shaping the nature of the relationship. One danger can be that this view implies that it is easy to change a relationship simply by seeing it differently. In Section 5, an extension of Kelly's theory will be outlined which suggests how partners' systems of constructs can become inter-locked in ways that make revisions of constructs and change difficult. Finally, in emphasizing the personal, or even the shared nature of constructs, PCT tends to minimize the wider societal influences which shape personal systems of meanings and identities.

3.2 Attribution Theory

Attribution Theory derives from an empirical research tradition which has attempted to examine systematically how people formulate explanations about other people's actions and their own. Whereas PCT is a wide-ranging theory which includes an account of how people explain events in a potentially infinite number of ways, Attribution Theory makes more specific generalizations about the types of explanations that people typically employ. There is an attempt to establish universal processes of how people formulate causal explanations, and in contrast to PCT these explanations are seen as based on a number of limited, core dimensions related to the organization of cognition and information processing. Attribution Theory adopts a nomothetic approach which tries to establish a general theory of causal explanations. However, it shares with PCT an emphasis on seeing people as actively trying to make sense of their relationships and, through forming causal explanations, on predicting how they will act in future. Attribution Theory, in emphasizing information processing and computation of explanations, diverges from a focus on meanings and the potentially infinite number of alternative ways of seeing events which is central to PCT. Furthermore, it does not emphasize the reflexive nature of human experiences, and in particular people's ability to transform and even transcend their experiences by constructing new or elaborated explanations of events.

ACTIVITY 3.5   Let us begin by looking at two examples of actions and how the participants in a relationship may explain these.

1   Marie had asked George to video record an episode of a television drama for her the previous evening as she was going out to a leaving party organized for one of her friends at work. George did not do so and offers the explanation that he 'forgot'.

2   Susan appears to have been rather withdrawn and unaffectionate for the last month. Whenever Peter suggests doing something together, such as going out for a drink or to the cinema, she always seems to find a reason for not being able to go.

Think for a few minutes about these two scenarios and try to put yourself in turn into each of these four people's shoes. Write down what explanations come to mind for the other's actions. You will probably decide fairly quickly that you need more information, but try and specify what type of information this might be.

Most partners – couples, colleagues or friends – are likely to admit that they can never be absolutely sure why the other has acted in a particular way. Despite this, if we were Marie or Peter we would probably make some attempts to find *causes* or *reasons* for our partner's actions and feelings. Heider (1958) proposed that people invariably make some attempt, consciously or unconsciously, to formulate theories or explanations about the causes for other people's actions. He argued that the need to find reasons or causes is extremely fundamental and illustrated this in a classic experiment in which people were shown a film of simple animated geometrical shapes and asked to describe what they saw in their own words. The reports typically included observations such as: the circle was 'following' the square, or in some instances one triangle 'chased' another 'because he was jealous of his relationship with the circle' (Heider and Simmel, 1944). If we make attributions to simple inanimate shapes, then how much more likely are we to make such attributions to people we are in relationships with? Heider suggested that we form two contrasting forms of explanations about others' actions:

- Internal/dispositional – explanations of causes in terms of people's wants, needs, intentions and personalities.

- External/situational – explanations of causes in terms of environmental causes, circumstances or situations in which an action is performed.

These two types of causes, he suggested, form the basis for our explanations of another person's actions. Examples of internal/dispositional inferences made by Marie might be that George forgot to video the programme because he is a forgetful person or that he deliberately did not video it because he wanted to 'get back' at her. Likewise, Peter's first thoughts to explain Susan's behaviour might be that she is a rather 'moody' sort of person, however, since her mood has persisted for some time he might also consider the possibility that she is becoming tired of their relationship. External/situational explanations they might make could be that the other is over-worked or ill, or that some external incident or trigger has caused Susan's mood, for example some problem at work or with her family.

Any action therefore can be seen as having a number of potential explanations and Kelley (1967) suggests that we operate rather like detectives and try to summarize a range of information, for example historical evidence, such as, 'has Peter or Susan acted like this before?'; consistency across situations – 'have they always acted like this at home but not elsewhere?'; was there some triggering event – 'when did it start, how often does it happen?' and so on. We try to predict how unusual or consistent their behaviour is, and whether other people see it in a similar way to us.

Actor-observer differences

One of the most important observations to have resulted from attributional approaches is the consistent finding that people offer different explanations for their own as opposed to others' behaviour: 'There is a pervasive tendency for actors to attribute their actions to situational requirements, whereas observers tend to attribute the same actions to stable personal dispositions' (Jones and Nisbett, 1972, p. 80).

This effect may be particularly marked, for example when we are making excuses or self-justifications for something having gone wrong. We may be more likely to want to claim the credit for ourselves when things have gone well.

However, not all situations involve blame and hence it is argued that this effect may also have a more general basis resting on differences between the information available to actors and observers. Specifically, actors will have greater access to their own covert thoughts and feelings, as well as knowledge about variations in their own behaviour at different times and places. We can know about our own intentions and feelings but we may know much less about another's (though in long-term relationships partners are more likely to have beliefs about how the other typically sees things). Hence, if our behaviour in the present interaction appears to be different from what we have done previously we are more likely to see it as due to factors outside ourselves, since we are likely to see ourselves as relatively stable. In addition, we cannot see ourselves in the same literal sense as an observer can see us. This is a central point for relationships, for example we cannot be continually aware what non-verbal signals we are sending which may be influencing the other. Instead, we can see the other person's actions, but may miss the point that these may, at least in part, be responses to our actions. An experiment by Storms (1973) nicely illustrates some of these features of relationships.

BOX 3.4   Seeing ourselves in interactions

Storms recorded a conversation between two people using two video-cameras. The cameras were directed over each partner's shoulder so that when the video was replayed, it could show each participant either the scene as it appeared to him, or the scene as it appeared through the other person's eyes. Storms compared accounts of the conversation from three different sources:

1   observers who were not involved but simply watched the interaction take place;

2   accounts from the participants before they had seen the videotape replay;

3   accounts from the participants after they had seen the videotape replay – two conditions (a) either showing their own view, or (b) showing the view 'through the other person's eyes'.

Storms found evidence of an actor-observer difference. Each participant initially said that the conversation was controlled more by the characteristics of the other person and/or the situation. When each partner subsequently viewed the interaction from their own (actor) perspective this bias continued, that is they saw themselves as reacting to the other. However, the group who were then shown the replay from the other person's point of view tended to see themselves as initiating and more in control and much less determined by the situation and/or by the characteristics of their partner.

3.3   Attributions and long-term relationships

Attribution Theory was largely developed in experimental situations with relative strangers like that described in Box 3.4. Spouses, lovers and friends, however, might be expected to have much more access to one another's 'covert' and historical information and therefore might be more likely to make attributions for their partner's behaviour similar to those they would make for their own behaviour. On the other hand, in close and long-term relationships there are more powerful motivational and emotional factors operating. Each participant's actions may have more profound and long-lasting effects. Findings suggest that couples can engage in either positive or negative distortions: couples who regard their relationships as satisfactory tend to make positive internal attributions, idealize and 'make allowances' by attributing to internal dispositions – 'maybe its due to her PMS', or to external factors – 'someone's been horrible to her at work', for negative behaviour. In contrast, in relationships which are felt to be in difficulty there is a tendency for partners to blame each other and ascribe negative internal/dispositional attributions, such as deliberate malevolence to each other:

> ...retaliation is most likely when the partner is seen to have violated *deliberately* a central relationship rule for which no extenuating circumstances can be found; the partner is most likely to be seen as behaving with malevolent intent or selfish motivation. Such a situation will generate the most intense anger and may lead the perceiver to view retaliation as the partner's 'just deserts'.
>
> *(Fincham et al., 1990, p. 174, emphasis added)*

Furthermore, studies have consistently shown (for example Cahn, 1992) that in distressed relationships there is a tendency to minimize positive events, for example 'He's being nice because he wants to have sex with me tonight' or, 'She's bought me a present just to make me feel bad about forgetting her birthday'. Such attributions can give rise to attempts at retaliation which can of course lead to or validate negative attributions in the other partner and lead to escalating cycles of negative interaction (Fincham et al., 1990). This also fits with Kelly's notion of pre-emptive construing discussed in section 3.1, the tendency to rigidly ascribe a limited way of explaining the other's actions. These in turn are driven by, and simultaneously drive, strong emotions in a relationship.

In established relationships, partners not only form attributions but discuss and compare explanations of their own and each other's actions. Partners are also likely to ask each other for explanations and may challenge or dismiss each other's explanations, justifications and so on. In fact the explanations given can serve as justification and as strategies for influencing each other.

A study by Lavin in 1987 (see Box 3.5) explored the attributions employed by married couples, and their strategic function.

BOX 3.5 Strategic attributions in married couples

Forty married couples were presented (individually) with nine written vignettes of hypothetical marital conflicts. These included situations such as a wife's lateness for a dinner engagement, satisfaction during sexual relations, a husband watching football on television, a wife's conversation with men at parties, the choice of evening entertainment and a husband's forgetfulness about taking out the rubbish. The couples were then brought together and asked to reach agreement on two questions from each vignette. Their discussions were recorded, after which each partner was asked to provide attributions for their own and their partner's behaviour during the discussion.

The results showed that partners overall perceived more positive than negative behaviours during the discussion. They also tended to make more internal/dispositional attributions for their own and their partner's actions. Lavin, however, distinguished between consistent/ stable and variable internal attributions: *stable* – 'that's the way I am', *variable* – 'I suppose I was just a bit down today'.

There were also significant gender differences found in the tendency to use attributions strategically. Men tended to attribute their own behaviour as being due to stable internal factors whether it was seen to be positive or negative. This allowed a 'no-lose' situation for them, so they could take credit for perceived positive behaviour and defend against negative, 'I can't help it, that's the way I am'. Conversely, they tended to attribute more of their wife's behaviour to variable factors, for example 'they were good this time but you can't count on that'. Lavin suggested that this offered them a strategic leverage to push for change, for example 'You can do better next time'. Women tended to make very similar attributions for both their own and their partner's actions. They also assigned similar levels of responsibility for them.

The main differences between the men and the women, however, were found in couples who had said that they were experiencing some difficulties in their relationship. This suggested that relationship difficulties may in part be related to styles of attributions which attempt to justify one's own actions and to blame the other's.

Initially, attributional approaches had tended to be laboratory based and rather artificial, for example presenting people with scenarios and asking them to form attributions about particular behaviours. In relationships, however, people are likely to have a rich base of knowledge about each other and, importantly, may have ideas about *each other's attributions* – or meta-attributions. These may be revealed in statements like, 'I know you think I did it deliberately but actually I broke it accidentally'. Explanations and understandings of each other's behaviour therefore may be more subtle and complex than the internal versus external attribution distinction can embrace. When people are asked about their relationships they attempt to fit events and actions into accounts which have a narrative or story form: 'I might have been awkward about helping out around the house but not anything like as much as she accused me of. I think she used to say those things just to make me feel bad, so she could play the martyr' (man quoted in Foreman, 1995).

Experiments in Attribution Theory typically attempt to extract the brief statements or justifications that make up such accounts. But even brief accounts such as the one above can be seen to form part of a wider 'plot' or story line, with characters, a time sequence, attributions and indications of feelings which comprise people's narratives (Harvey et al., 1992).

It is possible to extend or revise attributional approaches by examining a greater range of attributions, or exploring attributions in 'real life' rather than simply in laboratory situations. However, attempts to apply Attribution Theory in long-term relationships suggest that it is necessary to critically appraise and possibly extend Attribution Theory in the following ways:

1   The extent to which partners share attributions – it may be that partners in some instances hold mistaken assumptions about each other's explanations. Such misunderstandings may lead to difficulties such as pernicious cycles of arguments and misunderstandings. Attempts to clarify these have been the basis of many forms of counselling and therapy and possibly a contribution Attribution Theory could make would be to draw attention to the importance of the underlying assumptions about causes of behaviour held by partners.

2   Negotiation – partners' willingness to accept or agree with each other's attributions, or at least to accept them as valid alternatives. Partners may have varying levels of 'investment' in maintaining particular attributions. The bases of some of these may be profound unconscious, emotional patterns which have been established in earlier relationships or previously in the relationship in question (see Chapter 4). Also, there may be strategic reasons to use particular attributions, such as attempting to gain control, maintain perceived advantages and so on.

3   Processes over time – Attribution Theory has tended to take a rather 'frozen in time' view of relationships instead of considering the way that attributions evolve, change or become established over time. This theme of continual change is one of the themes of section 4.

4   Complexity – it is also likely that Attribution Theory over-simplifies some aspects of partners' understandings and explanations. For example, a dispositional attribution can mean both a view of the other person as acting on the basis of their unalterable personality or biology, *or* as due to their wilful choices. However, these hold quite different implications: the former almost becomes an external or situational explanation, in that the person is seen as having no real voluntary control or choice. In the other case, blame can be attached to wilful choices.

Such shades of meaning are the stuff of relationship accusations, justifications, and their counters and are acutely involved in the processes of accounting for our actions.

Accounts

Both Personal Construct and Attribution Theories address how people ordinarily attempt to make sense of and manage their relationships. However, both are somewhat removed from the way people actually talk and think about their relationships. How people discuss their relationships with others, and also what they say about their reflections on their relationships, suggests that these predominantly follow a story or narrative form. An important aspect of these stories is that they contain accounts which offer reasons, justifications and explanations in terms of a progression of events over time. Examples of such stories can be seen in the three accounts included as extracts in Chapter 1 of this volume. Researchers initially interested in people's attributions have begun to place more emphasis on these types of everyday relationship stories (for example, Harvey et al., 1992).

A study of relationships in terms of the stories that partners create raises many fundamental questions about the 'scientific' study of relationships (Gergen, 1985; Shotter, 1987). It is argued by Shotter that the study of relationships should become an enterprise of trying to understand the unique creations, systems of meanings, and unfolding production of stories that make up a relationship, instead of trying to form general models or make predictions, for example about the attributions in distressed versus non-distressed couples:

> What we need is a better story, a better way of formulating the nature of personal relationships than the current 'causal story', a story that makes 'rationality visible', so to speak, the processual, formative nature of such relationships ... and a story that fits with the *practice* of personal relationships, rather than with the established practices of science – for in personal relationships, too, we can check, evaluate, and elaborate the truths we make, as we see them.
>
> *(Shotter, 1987, p. 245)*

The role played by language and discourse in the accounts people give are of great importance. One essential feature is that accounts, and the words people use in giving them, reflect wider social constructions of broad cultural and ideological themes. Consequently, people's accounts of relationships can be seen to be not just 'personal', as PCT and Attribution Theory tend to emphasize. Instead, accounts reflect how our experiences in relationships are inevitably both personally and simultaneously culturally shaped. More specifically, a perspective based on accounts can be seen to contain three further components which to some extent are shared with PCT and Attribution Theory:

1 Time – accounts and narratives in everyday life tend to contain a story or plot which serves to connect events over time. An account or narrative tends to have a beginning, a middle and an end where the logic of the beginning, middle and end come to structure our constructions of events.

2 Justification – accounts contain attempts to explain events and, in particular, personal accounts in relationships serve to justify, exoner-

ate, protect and make excuses, in short to ascribe blame or responsibility. Accounts and constructions are always for some purpose.

3 Variability – the accounts that we give may differ, or may be adjusted according to the situation we are in, and to whom we are giving the account. For example we may give a different account of our role in the photocopying machine breaking down to our boss, to a friendly colleague and to ourselves.

Another way of viewing this is to suggest that accounts serve various purposes, they do important *work* in managing our relationships. In regard to this, Planalp and Surra (1992) suggested that the making of accounts involves a number of stages:

Figure 3.4

A precipitating event may be caused by external events, such as the loss of a job. This will result in some form of interpretation being made, such as the event being seen as either desirable or undesirable, how we think others feel about it, and what will be likely to happen (for example whether it will damage our self-esteem, damage family relationships, cause financial stresses or, alternatively, offer some new opportunities for change). These interpretations can help to make sense of, and even to transcend difficulties. They also embody the process of change whereby we select and develop some interpretations to form a dominant account which will help us eventually to think about the precipitating events in a more positive way and to develop alternative avenues of action. An obvious example might be to form an account which puts less emphasis on work in our lives and concentrate more on family or outside work activities. However, the possible narratives that can be contemplated are constrained by the societally shared narratives available. In some cases these may promote conflict, distortions of experience and self-blame, for example the narrative that 'able people do not lose their jobs and people are lazy if they cannot quickly find another'.

Harvey et al. (1992) stress that the development of an account is an especially important component in dealing with problematic or traumatic events, resolving crises in a relationship and so on. For example, a couple may be distressed by their continual conflict and arguments but start to construct an account of this as 'going through a bad patch' and subsequently as 'having grown from the experience'. It is interesting to note that this kind of spontaneous reinterpretation has also been found to be an effective therapeutic intervention, referred to as 'reframing' (Dallos, 1991; Watzlawick et al., 1967, 1976) with people in distressed relationships.

However, an important aspect of the effectiveness of such account making processes is the reactions of others to our attempted accounts. Harvey et al. (1992) stress that we typically 'try out' our attempted accounts on others first, for example friends and relatives. Their positive or affirmative reactions were found to be of central importance. This did not simply mean blind agreement, but a tolerant, non-judgemental approach to people's attempts to account for relationship difficulties, for example, they helped people to formulate effective new ways of making sense of and 'coming to terms with' these changes.

Most importantly, some of the research in this area has explored how relationships are shaped by the internalization of wider societal discourses, for example about what is 'good', 'normal' and 'desirable' in relationships. For example, White and Epston (1990) have developed a model of therapy which attempts to discuss how problems have evolved within a relationship and are maintained by the way participants have come to regard each other within such dominant discourses. Examples are that 'problems' are predominantly due to personal failures or inadequacies, or what is 'normal' sexual activity, or how a 'good' relationship should develop. Consequently, people may experience their relationship as 'wrong' or 'problematic' if aspects of their experiences in their relationships do not appear to fit with these dominant discourses.

Review of section 3

The approaches discussed in this section can be seen to capture different aspects of participants' construction of meanings in relationships:

- Attribution Theory offers a nomothetic approach which allows some generalizations and focused and detailed analyses of participants' explanations.

- Personal Construct Theory (PCT) is more able to capture the complexity and uniqueness of partners' meanings but it is difficult to derive specific generalizations from it. However PCT's emphasis on sociality and commonality highlights the essentially inter-personal nature of our understandings.

- Both PCT and Attribution Theory in turn tend to simplify or reduce meanings to either a few dimensions of attributions or to bipolar constructs. This misses the story-like nature of ordinary accounts and explanations.

- PCT and Attribution Theory both underemphasize the link between participants' systems of meanings, explanations, understandings and the wider societally shared discourses that shape partners' accounts. In effect both PCT and Attribution Theory may be accused of over-emphasizing the unique and personal nature of relationships at the expense of a recognition of the power of societal definitions and discourses, which an analysis of accounts embraces.

4   Negotiation and shared understandings

In this section we will discuss the link between patterns of actions in relationships and the personal and shared meanings held by partners. To start with, we will examine attempts to develop a model of the patterning of actions between people in relationships and subsequently to explore how these connect with their patterns of beliefs. Research and therapy with families and those in other relationships lead to the observation that groups of people involved in repeated interactions over time appear to develop repetitive and predictable patterns of relationships. The term *systemic* is employed to embrace the perspectives, originating in systems theory, which have been developed to describe and explain some aspects of such jointly constructed patterns.

4.1   Systemic perspectives

As we saw in section 2, Brazelton suggested that mothers and infants appeared to interact so that stability was maintained – the baby was not over or under-aroused and the mother felt connected and close to, but not over-whelmed by the child. In a similar way, Jackson (1957) proposed that families and other long-term relationships could be seen to establish and maintain balance or stability over time.

Originally developed in the biological sciences, systems theory proposed that various activities of the body could be seen as composed of interconnected but distinct systems of components which operated together in an integrated and coordinated way to maintain stability (Bertalanffy, 1968; Bateson, 1972). The coordination is achieved through *communication* between the components or parts of the system. To take a simple example, the regulation of body temperature involves an interaction between the sweat glands and perspiration, bodily activity, breathing rate and control mechanisms in the brain. These components appear to act together to maintain the temperature of the body within tolerable and 'safe' limits even when large changes occur, for example alterations in climate or physical activity. This led to the idea of such groupings of components as constituting a *system:*

> A system is a set of objects together with relationships between the objects and between their attributes … Every part of a system is so related to the others that a change in one part will cause a change in the other parts and in the total system. A system is not a composite of independent parts but a coherent and inseparable whole.
>
> *(Hall and Fagan, 1956)*

Human social systems cannot be simply described in the same way as biological systems, in particular the communications are more complex, they involve language, conscious intentions, attempts to exert influence by various strategies, and people are often acting within roles and so on. Furthermore, it is much more arbitrary where we draw the *boundary* of a system, for example who is in or outside a family system. Nevertheless, the theory did help to model some of the escalating and regulatory processes that had been observed in social grouping of various sorts. Box 3.6 describes an example of the application of a systems theory perspective in a clinical/experimental investigation of family dynamics.

BOX 3.6 Family processes and emotional arousal

Minuchin (a family therapist and researcher in the USA) offered a demonstration of the inter-connection of actions and feelings in a family where both the daughters suffered from diabetes. The intention was to explore how changes in the relationships in a family are experienced at a physiological level and how these changes can be stabilized by the patterns of family dynamics.

In order to demonstrate this, Minuchin employed a physiological measure of emotional arousal – the free fatty acid (FFA) level in the bloodstream. Changes in FFA levels have been found to relate closely to other measures of emotional arousal, such as self-reports and behavioural evidence. It was used in this experiment because it was seen to provide a reliable and sensitive measure of arousal. The samples were drawn in a way that did not interfere with the ongoing interactions.

Both of the children in the family were diabetic, Dede (a 17-year-old) had had diabetes for three years, her sister Violet (12) had been diabetic since infancy. There was no obvious difference in the girls' individual responsivity to stress but Dede suffered much more severely from diabetes and had been admitted to the hospital for emergency treatment 23 times. Violet had some behavioural problems that her parents complained of, but her diabetes was under good medical control.

Minuchin interviewed the parents for one hour (9-10 a.m.) while the girls watched from behind a one-way mirror. From 9.30 a.m. onwards he deliberately encouraged the parents to discuss an issue of conflict between them, which led to some experience of stress, in order to see how this affected the children. Although the children could not take part in the conflict situation, their FFA levels (stress levels) rose as they observed their stressed parents. At 10 a.m. the children joined their parents and it became apparent that they played different roles in the family – Dede appeared to be trapped between her parents. Each parent tried to get her support in the argument with the other parent, so that Dede could not respond to one parent's demands without seeming to side with the other. Violet's allegiance was not sought. She could therefore react to her parents' conflict without being caught in the middle.

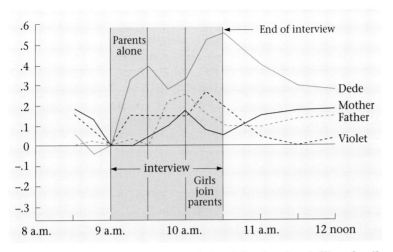

Fig 3.5: Change in free fatty acid (FFA) levels, the Collins family
Source, Minuchin, S. *Families and Family Therapy* (1974), Harvard,
Harvard University Press.

The effects of these two roles can be seen in the FFA results. Both children showed significant increments during the interview, between 9 and 10 a.m., and even higher increments between 10 and 10.30 a.m., when they were with their parents. At the end of the interview at 10.30 a.m., however, Violet's FFA returned to baseline promptly, but it took an hour and a half for Dede's level to return to normal.

The parents' FFA levels increased from 9.30 to 10 a.m., confirming that they were experiencing stress, but their FFA decreased after the children had come into the room. It appeared that their conflict was reduced or *detoured* through the children. However, the children paid a price for this, as shown by the increase in their FFA levels and by Dede's inability to return to baseline. 'The inter-dependence between the individual and family ... is poignantly demonstrated in the experimental situation, in which behavioural events among family members can be measured in the blood-stream of other family members' (Minuchin, 1974, pp. 7–8).

Examine the graph in Figure 3.5.   ACTIVITY 3.6

(1) What appears to occur, while the parents are being interviewed, to each person's stress levels?

(2) How does this change when the girls join their parents at 10.00 a.m?

(3) What differences in Dede's and Violet's responses can you detect before and after they join their parents?

In the Collins family, Minuchin makes clear that he sees *all* of the family members as caught in a web of powerful relationship forces which leads to some characteristic interactional patterns in the family and which, possibly, none of them can individually overcome. A pattern which can be seen in the Collins family is that when there is conflict between the parents then one of the children (more usually Dede) is drawn in. This may occur at a largely unconscious level so that all of them may be unaware that she is repeatedly involved in this way. Such repetitive patterns have been termed *circularities,* stressing a continual and mutually determined pattern of action over time.

Circular versus linear causation

Systems theory distinguishes between linear and circular models of causation to account for these patterns of mutual influence. *Linear* explanations have featured strongly in social psychology and emphasize that one person causes another to feel or act in a particular way. In contrast, *circular* explanations emphasize that causes reside in the interactional processes between two or more people. Relationship dynamics are explained, not simply in causal chains of events – what one person does to another, their internal dispositions and so on, but in terms of recursive spirals of mutual influence over time. When two or more people interact, each person's actions are seen as both a stimulus for *and* a response to the other. Each person is both simultaneously reacting to the other and proactively stimulating the other to react to him or her. We are seen as continually involved in a flow of interactions.

In the Collins family it appears that the actions, communications and feelings of each member of the family were inter-connected in a circular chain of causation. At one level we can see that the parents' conflict had an influence on the girls' levels of stress, but likewise the girls' illness may in turn have caused the parents to experience stress. Dede's repeated visits to hospital must have been a considerable source of worry for them.

Feedback and escalation

In the Collins family it is possible to see not only patterned and repetitive action over time but also escalation. The level of conflict between the parents increases and so does the level of stress in the girls. The concept of feedback proposes that information about the result of actions 'loops back' and can alter subsequent performance. This feedback may operate at a largely unconscious level, so that we can be unaware that our actions are changing in response to other participants in the interaction in this escalating manner.

Observations of relationships have suggested that feedback in relationships could operate to produce not just escalation but also maintenance of the status quo (Bateson, 1972; Keeney, 1987).

Open systems operate such that the feedback serves to produce escalation, an example here might be an escalating argument between two people which runs out of control, leading to physical conflict and/or perhaps the termination of a relationship.

Closed systems on the other hand appear to function so that over time the feedback reduces any major deviations from their normal pattern. These tend to display stability and maintenance of existing patterns.

These two patterns can be seen to exist simultaneously in the Collins family. The parents demonstrated an open system pattern as their conflict escalated. However, as a family they displayed the characteristics of a closed system since the escalating interaction in the parents became defused by the girls' involvement. In order for a relationship to function or be viable as a social unit, it needs to contain and be able to alternate between these two patterns. Functioning as an open system could bring about change and adaptation to alterations inside or outside the system, as long as the escalation did not proceed so far as to destroy the system. Alternatively, a system which was rigidly closed would be unable to adapt to novel demands and changes in the environment. Positive examples of mutual escalation in relationships are also possible, for example mutual joking, flattery or mutual sexual arousal.

The concept of feedback encapsulates the idea of reflexivity – a system has the capacity to monitor or reflect on its own actions (whether consciously or unconsciously). It is possible to build simple mechanical systems to demonstrate some adaptability (for example a central heating system) but in human relationships the notion of a system contains the idea of assessing what the needs of a particular situation or relationship are and adjusting to deviations from attaining these. An important point to note, though, is that because people in a relationship are *capable* of reflexivity it does not mean that the most effective, functional or 'healthy' course of action is always pursued. The experience of various forms of therapy reveal that 'insight' into problems does not always guarantee the ablity to change them. As we will see later, reflexivity is based upon a set of underlying premises or beliefs that we hold and these may function in an unconscious or automatic self-fulfilling way so that problems are maintained or even aggravated.

Systemic concepts were developed through the study of clinical problems which appeared to display rigidity, or lack of ability to adapt and change or avoid excessive escalations. Don Jackson (1957) suggested that relationships which contained such 'pathology' could be seen to function as closed systems. These operated so that any change appearing in the person presenting symptoms would be met by actions in the others which would have the sum effect of reducing, rather than encouraging, change. Systems theory suggests that, despite expressing a desire to change, in some sense the symptoms had been incorporated into the relationship dynamics; and the habitual behaviour in relation to the symptoms served to maintain, rather than change the problems. Jackson borrowed the term *homeostasis* to describe this process and added the idea that relationships could be seen 'as if' governed by a set of *rules* (largely out of awareness) which guided people's actions and embodied the homeostasis.

Various relationships; friends, lovers, families or work groups can all be seen to evolve into predictable patterns of actions or processes. This emphasis on pattern has tended to pay secondary importance to the content of the relationship. It might be observed, for example, that one person invariably initiates discussions and talks the most or that a group sub-divides into predictable coalitions. In such cases the focus is not so much on the *content* of what is under discussion (for example whether the discussion is about politics or domestic chores) but on the *process* – how the people concerned are interacting, what is going on between them.

This focus on pattern and process has been central to systemic perspectives. However, it has also been extensively challenged, especially by social constructionist approaches, for under-estimating the importance of meanings contained in the discussions, the importance of language and the embededness of relationships in wider cultural meanings and discourses. As an example, in heterosexual couples the terms 'neurotic' and 'nagging' may be applied more frequently to women, whereas 'withdrawing' and 'irresponsible' are more likely to be applied to men. These culturally shared stereotypes may function in a relationship to promote an escalating pattern of the woman attempting to make contact and the man withdrawing (Cahn, 1992; Watzlawick et al., 1974).

On the other hand, in agreement with social constructionist views, systemic perspectives argue that relationships are inevitably unique creations. When two or more people interact they are seen to be involved in a creative process – a *joint construction* of actions and meanings. It is argued that it is not possible therefore to fully predict how two or more people will interact, how they will 'get on', what sort of relationship will emerge. The nature of the relationship and how it develops is seen as *emergent* and evolving rather than as determined by the individual characteristics of the people involved. Each and every interaction is therefore seen as being to some extent unique, even though it may superficially appear to share similarities with other relationships.

4.2   Patterns of actions in triads

Much of the work on relationships has focused on studies of dyads or pairs of people. However, in the example of the Collins family (Box 3.6 above) we see an important new theme, how a third person (Dede) could be seen to play an important role in managing the relationship between a pair of others (her parents):

When therapists observed that what one spouse did provoked the other, who provoked the first in turn, they began to see that a dyad was unstable and it required a third person to prevent a 'runaway'. For example, if two spouses competed over who was most ill, total collapse could only be prevented by pulling in a third party. Rivalrous quarrels that amplified in intensity required someone outside the dyad to intervene and stabilise it. If a third person is regularly activated to stabilise a dyad, the unit is in fact not a dyad but is at least a triad, With this view, the unit becomes a unit of three people. Similarly if a husband and wife regularly communicate to each other through a third person, the unit is three people instead of a married 'couple'.

(Haley, 1976, p. 153)

Research and therapy from a systemic perspective led to the important (though not surprising) observation that the relationship between two people could have a powerful influence on a third. In the case of the Collins family in Minuchin's experiment we can see that Dede was extremely sensitive to the escalating conflict between her parents. In turn, her parents stress appeared to be reduced when they were able to re-direct their attention away from each other onto her and each of them made attempts to solicit her support. Families of course may consist of more than three people (as, indeed, in the Collins family) but it may be that at any given time an important dynamic is predominantly occuring between three of them. Also, at times a system may operate with two or more people acting as one group in relation to two individual others, such as of two parents in relation to 'the children'. Systemic approaches have developed a number of concepts to describe and explain the processes in triads.

Conflict detouring

Conflict detouring is an example of triangulation whereby the emotional conflicts between two people may be detoured or channeled through a third person. The Collins family was an example of this process in a family whereby Dede appeared to be the emotional conduit for the conflicts between her parents. However, similar patterns can occur in various relationships, for instance between colleagues or friends:

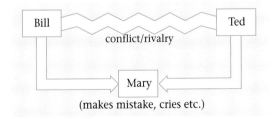

Figure 3.6 *Detouring of conflict through a third person*

In Figure 3.6, Mary, a young assistant, may respond to the conflicts between her superiors Bill and Ted by making some minor errors and becoming emotional herself. This may temporarily distract the men from their conflicts. The focus may then move to Mary and 'her problems' leading them, perhaps initially, to try to protect her and possibly accuse each other of upsetting her. However, if they are stressed, overtired and irritable they may find it hard to avoid eventually blaming her for being 'over-emotional' or 'weak'. Mary's distress consequently may escalate to the point where she develops 'a problem' perhaps taking time off work and so on. The focus of the difficulties may now move firmly to Mary's problems, perhaps even more generally about the 'difficulties of working with women', 'women's high level of emotionality' and so on and the conflict between Bill and Ted becomes submerged, except perhaps over disagreements about how to deal with the situation, whether she should be replaced and so on.

A person in a conflict detouring position becomes drawn into the relationship between another two people but then their involvement can also serve to prevent resolution of the underlying problems and conflicts. Related to the emotional processes are likely to be changes in perceptions, where Bill and Ted in the example above come to see themselves as similar – as male, less emotional and more free of problems than Mary.

4.3   Creating patterns and meanings

Early systemic approaches were criticized for seeming to assume that relationships could be observed in some objective sense from the 'outside' (Hoffman, 1990, James and McIntyre, 1983). It has since been argued that the observation of patterns in relationships are *inferences* made by observers of a relationship and not some objective quality of the relationship. Since people in relationships have their own ideas about what is going on, it is essential to try to gain some grasp of these ideas, since the patterns of actions observed will be a manifestation of their beliefs and understandings. This has led to an analysis of relationships as not just patterns of actions but as systems of beliefs and meanings.

This view has resulted in a revised version of systemic theory which recognizes relationships as consisting of multiple meanings and emphasizes the act of observation as active and propositional. That is, we can only make subjective inferences about the patterns of actions, feelings and beliefs in a relationship. It has also been suggested that observing inevitably entails some involvement with a system and hence the observations can be seen as a function of a higher-order system, that is, the system of the observer and the observed. However, this perspective still emphasizes that meanings, like actions, are jointly created through circular processes of feedback.

It could be argued that although patterns of actions can be more or less objectively observed, there can be much less certainty about what underlying meanings shape these. Furthermore, a focus on meanings suggests that concepts such as triangulation, escalation and homeostasis employed to describe the apparent patterns in relationships are themselves metaphors for making sense of relationships. The status of these metaphors may therefore be in terms not of their objective truth but of how useful they are, for example in assisting the process of therapeutic change in families.

In viewing people as actively shaping the actions and meanings in their relationships it is nevertheless possible to suggest that when people interact with each other over an extended period (as in friendships, families and other long-term relationships) they can be seen to develop a web of shared anticipations, not only about each other's behaviour, but about each other's feelings and thoughts. Included in these are meta-perspectives (Hoffman, 1993; Laing, 1969; Watzlawick, 1974), that is, ideas about how each person sees the other(s), and how they see their relationships with each other. Through discussions, comments and disclosures the people in a relationship may form a set of shared beliefs, assumptions, explanations and concerns which in turn come to regulate their interactions, producing predictable patterns of actions, emotional responses and thoughts (Dallos, 1991; Procter, 1981, 1985). Partners may hold competing explanations and stories about the meaning of what is going on between them or what should be going on. A number of writers, therapists and researchers have argued that the conflicts in relationships are fundamentally 'struggles over meaning' (Haley, 1976; Hoffman, 1993; Watzlawick et al., 1967, 1974). Meanings, like actions, can be seen as interactional and potentially as escalating, for example an interaction which involves a negative frame of 'blaming' can be seen to escalate to a dangerous degree so that a more positive frame is introduced to protect the group from collapsing into bitter dispute. This idea of meanings in relationships as changing and escalating adds to the PCT and attribution perspectives discussed earlier.

The following extract is taken from a piece of clinical research with couples (Foreman, 1995). Diane and Stuart in an interview described a typical interaction between them when they go out as a family. As you read this extract try to note the following:

ACTIVITY 3.7

1   What appear to be the underlying patterns?

2   How do they appear to be trying to exert influence over each other?

3   How are these patterns and tactics shaped and maintained by each partner's underlying assumptions?

Extract 3.1

Stuart: I enjoy going for walks but Diane doesn't seem to. We were out for a walk the other day and she said. 'I want to go back now,' not 'shall we go back?', and I know if I say 'I'd like to go a bit further' it would aggravate the situation, no reason for it. I wonder if you really like doing it or are you kidding me? I'm happy to admit I like doing things by myself but also as a family. I would like to know ... Do you enjoy going for walks?

Diane: You never ask ... you were furious about it

Stuart: No I wasn't furious, I thought you were angry...

Diane: No I wasn't...

Interviewer: Would you like to ask her now?

Diane: Do you want to know? Because we were walking along the cliff ... I'm petrified of heights and our two boys were running around but you are never very attentive, we have different standards of safety and I couldn't wait to get down. I get very anxious ... I didn't tell him because I knew it would really annoy him.

Interviewer: Did it ?

Stuart: Uhhhmn ... I think it does. I've become more aware of her problems ... doesn't like heights etc. but its a threat to my great love of life, open spaces, climbing ... She thinks I'm irresponsible, makes me feel mad. I feel perfectly confident. I've been mountaineering etc.

Source: Foreman, 1995, appendix 2

As you can see, the short extract from Diane and Stuart's account starts to reveal both some of the complexities of a relationship and also some patterns.

- Diane complains about Stuart being away so much and not doing things together and so she initiates some joint activity.

- Stuart somewhat reluctantly agrees but picks an activity which suits him. He harbours some resentment but avoids confronting the issue.

- Diane joins in the activity, although she does not feel happy with it, because at least it is time together. As the activity progresses she feels dissatisfied with it and eventually complains.

- Stuart complies with ending the activity but then feels annoyed and less inclined to spend such time together again so he withdraws and avoids contact.

- Diane feels frustrated that her attempt has failed and has not helped to make them closer and so she is likely to complain again.

The couple explained that this pattern had occured many times and, with slight variations, represented some fundamental patterning of their relationship over several years. There are various themes running through it, misunderstandings, inferences about intentions and feelings, different interests, trust and so on. The couple have quite different interpretations of the situation described, especially their ideas about each other's motives, intentions, thoughts and feelings.

This account also suggests an example of an escalating cycle. Both of them became increasingly unhappy with the walk, Diane becoming increasingly worried and Stuart increasingly annoyed at being prevented from carrying on. The interactional cycle might have continued to escalate, for example leading to a row, but this was avoided by Diane indicating that she wanted to go back and Stuart reluctantly complying. However, the negative feelings stayed unresolved. In effect, their relationship seems to have returned to stability in that further escalation is avoided, however the cost is that both remain in a state of anger and resentment. Stabilization around some such unpleasant and unsatisfactory emotional state characterizes relationships which are often perceived by the partners (and others) to be problematic.

Punctuation

From within a relationship it is possible that events are interpreted in different, and possibly conflicting ways by the participants. Watzlawick et al. (1967) suggest that a relationship can be seen as a seamless flow of events and that how each partner explains what is happening at any one time can be seen as a 'punctuation' which segments or divides it up in just one of a number of possible ways. By analogy, where we place the punctuation marks in a sentence can alter its meaning, similarly how we punctuate the flow of the interaction we are in can likewise cause it to be seen in different ways. For example, a typical difference in punctuations is where each person sees his or her own actions as caused by or as a response to the other person rather than their own responsibility.

Watzlawick et al. (1967, 1974) suggested that partners may develop a set of self-fulfilling perceptions which can interlock, like the pieces of a jigsaw puzzle, to produce repetitive patterns. In relationships each person's actions form the basis for the other's constructs and so on. Returning to Diane and Stuart's interaction, it displays a common pattern of interaction that many couples often get caught up in. This is a pattern of approach/avoid :

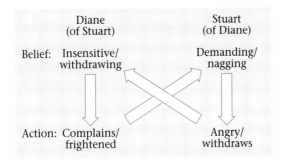

Figure 3.7 *Beliefs and actions maintaining an international pattern*

These constructions embody the competing story that each partner holds about the other:

Stuart: I'd want to spend more time with Diane if she wasn't so demanding, she's always going on at me and being critical, as it is I need to get away to be able to think and be myself

Diane: I'm not sure Stuart wants to be in a relationship, he's always wanting to get away on his own, I wouldn't go on at him so much if he showed he wanted to be with me sometimes

Together, their individual stories can interlock to form a joint narrative that their relationship is in difficulty, even though they both profess to care about each other. With many relationships such a repetitive, apparently 'stuck' pattern of acting and thinking can be the basis of feelings of desperation, a perception that the relationship is not working and contemplation of separation. Since they spend considerable time together, share similar experiences and communicate continually (even if not very successfully) with each other, partners come to form a web of mutual anticipations. For Stuart and Diane their mutual beliefs about each other, including how each of them thinks the other sees things, can be traced back through their relationship and what they had disclosed to each other about their childhood experiences and their original families. Stuart had revealed that he had come from a rather 'cold', emotionally distant family and Diane that her family had been very sociable but that she had been very 'emotionally insecure' before she met Stuart. Their relationship appeared to have activated just those aspects of themselves that they hoped their relationship would change, but had now become marooned upon. (In Chapter 4, questions of how relationships are influenced by earlier emotional experiences of other relationships are discussed in detail from a psychodynamic perspective.)

ACTIVITY 3.8   Try to think of an example from your own relationships, or of one that you have observed, which appears to display a pattern of interlocking punctuations. You may like to take a few minutes to draw this schematically (as was done with Diane and Stuart's relationship, in Figure 3.7).

Consistent with Kelly's ideas of reflexivity (see section 3.1), recent systemic theorists have emphasized the idea that the flow of relationships moves through levels of meanings and communications. The partners do not simply punctuate events but may also discuss their own and each other's punctuations and the presumed intentions underlying each other's communications. As an example, Stuart and Diane had tried to discuss how they communicated with each other, that is, they had not only had conversations but had conversations *about* their conversations. These higher-order meanings and communications have been called meta-communications and are regarded as playing a significant role in managing relationships (Watzlawick et al., 1967, 1974). In fact this multi-layered appraisal may be one of the distinguishing features of long-term relationships. The reflexivity or meta-communication in a relationship system can therefore be seen to be at ascending levels with each higher level defining those below:

Stuart: Do you enjoy going for walks?

Diane: You never ask ... you were furious about it.

Stuart: No I wasn't furious, I thought you were angry...

Diane: No I wasn't...

Stuart and Diane each punctuate the communication and intentions of the other, either deliberately or inadvertently attributing intentions to each other which may be incorrect or undesired. For example, when Stuart asks if Diane likes walks her answer starts with a meta-communication about their style of communication (that he never asks about her feelings). She then also adds an interpretation (that he was angry) which Stuart corrects with another meta-communication (about how his communication was related to the inference that he thought that *she* was angry). The discussion starts to clarify that each of them is working on the assumption that *the other* was angry or communicating anger and that they were merely responding to this. A third person, such as the interviewer in this extract, may attempt to assist such clarification by encouraging it or making observations, such as whether one or the other has been misunderstood. However, such attempts to encourage clarification may be a difficult task when a couple are angry and only wish to draw in a third person to decide which one of them 'is in the right'.

A relationship can be seen as simultaneously existing in the past, present and the future. Frequently, conflicts may be seen in terms of cycles of mutual accusations and justifications about previous actions. In contrast, people may also remember the 'good' parts of their history together. At any particular point of time an action or episode of comunication in a relationship derives its meaning not only from the content of the communication, but also from its historical context (Pearce and Cronen, 1980; Watzlawick et al., 1967; Wilmot and Baxter, 1983). Partners have available a repertoire of memories which they employ to anticipate present and future interactions between them. So, for example, a couple may be involved in an argument and the inferences they form will be dependent on how they see their relationship (its accumulated history). For example, if they see their relationship as already being 'in difficulty' they may see an argument between them as yet another example of this difficulty, and therefore as indicating a potential crisis. In contrast, if they see their relationship as quite good overall, they are more likely to see this argument as an example of 'just a bad patch'. In Stuart and Diane's case it appeared that the weight of history, or memories of negative experiences, rows, conflicts and upsets had started to dominate and colour their current interactions so that they were predominantly seeing all of each other's actions in negative terms.

4.4   Societal contexts

Systemic perspectives, in emphasizing the dynamic processes and patterning in relationships have been criticized for ignoring the wider societal structures and ideologies that shape relationships and, in particular, the issue of inequalities of power in relationships (Williams and Watson, 1986; Goldner, 1991; James and McIntyre, 1983). It has been suggested that some of the patterns that may be observed within relationships are guided by structural factors such as economic conditions, and societally shared ideas about relationships. In particular, individual participants in a relationship may differ in the amount and type of power they have available to influence the nature of the relationship.

One example of a frequently observed pattern seen in many western family relationships is that of a woman who is much more involved with the children and the domestic and emotional sphere of the family, with the man engaged outside the home, having much less to do with the family. The woman in this case may make repeated attempts to involve him, perhaps leading to patterns of angry confrontations and further withdrawals. Rather than seeing this pattern as predominantly produced by the participants, however, it can be seen to be shaped more broadly by the wider societal factors of power, economic structures and ideologies, including expectations and norms about family relations.

ACTIVITY 3.9   Now read *Reading E:* 'A sociological perspective' by Graham Allan. In it, Allan discusses the influences on personal relationships of societal factors. Note how he argues that wider social influences can affect not only marriages but also other relationships such as friendships.

As Allan makes clear, despite social changes women are still more likely than men to carry the burden of care for children and to be more centred around the home than men. This is *not* simply a personal choice, but one shaped by a variety of economic and practical necessities dictated by the society in which they live (Hollway, 1983; Williams and Watson, 1986). A web of discourses or ideologies, such as that women are 'naturally maternal', and hence a set of roles and beliefs about family life may become reproduced across the generations (these issues are discussed further in Chapter 6 of this volume).

These factors place some broad constraints on the types of relationship that partners may be able to construct. In addition, the differences between the power that participants possess may further constrain the dynamics and even the moment-to-moment flow of their relationship. In particular, it has been suggested that there are differences between men and women in the types of power that they possess and consequently the means they have available to influence each other.

ACTIVITY 3.10

Consider the types of power and influence that men as opposed to women may be able to exert in relationships with each other. You may like to consider some examples from your own experience as well as some of the examples employed in this chapter.

Arlene Vetere, in *Reading B* at the end of this book, suggests that men and women differ in the types of power that they possess:

> Women are believed to influence others more indirectly and to rely on their own personal resources, such as, perceived attractiveness, empathy, kindness and close interpersonal relationships for the exercise of power. Whereas it is believed that men have access to and are therefore able to utilise a different set of resources, such as, strength, skill and competence in the public domain and tend to be less likely to rely on interpersonal and intimate relations for the exercise of power.

As a result of these different resources held by men and women, it is argued they are likely to act in different ways in relationships and this in part contributes to shaping the characteristic patterns that are developed. However, in addition it can be argued that not only are their sources of power different but that they are also unequal. Specifically, men's power bases can be seen to be more objective, valued and allow them greater independence whereas women's power bases are more subjective and 'relational', for example a woman's attractiveness is dependent on her partner continuing to find her attractive. This may imply that one partner may have more ability to determine the nature of the relationship, for example to make important decisions or even to leave the relationship should they so wish (Foreman, 1995). However, this is a complex area and part of the problem has been that it is very difficult to define 'power' in relationships (see Vetere's Reading for a further discussion of these issues). Physical strength, economic resources, expertise, education and so on may appear to offer a clear objective base of power. Yet these can seem minimal in some cases where the other partner dominates emotionally or sexually or is more skilled at influencing the other or the children. (For a further discussion of the perception of male power see Watson, 1996.)

Williams and Watson (1988) argue that as a consequence of women's restricted access to material forms of power, it is likely that they employ covert and emotional means to exert influence in relationships with men. In turn this positioning of women as emotional and nurturant and men as unemotional and practical lays the basis for some frequently observed relationship patterns, such as women attempting to exert influence and establishing intimacy through emotional involvement and men seeking to minimize or avoid emotional intimacy since they feel vulnerable and less powerful in this area (Gottman, 1991). This pattern is not restricted to male-female relationships but can be seen more broadly in other relationships where there is an inequality of power. In relationships beteeen adults and children it is likely that a child will employ more indirect and emotional means than the adult to get what he or she wants. Williams and Watson (1988) have argued that women's dependency in relationships may compel them into just such a 'childlike' role. This will be taken up further in the following chapter.

Systems theory's inability to take account of such wider societal factors that shape the patterns of interactions has been seen by some as a major indictment and testimony of its failure (James and McIntyre, 1983; Williams and Watson, 1988). However, it has been suggested in contrast that in fact it *is* possible for systemic perspectives to incorporate an analysis of societal contexts (McKinnon and Miller, 1987). In considering the patterning of meanings in relationships, it is possible to incorporate an analysis of how each partner's beliefs are derived from wider societally shared narratives. The relationship patterns that emerge can therefore be seen to be the result of an interaction of a multiplicity of factors – the wider societal discourses, material circumstances and also the unique combination of the partners, including how they have internalized and translated the societal discourses into their personal and shared belief systems.

Review of section 4

- Relationships appear to present us with a dilemma: on one hand partners engage in repetitive and predictable sequences of actions and on the other hand, each person has the potential to act autonomously, to make choices based upon their understandings. The theories in earlier sections of the chapter which consider people as actively formulating meanings about their relationships can be integrated with recent systemic perspectives which emphasize relationships as characterized by recursive, circular sequences of actions.

- Systemic perspectives emphasize the following points:

  - that partners mutually influence each other: each person's actions are both a stimulus for and a response to the other's actions;

  - over time the participants' actions become patterned and may display cycles of escalation;

  - actions and meanings in relationships are connected in a mutual, dialectical fashion – each shaping the other;

  - the patterning of action and meanings can become interlocked into patterns of 'punctuations' which are self-maintaining;

  - escalating processes and conflict in a pair may be stabilized by the involvement, or drawing in of a third person.

- It is possible, and indeed necessary, to extend systemic perspectives to consider the influence of wider societal discourses, especially in relation to power, in shaping interactional patterns.

5 Discussion and conclusion

This chapter has attempted to draw together attribution theory, personal construct and systemic theories, stressing the continous recursive interplay of actions and beliefs. The emphasis has been on how relationships are actively constructed at both the level of actions and meanings. It has been argued that even the earliest relationships consist of mutual influence which develops into regular and predictable patterns. Apparently fundamental even to these early relationships is an attempt by infants to exercise some degree of control and influence over the adult. The experience of mutual influence appears to generate a sense of emotional well-being for both partners and to form the basis of a developing sense of autonomy for the infant. This development of control seems to centre around attempts to define meanings about what is going on in the relationship.

In adult relationships, these themes of control and influence, patterning of action over time, active struggles over meanings, reflexivity and levels of communication are increasingly central. It is possible that adult relationships are based in part on the generalizations from early patterns of relating. A further discussion of the influence of such early experiences is the theme of the next chapter in this book. People are generally involved in a range of relationships at any one time.

Early relationships also form the basis of individual beliefs, attributions and narratives which partners carry into the melting pot of later relationships. Through a process of negotiation these shape the development of the relationship. The pleasure and satisfactions of relationships as well as the problems and conflicts can be traced to the core constructs, the understandings, beliefs, expectations and explanations that we have about the people with whom we are interacting and about our relationship with them. Over time we develop sophisticated understandings of how the other will act, think and feel, and about what paths and patterns we anticipate our relationship is likely to follow.

In addition, relationships do not take place in a vacuum but within a social/cultural context. A significant aspect of this context is that it embodies inequalities of power. This can affect relationships in several ways, it may influence the kinds of relationships and roles that are possible and also the influence strategies that can be used in these. It also tends to affect the type of interactional patterns that emerge, and it may operate so that the more powerful can prevent certain issues being discussed or resolved. Finally, it affects how these issues are talked about – the language and counter arguments that are available in society generally. This is pursued further in the final chapter in this book. Let us finish this discussion with a metaphor. A relationship can, perhaps, be seen as like a snowball rolling in the snow: where it has rolled and what is has incorporated into it affects how it behaves in future, what more it can absorb and how much it can grow. The wider context, such as the climate, affects whether it breaks, and how easily it thaws and melts.

Acknowledgement

With grateful thanks to John Oates for his advice and assistance with section 2.

Further Reading

Anderson, H. and Goolishan, H.A. (1986) 'Problem determined systems: toward transformation in family therapy', *Journal of Strategic and Family Therapy, 4,* pp. 1–13.

Integration of systemic and social constructionist perspectives within therapy.

Brazelton, T.B. and Cramer, B.G. (1991) *The Earliest Relationship: Parents, Infants and the Drama of Early Attachment,* London, Karnac Books.

Good overview of mother-child research.

Dallos, R. (1991) *Family Belief Systems, Therapy and Change,* Buckingham, Open University Press.

Integration of PCT and systemic theory with reference to therapy with couples and families.

Hoffman, L. (1993) *Exchanging Voices,* London, Karnac Books.

Very readable. Laden with quotes of developments in theory and application of systemic and narrative approaches in therapy.

Minuchin, S. (1974) *Families and Family Therapy,* Harvard, Harvard University Press.

Seminal and fascinating book on family structure, theory and practice of family therapy.

Trevarthen, C. (1992) 'The function of emotions in early infant comunication and development' in Nadel, J. and Camioni, L. (eds) *New Perspectives in Early Communicative Development,* London, Routledge.

Excellent review of work on communication and emotions in mother-child interactions.

References

Bannister, D. (1960) 'Conceptual structure in thought disordered schizophrenics', *Acta Psychologia, 20,* pp. 104–20

Bateson, G. (1972) *Steps to an Ecology of Mind,* New York, Ballantine.

Bertalanffy, L. von (1968) *General Systems Theory,* New York, George Braziller.

Bertalanffy, L. von (1988) 'General systems theory – a critical review' in Buckley, W. (ed) *Modern Systems Research for the Behavioural Scientist*, Chicago, Aldine.

Brazelton, T.B. and Cramer, B.G. (1991) *The Earliest Relationship: parents, infants and the drama of early attachment*, London, Karnac Books.

Brazelton, T.B., Tronick, E., Adamson, L., Als, H. and Wise, S. (1975) *Early Mother-Infant Reciprocity*, Ciba Foundation Symposium 33, Amsterdam, Elsevier.

Bruner, J.S. (1977) 'Early social interaction and language acquisition' in Schaffer, H.R. (ed) *Studies in Mother-Infant Interaction*, London, Academic Press.

Cahn, D.D. (1992) *Conflict in Intimate Relationships*, New York/London, The Guildford Press.

Dallos, R. (1991) *Family Belief Systems, Therapy and Change*, Buckingham, Open University Press.

Duck, S. (1988) *Relating to Others*, Buckingham, Open University Press.

Duck, S. (1994) *Meaningful Relationships*, London, Sage.

Fajardo, B.F. and Freedman, D.G. (1981) 'Maternal rhythmicity in three American cultures' in Field, T., Sostek, A., Vieze, P. and Leiderman, P.H. (eds) *Culture and Early Interactions*, Hillsdale, New Jersey, Erlbaum.

Fincham, F.D., Bradbury, T.N., and Grych, J.H. (1990) 'Conflict in close relationships: the role of interpersonal phenomena' in Graham, S. and Folkes, V. (eds) *Attribution Theory: Applications to Achievement, Mental Health and Interpersonal Conflict*, Hillsdale, New Jersey, Erlbaum.

Fivas-Depeursinge, E. (1991) 'Documenting a time-bound, circular view of hierarchies: a microanalysis of parent-infant dyadic interaction', *Family Process*, no. 30, pp. 101–20

Foreman, S. (1995) *Inequalities of Power, Strategies of Influence and Sexual Problems in Couples* (unpublished Ph.D. thesis) Milton Keynes, The Open University.

Gergen, K.J. (1985) 'The social constructionist movement in modern psychology', *American Psychologist*, March.

Goldner,V. (1991) 'Sex, power and gender: a feminist analysis of the politics of passion', *Journal of Feminist Family Therapy*, no. 3, pp. 63–83.

Gottman, J.M. (1991) 'Predicting the longitudinal course of marriage', *Journal of Marriage and the Family*, 17, pp. 3–7.

Haley, J. (1976) *Problem Solving Therapy*, San Fransisco, Jossey Bass.

Hall, A.D. and Fagan, R.G. (1950) 'Definitions of systems' in Hall, A.D. and Fagan, R.G. (eds) *General Systems*, 1, New York, Bell Telephone Laboratories.

Harvey, J.H., Orbuch, T.L. and Weber, A.L. (eds) (1992) *Attributions, Accounts and Close Relationships*, London, Springer-Verlag.

Heider, F. (1958) *The Psychology of Interpersonal Relations*, New York, John Wiley & Sons.

Heider, F. and Simmel, M. (1944) 'An experimental study of apparent behaviour', *American Journal of Psychology*, no. 57, pp. 243–59

Hoffman, L. (1990) 'Constructing realities: the art of lenses', *Family Process*, vol. 19, no. 1, pp. 1–13.

Hoffman, L. (1993) *Exchanging Voices*, London, Karnac.

Hollway, W. (1983) 'Heterosexual sex: power and desire for the other' in Cartledge, S. and Ryan, J. (eds) *Sex and Love: New Thoughts on Old Contradictions*, London, The Women's Press.

Jackson, D. (1957) 'The question of family homeostasis', *Psychiatry Quarterly Supplement,* no. 31, pp. 79–99.

James, K. and McIntyre, D. (1983) 'The reproduction of families: the social role of family therapy?', *Journal of Marital and Family Therapy*, vol. 9, no. 2, pp. 119–29.

Jones, E. E. and Nisbett, R. E. (1972) 'The actor and the observer: divergent perceptions of the causes of behaviour' in Jones, E. E. and Nisbett, R.E. *Attributions,* New Jersey, General Learning Press.

Keeney, R. (1987) *Aesthetic of Change*, New York, Guildford Press.

Kelley, H. H. (1967) 'Attribution theory in social psychology', *Nebraska Symposium on Motivation,* 15, pp. 192–238.

Kelly, G. (1955) *The Psychology of Personal Constructs,* vols. 1 and 2, New York, W. W. Norton.

Laing, R. D. (1969) *The Politics of the Family and Other Essays,* London, Tavistock.

Lavin, T. J. (1987) 'Divergence and convergence in the causal attributions of married couples', *Journal of Marriage and the Family,* no. 49, pp. 71–80.

McKinnon, L. K. and Miller, D. (1987) 'The new epistemology and the Milan approach: feminist and sociopolitical consideration', *Journal of Marital and Family Therapy*, vol. 13, no. 2, pp. 139–55.

Minuchin, S. (1974) *Families and Family Therapy*, Harvard, Harvard University Press.

Murray, L. and Trevarthen, C. (1985) 'Emotional regulation of interactions between two-month-olds and their mothers' in Field, T. M. and Fox, N. A. (eds) *Social Perception in Infants,* Northwood, New Jersey, Ablex.

Newson, J. and Newson, E. (1977) 'Intersubjectivity and the transmission of culture: on the social origins of symbolic functioning', *Bulletin of the British Psychological Society,* no. 28, pp. 437–46.

Oates, J. (1994) 'First Relationships' in J. Oates (ed) *The Foundations of Child Development,* Oxford, Blackwell/The Open University.

Pearce, W.B. and Cronen,V.E. (1980) *Communication, Action and Meaning*, New York, Praeger.

Planalp, S. and Surra, C.A. (1992) 'The role of account-making in the growth and deterioration of close relationships' in Harvey, J.H., Orbuch, T.L. and Weber, A.L. (eds) *Attributions, Accounts and Close Relationships,* New York, Springer-Verlag.

Procter, H.G. (1981) 'Family construct psychology, in Walrond-Skinner, S. (ed) *Family Therapy and Approaches*, London, Routledge & Kegan Paul.

Procter, H.G. (1985) 'A personal construct approach to family therapy and systems intervention' in Button, E. (ed), *Personal Construct Theory and Mental Health*, London, Croom Helm.

Schieffelin, B.B. and Ochs, E. (1983) 'A cultural perspective on the transition from prelinguistic to linguistic communication' in Golinkoff, R.M. (ed) *The Transition from Prelinguistic to Linguistic Communication*, New Jersey, Erlbaum.

Shotter, J. (1987) 'The social construction of an "us", problems of accountability and narratology' in Burnett, R., McGhee, P. and Clarke, D.D. (eds) *Accounting for Relationships*, London, Methuen.

Stern, D. (1985) *The Interpersonal World of the Infant*, New York, Basic Books.

Stevens, R. (1996) 'The reflexive self: an experiential perspective' in Stevens, R. (ed).

Stevens, R. (ed) (1996) *Understanding the Self*, London, Sage/The Open University (Book 1 in this series).

Storms, M.D. (1973) 'Videotape and the attribution process: reversing actors' and observers' "point of view"', *Journal of Personality and Social Psychology*, no. 27, pp. 165–75.

Sylvester-Bradley, B. (1981) 'Negativity in early infant-adult exchanges and in developmental significance' in Robinson, W.P. (ed) *Communication in Development*, London, Academic Press.

Toates, F. (1996) 'The embodied self: a biological perspective' in Stevens, R. (ed).

Trevarthen, C. (1974) 'Conversation with a two-month old', *New Scientist*, vol. 2, May.

Trevarthen, C. (1977) 'Descriptive analyses of infant communicative behaviour' in Schaffer, H.R. (ed) *Studies in Mother-Infant Interaction*, London, Academic Press.

Trevarthen, C. (1980) 'The foundations of intersubjectivity: development of inter-personal and cooperative understanding' in Olson, D. (ed) *The Social Foundations of Language: Essays in Honour of J.S. Bruner*, New York, W.W. Norton.

Trevarthen, C. (1992) 'The function of emotions in early infant comunication and development' in Nadel, J. and Camioni, L. (eds) *New Perspectives in Early Communicative Development*, London, Routledge.

Watson, D. (1996) 'Individuals and institutions: a case study of the work place' in Wetherell, M. (ed).

Watzlawick, P. (1963) 'A review of the double-bind theory', *Family Process*, vol. 2, no. 1, pp. 132–53.

Watzlawick, P., Beavin, J. and Jackson, D. (1967) *Pragmatics of Human Communication*, New York, W.W. Norton.

Watzlawick, P., Weakland, J. and Fisch, R. (1974) *Change: Principles of Problem Formation and Problem Resolution*, New York, W.W. Norton.

Wetherell, M. (ed) (1996) *Identities, Groups and Social Issues*, London, Sage/The Open University (Book 3 in this series).

Wetherell, M. and Maybin, J. (1996) 'The distributed self: a social constructionist perspective' in Stevens, R. (ed).

Williams, J. and Watson, G. (1988) 'Sexual inequality, family life and family therapy' in Street, E. and Dryden, W. (eds) *Family Therapy in Britain*, Buckingham, Open University Press.

White, M. and Epston, D. (1991) *Narrative Means to Therapeutic Ends,* London, W.W. Norton.

Wilmot, W. and Baxter, L. (1983) 'Reciprocal framing of relationship definitions and episodic interaction', *Western Journal of Speech Communication,* no. 47, pp. 205–17.

Wolf, P. H. (1969) 'The natural history of crying and other vocalisations in early infancy' in Foss, B. M. (ed) *Determinants of Infant Behaviour,* vol. IV, London, Methuen.

CHAPTER 4
THE PSYCHODYNAMICS OF RELATING

by Kerry Thomas

Contents

1   Introduction

Have you ever felt that an argument you are having with a close friend or a sexual partner is not really to do with the other person – that it seems to have come from somewhere else? Have you perhaps felt as though you are driven compulsively to say and do certain things and to relate in destructive ways? Have you ever felt as if you are mixed up with another person so that it is difficult to tell sometimes where you end and the other person begins? Have you ever wondered about the force of an attraction to someone, sexual or otherwise? Or have you ever wondered what happens when intense love suddenly gives way to disillusionment? Have you heard yourself complaining bitterly about another person and then realized that you were talking about an aspect of yourself? Theories of psychodynamics can offer explanations for these mysterious phenomena; and the practice of psychoanalysis, including the relationship between patient and analyst, can provide the evidence. We shall draw heavily on this evidence in the present chapter. The explanations are based on *unconscious psychological processes* which are thought to be a crucial part of our intimate relationships: mothers with infants, parents with children, in friendships and between sexual partners.

Unconscious processes are the focus of this chapter. They operate in the present but they are profoundly influenced by the past. The earlier chapters of this book have stressed what is created between people in their interactions and their relationships in the *here and now* and over the *history of the particular relationship*. For example, in Chapter 2 there are many 'here and now' analyses of non-verbal and verbal interactions (see the husband and wife in section 4, Box 2.7 and the 'face saving interaction' in section 6.3). In Chapter 3, section 4 the discussion of Stuart and Diane looked at what is happening in the present and what has been established over the course of their relationship. In contrast, the psychodyamic perspective places a great deal of emphasis on the continuing and constant influence of the past, on the determining influence of past relationships on virtually all current interactions and relationships. In this view, our everyday relationships are motivated and shaped to a large degree by what is carried over from early and very early experiences.

The earlier chapters also differ from the present one in placing most of their emphasis on features of interactions and relating that are conscious, or potentially conscious, for the participants. There is an underlying assumption that what is going on can be talked about and described by the participants, reflected upon and negotiated. In Chapter 3, Kelly's work on personal construct theory, attributions in long term relationships, and systemic theories all focus on conscious beliefs and expectations – which can be changed.

According to psychodynamics, relationships are driven by unconscious forces, many of which concern our *use of other people,* in our relationships, to satisfy needs which first surfaced in childhood and may have been repressed ever since. Within our relationships, especially intimate and sexual ones, we re-experience gratifications and frustrations of a primitive and often highly emotional kind. These re-experiences are not just passive. We make (unconscious) efforts to seek out opportunities and particular others who will (unconsciously) facilitate the creation of new relationships that carry the stamp of past experiences of significant others, and familiar patterns of relating from long ago, particularly from childhood. These are called *transferences.*

Section 2 of the chapter discusses first the centrality of relationships in psychodynamic theories, from the biological functions of early relating to the ideas of object relations psychoanalysts who believe that relating in itself is a fundamental human motivation. Second, we shall show how evidence from early clinical psychoanalysis – largely the ideas and work of Freud – began to reveal unconscious forces that can inform our understanding of ordinary relating. In particular, we shall examine early versions of the concept of transference – the unconscious transfer to someone in the present of feelings and ways of relating that come from experiences of others and of relationships in the past.

Sections 3 and 4 of the chapter, respectively, are structured around the two central concepts of modern psychodynamic theory and clinical practice: *transference* and *unconscious communication*. We shall use these concepts to help us understand relating and relationship choice in ordinary life.

Section 3 focuses on the process of transference as it is understood now. Transferences may be triggered by something specific in a current situation or by a particular kind of other person. Or it may be the endless repeating of attempts to regain something you once had and then lost. It could be an attempt to regain something good, or exciting or, paradoxically, something that was frightening and hurtful. The process of transference may lead to satisfying and more or less appropriate relationships in the present. But it may lead to difficulties, ranging from irritating misunderstandings to seriously inappropriate and damaging misalliances.

Chapter 2 has discussed the influence of norms and rules on interactions in general, and Chapter 3 has shown how beliefs and ready-formed expectations and meanings can influence choice and conduct of relationships, whether these originate in our personal constructs or are more culturally defined. But, in the psychodynamic view, although transferences may encompass norms, beliefs and expectations, they have a different quality from these ordinary residues of experience. First, in contrast with the beliefs and meanings discussed in the earlier chapters, transferences are largely unconscious. Second, transferences often have a powerful emotional content. Third, they are frequently more than just a feature of a relationship – a transference can be the *essence* of a relationship, for example, where one person is dependent on the other. These aspects of transference can give rise to short term, unexpected and intense happenings in an interaction, but they can also have a crucial determining effect on how we conduct our relationships in general.

Section 4 of the chapter explores unconscious communication. All manner of forms and channels of communication have already been discussed in this book (see most of Chapter 2 from section 3 onwards, especially 4.4 and 4.6 and Chapter 3, especially 2.1 and 4.3). Unconscious communication encompasses much of what has already been introduced, but it goes further. It includes but goes beyond the gaps, confusions, veiled attacks, double binds, the making of impressions and other hidden messages buried in the content and structure of communications. It also goes beyond the complexity and sheer volume of the non-verbal information that we absorb and process outside awareness during interactions. In psychodynamic theory, unconscious communication is thought to use modes of communication that are rather different, such as the apparent transfer of emotional states between people. Trevarthen's work on intersubjectivity and the role of emotion (see Chapter 3, section 2) was an example of how unconscious communication leads to the beginnings of intersubjectivity, created between mothers and their infants long before the infant has language. In section 4 we shall see that this process continues throughout life, creating intersubjectivity between adults – the first step in negotiating meanings and joint action.

It should be clear by now that the psychodynamic approach to relating is very different from what has been put forward in the two previous chapters. Relationships are not necessarily what they seem to be in the present, nor are the participants necessarily doing what they think they are; and a great deal is communicated unconsciously. According to psychodynamics, participants in relationships unconsciously influence others to behave in ways that will help them to realize unconscious goals, and no one has much *conscious* control over what happens. Unconscious intentions, hidden meanings, unexplained passions – positive and negative – are seen as a function of earlier experiences in relationships being played out like scripts from the past. During the *process* of psychoanalysis, analysts try to 'break into' the unconscious spirals that commonly build up in ordinary relationships, using their own reactions to transferences from their patients (countertransference) to examine unconscious communications. But, in everyday life, this level of awareness is rare. What usually happens is that interactions escalate, partners collude with each other unconsciously, patterns get repeated and bewilderingly stultified. It is difficult to move into new ways of relating when the underlying forces are unconscious.

Section 5 emphasizes the idea of the *relational mind* and its implications for relating throughout life. In modern psychodynamic theory, the holistic and compulsive quality of transferences suggests that we are *made up of other people,* that our minds are structured, from infancy, by internally represented versions of the other people (objects) and their relations (object relations) with ourselves and with each other. These other people and relationships are taken in (introjected) to create internal worlds furnished with internal objects and internal object relations. From this it follows that not only do our early experiences of relating drive relating throughout life, but that these experiences, these versions of other people and ways of relating actually constitute our *selves.*

Aims of the chapter

1   To discuss the basic assumptions that psychodynamic approaches make about what drives relating and relationships.

2   To use the psychoanalytic setting and the relationship between analyst and patient as evidence of how unconscious motivations and internalizations of early experiences of others and of relationships drive relating in the present – through the concept of transference.

3   To use the analytic encounter and the analyst's countertransference experience to explore processes of unconscious communication, empathy and intersubjectivity.

4   To use object relations theories to understand relationships in ordinary life and explore the importance of relating and relationships throughout life for the construction, maintenance, expression and modification of the self.

2   Early relationships and their residues in adult life

This section begins by looking at psychodynamic ideas about the general impact of infancy and childhood on personality and psychological well-being. We then move on to the idea that residues of our experiences in infancy and childhood act as more specific templates for relating in later life – the concept of *transference*.

The general and lasting impact of infancy and childhood is central to psychodynamic theory and it is an aspect of psychodynamic determinism that has had considerable influence on our culture. We take this idea so much for granted now that it is easy to forget that it is relatively new. Reading about child rearing and how to influence babies' behaviour and ensure their future psychological health is now a part of ordinary parenting. Implicit in these concerns with successful breast feeding, toilet training, dealing with children's aggressive impulses, masturbation and so on is an assumption that infants' first experiences of other people have profound implications for how successful and happy they are in their relationships in adult life.

Both Freud and Klein put forward versions of psychodynamics that are instinct theories, with a firm biological basis. The essential functions of relating and relationships are seen as the satisfaction of biological need states. In this view, relating and relationships throughout life are motivated by the search for another person who can provide the means for, or facilitate, the release from physical tensions such as hunger, thirst, discomfort and especially erotic desire. Relationships are either the means to these ends or by-products of instinctual searches for biological satisfaction.

In this classical Freudian approach, relationships throughout life are closely linked to biology and to sexuality. But this viewpoint has since been modified to stress the importance of relating and relationships for their own sake. This shift in direction comes from the work of the object relations psychoanalysts, and will form a basis for most of what follows in sections 3, 4 and 5 of this chapter.

2.1 From biology to relating for its own sake.

All psychodynamic theories have a grounding in biology. During development the mind becomes structured in conjunction with the physical maturation of the body. And as the mind-body (that is, the 'psyche-soma') develops, the infant, child or adolescent is faced with a range of more or less age-specific opportunities to relate, each with a characteristic socialization conflict to be surmounted.

In classical Freudian theory, consummations and/or frustrations of biological needs by specific other people in the early environment are focused on the sequential emergence of erogenous zones of the body – mouth, anus, urethra, clitoris/penis. At each of these psychosexual stages, typical difficulties can arise for the child which are largely social and relational and to do with impulse control. Failures in resolving these difficulties lead to fixations in adult life – fixations that affect personality and are associated with the body zone concerned. For example, in Freudian theory the result of conflict with primary carers in the anal stage, perhaps associated with too early, too rigid and too controlling toilet training, leads to an obsessional, over-controlling, rigid, and retentive 'anal personality'. We might hypothesize that such a person would have some degree of difficulty in forming and sustaining relationships in adult life.

In Freudian theory, throughout childhood the fundamental difficulty is the control of erotic impulses, that is, sensual and sexual excitements associated with each erogenous zone. By the age of 4- to 5- years, in the phallic stage, impulse control is associated with intense love for the parent of the opposite sex, the Oedipus and Electra complexes in boys and girls respectively, and with the fear of punishment for this love. According to Freud's theory this fear centres on fantasies of castration and leads to a defensive internalization of a judgemental superego figure, usually based on the father. From this stage on, sexual desires are repressed and the child enters the latency period. According to Freud, sexuality returns in the genital stage as the adolescent begins to integrate erotic impulses within adult sexual relationships. *But forbidden childhood desires do not go away.* Throughout life, energy has to be expended to keep them out of consciousness. In certain settings (such as psychoanalysis), in interactions or close relationships where power differentials might make one feel diminished or childlike (regressed), and under stress, these early wishes can re-appear *transferred* to the analyst in psychoanalysis or to partners or other people – sometimes quite inappropriately.

In quite ordinary discourse we now use Freudian concepts to account for relationship choices and problems. There is the idea that difficulties in resolving the mother-father-child triangle (the Oedipus Complex) in childhood can affect adult relationships. It is quite commonplace to hear remarks about someone marrying a person who 'is just like her father' or who ·'treats him just like his mother did'. More complex versions of this might be replays in adult sexual life of the early Oedipal triangle – the woman who repeatedly gets entangled with unavailable married men – or (unconscious) life-long searches for relationships which repeat experiences with a parent of the opposite sex – such as a controlling father or a tantalizing mother.

There is another kind of childhood experience with implications for psychological well-being in adulthood that has caught the public eye: early separations of infants from their primary carers. Bowlby was a psychoanalyst who studied and wrote about attachment theory, separation anxiety and the lasting effects of separations in infancy and childhood. Other psychologists took up these ideas and studied them in a more traditionally empirical way, showing difficulties in relating that seem to follow from early institutionalization and/or a lack of consistent and stimulating one to one care in infancy. Institutionalized upbringing was shown to have repercussions on the capacity for adult relationships. Bowlby's work has been used to understand adult relationships in terms of attachment, affectional bonds, dependency, separation and loss and the *transfer* of patterns of attachment experienced in childhood to adult relating (see Bowlby 1971, 1975, a review in Slade and Aber, 1992 and Rutter, 1995).

Work deriving from attachment theory has shown that the earliest relationships are not just a matter of physical survival. Although attachment behaviours originate as biological drives (an instinct theory), in humans at least they have become elaborated. Physical closeness with another, not necessarily of an erotic kind, is in itself rewarding. This idea is close to what the object relations analysts believe to be the fundamental human motivation – that of relating with other people – for the pleasures of intimacy and intersubjectivity.

The move in psychodynamic theory away from biological drive reduction as a motive for relating and towards relating in its own right for its own rewards of intimacy, shared meanings and emotions, gives a completely new colour to theories of early experiences in relationships and their implications for relating throughout life. Now what becomes important is the *quality* of the earliest interactions; and the success of interpersonal 'attunement' between mother and infant. For example, it now becomes important to ask how successfully infant and mother create an intersubjective space in which the infant can communicate using emotions and then begin to share and thus construct meanings. (See the work of Trevarthen, discussed in Chapter 3.) The infant's experience of relating with others, and the tone of other ongoing relationships in the immediate environment, become internalized as templates or scripts for relating throughout life.

Malattunments between infant and mother can occur through something in the baby's innate constitution, its physical health, or some difficulty experienced by the mother such as post-natal illness or depression, or something in the environment – stress, poor living conditions, or various combinations of these factors. In psychodynamic theory, malattunement in infancy can have far reaching effects. The psychoanalyst Balint placed his developmental emphasis on what he called 'the basic fault.' He was not referring here to blame, but to fault as in a geological fault line, a kind of fundamental discontinuity brought about in the very early stages of development when something goes wrong between mother and infant. His evidence came from his psychoanalytic patients who, he found, frequently expressed a feeling that 'something is wrong', 'something is missing inside'. Balint believed that infants thrive only when they have experiences of intense relatedness, and that they have to pass through a critical phase of adequate attunement, in which their needs are met by their carers in appropriate and pleasing ways, in order to learn ways of relating to others and so develop socially (Balint, 1968).

Within psychodynamics, the object relations approach emphasizes the crucial importance of other people and experiences of relating for the development of the structure of the infant's mind. In this view, the building blocks of the infant's internal world are versions of significant others and the patterns of relating that are taken in (introjected) in the course of the earliest relationships. According to psychodynamic theories and as demonstrated in the analytic relationships between analyst and patient, these residues of early experiences of other people and ways of relating provide templates and scripts which, in later life, are continuously re-enacted with new people and in new and on-going relationships through the process of transference. The remainder of this chapter takes as its primary source of evidence the encounter between patients and their analysts in the course of psychoanalysis to explore the basic psychological process of transference and to unpack processes of unconscious communication.

2.2   Using the psychoanalytic encounter as a 'laboratory'

In the past, 'transference' has been a psychoanalytic and clinical concept, kept for transferences within the psychoanalytic consulting room. That is, the transference (by the patient) of earlier ways of relating on to the figure of the analyst. However, with increased understanding of the unconscious processes involved, it has become clear that transferences are general psychological phenomena that play an important part in everyday life. But, because they are unconscious, they cannot be studied in the context of ordinary life, nor by the methods that are used by other approaches to the study of relating. The previous two chapters have described and explained interactions and relating using evidence that can be gained by *observing interactions from outside* and by using the *verbal accounts* that individuals and couples give of their experience of being in relationships. But attempts to describe, understand and theorize about transferences and other unconscious processes require special methods in a very unusual setting. Therefore, this chapter will be based on evidence from psychoanalysts' observations, and their experiences of their patients' attempts to engage them in relationships that are based on transferences.

Interactions and communications of this kind (during psychoanalysis *and* in ordinary life) are not directly available to consciousness and therefore cannot be part of patients' (or others') accounts of what is happening; nor can they be observed from the outside by non-participant observers. Interviews or video recordings of partners interacting may give some clues as to the underlying unconscious processes at work in the interaction. But it is only by being part of the unconscious relating processes, that is, only by allowing oneself to be used as an object of the transferences and as a receiver of the other's unconscious communications, that the processes can be fully accessed and studied. (See the discussion of what constitutes communication in Chapter 2, section 4.4)

It is this difficult procedure of simultaneously being *in a relationship* and far enough *outside it* to be able to observe it and observe oneself, that is the essence of modern psychoanalysis and psychoanalytic psychotherapy. In a carefully circumscribed way the psychoanalyst observes, experiences and tries to understand the transferences and communications through her/his own *countertransference*, that is, the totality of the effects of these unconscious communications upon the analyst. This chapter uses the analytic encounter as a kind of 'laboratory', which comprises the *psychoanalytic setting* and the details of the *encounter* between analyst and patient. (See Box 4.1 for a description of the setting. Boxes 4.4 and 4.5 below describe the other kinds of evidence that are used.)

BOX 4.1   The psychoanalytic 'laboratory'.

Part One – the setting

The analytic encounter has unique features that can reveal processes of relating. There are many *constant* factors which are like controlled variables – the same two people, meeting at the same time of day for fifty minutes, several times a week sometimes for several years. The physical setting remains constant and there is minimal interference from information about the analyst (or his/her family). There are no demands on the patient (other than no physical contact or damage to property), no ordinary task orientations and no social obligations. Social cues are minimized. In most cases eye-contact and other face-to-face cues are removed since the patient lies on a couch with the analyst sitting behind, out of sight. There is rarely a 'contract' and the analyst does not initiate any interactions nor have an agenda, but follows the material the patient brings. Normal conversational rules are broken during the sessions – the analyst, for example, will rarely answer a question and will not be drawn into discussions or arguments. There is no pressure for the patient to make sense, and 'free association' is encouraged. In addition, the analyst offers confidentiality and a non-judgemental attitude, and a 'container' in which intense emotions can be thought about and talked about safely but never acted upon. Analysts often hear about primitive emotional states and sexual relating in a way that is probably unique. All these arrangements maximize the 'space' available for unconscious phantasies (the 'ph' spelling denotes that they are unconscious), conscious fantasies and replays of relating – the transference.

In this setting the analyst, who is a trained, consistent and constant observer and interpreter of what is happening, has the opportunity to collect data, formulate hypotheses and test them with the same person over many occasions extending sometimes over several years.

The relationship between patient and analyst has another feature of a laboratory. By not responding, and thus avoiding the ordinary interactive responsiveness of relating, and by not colluding with the patient's unconscious (and conscious) demands but instead *interpreting* what is happening, the analyst makes a clinical intervention. These interventions have features of what, in an experimental setting, would be called a manipulation. The effects of interpretations are closely monitored, within the analysis and in the patient's reported behaviours in the external world. The outcome is, hopefully, a new understanding.

2.3   Freud's discovery of transference

Freud first encountered the phenomenon of transference early in his career whilst he was still using hypnosis:

> One day I had an experience which showed me in the crudest light what I had long suspected. It related to one of my most acquiescent patients, with whom hypnotism had enabled me to bring about most marvellous results ... As she woke up on one occasion, she threw her arms round my neck. The unexpected entrance of a servant relieved us from a painful discussion ... I was modest enough not to attribute the event to my own irresistible personal attraction, and felt that I had now grasped the nature of the mysterious element that was at work behind hypnotism.
>
> *(Freud, 1925, p. 27)*

What Freud had experienced was *erotic transference*. At that time, patients 'falling in love' with the doctor, the psychiatrist, the hypnotist or the psychoanalyst was a well documented hazard, especially with patients diagnosed as hysterics. We shall explore the relevance of this for everyday relating in the next section.

Freud was shaken by his experience of being the object of an erotic transference. Whatever had happened was unexpected, highly emotional and had a compulsive quality. There were sufficient sexual connotations to make him fear that, whatever it was, it might continue and intensify if the treatment continued. Freud was concerned that he might have caused it – through his own personality or attractiveness. Erotic transference was recognized to be dangerous for practising clinicians and notoriously exploited by some hypnotists, consequently Freud felt that he had to distance himself. At the same time, he tried to fit the observation into his own psychoanalytic theory.

First, he took the position that the transference was entirely due to something *inside* the patient, erupting from the past and essentially illusory – a misperception with respect to the current therapeutic encounter, something pathological. This is a statement of an *intrapsychic* view of transference – that transference is not a function of the current relationship between analyst and patient.

Second, Freud explained these 'illusory perceptions and misplaced emotions' in terms of 'false connections' that lead to transference onto the figure of the psychoanalyst/psychiatrist of forbidden and *repressed* (unconscious) erotic wishes from childhood – often erotic desires for the mother or father. Freud understood what was happening in terms of residues of the past erupting into the present and being placed, unconsciously, on to another person.

Freud believed that childhood experiences, in particular early, forbidden, sexual events and feelings, continue to exert an influence on the developing psyche and then on adult behaviour and symptoms. Since, even in childhood, it is the erotic longings that are thought to be the most powerful and the most prohibited, defences against erotic phantasies and impulses and the associated anxieties need to be massive. The figure of the analyst and the intimate setting of analysis can release powerful erotic feelings that are transferences of the original repressed wishes. Freud's clinical theory took a big step forward with the discovery of transference. Here was the clear manifestation of the hidden wish – transferred to the analyst.

Erotic transference was the first aspect of transference to be systematically observed in the psychoanalytic setting, but it is certainly not the only manifestation of transference. Within the psychoanalytic setting and *also in everyday relating* transference is a much more generalized phenomenon.

2.4   Transferences: templates for interactions and relationships

Freud gave up using hypnosis. But he found that even without it his patients still formed strong attachments to him, although not necessary erotic. In his writing on transference (of which there was not very much), he began to refer to other kinds of transference. He developed the idea that transferences are built upon 'a stereotype plate (or several such)' which serve as a prototype for particular patterns of close relationship 'constantly repeated – constantly reprinted afresh – in the course of a person's life' (Freud, 1912, p. 100).

> What are transferences? They are new editions or facsimiles of the impulses and phantasies which are aroused and made conscious during the progress of the analysis; but they have this peculiarity, which is characteristic for their species, that they replace some earlier person by the person of the physician … Some of these transferences have a content which differs from that of their model in no respect whatever except for the substitution. These then – to keep the same metaphor – are merely new impressions or reprints. Others are more ingeniously constructed; their content has been subjected to a moderating influence … and they may even become conscious, by cleverly taking advantage of some real peculiarity in the physician's person or the circumstances and attaching themselves to that. These, then, will no longer be new impressions, but revised editions.
>
> *(Freud, 1905, p. 116)*

The idea of transference templates meant that Freud could think of some of the transferences that occured in psychoanalysis as 'turning for help to a wise father (or a kind mother)'. This move also meant that negative transferences could exist. One person's version of a father transference might be benign but for another it might be frightening, for example a transference from a punishing, critical father. In analysis, these two patients would experience very different kinds of feelings and impulses towards the analyst in the transference. When patients experience their analysts as kind, helpful and wise, Freud was less insistent on the entirely intrapsychic nature of the transference, hinting at some influence of the 'real' therapeutic relationship. The assumption here is that such a transference is a positive and unproblematic transference of affectionate feelings – originally for a father or mother – which would help the psychoanalytic process. This is what we now call the therapeutic alliance. Freud did not elaborate this re-appraisal of benign forms of transference, nor did he take up the more complex and *interpsychic* view of transference that will be discussed later in this chapter.

Freud suggested that these helpful transferences happen outside the psychoanalytic setting with other kinds of doctors and professionals, male or female. But what is it in the process of psychoanalysis and in the structure of certain other professional relationships that elicits transferences? Apart from the person and general manner of the analyst, doctor or lawyer etc., psychoanalytic and professional settings are structured in terms of *power*. There is expertise and professional status on the one hand, and lack of knowledge and perhaps dependence on the part of the patient/client; and it is probably this that promotes transference via a re-creation of the power differential of the parent-child relationship. And amongst professional relationships, it is probably in psychoanalysis that this power dimension is most obvious and profound – the whole enterprise rests on the patient asking for help and for the benefit of superior knowledge. These factors are potent cues for child-like feelings and behaviours; and in many respects the analyst does take a parental role. But, in psychoanalytic terms, transferences are not roles, they are the return of repressed childhood or infantile feelings and wishes. Sometimes there is a more powerful regression to infantile states of mind. In such a setting, where ordinary task orientation is absent, and the other person is more or less blank – providing a space for the patient to fill – it is perhaps not surprising that all manner of repressed child-like feelings and behaviours arise, including repressed erotic feelings. In Freud's theory, erotic transference is not 'grown up' loving but the resurrection of a childhood erotic impulse or attraction to father, mother or some other figure.

This discussion of transference has probably reminded you of the potential hazards of therapeutic encounters, and of some non-therapeutic ones. Intense attachments – and openness to influence – are possible outcomes of many kinds of therapy, perhaps hypnotherapy most of all. You will see from the evidence throughout this chapter that the psychological effects of the setting of psychoanalysis, other therapies and *other professional relationships* can place the professional in a powerful position. Patients and prospective clients of therapy need to be aware of this and try to ensure that they find appropriate, well-trained and well-analysed therapists so that the feelings that are aroused can be 'thought about' and worked with, *without being enacted*. (See, for example, the discussion by Masson, 1988.)

ACTIVITY 4.I

Pause here for a moment and think about some of the professional and the more intimate relationships that you have experienced. Did you ever feel childlike? Try to write down how *you* think the power differential affects interactions and relationships. Can you list any other features of the situation or the actual people involved that might interact with the power differential?

Do you think that there has to be a power differential for one or other of the participants to feel childlike, or to be childlike some of the time? In terms of your own experiences, do you think transferences will still happen where there is no question of one person being ill and one well, one the helper and one the helped, or one the teacher and one the taught? What do you think would happen when it is the woman who is the lawyer and the man the confused client? Compare what you have listed and written with the discussion in Chapter 3, section 4.4.

It is fairly common for dependencies, unreasonable demands, hostilities, feelings of infantilization and sometimes erotic attachments to emerge from professional encounters that have a power differential. The power difference frequently maps on to gender difference, perhaps increasing the possibility of erotic feelings. In Freud's time this would have been even more salient since it was common for women to be much younger than their husbands and to be infantilized in marriage. The erotic culture of that time, and maybe all times, might predispose female clients/ patients to 'fall in love' with male doctors, male teachers, male analysts and to marry older, more powerful husbands. Women might be infantilized, but it also seems that the more powerful, and perhaps parental role (usually, but not invariably, male), carries an erotic charge based on dominance. The eroticization of dominance may be culturally constructed or biological or, of course, both. Issues about societal and socially constructed power differentials and how they impact on interactions and relationships were discussed in Chapter 3, especially in section 4.4, and will be raised again in Chapter 6.

ACTIVITY 4.2

A reference is made in Chapter 3, section 4.4, and again in *Reading B* to the work of Williams and Watson (1988). This is quoted to support the idea that economic and societal power differentials, which largely operate in favour of men, lead to women trying to maintain influence by covert and emotional means, rather in the way that children try to do in their relationships with adults. In Chapter 3 the discussion is in terms of roles and directly internalized social discourses. In the psychodynamic view the outcome is similar but the explanation is rather different. Can you articulate the difference?

How might transference as a general psychological process play a part in ordinary sexual relationships? It is quite common in close friendships, sexual partnerships and marriages for one person to be the 'teacher' or 'authority' for the other, or for one person to be more emotionally dependent than the other – conferring a form of power differential. There will be a tendency for the less powerful participant to be pushed (unconsciously) into childlike behaviours or actually to regress and feel childlike. Sexual coupling (heterosexual and homosexual) is often quite openly based on what look like parental roles, either with one partner consistently the 'parent' and the other the 'child' or with exchanges according to circumstances. In psychodynamic terms, in such relationships we might expect the infantilized partner not just to enact child roles but to *be engaged in a much more profound and intense process* – the transfer of needs and emotions from long ago, from real parental figures to the current partner. In turn, as we shall see in section 3, this transference (unconsciously) influences the other not just to enact a parental role but also to transfer ways of relating that were introjected in their childhood from a powerful parent – perhaps benign but perhaps autocratic or even sadistic. Thus the 'parental' partner is also resurrecting a childhood template. These *mutual transferences* may be erotic or they may be about other aspects of relating; most likely, however, they will be a complex entanglement which includes erotic elements. In psychodynamic terms, the transference elements will be largely unconscious and collusive, and they may be what *maintains* the relationship.

Erotic transference, as Freud originally described it, does have some bearing on relationships in ordinary life: it can help us to understand sexual attractions and 'falling in love'. One of the main features of a transference is its compulsive quality, we feel possessed by a particular *way of being* in relation with another person. And erotic transference, as Freud understood it, is intrapsychic – based on the individual's past rather than something created between two minds. We see another person in ways that other people cannot see and often dismiss. We may feel an inappropriate intensity or kind of emotion. This is rather like the way sexual attraction or 'chemistry' can suddenly draw us to another person. (Although characteristics of the other that are clear signals of availability, or culturally-sponsored markers of sexual attractiveness can have a similar effect.) It is as if we have put into the other person characteristics that originate in ourselves – we have projected some earlier experience or need into another person. Sometimes we are able to recognize these exaggerations or irrationalities – although, more usually, recognition comes much later and perhaps when we have 'got away' from the interaction. With some degree of reality testing, we find out what the other person is really like, and it becomes difficult to maintain the projections. The transference dissolves and we fall out of love – or convert the transference to a more realistic form of loving.

Early Freudian work on transferences has gradually been extended to the idea that *all* adult relationships are based on replays of much earlier relationships. Two psychoanalysts, Luborsky and Crits-Christoph (1990), have carried out empirical research on transference templates. They have monitored the narratives – the stories – that a wide range of patients tell about themselves and their relationships and found repeating patterns of 'core conflictual relationship themes' (CCRT). They have devised a method for measuring CCRT's and have found that they can capture the 'central pattern, script, or schema that each person follows in conducting relationships' (Luborsky and Crits-Christoph, 1990, p. 1). CCRT's are expressed in terms of the patient's wishes, the ways that other people in the stories react to those wishes and the patient's responses to the reactions. For each patient, the fundamental pattern is repeated across relationships with different types of people and is found in both waking narratives and in dreams. They also found that the basic CCRT for a patient is the same in the relationship with the therapist as with other people in the external world; and that the more therapists focus on the CCRT the more the patients benefit.

In so far as our real life relationships are based on transferences which are largely unconscious, how far are they affected by the *actual* other? If they are mere repeating projections of our internal worlds, of our early repressed need states, to what extent is there a relationship in the present? And how can we find new ways of relating? Are we only able to use the building blocks of old relationships? How can we change? How can we innovate? In Chapter 3 we saw that relationships can be affected by reflexive processes, and re-negotiations of meanings. But this can only happen when beliefs, expectations, personal constructs (and behaviours – what people are actually doing) and the constructions that participants have of their relationships as a whole – their narratives – are conscious. Because the templates and ensuing scripts set by transferences are largely unconscious, it can be very difficult to change a pattern of interacting or a relationship. This is even more difficult because relationship choices and patterns of relating over time tend to enmesh both partners in mutual transferences which reinforce each other – in unconscious collusion. As we saw above, those who need to re-enact a bossy parental figure from the past will choose and collude with someone who needs to be childlike.

ACTIVITY 4.3   Look back to Chapter 3, Activity 3.6 and section 4.3 – the use of the extract about Diane and Stuart. Read through the extract again but this time use the concept of transference to reinterpret this extract. Make brief notes on Diane and Stuart's possible unconscious transferences. When you have done this activity, look at Box 4.2.

BOX 4 . 2   Diane and Stuart: a psychoanalytic re-interpretation

The common marital interaction pattern exhibited by Diane and Stuart might be seen by a psychoanalyst as reflecting the experience of the two partners in their own families of origin.

For example, Stuart's resentment at having to spend time doing something his wife wants, as a duty, and especially her need for him to be open and communicative, could reflect Stuart's experience of his mother – a mother transference. We are told that Stuart said he came from a 'rather cold, emotionally distant family'. In this family duty might have taken precedence over doing things with another so that both feel good. This experience of distance and duty, represented in his internal world as a demanding and unrewarding 'internal mother' would be re-evoked in the present. Stuart might then, unconsciously, behave towards Diane as he did as a boy or adolescent with his mother – becoming more resistant and defiant and distant.

Diane is economically dependent on Stuart and we are also told that she brought with her into the relationship a feeling of emotional insecurity. These two factors together might have made her unconsciously feel infantilized. In the here and now, Stuart responds to her needs by striking a bargain (from a position of power – like a parent) in which Diane (like a child) has to agree to engage in activities (walking too far and dealing with heights) that are too much for her, too frightening, perhaps resonating with an early interaction pattern and feelings experienced with her parents. Her considerable concerns for her children's safety further amplify her own fears – she might be identifying with her children. Stuart's failure to be responsible and take care of the children in their attempts to do dangerous things, might make Diane feel frightened and even more infantilized.

This kind of explanation does not conflict with the idea of commonly found, and gender-specific patterns of withdrawal and advance/intrusion in marital couples discussed in Chapter 3. But it uses a different level of explanation to connect cultural expectations and family interaction patterns to the continuing unconscious influence in the present of very early experiences of relationships.

In ordinary life, the repeating patterns of relating that we find ourselves engaged in can sometimes give a clue (to others) of difficulties from the past of which we have no conscious awareness. *It is as if we are communicating about a difficulty through our transference.* In the example above, it is as if Diane is unconsciously communicating to Stuart her need for him to be a kind and attentive parent to the overburdened child she feels she is: 'I want to go home now. I've had enough. It's too much for me.'

Transferences may begin within one person but their expression is inter-personal. *A transference becomes an unconscious attempt to get the other to feel and behave in a particular way.*

In everyday relating, transference as a process is a form of communication. This view of transference and unconscious communication in relationships will be the main topic in sections 3 and 4 of this chapter, where the emphasis shifts from an intrapsychic view towards an inter-personal view of transference processes.

Review of section 2

- Psychodynamics approaches relating and relationships by emphasizing either biological need states (instinct theories) or relating for its own sake (object relations theories).

- Relating in infancy, childhood and throughout life is seen as determined by unconscious motivations and unconscious communication. In adulthood, primitive needs and emotions that have been repressed re-surface, usually unconsciously, and affect adult relating.

- Relating in adulthood is determined by early introjections of versions of significant others and relationships. These residues of early experience influence adult relating through the transference of emotional states and ways of relating from a figure in the past to someone in the present. A significant part of relating, especially in intimate relationships, is unconsciously driven by repetitions of infantile ways of relating.

- According to psychodynamics, conscious choices of partners, negotiations in current relationships, and attempts to be reflective are difficult and sometimes not possible.

- Early Freudian psychodynamics focused on erotic transferences, conceptualized as the reappearance of repressed childhood erotic wishes. The concept has been extended to cover transferences of other features of early experiences with other people and relationships.

3   Voices from internal worlds

In this section we shall explore modern ideas about transferences, between psychoanalysts and their patients, and in ordinary life. We move away from Freud's view of transference to examine what is broadly an object relations approach, although we shall also include some of the ideas of the child psychoanalyst, Melanie Klein.

3.1   An object relations approach

The argument in this chapter rests on two fundamental conceptual differences between classical Freudian psychodynamics and object relations theories.

Freud's model of the mind is constructed around the id, ego and super-ego, of which only the superego is thought of as an internalized *figure* (usually of a punitive father). And this internal object does not appear until the resolution of the Oedipus complex when the child is about 4- or 5-years-old. In contrast, Klein and the object relations theorists have shifted emphasis to the first five years of life. Psychoanalytic evidence from work with young children shows that lively, internal worlds develop very early in life. These worlds are peopled with representations (internal objects), variably accurate and/or phantastic, of significant others and their relationships with each other and with the child (represented as internal object relations). Long before the age of five these worlds are being constructed and elaborated out of relationships with parents, triangular oedipal tussles and sibling rivalries. Even earlier, from birth, internal worlds are being created out of the infant's relationship with mother, not as a person but as a source of nourishment and frustration, and with loving and punitive versions of mummies and daddies.

Kleinian theory, although not strictly part of the object relations approach, is crucial to the argument here because Klein introduced the idea that *transferences have a defensive function.* Klein's contribution to the concept of transference is outlined in Box 4.3. (A discussion of the 'defensive' self can be found in Thomas, 1996.)

BOX 4.3 Klein: Splitting, projecting, and transferring as a defence mechanism

Klein believed that transference is a *process* largely concerned with very early defence mechanisms – a defensive projection outward on to others of painful parts of the internal world. According to Klein, much of the developing structure of the mind follows an unfolding biological blueprint of unconscious phantasies (unthought knowns). In Kleinian theory, this development is driven by the life instinct (Freud's 'Eros' and his focus on sexuality) *and* by the death instinct, that is, by the infant's innate destructive drives, primitive hate, aggression and envy. Klein's focus on these negative aspects of children's inner worlds created what has been called a Bruegelesque inner landscape of caricatures: good or bad, nourishing or withholding, loving or punishing figures. Because of her emphasis on innate phantasies, this landscape has relatively little to do with children's actual experiences with other people. Using this focus, and clinical evidence from child psychoanalysis, she described how the mind is structured defensively in order to make the inner world a more tolerable place.

Klein concluded that children (and adults) deal with anxieties using a primitive defence mechanism called *splitting*. Splitting means that as the child constructs an internal world, the good and bad aspects are kept separate, internally, so that they do not contaminate each other – hence the idea of caricature. By this she means the 'good' is kept good and the 'bad' kept really bad. Splitting is then followed by a second primitive defence mechanism called *projection*, by which the bad internal objects are projected into representations of objects in the external world – in phantasy. The outcome is that the internal world may feel more comfortable but the bad feelings still exist, now, in phantasy, seeming to come from the outside and leading to a sense of persecution. In this Kleinian view, children in analysis use the analyst as a repository for projections of parts of their internal worlds, especially the painful and frightening parts.

Projections need to be 'received' and contained and also explained; and *negative transference is essential to the analytic process*. This view substantially changed the concept of transference. Klein, and many others since, have tested these ideas about negative transference in the clinical setting with children (and adults). Interpretation of the negative transference to the children – showing them in their own language what they are doing, feeling and representing symbolically in their play and in their relationship with the analyst – leads to a reduction in anxiety.

The second conceptual difference between classical Freudian theory and object relations theories concerns underlying assumptions about the *functions* of relating with other people. For Freudians (and Kleinians) the experience of relating with others is secondary to the libidinal rewards and tension release associated with the satisfaction of bodily needs that others can supply. In object relations theory, other people in themselves become more important. People are no longer 'signposts' to libidinal gratification; instead relationships are seen as motivated by the intrinsic rewards of actually relating.

The object relations approach leads to a fundamentally different view of object relating in internal worlds, of relationships in everyday life, and how the two domains connect through processes of transference.

In object relations theories, internal representations of other people, of their relationships with us and with each other, formed very early in life, are an essential part of the structure of our minds, and are crucial constituents of our *selves*. From this point of view, psychodynamic claims that relationships throughout life are unconsciously driven by residues of early experience take on much more force. We are no longer thinking of relatively encapsulated, repressed desires returning in adult relationships in an attempt to find – by this time largely irrelevant – gratification. Instead, we are dealing with the emergence of parts of the self, in the form of earlier 'others' and earlier relationships – the voices from internal worlds. Relationships become the forum for various unconscious processes which build and maintain the self. And relationships can now be seen as the stage on which we enact processes that construct, express, and defend our selves.

3.2   Who is speaking? And to whom?

It has been analysts' own experiences of being the 'receivers' of their patients' transferences that has led to a re-casting of the mind as a place peopled with versions of those with whom the infant and small child has actually enjoyed, or failed to enjoy, satisfaction and intimacy. This is one of the hallmarks of the British object relations psychoanalysts. Their theories are essentially concerned with the structure and content of internal worlds, and the resulting psychic reality in which we live, *as versions of real relationships experienced in infancy and childhood*. This leads to a more interpsychic and interpersonal approach to psychodynamics.

As these ideas became more acceptable in psychoanalytic practice, the variety and sometimes fleeting nature of transferences became more evident. Object relations analysts began to hear the different 'voices' speaking from their patients' internal worlds.

> In the early 1950s Paula Heimann ... posed a simple question that became crucial to the practice of psychoanalysis in what has come to be called the 'British School' of psychoanalysis ... When listening to the patient's free associations (or broken speech), and tracing the private logic of sequential associations as all psychoanalysts had done up until then, she asked: 'Who is speaking?' ... We can say that up until this moment it had always been assumed that the speaker was the patient who had formed a therapeutic alliance with the analyst, and

therefore that he was a neutral or working speaker who was reporting inner states of mind ... But Heimann knew that at any one moment in a session a patient could be speaking with the voice of the mother, or the mood of the father, or some fragmented voice of a child self either lived or withheld from life.

'To whom is this person speaking?' Heimann then asked. The unconscious admits no special recognition of the neutrality of the psychoanalyst and, given the unending subtleties of the transference, Heimann realized that at one moment the analysand was speaking to the mother, anticipating the father, or reproaching, exciting or consoling a child – the child self of infancy, in the midst of separation at age two, in the oedipal phase, or in adolescence. 'What is the patient talking about and why now?', she added.

Heimann and other analysts in the British School, all of whom had been deeply influenced by Melanie Klein, analysed the object relations implied in the patient's discourse ... the shifting subjects and others that were implied in the transference.

(Bollas, 1987, pp. 1-2, emphasis added)

The quotation raises three questions that we can use to structure our discussion of transference in the psychoanalytic setting *and* in ordinary life.

'Who is speaking?' This question alerts us to the potential variety of internal objects in a patient's internal world that are available for the patient to identify with and to *be* in the transference relationship with the analyst. It also suggests the variety or fluidity of voices from the past that can appear in ordinary relationships.

'To whom...?' This focuses attention again on internal structure, but now on the relationships between the patient's internal objects. A patient's particular voice is talking to a particular other from his or her internal world, projected into the analyst. This implies an attempt to reproduce externally an internally represented way of relating. Often the force with which the patient attempts, unconsciously, to create the appropriate other in the analyst, vividly demonstrates a need, an insistence for a repetition or a gratification.

In psychoanalysis, if this repetition were permitted or the need gratified, it would validate and/or strengthen an internal personality structure, strengthening some way of relating that is self-destructive or compulsive and that the patient consciously wishes to change. Where there is an attempt by the patient in the transference to force a repeat of a rigid and unhelpful or pathological relationship, the analyst's task is to see this and interpret it and not allow the re-enactment of past relating to actually happen. Sometimes, however, the simple fact of having a particular voice heard and understood is validating and healing. The patient may be demanding this form of gratification in the transference relationship because he or she has never, or only occasionally, or only tantalisingly, received it from the external world. This level of gratification – having a 'hearing parent' or a 'witness' can be helpful.

In ordinary interactions sometimes one can 'feel' another person trying to get one to be a particular kind of other with whom they can relate in a particular way, although usually it will be an unconscious influence process. In everyday interactions we may unconsciously gratify the demands of the other, thus reinforcing them. Or we may feel uncomfortable or angry without knowing why.

'What is the patient talking about and why now?' This question draws attention to the kinds of data that psychoanalysts use and the *meanings* that are generated in the psychoanalytic encounter, see Box 4.4. But the questions are also important for ordinary life. In everyday relationships *and* in quite transient interactions the question 'What is this person talking about?' and 'Why now?' might reveal hidden messages below the surface content of what is being said and done.

ACTIVITY 4.4

Read Box 4.4; you might wonder if transference interpretations like this, in psychoanalysis, can tell us anything about what we do outside the consulting room in everyday life. Suppose this woman, in the example in Box 4.4, who had been let down by the milkman's mistake was not in analysis, or that the analyst's holiday had extended for several days so that the patient did not have the opportunity to tell the story, and to have her feelings interpreted. What might have happened in her ordinary world of interactions and relationships? Try to think of at least two different outcomes.

The transference relationship with an analyst and the way it is revealed in behaviour can have direct parallels in ordinary life, although the consequences are likely to be rather different. If this same woman, in her ordinary world, was feeling sufficiently upset and lonely over the Bank Holiday, that is, regressed, *and* the milkman forgot to deliver her milk, then the 'miserable, abandoned child', unconsciously evoked, might complain to a friend and get indirect comfort from the telling. In ordinary life her friend might laugh at her for making a fuss – repeating what her parents had done and making her feel even worse. The friend's own transferences might now be evoked. He might have laughed, not because it was funny nor because he consciously wanted to hurt her, but out of his own transference. He might unconsciously attack her to defend himself against his own similar feelings of being let down at some point by some important other. This would be an example of mutual transferences influencing the interaction between the two friends. If the woman picked a fight with the milkman *acting* on her bad feelings, displacing them in an inappropriately emotional way, displacing on to him the emotional intensity of being let down long ago, he might retaliate

BOX 4.4   The psychoanalytic 'laboratory'.

Part Two – behaviour, meanings and the transference relationship

What kinds of data are generated in analytic settings? What do psychoanalysts use as evidence of unconscious processes? Broadly, there are three kinds of data: (1) sense data – the analyst's observations of patients' behaviours and physiology; (2) meanings; and (3) the evidence from psychoanalysts' own feelings and reactions to what is going on – countertransference data. Countertransference evidence will be discussed in section 4, Box 4.5.

What are these sense data? What kinds of behaviours might be observed? A patient who usually comes to sessions on time might suddenly begin to arrive late. A patient might suddenly give up a ritualistic pattern of removing shoes, taking coins out of his pockets, adjusting the pillows, lying in silence for a few minutes before beginning. A patient who has great difficulty in the external world in disclosing himself in speech beyond social niceties might, whenever he talks in the sessions, move about compulsively, crossing and uncrossing legs, moving arms, turning his head. There are patients who cut across interpretations, drowning out the analyst's words. There are non-verbal behaviours such as laughter or tears, changes in voice tone and loudness. Patients cannot hide physiological changes – sweat on forehead, increases in heart rate and respiration that show in chest movements. There is somatization – the patient who, when angry, has an attack of asthma; the patient who complains of palpitations when talking about frightening material. All of these provide sense data – they are clear pieces of behavioural evidence, although there will be dispute as to their exact meaning.

Meaning data are the essence of psychoanalytic encounters. There is the *content* of current happenings, memories, fantasies and dreams, but more important are the ways in which unconscious motives and underlying structure is revealed. Why is the patient talking about this particular incident *now*? Why does she switch between seemingly unrelated pieces of material? Each patient's own language of symbolism – their own idiolect – can be observed and learned. It is not the bald content of what is said that constitutes the data. The timing of the delivery of information, the resistances and what is *not* said, the 'jumps' from one topic to another and the repeating themes are frequently more informative than the content. Thus unconscious meanings shine through mundane 'here and now' examples of everyday life, and through the transference relationship.

The transference relationship itself is evidence, since it is the representative in the here and now of past relationships. Transference can be revealed in quite trivial-seeming incidents. For example: an analyst cancels a session because of a Bank Holiday, and the patient begins the next session by expressing anger that the milkman failed to deliver milk and she had to drink bitter black coffee. This fact *and the telling of it* might reveal that the patient has unconscious phantasies about the analyst failing to deliver – letting the patient down. The analyst might hypothesize that the milkman story is being told by a voice from the past, 'the miserable, disgruntled child who has been let down, through no fault of her own'. It has been told to the 'analyst/parent who went off having fun without her patient/child'. The conscious story reveals an unconscious story of anxiety and perhaps anger told by an abandoned child. This kind of interpretation of the material would not be made on the basis of one appearance of the theme. The patient might describe a dream or a film in which a child is on a railway platform waving good-bye to parents who are leaving on a trip. In the course of the analysis similar material would come up repeatedly – especially at holidays, when sessions are cancelled.

Hypotheses about meanings are kept in mind, tested and retested against further material, and interpretations are usually phrased as hypotheses and their *effects* observed. Was the patient able to listen to the interpretation? Did the patient seem relieved, or suddenly remember something else relevant, displaying an increased understanding? Was there a reduction in defensiveness?

No longer is transference necessarily a direct reference to the analyst; it is the *total situation* of the communication, including all kinds of everyday bits of material, triggered by the analytic setting and its transference implications.

(consciously or unconsciously) by 'forgetting' to deliver her milk again another day. The ordinary cycles of interaction and mutual transferences would reinforce the original hurt.

In ordinary life, the woman might act on her bad feelings within a more important and intimate relationship. Perhaps she was alone over the holiday weekend because her sexual partner had to work abroad, a fact that she might have accepted rationally, if sadly. The milkman event could have triggered current feelings of being let down, that she was defending against and could not consciously acknowledge in her current relationship, as well as the deeper, older feelings of abandonment. Since all this is likely to be going on unconsciously, when her partner returns she might pick a serious fight with him – perhaps overtly because he did not take an earlier plane – and they might both be surprised at what is happening. She would be enacting the bad feelings which originated in childhood, were then stirred up by abandonment by the partner (although consciously rationalized), exacerbated and brought to the surface by the milkman, and finally triggered by her partner failing to return on the earliest plane.

We have to remember that her partner is not a blank screen. He will bring his own reactions and responses into the situation. She might be provoking him, via her unconscious communication, to feel irritated and he might then 'resist' her dependence, thus making her experience further disappointment, or feel that abandonment is imminent. This irritability and resistance would be his countertransference – which, unlike psychoanalytic countertransference, would probably remain unconscious and not be reflected upon but would affect his behaviour. And/or he might bring his own transferences into the interaction, perhaps resisting her as a transference of his resistance to his clinging, dependent mother. Countertransferences and mutual transferences, in ordinary life, might lead to an escalation of the quarrel without either of them really knowing what is going on. The woman might have her unconscious template re-validated; she might become convinced that he will abandon her. And, if the fight is bad enough, he might.

In real life and in everyday relationships, similar features which centre around the idea of regression – of going back, to a greater or lesser extent, to child-like states of mind – may arise from time to time. Or they may characterize a particular relationship. Life events, such as death of a parent, or divorce or illness, can trigger regression and lead to behaviours and feelings that we thought had been outgrown long ago. Stress can intensify transferences. For example, a new job where we have to learn the ropes and meet many new people who know so much more about what is going on, can unconsciously revive 'starting school' and, with that, unconscious transferences to our partners. In our unconscious phantasies, a partner might become the nice teacher who helped or the cruel mother who sent us to school in the first place when we would much rather have stayed safely at home. All these can have unexpected and quite intense effects on relating.

These are relatively short-term everyday life examples. But our patterns of relating in long-term relationships can also be deeply affected by transferences. Sexual relationships, in particular, include intimacies that quite ordinarily have regressive aspects. The intimacies of close sexuality contain expressions of one's child self: baby talk, body contact and foreplay that arises from the earliest body care, nourishment and attention provided by mothers. Some sexual relationships are more generally regressive – where one partner parents the other in all kinds of ways – quite a commonplace kind of marriage. It is in the context of intimate relationships, especially when something goes 'wrong' – an infidelity or rejection or bereavement, or sometimes a seemingly insignificant event like a forgotten appointment – that intensely emotional and sometimes frightening transferences can sweep in. There are times in all relationships when things are very clearly not what they seem. And some relationships exist permanently in a state of mutual, collusive transferences.

In ordinary life we all, unconsciously, replay the structures of relating that are laid down in our minds at times when dependencies and attachments and very early sensual and sexual gratifications are what lead our psychological development. In later life, we all, to some extent, *use others* to express, compulsively repeat and perhaps repair these early templates.

Our relationships are communications with others – from our internal worlds and our psychic realities. In the next section we return to the detailed evidence of these kinds of processes to begin to examine the idea that relationships themselves are forms of unconscious communication – communication which often has a function more relevant to the past than the present.

3.3   Transference as a process of unconscious communication

In modern psychoanalysis, everything that patients say and do can be treated as a communication that defines and constitutes the transference relationship. Klein summed this up: 'transference as the total situation' (Klein, 1952, p. 55). With this conceptual step, transferences become more than specific templates, seeing someone as a figure from the past or a script for relating, originating in the past. *Transferences are an interpersonal process of communicating and influencing another person to engage in some aspect of a re-enactment.* In the course of psychoanalysis, the processes can be seen relatively clearly. Psychoanalysis is directed towards the mutual (that is, between analyst and patient) understanding of patients' current lives and relationships in terms of their established patterns of relating *revealed* in the totality of their communication with the analyst. In this view, patients are not simply talking in the presence of a 'blank screen' but working very hard (and largely unconsciously), in a variety of ways, to re-create a particular kind of relating with a particular kind of other (the analyst in phantasy). Sometimes several such dramas may be in repertory at one time, with the patient moving back and forth from one play to another within a session or over longer periods of time. By trying to recreate a relationship, by using their analysts in the transference, they are communicating something about their own predicament and their own self.

The two clinical extracts below illustrate 'voices from internal worlds' and 'transference as a communication'. In each vignette the patient is either *being* an object from their own internal world and/or trying to get the analyst to *be* the 'other' – the other half of a reciprocal internal object relationship. See if you can decipher the underlying communication in each extract.

ACTIVITY 4.5

Extract 4.1

A patient whose case history I had taken myself appeared always to break off love relationships after one year. It became clear to me that this had happened several times already, yet she was not really aware of it. After one year of analysis her behaviour became impossible – she no longer understood even the simplest interpretations. I began to doubt whether I should continue the analysis. Then I remembered that time and again she had broken off relationships, compulsively as it were.

I re-read the case history and discussed the phenomenon with her. I suggested that with me she might be repeating what she had done so often before: breaking up a relationship after one year. Then it appeared that – at least in her perception – she had had her father all to herself for only one year. That had been when she had been between 6- and 7-years-old, when her father always took her to and fetched her back from school. Then he died. In her fear of being let down she now actively ran away herself. She actively did what she passively feared would happen to her: being abandoned. Later this fear was transferred from her father to each of her successive partners and, during the analysis, to me. In the transference this was discussed and resolved.

Source: De Blecourt, 1993, p. 759

Extract 4.2

A patient described a mother who could never *take* any of his concerns. He was a man with passionate feelings, but his mother would always say to him, 'Yes, yes, darling', and quickly change the subject. This quality of his mother's absolutely exasperated him, for it was a manifestation of her inability to bear any of her child's anxiety. He described a mother who seemed unable to cope with any demands from her baby: once she found herself responsible for *her* baby she dumped him on to someone else. This for him was the unbearable response. Now I think it likely that his mother really *was* like this with my patient. Accordingly in the transference he perceived me in the same way. He was sure that I could not bear any demands from him, and he was certain I would drop him early on in treatment. After a time he began to feel that perhaps I would continue to treat him but only on condition that he was very compliant.

This was one aspect of the transference, but there was another. What was much more horrific for him was to discover that he was also identified with this hated object: to discover that as soon as I put some demands on him he would reject me. It then became clear that this hated figure or function was his own way of behaving, but obscured from his awareness. Therefore the question becomes: was this hated way of behaving a current aspect of himself or was it also the way his mother had actually behaved towards him? I believe that it is a combination of both: that there is an object part of the psychic structure that takes on the form of the external figure, in the same way that wax will take into itself the impression of a seal. This object part is then experienced as extraneous to the self, but at the same time the ego is identified with it; or rather, the ego becomes lured into the activities of this hated object, which Fairbairn called a 'bad internal object'. Therefore the analyst is perceived as the bad object, but he also becomes the recipient of the bad object's activity.

Source: Symington, 1986, p. 110

These clinical extracts show how someone can *become* different figures from their internal world, different aspects of object relations introjected long ago. The extracts also illustrate how hard patients work, unconsciously, at *using the object* – in this instance their analyst.

In Extract 4.1 the patient is unconsciously re-enacting with the analyst a painful event and *becomes* her 'object from the past', the rejecting other. In Extract 4.2 the patient re-creates the early situation with his mother. At first he is himself – as a child – and tries to make the analyst into someone (mother) who cannot bear his demands. But later he moves from this 'self representation' in the transference and instead *becomes* the object – the other person from the past. When his analyst made demands on him (*was* like his mother) the patient moved from *being* his child self to *become* his rejecting mother. So there are two aspects to this transference: first, the analyst is turned into the bad object, and then he is made into the rejected child self of the patient.

What were the communications in these two extracts? In Extract 4.1 the analyst is made to feel useless – the patient doesn't understand interpretations any more. The patient is unconsciously communicating her inability to continue the analytic relationship in which she has her father to herself. Her anxiety is that the analysis will end and she will feel abandoned as she did when her father died. In her conflict she is both taking the initiative and ending it herself (unconsciously and indirectly) and unconsciously asking for the outcome to be different this time, expressing a hope that this new relationship (with the analyst) will lead to a different outcome and some change (some degree of repair) in her internal world.

In Extract 4.2, the patient is unconsciously asking that his demands should be met by the analyst – something his mother could not manage. First he 'asks' in the way that he might have used as a child, by being a good boy; second, he 'asks' in a way that, in real life, would probably have had the opposite effect to that desired – being a bad boy, by *becoming* his rejecting mother. He rejects his analyst, unconsciously expressing the hurt and anger he felt as a child by making the analyst feel the way he had felt when rejected as a child.

These extracts illustrate transference communications; the processes that underpin unconscious communication of this kind will be explored in section 4.

The psychoanalyst has to keep in mind what it is that is being communicated – to what (unconscious) end. The force of these communications is such that one psychoanalyst has suggested :

> Every patient approaches an analyst with particular emotional expectations, and with the hope that the analyst will be able to respond to him or her in a way which was more satisfactory than the parents'. I think that in the initial consultation, therefore, every patient gives the analyst some instructions about how he or she wants him to function. In other words, the patient transfers on to the analyst all his or her developmental hopes…
>
> …the patient transfers on to the analyst responsibility for emotional development in a failed area.
>
> (Symington, 1986, pp. 110, 112)

What light can these psychoanalytic observations shed on relating and relationships in everyday life?

3.4 'Using' other people in everyday relationships

Transference as a communication – as an unconscious intention to *use the other* in some way – can be observed and experienced in everyday life. Much of the time, to varying degrees, we unconsciously choose others (certainly for our more important and personal relationships) primed with the same kinds of hopes and demands that patients bring to their analyses.

In ordinary life, our choices of other and the patterns of interaction are unlikely to be as clear as they are in the consulting room where the other is trained to observe and interpret rather than engage in the demands of the interaction. But refusals to collude can happen in ordinary interactions and relationships. Such refusals can be conscious, but often they happen without awareness on either part of what is going on. In ordinary relationships, two (or more) people often become mutually engaged in unconscious using of each other. Their unconscious demands might mesh with a beneficial outcome. More often, perhaps, this kind of unconscious fit will be damaging and lead to intense emotions and interaction cycles that escalate out of control.

ACTIVITY 4.6   Look back to the example of Diane and Stuart in section 2 and then try to think of other everyday examples of refusals to collude or of collusion and escalation.

Another person might be seen as (in fantasy or in unconscious phantasy) and induced to *be* a longed-for or a greatly-feared persecuting figure from the past. Another person might be 'made into' a part of the self in a past guise, such as an endlessly criticized child. In this instance the other might be cruelly and continually attacked verbally, with a stream of complaints about weaknesses and incompetence.

> The other person usually does have certain characteristics that trigger transferential communication. Does nagging occur irrespective of the nature of the other? Or do some people invite nagging – albeit unconsciously?

Some kinds of transferential use of the other that happen in everyday relationships may be easier to see (and perhaps easier to bear to look at) in the analytic setting. For example, an analyst might be 'turned into' unbearable parts of the patient's current self experience. A patient in an abusive marriage might say things (maybe sexual things) that *make the analyst feel abused* in some way. Outside the analytic setting this use of another person, to express or 'get rid of' or communicate pain in the hope of comfort, might engage and distress someone close to the couple. It might involve a child. Use of the other which makes the other feel and experience something for you will be discussed in section 4.

Some interactional manoeuvres are easier to understand than others. It is not difficult to imagine wanting to make another person *be* (a version of) a longed-for figure from the past. But the idea of turning a significant other into a *persecuting* figure from the past is not so easy to understand or accept. However, this is relatively common – especially in intense and sexual relationships where the intimacy might have elements of sado-masochism. It may be an occasional or partial aspect of the relationship. Or it may be a central feature that makes the relationship into an on-going battle, insidious or obvious. In an extreme form such a relationship almost always requires collusion from the other person. In less personal relationships, and usually in a milder form, this use of another is relatively common. For instance many people create 'monsters' – feared and judgemental others – out of teachers, bosses or religious mentors.

What about making the other person into a criticized part of one's own self? A relatively trivial example of this might be a man who makes an error at work and is criticized and humiliated, perhaps by his female colleagues. He might come home and enact this with his wife, criticizing her and making her feel like he had felt at work. But if the incident at work evoked childhood humiliations at the hands of his mother then a less than trivial quarrel might ensue, based on a transference. Such a man might relate to women in this way in general – making them feel incompetent at every opportunity.

When someone has had a physically and/or sexually abusive relationship in childhood, especially with a parent, this abusive way of relating can have a profound effect on adult relating. Sometimes the person may have difficulty in forming relationships at all. Sometimes the abusive relationship is re-created in reverse, with another person being abused and made to feel the disgust, humiliation and pain. This is a very extreme example of a process that most of us use, at least some of the time. We make use of others as recipients or receptacles for our own painful feelings, for the persecuting internal objects that we want to be rid of. This is a defensive function in which we expel the painful phantasies from the inner world on to real others in order to find relief. Often this relief is short lived since it now feels as if the 'persecuting, bad other is out there and still causing pain'. And, of course, the other person might refuse to take the projection, might refuse to be 'dumped on', blamed or abused. Then there might be a breakdown of the relationship or it might lead to continuing quarrels and escalation, depending on the unconscious and conscious agenda of the other person.

Most of the examples that we can identify in everyday relating are of transference of painful object relating because the process can be easily extracted from the flow of relatively successful relating, where the patterns of pleasure and reward are more simple. Some negative transferences may sound like serious psychological disturbance. And of course sometimes they are. We might consider them to be pathological if they are incessant, if they take over a relationship, if they are compulsively repeated, or prevent relationships even starting. And, clearly, they are going to have a much quicker and more dramatic effect on a relationship when they concern projections of bad internal objects than idealized ones. But, in the psychodynamic perspective on relating, all these processes have quite an ordinary place in everyday relationships. Most of them are relatively fluid and relatively benign. They either only make appearances now and then and in mild forms, or they constitute the relationship because they exist in forms that are mutually gratifying and self-expressive. Although transferences are largely unconscious, sometimes we do get a hint of what is happening. Sometimes we register the sudden intensity of a reaction or unexpected event that happens with a partner (after the event) and recognize that it is out of the ordinary. We can then do some reality testing and/or return relatively easily to the current reality of the other people around us in the relationships we are engaged in.

In the analytic setting, the to-ing and fro-ing of response and reaction in ordinary life is removed. This removal of real life contingencies and the neutrality of the analyst enables something else to emerge: Joseph (1985) described the force with which *use of the object* can happen.

> Much of our understanding of the transference comes through our understanding of how our patients act on us to feel things for many varied reasons; how they try to draw us into their defensive systems; how they unconsciously act out with us in the transference, trying to get us to act out with them; how they convey aspects of their inner world built up from infancy – elaborated in childhood and adulthood, experiences often beyond the use of words, *which we often can only capture through the feelings aroused in us, through our countertransference…*
>
> (Joseph, 1985, p. 447 emphasis added)

Joseph focuses on the idea that analysts *do* feel the pressure of the patient's demands, do have feelings in response to the transference. This whole internal response of the analyst is called countertransference. In section 4 we shall see that countertransference is a term used in different ways, a conception that, like transference, has changed dramatically since Freud's time, and that countertransference in the analytic setting can be used to understand processes of unconscious communication in relationships in general.

Review of section 3

- In object relations theories, internal representations of other people and relationships, largely from our early life, are what make up our selves. These internal objects and internal object relations are transferred into current relating.

- Relationships become the means to construct, repeat, express, defend, repair, modify and develop our internal objects and internal object relations – our selves.

- In Kleinian theory, transferences can be defences – getting rid of painful or frightening internal objects to reduce anxiety. In phantasy, these internal objects are projected into other people. This defensive process will have an effect on current relating and relationships.

- Transferences can be thought of as voices from internal worlds and unconscious requests to the other to *be* and to behave and feel in particular ways.

- What is transferred on to the other can be a version of the self, in a past guise, or the other from the past. Transference as unconscious communication demands a replay of the past relationship, a replay of the internal object relationship.

- Psychoanalysis provides the clearest evidence of transference and other unconscious processes. The kinds of evidence we have examined so far are analysts' observations of patients' behaviour and 'meaning data'.

- In ordinary life, we use others, unconsciously, in a variety of transferential ways. Mutual transferences may be beneficial; or they can bind people into collusive repeating cycles of destructive reciprocal behaviours.

4 Unconscious communication in relationships

In the last section we looked at modern views of transference and the part that transferences play in everyday relationships. There the focus was on the unconscious effect of the past on the present; now we re-focus on the minutiae of relating in the present and on what happens in the intersubjective space between two people. Intersubjectivity, between mothers and pre-verbal infants, was introduced in Chapter 3, section 2; here we shall examine the processes of unconscious communication through which adults (and children) influence each other and create intersubjectivity. Once again the psychoanalytic encounter supplies the evidence. So far (see Box 4.4 above) we have used evidence from external observations of patients' behaviours and patients' accounts, and the way that analysts convert these surface forms to meaning data. For the study of unconscious communication, we need to add another form of evidence: the analyst's experience (in all senses) of being a *receiver* for unconscious communications.

Most of us know, as ordinary humans who relate in everyday ways, that extraordinary and powerful things can happen in relationships, especially in intimate encounters. What *is* going on when a mother seems to understand and communicate with her baby without language? What *is* happening when we experience a sense of loss of separateness – a loss of boundaries – with another person, either momentarily or over a longer period of time? These are processes that cannot be fully studied from outside the interaction. They need to be observed *and experienced* by a participant who can receive the communications, make them conscious and then unpack what constitutes the processes. Psychoanalysts use their countertransference for this purpose.

4.1 What is countertransference?

Freud and his colleagues took the position that analysts are objective, observing (and correct) scientists who neither create transference nor in any other way impose their own subjectivity, including their own feelings and phantasies and conscious imaginings, onto the material.

Initially there was also an implicit notion that the analyst is not emotionally affected by the material – a blank screen in every sense. But a closer reading shows that Freud did not deny how difficult it can be for the analyst – a way of acknowledging that analysts are not immune to patients' feelings and communications. He believed that patients could unconsciously affect their analysts by resonating with something in the analyst's own unconscious; and that at a conscious level the analyst could and must monitor and then control and banish any feelings.

This suggests that Freud thought of countertransference as a contaminant to be eliminated; that the analyst should look within himself and find the parts of his own pathology that hinder the process of *objective* analysis.

You might wonder how this was to be done; and indeed if it is possible. Freud and others, notably Jung, began to insist that prospective analysts must be psychoanalysed themselves, a process of 'psychological purification' to eliminate 'blind spots.'

But Freud's comments on countertransference are contradictory. Elsewhere he seems to suggest that analysts can *make use of* their conscious feelings and unconscious processes *vis-à-vis* the patient's communications, providing great care is taken to discover why, and in what manner, the patient is able to affect their unconscious. In other words, they must be well analysed, have no blind spots and be continuously vigilant. Nevertheless, for a long time the overall attitude remained the same – that countertransference will happen, it might be helpful, but with care it can be minimized.

As the concept of transference changed, countertransference has been re-cast in a much more positive light. Why? Because, as we saw in the last section, the transfer of a wish or projection of a feared object implies a communication and/or an attempt to compel the other to *be* something, to say something, or to re-enact a way of relating – as a lover or a punitive father/teacher/mother. The patient, in making this unconscious communication, may enact, in very subtle and usually unconscious ways, the seducer or the frightened or passive or provocative or masochistic child/pupil etc. Once transference is recognized as communication, then psychoanalysis becomes a form of interpersonal psychology.

Do you think it is possible for a human being in an interactional setting, however contrived (as the analytic setting is), to be completely unaffected by the other person? Does it make any sense to think of psychology – in any form – as essentially *intra*psychic?

Since the mid 1950s it has been suggested by several analysts that countertransference can have diagnostic and therapeutic value; that analysts should monitor their own feelings and consider what effect the patient's particular attempts to relate are having. *When I am with this patient, at any given moment what am I feeling?* 'Feeling' here is used loosely; what is being suggested is that the analyst, as a human who is equipped, raised and practised in relating in ordinary life, can and should use these skills to act as a receiver for the patient's communication. Freud wrote: 'It is a very remarkable thing that the unconscious of one human being can react upon that of another, without passing through the consciousness' (Freud, 1915, p. 194).

For most modern analysts, countertransference has become a major diagnostic tool and a guide to therapeutic intervention. In this view, countertransference encompasses all the analyst's reactions and feelings and thoughts and fantasies: '...the analyst's emotional response to his patient within the analytic situation represents one of the most important tools for his work. The analyst's countertransference is an instrument of research into his patient's unconscious' (Heimann, 1950, p. 81).

It is important to note that not all analysts take this view. And, in any case, a crucial problem remains. What can justifiably be counted as useful countertransference and what remains part of the analyst's pathology? How can you ever know what belongs to the patient and what to the analyst? How can the analyst ever know?

Of course another caveat remains: that analysts will monitor themselves for emotional and physiological reactions, for imagery, for their own free associations *but not act upon them.* The only permissible action is a thera-peutic 'speech act'. After thought, and sometimes after a 'cooling down period' in which the feelings subside, and only when the patient is judged to be able to use what is said, the analyst can make an interpret-ation. The analyst formulates and describes, in as neutral a tone as poss-ible, what the patient seems to be doing/communicating, or the way of relating that the patient is demanding, whether consciously or uncon-sciously, verbally or by any other means *in the present*, and links it to what is known or hypothesized about the past.

In this interpersonal approach, transference and countertransference can-not be separated, they are a reciprocal process of unconscious communi-cation; illustrations of the process are presented in Extracts 4.3 and 4.4 below.

Extract 4.3

One patient, over a certain period, used to fall into a deep sleep in the course of the analytic hour. I kept my patience and was fascinated by this phenomenon. At a certain moment, however, I became aware of thoughts like 'suppose that now something crashes to the floor with a bang', or if I were to cry: 'Hey, wake up!' Then I realized: of course, he wants me to get angry. After that I became aware of a slight feeling of irritation. From this point the interpretation could be given. I did not have to get angry, but could say: 'Could it be your intention to irritate me by falling asleep?' My patient was suddenly wide awake, sat up, raised his hand and said: 'Ah, but now you must have felt something'. I replied that I could imagine the possibility. Then the patient's keen insight in the analysis became obvious: he lay down again, stretched comfortably and said 'Analysis is a fine job, isn't it? Unconsciously I want to irritate you. And you get a bit angry, but you do not abreact your anger on me – you use that feeling to show me that I want to make you angry, and now I feel that this is really true. My father always got angry with me immediately.'

Source: De Blecourt, 1993, p. 763

Extract 4.4

I found myself in a curious position when Helen, a woman in her mid-twenties, started her analysis. She would begin to describe a situation, such as going to meet a friend, and then she would stop her account in mid-sentence. She would pause for a long time, often as much as several minutes, and the she would resume her account as if there had been no interruption. Initially I focused, as I always do with someone new to analysis with me, on how difficult it was to speak to a stranger and how hard it was to entrust the simplest things to him. Her anxiety about being in the analytic situation was very apparent, and this interpretation of the transference was necessary and to some degree accurate. But nevertheless, her long pauses continued, and I knew I had not fully understood the situation...

I knew I would have to settle into this situation and accept it as the sort of environment she creates in which both she and her objects live. Increasingly I asked myself how I felt as an object of such a transference.

I knew that I felt irritated on occasions, but equally I felt that there was no way in which to utilize this irritation for some kind of alteration of the environment. As it was very difficult for me to follow her line of thinking, because of the many interruptions and long pauses, I was aware of being confused by her. I found as the months passed that I would 'wander off' during these pauses, and when she would resume talking it might be a few seconds before I had returned to listen...

I thought a lot about what this might all mean within the transference-countertransference idiom, and I entertained the idea that she might be transferring to the analytic situation the nature of her mother's idiom of maternal care, and that I – the infant-object of such a care system – was an existential witness to a very strange and absent mother. I decided that the material expressive of the patient's mental life was now in me, insofar as my countertransference began to dominate the clinical situation, at least in my mind. I knew I would have to find some way to make the material available to her. After several months of analysis, when I thought the patient was ready to receive an indirect expression of my countertransference, I told her that I was aware of something taking place in me that I thought was of interest, and I wanted to put it to her for reflection and ultimately for analysis. I proceeded to tell her that her long pauses left me in a curious state, one in which I sometimes lost track of her, and it seemed to me that she was creating some kind of absence that I was meant to experience. A bit later in the session I said to her that she seemed to disappear and reappear without announcement of either action.

The patient was immediately relieved when I spoke up for my own subjective state. She said that she had long known about this habit, but she did not understand it herself, since it was not occasioned by anxiety, and that she would often experience a kind of despair about being inside this habit, frequently wondering if there was any point in continuing to talk.

In speaking up for the situation I found myself in, I was also aware of my own personal relief. No analyst should only interpret in order to relieve himself of the psychic pain he may be in, but equally neither should he be ignorant of those interpretations that cure him of the patient's effect. In making my experience available to the patient, I put in the clinical potential space a subjective scrap of material that was created by the patient, and by expressing myself I gave a bit of something of Helen's self back to her.

In the first year of her analysis, Helen was extremely secretive about her relation to her mother, and I did not push her … When she was clearly ready to do so, she told me how distracted and otherworldly her mother was, and how the mother had only been able to relate to a small portion of her as a child, leaving Helen to live through her childhood in secrecy and in dread of her true self. Her mother's impingement on her true self was her absence from relating, just as, I suppose, I experienced Helen's silences and absences as impingements in the clinical situation. This was not the case of a daughter hating her mother or of a mother being a hateful person. She was a kindly and loving woman who, nevertheless, absented herself from her children's lives for a number of reasons and left each of her several children severely confused.

Source: Bollas, 1987, pp. 211–14

There is considerable controversy about whether an analyst or thera-pist should ever, in any form, disclose countertransference thoughts or feelings to the patient. Countertransference can be used without any disclosure by wording interpretations in an abstract, and hypo-thetical way.

It is the analyst's restraint and constant self-monitoring that is so differ-ent from interactions in ordinary life. Participants in everyday interac-tions commonly express their feelings, either verbally or by giving vent to their emotions, or by some action. This kind of 'giving back' is thought by some to be part of being 'authentic' (see *Reading D: 'A humanistic approach to relationships'* by Richard Stevens at the end of the book). Many people, including some couples therapists, assume that this is a beneficial process of feedback. We are urged to communicate and talk about our communications (metacommunication). But it is not easy to be fully aware of what is going on in an interaction in which you are an engaged participant. Also, since much that passes between people is unconscious and is unconsciously reacted to, it can be very difficult to negotiate what is happening, or to intervene in the spirals of expectations and emotions that often ensue. 'Giving back' can be detrimental. In psychoanalysis, because one of the participants is trained to stop to think rather than spontaneously engage, he or she can avoid colluding with the patient's compulsive patterns of relating, and can break the expectation of validation that the patient has met, and may still be meeting, in the external world.

4.2   Studying unconscious communication

Psychodynamic clinicians are prepared to accept evidence that is rather different from that used by other scientists who have studied communication and relating, in humans or animals. Because of this, psychoanalysts have gone much further in their attempts to understand the capacity of the unconscious mind to act as a receiver for unconscious communications from another person.

At this point you might want to look back to the methods that were used in   ACTIVITY 4.7
the studies of interaction described in Chapter 2 and in *Reading C:* 'The
experimental study of relationships' by Argyle at the end of the book. Try to
make a list of the main categories of method and the kinds of data that each
method generates. Are these methods equally useful for studying all kinds of
interaction? Or is it necessary to use different methods for different levels of
intimacy such as social relationships, personal relationships, short and long-term
relationships?

Processes of unconscious communication are not well understood, but it is important that they are treated as phenomena which are open to rigorous study – albeit by methods that are not always acceptable to traditional science. These processes may be mysterious but they are not mystical. They are not ESP; they are based, ultimately, on sense data (often received unconsciously). In so far as these can be made conscious, they can be converted by conscious thought to meaning data (see Box 4.5).

Part of the mystery lies in the sheer amount of information and the subtlety of the cues that pass between people, most at an unconscious level. It is commonly accepted that a great deal of complex information reaches our senses without any awareness; and that this is especially true during social interactions with others. This has been studied within a more conventional scientific paradigm (Lewicki, 1986). But what happens to this information? Might it be processed and stored and/or inform some 'out of awareness' response? Sometimes one is aware of registering something and immediately losing it from consciousness, but if reminded later there is a sense of 'yes I did see that'. Unconscious communication can involve this ordinary 'out of awareness' that is associated with much cognitive processing, but it also includes the more organized, motivational aspects of the psychodynamic unconscious. Unconscious communication may be driven by plans and goals that are temporarily out of awareness, but more often it is driven by unconscious motivations such as forbidden desires, defences, unconscious phantasies and many other attempts to establish, maintain, or repair the self.

BOX 4.5   The psychoanalytic 'laboratory'.

Part Three – the analyst's own feelings and reactions

Psychoanalysts observe patients directly (see Box 4.4) and *indirectly* through their countertransference experiences. Analysts are available as receivers of conscious and unconscious communications and projections, thus using their own minds and bodies as tools.

> …What distinguishes this relationship from others, is not the presence of feelings in one partner, the patient, and their absence in the other, the analyst, but above all the degree of the feelings experienced and the use made of them, these factors being interdependent. The aim of the analyst's own analysis, from this point of view, is not to turn him into a mechanical brain which can produce interpretations on the basis of a purely intellectual procedure, but to enable him, to *sustain* the feelings which are stirred in him, as opposed to discharging them (as does the patient), in order to *subordinate* them to the analytic task in which he functions as the patient's mirror reflection.
>
> *(Heimann, 1950, pp. 81–2)*

Countertransference reactions produce sense data: sensations of sleepiness, sadness, irritation, feeling threatened or humiliated, sudden impulses to comfort, or retaliate with attacking remarks. And there are patients whose sessions correlate with somatization in the analyst – headaches or stomach pain. Such reactions in the analyst are initially largely unconscious. They have to be brought into consciousness, monitored and thought about. These responses in the analyst are the result of patients' unconscious attempts to relate in the transference in particular ways. For example, many analysts have experienced and written about countertransference feelings of sleepiness and inability to concentrate when the patient is (consciously or unconsciously) withholding important, that is, emotionally charged, material. There is also a frequently reported phenomenon of countertransference 'at one remove'. Detailed reports of what happens in a session (written or recorded) have been read out or played back to supervision groups – without interpretation or the analyst's self-report on countertransference. It has been found that members of the group often experience the same feelings, the same anxiety, the same sleepiness etc. as the analyst (see Joseph, 1985; and Tansey and Burke, 1989).

4.3   Processes underlying unconscious communication

The unconscious processes that are involved in transference/countertransference centre on the concept of identification. Identification involves some loosening of the boundaries between self and other to permit experiences of *being* aspects of the other, either fleetingly or for longer periods. And this experience of *being* the other is a large part of the process of entering each other's subjectivity – the creation of intersubjectivity.

4.3.1   Imitation and identification

Imitation can be consciously contrived, but it also has an unconscious and almost compulsive form. How often have you found yourself watching someone intently and imitating their facial expressions or their movements? Mothers imitate their babies as often as they are imitated, in an automatic, irresistible way. This kind of imitation seems to be a primitive, preverbal way of communicating a 'sameness', by creating sufficient likeness to the other in gesture, expression, movement and position to evoke in the self an emotional state or intention which belongs to the other. The analyst Joseph Sandler has described this identification:

> ...One sees it best perhaps at a children's cinema performance ... where the motions of the hero on horseback seem to be mirrored in the involuntary movements of the children in the audience. I want to stress that this is a completely automatic and reflex effect. I want to emphasize too, that this is a process that occurs all the time in everyone ... we cannot perceive a movement or an expression in another without unconsciously duplicating it in ourselves, although the duplication will be well below the threshold of conscious experience. Indeed if we did not have an effective mechanism to inhibit this tendency we should find ourselves madly duplicating the behaviour and feelings of everyone around us, a phenomenon of confusion between 'self' and 'other' which we can often observe in one form or another in hospitalized and deteriorated schizophrenics, in whom the capacity to differentiate 'self' from 'other' has been weakened or lost.
>
> *(Sandler, 1993, pp. 1101–2)*

Sandler uses the term *primary identification* for temporary identification with another person which ends with an easy separation of self and other, that is, an easy disidentification. He draws attention to the developmental function of primary identifications: from infancy they provide a route to learning about others and eventually to a more permanent kind of identification, called *secondary identification*, which creates self-representations and constitutes identity.

4.3.2   Internalization, introjection and introjective identification

Internalization is a general term for the process by which features of the external world become represented in a relatively enduring form in the internal world. Introjection is a more specific term which tends to be kept for the 'wholesale' internalization of versions of other people and of their relationships. When internal objects and internal object relations are referred to as introjects this emphasizes the 'having been taken in as an entity' and 'available for use as an entity' – a chunking of information to form the building blocks of intrapsychic structure and constructing the self. Introjects are potentially available for identification – introjective identification – although they may not be identified with but kept encapsulated, sometimes for defensive reasons. They may be identified with in a transient way, briefly becoming a part of the self; or they may become merged with the self representations through secondary identification to become an enduring part of the self. During interactions, the same processes of introjection and introjective identification occur *from moment to moment,* usually with far less effect on internal objects and the sense of self. In interaction, according to Tansey and Burke (1989), what is taken in and identified with can be 'models of the self and other(s) in interaction'. These models can be constantly updated by the ongoing interaction, a continuous interpersonal process of transient introjective identifications.

In psychoanalytic countertransference these transient introjective identifications enable the analyst to 'know' what it is that the patient is making available (through the transference) to be 'known', what it is that the patient is forcing into the analyst – using the unconscious process of projective identification.

4.3.3   Projective identification

We have seen that projection is essentially a defence mechanism. It may refer to externalization of an internal conflict such as in Klein's psychoanalytic work with children, where the enactment of conflictful relationships projected into toys relieved the child of anxiety (see Box 4.3). Projection may also refer to the mechanism of locating in the external world one's own inadmissible impulses such as aggression. Klein went on to develop another, related concept – that of projective identification.

In projective identification, a part of the self is projected along with the bad internal object so that the projector feels 'mixed up' with the recipient of the projection and achieves some feeling of control over what is being projected and over the recipient. According to Klein, projection and projective identification are primitive defence mechanisms used to get rid of bad internal objects *in phantasy;* they are intrapsychic and do not involve communication with others *in reality.* Projective identification of this kind is sometimes called first stage projective identification. It has been gradually replaced by a concept which is similar, but has direct *interactional effects:* second stage projective identification. The projector has the phantasy of getting rid of something painful, an unwanted internal object or an unwanted part of the self, by projecting it and depositing it in another person with whom she or he is *actually interacting*. Then, through unconscious interactional efforts, the projector influences the recipient to 'think, feel and behave in a manner congruent with the ejected feelings and self and object representations...' (Ogden, 1982, p. 2).

4.3.4 Projective identification as unconscious communication

In second stage, interpersonal projective identification real pressures, albeit unconscious, are exerted by the projector in the interaction. The recipient may be unconscious or only partially conscious of what is happening. An example is given by Ogden (1979). The projector is a patient on a ward and the recipients are the other people around her, especially her therapist.

> A 12 year old in-patient, who as an infant had been violently intruded upon psychologically and physically, highlights this aspect of projective identification. The patient said and did almost nothing on the ward, but made her presence powerfully felt by perpetually jostling and bumping into people, especially her therapist. This was generally experienced as infuriating by other patients and by the staff. In the therapy hours (often a play therapy), her therapist said that he felt as if there were no space in the room for him. Everywhere he stood seemed to be her spot. This form of interaction represents a form of object relationship wherein the patient puts pressure on the therapist to experience himself as inescapably intruded upon.
>
> *(Ogden, 1979, p. 359)*

One of the functions of this interpersonal form of projective identification seems to be the creation in another person of a state of mind as a means of communicating with the other person about this state of mind (Hinshelwood, 1991, p. 184).

4.4 Empathy and intersubjectivity

In this section, the interpersonal transference/countertransference process is used to unpack the intersubjective process of empathy. We shall take the perspective of the analyst's countertransference, shifting the focus from the unconscious communications of the projector (patient) to the unconscious and increasingly-made-conscious processing of the recipient (analyst).

Whilst it is not usual in ordinary relating for one of the participants to monitor the effect of the other's unconscious communication, it is possible. Individual and couples therapy can encourage participants to 'hold' the feelings that are induced in them by the other and to think about them before reacting and enacting. This is a rather different viewpoint from what is often endorsed – that we should express our feelings and be 'authentic'.

Countertransference includes all the reactions the analyst has to the patient. These include simple trial identifications with the patient; or the receipt of projective identifications from the patient, followed by trial introjective identification on the part of the analyst. In both cases, the final stage is a disidentification which allows the analyst to think consciously about what is happening. The subjective experience of these stages is usually a holistic feeling of empathy (Tansey and Burke, 1989). Empathy has been defined by Schafer as '...the inner experience of sharing in and comprehending the momentary psychological state of another person' (Schafer, 1959, p. 345). However, in psychoanalysis, empathy in itself is not sufficient. It has to be translated into words. It has to be an interpretation in *empathic and intellectual* terms which will relieve the patient and/or provide clarification and a spur to think and process more deeply, leading to change – the so-called mutative interpretation. By understanding this through the 'unpacking and making conscious' processes that psychoanalysts need to use, we can learn more about empathy and empathic communications in general.

In psychoanalysis, to achieve an empathic outcome and a good interpretation, it is crucial that analysts do not remain caught up in the identifications, unconscious of the boundary between themselves and their patients; disidentification is essential. The re-establishment of the boundary between two participants enables the analyst to begin to *think about the patient* rather than *think and feel with the patient* (Beres and Arlow, 1974).

> When the analyst becomes aware that the mood or thoughts he has been experiencing represent commentaries on the patient's material, he has made the transition from simple identification to empathic comprehension. If the analyst fails to take that step and remains in the state of identification, he is sympathetic but not empathic ... *Thinking with the patient is quite different from thinking about the patient.*
>
> (Arlow, 1993, p.1149, emphasis added)

The feelings associated with trial identifications, providing that they remain temporary and controlled, can be used as 'signal affects' (Schafer, 1959) that inform the analyst about the inner experience of the patient. For example: '...a patient arrives for his session and begins to sob over the sudden death of a beloved pet on whom he has relied for several years as a companion. In response, the therapist notes in himself a growing feeling of sadness and a suppressed impulse to cry' (Tansey and Burke, 1989, p. 61). In examples like this, a trial identification with the feeling state of another can lead to an empathic outcome with relatively little processing, so long as the analyst is not submerged in his own painful feelings about loss and can still disidentify. Where analyst and patient feel the same feeling, as in this example, it is often called *concordant identification* (Racker, 1957). However, concordant identification *can* lead to a failure of empathy if the disidentification does not follow. Suppose the sad feeling state of the other was continuous and all pervasive, as opposed to the discrete instance of sadness following a bereavement, then the analyst's trial identification could become overwhelming and fail to reach an empathic outcome. For example, working over a long period with a patient who feels hopeless, the analyst might unconsciously identify with the patient and experience the work with the patient as a state of hopelessness, leading to countertransference turmoil.

Disturbing, even painful, countertransference is more common when a patient uses projective identification. Here the patient is not only communicating an emotional state but using this communication unconsciously to control the analyst. The intensity of the projection will depend on the clinical state of the patient. What the analyst experiences can be very unpleasant and difficult to disidentify from and process empathically. For example:

> …a patient begins the session with a scathing criticism of the therapist's office decor, noting with sarcasm the lack of sophistication in various paintings and the incongruence between types of furniture. Under the continuous pressure of this criticism, the therapist recalls the time when he selected his office furnishings and remembers his feelings of inadequacy in coordinating various pieces. His reawakened sense of incompetence grows as the patient's critical eye moves from one item in the office to another. The therapist's experience gradually shifts to a feeling of anger toward the patient.
>
> *(Tansey and Burke, 1989, p. 61)*

This kind of identification more commonly leads to disturbing countertransference. It is called *complementary identification* (Racker, 1957) because *both* sides of the object relationship that preoccupies the patient are involved. Identification can shift from one side of the dimension to the other. The sado-masochistic object relationship is one of the clearest examples: in the clinical illustration above, the analyst's identification moves from 'victim' towards 'aggressor'. This can happen, in the same way, in ordinary life. Someone with a sado-masochistic preoccupation, whose life and relationships in general are organized in these terms, will be familiar with *both* sides of the relationship 'victim' and 'aggressor', because of childhood experiences of this dimension of relating. Such a person will have introjects of a sadistic object and of a masochistic object, and of sado-masochistic object relations. The person's self-representation may have been consolidated as essentially 'victim' or 'aggressor', or it may oscillate between the two depending on circumstances. Such a person might, in an interaction, unconsciously work hard to elicit critical responses and provoke anger (*being* the 'victim' and making the other the 'aggressor'); but equally the interactional effort might be to *be* the aggressor and make the other feel victimized. In ordinary life we are quite likely to be drawn in, rather than being able to disidentify from our own countertransference identifications and use the emotional insight (a mixture of feeling and intellectually knowing) for empathic understanding of what is going on.

Review of section 4

- The study of unconscious communication requires a receiver – someone who is a participant but at the same time is only partially engaged in the interaction. Psychoanalysts use their countertransference reactions as tools for understanding, but in ordinary life this level of monitoring is rare.

- The processes involved in unconscious communication centre on the concept of identification.

- Introjections of other people can be identified with temporarily – from moment to moment – or longer term. This can happen during interactions leading to a continuous interpersonal process of transient 'cross over' of self and other.

- Longer term identifications may become part of the self-representation.

- Kleinian projective identification is a defence mechanism that involves getting rid of unwanted internal objects and parts of the self – in phantasy. It is intrapsychic, not a communication, although it may have an effect on others.

- In communicative projective identification, the projector, through unconscious interactional efforts, influences the thoughts, feelings and behaviour of the recipient so that they become congruent with what has been ejected. Its function is to create in the other a particular state of mind as a way of communicating with the other about this state of mind. This is the essence of intersubjectivity.

- The subjective experience of intersubjectivity is empathy.

- Concordant identification is when one person experiences the same state of mind as the other. In complimentary identification, usually the outcome of projective identification, person and other experience reciprocal aspects of a way of relating.

5   The relational mind

The use of the psychodynamic perspective to examine relationships suggests that our capacity to relate, and our continuing need to relate, are not to do with survival in a physical sense but about something else – something that only other people in close relationships can provide. Whatever it is, this seems to be an essential feature of our humanness, and invites speculation about the structure of human minds. This final section discusses several ways in which the human mind might be thought of as relational.

The process of psychoanalysis has revealed, through transference, how other people and their ways of relating are represented in our internal worlds in many versions, not necessarily accurate and certainly adjusted by phantasy. This lively 'dramatis personae', introjected as entities from our experiences of others, functions as a series of templates and scripts for relating, remaining available throughout life for casting in various dramas. *We are made up of other people.* We live out their voices and their ways of relating, in various combinations and permutations. Some of these voices stabilize into self-representations; some are more fleeting, elicited by situations, by particular others, and in particular relationships. This view of a relational mind is derived from object relations theory and, to a lesser extent, Kleinian and Jungian psychodynamics. It is very different from notions of personality as biologically and temperamentally constituted, although the two approaches are not incompatible. The relational mind is somewhat compartmentalized: self experience is more fragmented, labile, and perhaps situation-specific and other-specific than is generally conveyed by cultural representations of selfhood. Effort is required to maintain a sense of identity and continuity and to construct a coherent narrative by which to live.

Central to this approach to the relational mind is the idea that it is introjections of other people and ways of relating – that form in infancy and early childhood when language has not yet developed or is very limited – that are the raw materials of our selves. It is these primitive building blocks that stay with us, and exert a largely unconscious effect on our relationships and our lives more generally. These building blocks tend to hold their original emotional charge – early emotions are resurrected in new settings (transferred), often in polarized and *primitive* forms.

In western culture, 'primitive' is a somewhat pejorative word. And this chapter has demonstrated that interactions and relationships have a large unconscious component which can indeed have unpleasant and compulsive effects on our lives. Things happen that are 'primitive' in the sense of being emotional, non-verbal, body-related and not available to conscious reflection and rationality. But unconscious communication – a primitive form of mutual influence – can transmit effective and complex messages about our selves, our needs, our states of mind and about relating, and can carry important messages about the nature of a particular relationship.

You might like to compare this psychodynamic approach to unconscious communication as a way of defining a relationship with the
discussion in Chapter 2, section 7 of some of Goffman's ideas.
Goffman distinguished between what is 'given' and what is 'given
off'. And he also used the idea of displays which ' ...don't communicate in the narrow sense of the word ... They provide evidence of the
actor's alignment in the situation...' (Goffman, 1976, p 69).

The processes described in this chapter as unconscious communication
are also 'primitive' in that we begin life equipped with the capacity to
communicate in this way. Before conscious thought and language,
infants use unconscious communication to gain direct access to other
minds. This is the start of intersubjectivity and the beginning of the process of relating. The study of the primitive modes of communication has
been largely confined to how intersubjectivity is established very early in
life through the cross-over of emotional states between mother and
infant (see Chapter 3, section 2). Trevarthen (1993) explored how intersubjectivity between mothers and their pre-verbal infants is achieved and
the distress that follows when it breaks down. But the use of unconscious
communications – with or without the addition of language – continues
into adulthood as an effective means of transmitting complex messages.
These messages are received unconsciously but provoke emotional states
which can have a considerable influence on mind, and behaviour. (For a
discussion of these largely unconscious outcomes of the use of language
from a different point of view – that of discourse analysis – see Potter,
1996.)

Why has the study of unconscious communication (outside the psychodynamic perspective) been restricted to infants and mothers? Most adults
would accept that they have experienced identification and projective
identification – mix ups with other identities, the establishment of intersubjectivity, the pleasure and excitement of this kind of intimacy and the
'oddness' and the pain of its breakdown *in adult relationships*. The lack of
attention to these unconscious processes is partly due to methodological
difficulties – for those outside the psychodynamic paradigm. But it is also
because of the pejorative slant of the term 'primitive'. And perhaps it is
because human reliance on others for well-being tends to be diminished
in a culture where individual autonomy and boundedness is valued.
From the standpoint of the relational mind, if we ignore (and/or deplore)
primitive processes of imitation, introjection, identification and projective identification, and the unconscious nature of a large part of communication between humans, then we rule out of court much of the
vital part that other people and relationships can play in the modification of internal worlds, with and without the medium of language
itself. Humans *need* other people in a profound way. The relational mind
is made up of other people and relationships (see also Wetherell and
Maybin, 1996; Morgan and Thomas, 1996). It can be supported, repaired
and changed essentially through the intervention of other minds. And
other minds can be used in defensive manoeuvres to maintain selves. Of
course, the conscious, rational, informational content of the world has a

part to play; but coping with strong emotions, creating new 'frames' on the world, and structural changes in the self need the containment of other minds and the introjection of new voices, new or modified versions of who to be and how to be.

Evidence from the analytic setting has shown how patients use their analysts to express and to communicate parts of the self in the transference relationship. Projective identification in this sense has been described as the patient's interactional efforts to induce in the analyst 'aspects of his [the patient's] own inner states, so as to externally manage them and to evoke adaptive responses for reintrojection' (Langs, 1976, p. 277). This is an example of using a relationship – using another mind – to help cope with emotions and modify the internal world. In the context of psychoanalysis with disturbed patients, projective identification is likely to be urgent, intense and disturbing; but it is now clear that, as a means of communication, it is used quite commonly in ordinary interactions, especially in close relationships. Using other people's minds seems to be a general psychological process by which painful feelings can be got rid of, as when a child in distress uses its mother. The unconscious intent of the projective identification seems to be to force the other person to give feedback about the state of mind that has been communicated, to modify the projection and return it in a form that can be reintrojected and 'more easily digested' by the original projector. This model of intersubjectivity is known as the *container-contained*. Jung used the idea in an early discussion of marriage partners (Jung, 1925), and it is best known in the version described by Bion (Bion, 1962).

When people in close relationships use each other in these kinds of ways – mostly unconsciously – one of the participants may be 'obviously' the one that is learning or the one that is distressed, or seeking support. But the processes will affect both. Again, this kind of mutual transformation is a phenomenon that many of us have experienced. But, again, it is in the analytic setting that it has been studied, and discussed. The primary function of the psychoanalytic encounter is to provide a relationship through which change can occur. The analyst can try to expand the consciousness of the other by bringing into consciousness unconscious processes and motivations – increasing awareness and information. But the analyst is also available to be used for the creation of an intersubjective space in which *new* ideas, *new* identifications and the cross-over of knowledge can occur. This is an example of the use of one mind for the expansion of the other. In Jungian analysis, the analytic encounter has been called a crucible – because *both* the participants who engage in this level of interaction and intersubjectivity must emerge changed to some degree.

BOX 4.6   The crucible

In Jungian analysis, the metaphor of the analytic setting as a crucible highlights the idea of a vessel within which two people produce something new, whilst both are changed by the experience. It is a mysterious process which has unfortunately been further mystified by misreadings of Jung's elaborate discussion of mediaeval philosophy and the alchemical metaphor. Jung was one of the first analysts to suggest that it is not possible for one person, in the analytic encounter or any other close encounter, to influence another without also being changed.

> ...psychotherapy is not the simple, straightforward method that people at first believed it to be, but, as has gradually become clear, a kind of dialectical process, a dialogue or discussion between two persons. Dialectic was originally the art of conversation among the ancient philosophers, but very early became the term for the process of creating new syntheses. A person is a psychic system which, when it affects another person, enters into reciprocal reaction with another psychic system...
>
> *(Jung, 1935, para 1)*

Much more recently, Symington has written

> ...the emotional upheaval of the very first encounter changes the two participants, who will never be the same again. I also believe that a new entity is forged; a new reality emerges. The two people do not remain independent entities ... analyst and patient are sucked into each other's worlds. When two people meet there is a new world-being. This is because the other person is not just an object like a stone, a plant or an animal, but *because the knowingness of one is in the world of the knowingness of the other's knowingness. This allows a special knowledge between human beings.*
>
> *(Symington, 1986, p. 30 emphasis added)*

The analytic setting is unusual in that a great deal of time is given to explorations of what is newly formed in the intersubjective space between the two participants; and the setting provides a safe container for these ideas to be thought about. But in ordinary life the same processes of mutual change occur, even if we do not ordinarily spend time thinking and talking about them. There are occasions in ordinary life when this kind of exploration and the intensity of the experience of intersubjectivity is central to the relationship – intimate sexual relationships are perhaps the obvious example, but other close friendships can also have this quality. The idea of the relational mind emphasizes the general point that other minds are the means to achieve structural change in internal worlds and the self.

In this section so far, speculations about the relational mind have focused on the psychodynamic version: introjections, identifications and unconscious processing. But there are links between this version of a relational mind and somewhat similar movements in other areas of psychology. A recognized characteristic of the human mind is its ability to model other minds, although this skill is usually thought of in terms of rational, conscious, information processing. The aim of these skills is thought of as learning about other people's view of the world in order to be able to predict their plans and intentions. These models can be specific to another person in an interaction or relationship, or can be about other people in general.

Attribution theory, which is discussed in Chapter 3, section 3 of this book, and parts of Kelly's personal construct theory, especially the sociality construct (see Chapter 3, section 3.1.2), are versions of this approach, although from very different theoretical perspectives.

It is only by learning how to take on other people's views of the world and infer their intentional states that social life can proceed. Piaget, Mead and others have studied the development of this process. Where there are deficits in this ability, as perhaps in autism, social encounters are very difficult, and the development of selfhood is impaired.

The philosopher, Dennett (1987), believes that modelling other minds is what characterizes humans, and to develop this skill, assumptions have to be made about intentionality in others – *the intentional stance*. By this he means that we have to believe that other people have beliefs and desires that can be used to deduce their intentions (see also Freud, 1915, p. 169; Wollheim, 1993). In this view we also have to assume that people are rational – in the sense that they will maximize good outcomes where possible and are capable of following simple logical propositions. (This does not imply that they necessarily have to be conscious of the rules they are using, or able to articulate the rules of logic.) The psychodynamic approach to the relational mind draws on different processes – the crossover of emotional states, and projective identification as an unconscious communicative process. It may be that these methods are particularly important as a starting point – in infancy and perhaps in the earliest stages of relationships when little mutual knowledge of the other can be articulated. Thereafter, modelling of the other's mind can be built on further identificatory 'crossovers' *and* the use of language *and* more ordinary sources of information. Once the process of modelling another person's mind begins, then communication of all kinds can take a leap forward in complexity.

Outside the psychodynamic paradigm another approach to the relational mind is the increasing focus, in many areas of psychology and artificial intelligence, on the embedded and dynamic nature of our internal representations. Robotics emphasizes continuous modelling and re-modelling of the world *in relation to* actions on the world and their outcomes. There is a revival of interest in some of the ideas of Piaget and others that *static* representations of the external world are not our primary experience. Instead, as the world is experienced, it is modelled provisionally and dynamically *in relation to* actions on and interactions with the world. Whilst robotics might need to concentrate on the physical world, for humans it is the social world of other people that is most salient, rewarding and complex. Other people *are* the environment for the early, dynamic structuring of the mind. Several psychologists and psychodynamic theorists have suggested, each in their own particular vocabularies, that ways of relating to other people and ways of being related to – interactional structures – are the dynamic units of psychic organization and the building blocks of the core self (Emde, 1988; Fast, 1992; Schank and Abelson, 1977; Stern, 1985). Thus, the world and the objects in it (primarily the people) are represented internally, at least at first, as the sources and outcomes of particular modes of interaction – tenderly, lovingly, cruelly, fearfully. This is close to object relations theory and Kleinian multiple representations of objects and self-fragments where each is qualified or characterized by adjectives that refer to actions, effects and functions – 'nourishing mother and full-fed self'; 'exciting mother and agitated self'; 'critical father and humiliated self'. Versions of objects and selves emerge from engagements in a series of *interactional events*, are then multiply represented and later activated by particular situations; although over time this level of differentiation reduces to more integrated images. This 'event structure' view of the rela-tional mind is suggestive of our fascination with narrative.

The concept of relational mind encapsulates much of what is essentially human: our long period of development and dependence, hand in hand with our capacities for symbolization, including modelling other minds, intersubjectivity, and communication. It highlights what seem to be intrinsic rewards of intimacy and the importance of the initial 'programmers', and the relational and interactional context in which infants and children exist. And it emphasizes our need for others *and* how and why it is so.

Further reading

Symington, N. (1986) *The Analytic Experience*, London, Free Association Books. This is an excellent introduction to the psychodynamic way of thinking, easily accessible, with many clinical examples.

Bollas, C. (1987) *The Shadow of the Object*, London, Free Association Books. This is another beautifully written book on the psychoanalytic encounter. It is a more advanced discussion, again with clinical vignettes and it concentrates on an object relations approach.

For those who are particularly interested in the developmental approach to relating and the self, it is worth reading about Trevarthen's research first hand: Trevarthen, C. (1993) 'The function of emotions in early infant communication' in Nadel, J. and Camaioni, L. (eds), *New Perspectives in Early Communicative Development*, London, Routledge. Stern, D. (1985) *The Interpersonal World of the Infant*, New York, Basic

Books, makes some crucial links between psychoanalytic ideas and modern developmental psychology. This fascinating book is highly recommended by everyone.

If you need to check the meaning of some psychoanalytic concepts, there are several useful dictionaries: Rycroft, C. (1968) *A Critical Dictionary of Psychoanalysis*, London, Penguin, is the most basic one. Laplanche, J. and Pontalis, J.B. (1988) *The Language of Psychoanalysis*, London, Karnac Books, is the classic, more advanced dictionary. There are also two specialized ones. The first concerns Kleinian terminology: Hinshelwood, R.D. (1991) *A Dictionary of Kleinian Thought*, London, Free Association Books. The second is a dictionary of Jungian concepts: Samuels, S., Shorter, B., and Plaut, F. (1986) *A Critical Dictionary of Jungian Analysis,* London and New York, Routledge and Kegan Paul.

Those who are interested in relationship therapy could start with Scharff, J. S. and Scharff, D.E. (1992) *Scharff Notes: A Primer of Object Relations Therapy*, Northvale, New Jersey and London, Jason Aronson Inc. This is a simple introduction. More advanced texts by the same authors are: Scharff, J.S. and Scharff, D.E. (1992) *Object Relations Family Therapy*, Northvale, New Jersey and London, Jason Aronson Inc.; Scharff, D.E. and Scharff, J.S. (1991) *Object Relations Couple Therapy*, Northvale, New Jersey and London, Jason Aronson Inc.; and Scharff, J.S. and Scharff, D.E. (1994) *Object Relations Therapy of Physical and Sexual Trauma,* Northvale, New Jersey and London, Jason Aronson Inc.

References

Arlow, J. A. (1993) 'Two discussions of "the mind of the analyst" and a response from Madeleine Baranger', *International Journal of Psycho-Analysis,* vol. 74, pp. 1147–54.

Balint, M. (1968) *The Basic Fault,* London and New York, Tavistock.

Beres, D. and Arlow, J. A. (1974) 'Fantasy and identification in empathy', *Psychoanalytic Quarterly,* vol. 43, p. 2650.

Bion, W. R. (1962) 'A theory of thinking', *International Journal of Psycho-Analysis,* vol. 33, pp. 306–10.

Blecourt, A. De (1993) 'Transference, countertransference and acting out in psychoanalysis', *International Journal of Psycho-Analysis,* vol. 74, pp. 757–74.

Bollas, C. (1987) *The Shadow of the Object,* London, Free Association Books.

Bowlby, J. (1971) *Attachment,* Harmondsworth, Pelican.

Bowlby, J. (1975) *Separation, Anxiety and Anger,* Harmondsworth, Pelican.

Dennett, D. C. (1987) *The Intentional Stance*, Cambridge Mass. and London, MIT Press.

Emde, R.B. (1988) 'Development terminable and interminable', *International Journal of Psycho-Analysis,* vol. 69, pp. 23–42.

Fast, I. (1992) 'Object relations: towards an object relational model of the mind' in Barron, J. W., Eagle, M. N. and Wolitsky, D. L. (eds) *Interface of Psychoanalysis and Psychology,* Washington DC, American Psychological Society.

Freud, S. (1905) 'Fragment of an analysis of a case of hysteria', *Standard Edition 7,* London, Hogarth Press (1953).

Freud, S. (1912) 'The dynamics of transference', *Standard Edition 12,* London, Hogarth Press (1958).

Freud, S. (1915) 'The unconscious', *Standard Edition 14,* London, Hogarth Press (1957).

Freud, S. (1925) 'An autobiographical study', *Standard Edition 20,* London: Hogarth Press, 1959.

Goffman, E. (1976) 'Gender advertisements', *Studies in the Anthropology of Visual Communication*, vol. 3, whole no. 2.

Heimann, P. (1950) 'On countertransference', *International Journal of Psycho-Analysis,* vol. 61, pp. 81–4.

Hinshelwood, R.D. (1991) *A Dictionary of Kleinian Thought*, London, Free Association Books.

Joseph, B. (1985) 'Transference: the total situation', *International Journal of Psycho-Analysis,* vol. 66, pp 447–54.

Jung, C. (1925) 'Marriage as a psychological relationship' in *Collected Works vol. 17,* London: Routledge.

Jung, C. (1935) 'Principles of practical psychotherapy' in *Collected Works vol. 16,* London, Routledge.

Klein, M. (1952) 'The origins of transference' in *Envy and Gratitude, Collected Works vol. III,* London, Karnac Books (1993).

Langs, R. (1976) *The Therapeutic Interaction: vol II,* New York, Aronson.

Lewicki, P. (1986) *Nonconscious Social Information Processing*, London, Academic Press Inc.

Luborsky, L. and Crits-Christoph, P. (1990) *Understanding Transference: The Core Conflictual Relationship Theme Method,* New York, Basic Books Inc.

Masson, J.M. (1988) *Against Therapy: Emotional Tyranny and the Myth of Psychological Healing*, New York, Atheneum.

Morgan, H. and Thomas, K. (1996) 'A psychodynamic perspective on group processes' in Wetherell, M. (ed).

Ogden, T. H. (1979) 'On projective identification', *International Journal of Psycho-Analysis,* vol. 60, pp. 357–73.

Ogden, T. H. (1982) *Projective Identification and Psychotherapeutic Technique,* New York, Aronson.

Potter, J. (1996) 'Attitudes, social representations and discursive psychology' in Wetherell, M. (ed).

Racker, H. (1957) 'The meanings and uses of countertransference', *Psychoanalytic Quarterly,* vol. 26, pp. 303–57.

Rutter, R. (1995) 'Clinical implications of attachment concepts: retrospect and prospect', *Journal of Child Psychology and Psychiatry,* 36, pp. 549–71.

Sandler, J. (1993) 'On communication from patient to analyst: not everything is projective identification', *International Journal of Psycho-Analysis,* vol. 74, pp. 1097–107.

Schafer, R. (1959) 'Generative empathy in the treatment situation', *Psychoanalytic Quarterly,* vol. 28, pp. 342–73.

Schank, R. C. and Abelson, R.P. (1977) *Scripts, Plans, Goals and Understanding.* Hillsdale N.J., Erlbaum.

Slade, A. and Aber, J.L. (1992) 'Attachments, drives and developments: conflicts and convergences in theory' in Barron, J.W., Eagle, M.N. and Wolitsky, D.L. (eds) *Interface of Psychoanalysis and Psychology,* Washington D.C., American Psychological Association.

Stern, D. (1985) *The Interpersonal World of the Infant,* New York, Basic Books.

Stevens, R. (ed) (1996) *Understanding the Self,* London, Sage/The Open University. (Book 1 in this series)

Symington, N. (1986) *The Analytic Experience,* London, Free Association Books.

Tansey, M. J. and Burke, W. F. (1989) *Understanding Countertransference,* Hillsdale, N J, The Analytic Press.

Thomas, K. (1996) 'The defensive self: a psychodynamic perspective' in Stevens, R. (ed).

Trevarthen, C. (1993) 'The function of emotions in early infant communication', in Nadel, J. and Camaioni, L. (eds), *New Perspectives in Early Communicative Development,* London, Routledge.

Wetherell, M. (ed) (1996) *Identities, Groups and Social Issues,* London, Sage/The Open University. (Book 3 in this series)

Wetherell, M. and Maybin, J. (1996) 'The distributed self: a social constructionist perspective' in Stevens, R. (ed).

Williams, J. and Watson, G. (1988) 'Sexual inequality, family life and family therapy' in Street, E. and Dryden, W. (eds) *Family Therapy in Britain,* Buckingham, Open University Press.

Wollheim, R. (1993) 'Desire, belief, and Professor Grunbaum's Freud' in *The Mind and its Depths,* Cambridge Mass. and London, Harvard University Press.

CHAPTER 5

CHANGE AND TRANSFORMATIONS OF RELATIONSHIPS

by Rudi Dallos

Contents

1   Introduction

It is argued in Chapters 3 and 4 that one of the key features of a relation-ship is having extended interactions *over time*. People in relationships develop a joint history; things they have done together, their conver-sations, shared feelings and fantasies. This chapter is concerned with how people and their relationships change over time. Despite develop-ments and changes, each of us can also perceive threads of continuities reaching back in our lives. This may be expressed in terms of a narrative or a story which we construct and which connects the events and our sense of self into a meaningful pattern through time. We may adhere to a view of our self as being constant, a sort of core 'personality', some sense of a unified 'self' which remains essentially the same across the years. Alternatively, we may become aware that we change according to the situations we are in, for example we are sometimes surprised by how our feelings and actions may alter depending on who we are with – the relationship we are presently involved in. 'The personalities of the indi-vidual affect the nature of the relationship, but so also does the relation-ship affect, to a greater or lesser degree, the participants. We not only contribute to the relationships in which we are involved, we are changed by them' (Hinde, 1979, p. xi).

The examination of continuities and change in relationships has been of considerable interest, not only for social psychologists but also for applied psychologists, such as clinicians who have been interested in both the positive and the negative aspects of relationships; in how and why relationships sometimes appear to deteriorate leaving people unhappy, unable to make progress in their lives and feeling 'stuck'. Observations and clinical work with families have generated models of the development of relationships, including views of 'normal' and satis-factory paths of change, and how these involve a variety of key stages or transitions that have to be negotiated. This idea of a progression through stages (common to many psychological theories of development, for example Piaget, 1959 and Freud, 1940) has shed some light on relation-ships but runs the risk of assuming that relationships do in fact have some pre-ordained directions, stages and set of goals. Instead, relation-ships might be more accurately considered as having a number of *trans-formations*, whereby the nature of a relationship; what it means to the participants, how they feel about the relationship and about themselves, changes radically. As Duck (1994) suggests, 'Living in a relationship is thus also living ... in a world of changing possibilities, not living with finalities and unchanging certainties ... Getting married, for instance, does not answer once and for all the question of whether the partners will stay together' (p. 52).

1.1   Forces for change

All of us change, whether we like it or not, physically, emotionally and intellectually, due to the inevitable processes of growth and ageing. Obvious examples of such changes are puberty and the menopause. These involve major changes in the functioning of the body, such as hormonal balances, body shape and functioning. In addition there are the more gradual continuous changes, such as in increasing (or decreasing) strength, dexterity, size, perceptual and intellectual abilities. There has been considerable debate about whether these changes cause our actions, for example whether the increasing production of the hormone testosterone in adolescence causes aggression and sexual desire. By and large the evidence for any direct causation is at best inconclusive (Toates, 1996). The biological changes appear to be mediated by personal and societally shared constructions.

The biological imperatives of growth, change and development form the background to the discussions of change in this chapter. Though these biological changes may be important, they are allocated socially constructed meanings which vary, at least to some extent, between and within cultures (Hsu, 1981; Wetherell and Maybin, 1996). In part, these can be seen in common expectations of how relationships should change which we have learned from direct observation of our own families and friends, but also the wider societally shared ideas of 'normal' development. These shared assumptions are embodied in a variety of societal practices and institutions which prescribe the routes of change, for example when children start and finish school, leave home and start work, expectations of when marriage and childbirth should take place, and expectations of financial duties and obligations. Relationships and their paths of progress and change are embedded in the material and ideological features of the culture they are located within. These may set limits of what the relationship can be, and how it can change. These discourses of change may also be seen in people's statements about lack of change in their relationships, whether they seem to be 'not going anywhere', have 'reached a plateau', are 'going round in circles' or 'going too slow' (Baxter, 1992). Implicit in these descriptions are evaluations and beliefs about how the relationship *should* be developing and changing. These evaluations may reflect not only the state of a relationship but also the influence of shared cultural beliefs or discourses which we have absorbed about the 'normal' course that a relationship should take.

> Every culture marks off stages of living, each with its appropriate experiences ... Age norms, for example, get internalized and translated into psychological expectations for self and others, lending a sense of being on time or off time, of being early or late while undergoing life events. Remaining single until her late twenties would not lend an Irish woman a sense of being 'late' nor earn her the label of 'spinster' as it would in Latin American cultures ... Divorce in a

middle-aged Italian couple requires a more difficult shift in extended family loyalties than for an English couple ... In contrast to Anglo-American values, identity seeking or 'finding oneself' is not a primary concern for Mexican-American adults. The impetus for individuation is expressed or submerged in the dyadic context of forming a marital system with a common goal and negotiation of values, priorities and everyday routines.

(Falicov and Karrer, 1981, pp. 384 and 394)

I hope you have gathered, from Falicov and Karrer's brief examples, that the stages of personal development which are picked out as important transitional points by one culture – and the timing and the meaning allocated to them – may be completely different for other cultures. Though biologically determined changes do present people with important issues to be dealt with, such as puberty, childbirth or loss of health, there is considerable variation in what meanings are attached to them and what social consequences result.

Images of change

Ways in which we can improve, manage and change our relationships with others abound in popular literature, newspapers and magazines and on television and radio – and they all have an influence in shaping our beliefs. We are continually bombarded with ideas, expectations and advice about how to conduct relationships, not least being the discussions of relationship 'problems' in the 'agony' columns of the tabloid press. Some of this popular 'knowledge' is fuelled by findings from psychological investigations and the 'helping professions' – counselling, clinical psychology, family and marital therapy and so on. What is defined as a 'problem' reveals some of the assumptions that are current and influential in professional and lay circles. The combination of these ideas, assumptions and explanations can be seen as embodying popular discourses on relationships and change. A number of researchers have explored the extent to which these ideas have influenced the thinking of couples (Baxter, 1992; McCall, 1982). Baxter suggests that popular images of relationships are encapsulated in the metaphors that couples employ (see Box 5.1)

A theme that runs through many of these metaphors is that of the idea of continuity and progression – that relationships are 'going somewhere', that is, that there is a linear progression to some ideal end-point. This idea of a progression, for example of increased emotional intimacy and understanding, is also embedded in popular notions and advice about relationships (McCall, 1982) and to some extent in life cycle theories which will be considered in a later section.

BOX 5.1   Metaphors of relationship development

Baxter (1992) has explored the metaphors that couples employ to describe their romantic relationships and how these were perceived to change and develop. Couples were asked to provide a description, in their own words, of the development of their relationship. Researchers then independently categorized the metaphors employed in the descriptions. The following were the most prevalent:

Relationship development as work – 'we worked through our problems', 'it was hard going at first'.

Relationship development as a voyage of discovery – 'keep finding out new things', 'still getting to know each other' as opposed to more negative metaphors, such as 'going on automatic pilot'.

Relationship development as an uncontrollable force – 'the relationship engulfed us totally' or 'I just couldn't help it'.

Relationship development as danger – 'need to be cautious at first', 'playing with fire', 'I have to have my guard up'.

Relationship development as economic exchange – 'we make compromises', 'we split everything equally'.

Relationship development as a living organism – 'birth of the relationship', 'growth to maturity' etc.

Relationship development as a game – 'we play cat and mouse', 'a mind game', 'I won him over' etc.

Baxter argued that these metaphors contained complex ideas about expectations of change, the causes of development or stagnation. She suggests further that these functioned, not only to describe the relationship, but also to actively construct what had happened; the current relationship had implications for the nature of future change and development.

Change – transitions and transformations

The following three sections of this chapter will explore three significant points of change in relationships:

1   initiating relationships;

2   first time parenthood;

3   children leaving home.

We will attempt to consider, through these three examples, some common features of a variety of other transitions, such as starting a sexual relationship, getting married or deciding to cohabit, grandparenthood, bereavement, separation or divorce, and so on. One common concept is the view of change as a *process* – something that occurs over time rather than predominantly as a sudden 'overnight' transformation. This is not to say that sometimes significant changes may not happen quickly or spontaneously, for example a sudden bereavement or apparently impulsive decision, but that in general there is a period of preparation, contemplation and discussion prior to the change. Also, in every case there is a period of consolidation following a change, appraisal of the consequences and perhaps even thoughts about further changes.

These three transitions also illustrate a range of other features common to transitional periods. Usually there is some change in roles, for example acquaintances take on a new role with each other as friends, with the arrival of a child a couple have to adopt new roles as parents, with the departure of children the roles may change back from predominantly being parents to being a couple or even to becoming grandparents. Transitions also commonly involve significant alterations in people's social networks (see also the next chapter in this volume), for example the development of a friendship is likely to lead to the partners spending less time with others. Likewise, the arrival of a child may mean a couple have less time for friends or former colleagues and see more of their own parents and/or start to seek out the company of other new parents, and so on.

Changes in emotions are also likely, for example the arrival of a child may elicit feelings of both joy and distress at the responsibilities, friendship may bring a sense of feeling cared for, being less lonely and so on. Strong emotions, such as jealousy, may be attached to having to 'share' a partner with a third person when he or she takes on a carer's role. A wide range of other more practical factors, such as financial implications, organization of time and activities, physical activity, stimulation and so on may also accompany and influence these and other changes.

Finally, there are likely to be changes in power, for example, leaving home involves a change of status in a family for a young person – from a child to an adult. Two people becoming good friends may mean shifts in power so they feel supported and stronger, able to rely on each other. Such emotional factors may be important throughout relationships but may be particularly so at transitional points.

ACTIVITY 5.1   Now read the first part of *Reading E*: 'A social perspective' by Graham Allan. To what extent do you agree with his suggestion that we are constrained in the choices we make about our relationships?

These three transition points have also been chosen because they enable us to consider relationships between pairs of people (dyads) and also those in threesomes (triads). Evidence will be considered which shows that change in a pair of people in a relationship is frequently prompted by the entrance of a third person, for example the birth of a child, a new friendship, an elderly relative coming to live with his or her adult children and so on. Similarly, the exit of a third person may be associated with significant changes, for example a child leaving home, the death of an elderly relative, or the moving away of a close friend or colleague. In particular, the study of change in clinical work with families has suggested that the movement from a twosome to a threesome (and vice versa) is of great importance, and that the massive adjustments required may precipitate a variety of emotional reactions. In some cases these may be pleasant, in others stress, conflict and problems may result.

The following three sections will offer evidence from descriptive and empirical studies: experimental, self-report and questionnaire-based approaches, as well as qualitative approaches, such as the those employing personal accounts of change. In section 5 the contribution from interactional approaches, such as systems theory (discussed in more detail in Chapter 3 in this volume) and its application in clinical practice will be explored within the framework of the concept of the family life cycle.

Aims of the chapter

1 To outline the nature of change (whether transitional or transformational) in relationships.

2 To examine change in terms of a number of central themes: changing roles, shifts of power, alterations in intimacy and independence, and connections with others.

3 To explore the shifts in power as relationships progress, deteriorate or transform.

4 To examine the interdependence of the themes outlined in (2) and (3) above.

5 To offer an outline and critical appraisal of family life-cycle models of change.

---

2 Casual to close relationships – becoming friends

An obvious starting point for a study of change in relationships is to consider how and why they start. One popular assumption has been that we choose to have relations with people that we like, based on similar interests, physical attractiveness and so on. In this section, we will consider the development of friendships – the transition from simply interacting with someone, an acquaintance perhaps, to becoming friends. However, it is important to note that many relationships do not fall neatly into any category. There are some relationships, for example, where we have little or no choice about whether we enter into them and stay in them or not. Family relations are a case in point. A baby does not choose his or her parents and there are strong prohibitions against our totally rejecting other family members. Likewise, there are many situations such as work where we are more or less forced (if we want to keep our job) to enter into relationships with people we might not otherwise choose even to spend much time with.

ACTIVITY 5.2   Note down two or three of your relationships: with perhaps a friend, a colleague, or a lover. Think back to how you first met and how the relationship started to develop. To what extent were you free to choose to interact with the other person? How did the amount of choice available influence the development of your relationship?

There may be considerable variation in the extent of the choice we have in different situations. It is also possible that we exercise some degree of choice even in constrained or 'closed' situations, such as at work, in *how* we choose to interact with people. By various verbal and non-verbal means we may be able to make it clear that we are prepared to be friendly, or alternatively, that we wish to keep contact formal and to the minimum in intimacy.

2.1   Choosing friends

What do we mean by 'friendship'? Predominantly, we mean a relationship in which we like a person, in which the other's company is in itself a source of pleasure. This excludes relationships where we are 'being friendly' with someone to gain perks, promotion, or sexual favours. Our friends may also give us things we want; lend us money, help us out, listen to our problems, but at least some of what we enjoy and derive from them is 'intrinsic to their person', from the pleasure of their company (Rodin, 1982).

ACTIVITY 5.3   Think of two or more of your friends (either present ones or past ones). What are some of the characteristics that you like about them? How do they differ from each other? Has what you like about them changed over the course of your relationship?

What we seek from friendships appears to alter according to a variety of factors. Burleson (1994) suggests, for example, that young children describe friendship in concrete physical terms: engaging in mutual activities and games and sharing toys. In contrast, older children describe friendships more in terms of sharing intimate thoughts and feelings, being psychologically similar and engaging in mutual self-exploration and validation. These changes may be related to children's growing cognitive capacities which enable more sophisticated understandings and needs to develop. In adult relationships we tend to seek different things from a friendship as the relationship progresses, due to our changing life circumstances and needs.

Field of eligibles and liking

The term 'field of eligibles' was introduced by Winch (1958) to describe the idea that each of us has a set of people with whom we regularly come into contact – at work, at leisure, while shopping, friends of the family. There is the potential therefore for us to select from amongst this group of people some to become our friends. There may, of course, be a variety of factors that determine how large or how small this set of people may be, and this may influence our decisions. Further, there may be varying amounts of similarity 'built in', for example people working together or attending the same club may have a considerable amount in common with each other.

Traditionally, research on relationship initiation has emphasized the idea of personal choice, but this may represent a cultural bias. Relationship development based on choice can be seen to imply an individualistic orientation associated with much of modern Western culture as opposed to collectivism as exemplified, for example, in Chinese culture. This difference is nicely summarized by Hsu commenting on the development of romantic relationships, 'An American asks "How does my heart feel?" A Chinese asks, "What will other people say?"' (Hsu, 1981, p. 50).

A considerable amount of research on friendship choice has proceeded on the proposition that we select some and reject others for possible friendships from this 'field of eligibles'.

Turn back to Chapter 1 of this volume and look again at the accounts of friendship offered. To what extent do these strike a chord with some of your own experiences? How many of your friendships have arisen from simply being in proximity to people at school, at work or with your neighbours? What differences does the extent of choice we have in developing a relationship make to the nature of the relationship?   ACTIVITY 5.4

Though perhaps capturing *some* aspects of friendship formation, the notion of choice and the related idea of a 'field of eligibles' ignores a variety of structural and practical considerations. One extremely reliable finding in friendship formation has been that of 'proximity', that is we tend to make friends with people who happen to be close to us – with work colleagues, neighbours and classmates. Murstein (1977) has termed this a 'closed-field', in that individuals may be 'forced' to interact whether or not they wish to. Such 'closed' situations as school or college 'throw' people together and it may be that as a result of spending time together people get to know each other and become friends almost without any conscious awareness of this happening or of making any deliberate choices. As the young friends in Chapter 1 commented, 'I just sort of bumped into him through the playgound ... a larger group of us would hang out ... I think it was within that nexus of a larger group of people that we were able to establish a sort of common interest (Alex). 'We became friends at my old school because she was friends with some of my friends, and then when we went on to high school we became good friends because she was the only person I knew in my class' (Jenny).

Dating agencies and personal columns of newspapers may represent one area where decisions are made consciously and deliberately. However, more generally the field of eligibles is often determined for us, and there may even be an element of 'match-making' so that people are introduced to each other by relatives, mutual friends, colleagues and so on. It can be argued further that it is functional or adaptive to attempt to get on with people with whom we have no choice about interacting, such as at work, or at school. How many other friendships a person possesses (their sociability and popularity), or how confident they feel that others like them may influence how 'choosy' they are in regard to with whom they are prepared to become friends.

The notion of choosing relationships implies that decisions are being made deliberately at a conscious level. Yet we hear people speak of feeling some sort of attraction for someone even if initially they do not quite appear to get along.

The development of friendships can be seen in terms of powerful emotional undercurrents and needs which may compel someone to choose a friend who they do not consciously like. Indeed, psychoanalytic theorists have argued that many of our actions and feelings may be shaped by powerful unconscious influences. Various unconscious processes have been described and may be significant in the formation (and maintenance) of relationships and these were discussed further in Chapter 4.

ACTIVITY 5.5

1   *Someone you like*

(a) Think of someone you like very much and write down one or two things that you like best about that person.

(b) Now ask yourself whether you can think of someone you do *not* like who has one or more of these qualities.

2   *Someone you dislike*

(a) Think of someone you dislike and likewise note one or two of the qualities you most dislike about that person.

(b) Now ask yourself if you can think of anyone you *like* who has these qualities .

Source: Rodin, 1982, p. 33

What did you learn from this activity? Some people find it much harder to think of someone they dislike, possibly because we are unconsciously 'defending' ourselves against thinking about them (see also Chapter 4). Rodin (1982) argues that when people carry out this exercise there is usually an asymmetry: most people can find someone they dislike who shares some of the best qualities of people they like but find it much harder to find people they like who share some of the worst qualities of people they dislike; 'Disliked others may have some likeable qualities but liked others seem never to have disliked qualities' (Rodin, 1982). This is not to say that we find our friends to be perfect but that it is unlikely, she argues, that we see them as having qualities that we most dislike, that is as having the most salient features of people we dislike. Rodin suggests that liking and disliking work in different ways, so that once we have decided that someone meets our dislike criteria then we dislike them regardless of any likeable qualities they may also possess.

Validation

At first sight, Rodin's findings appear to support popular ideas that first impressions are important and perhaps hard to alter. However, it is possible that we may like someone at first and then discover some aspect about them we do not like – a dislike 'criterion'. But what is the basis for our liking or disliking a person? One approach is to consider that central reasons for liking someone are the linked concepts of validation and similarity. George Kelly's Personal Construct Theory (1955, see also Stevens, 1996 and Chapter 3 of this volume) emphasized that one of our most vital psychological needs is to gain *validation*. By this he meant that we have a need to have our view of the world, including our view of ourselves, affirmed by others. This can also be described as personality support or validation of our identity (Duck, 1977). Validation means more than mere agreement or sympathy. It contains the idea of 'tolerance' so that the partners may disagree yet see each other as having a commitment to trying to understand each other, learn from each other and so on. In Kelly's terms, the partners are also likely to anticipate that their future interactions will continue to provide such validation.

It would follow therefore that we start friendships with others who appear to be reasonably similar to us, on the assumption that they are most likely to offer us such validation. If I judge someone to have diametrically opposed views to me, for example, regarding our views on education or race, I might assume that he or she disagrees with my political views, which are very important to me, and therefore that I would not find their company rewarding and that we would not get on. The concept of validation is central for the following discussion of theories of liking and of the stages of achieving intimacy. This idea of similarity as being rewarding was initially explored by Byrne (1961) in a study which came to be known as the 'bogus stranger' experiment.

BOX 5.2 The bogus stranger experiment

In the 'Bogus stranger experiment' Byrne invited a volunteer to come to his office to take part in an experiment, but gave no details of what form the experiment would take. When the volunteer arrived he was told that a second volunteer of the same age and sex would also be taking part in the experiment but had unfortunately been delayed. While he or she was waiting, Byrne asked the volunteer to fill in a questionnaire (which assessed the volunteer's attitude to a number of important issues, such as political views and attitude towards drugs). When the volunteer had completed the questionnaire, Byrne made an excuse and left the room, taking the questionnaire with him.

After a short time Byrne returned with another questionnaire which he claimed had been completed by Volunteer II. He asked Volunteer I to read through the questionnaire and then to rate Volunteer II on a scale of 1 to 7 using the Interpersonal Judgement Scale (IJS). This scale consists of seven points assessed from the answers to a number of questions such as: How much would you enjoy working with the person who completed this questionnaire? and How much do you like the person who completed this questionnaire?

In fact, Volunteer II did not exist. Byrne simply took Volunteer I's completed questionnaire and made up a fake questionnaire with answers which were similar in varying degrees to it. Some of the responses he made 80 per cent similar to those of Volunteer I, some 50 per cent similar and some only 20 per cent similar. In this way he was able to manipulate the extent of the similarity between Volunteer I and the 'bogus stranger'. He did this in order to assess the effect the varying degrees of attitudinal similarity had on the volunteer's ratings of liking for the 'stranger'.

As expected, Byrne found that the greater the perceived similarity between the subject and the 'stranger' the higher the ratings on the liking scale. One conclusion was that attitudinal similarity is rewarding and can predispose us towards liking someone, even if we have never met them.

Though Byrne's work lent support to the idea that perceived similarity is fundamental to liking, studies such as the 'bogus stranger' experiment have many drawbacks. For one thing they are artificial, since we usually meet potential friends face-to-face and the meeting is likely to occur in a social setting which may have its own rules and demands, such as at work or at a club. We may be introduced by a mutual friend, whose presence may influence our perceptions of the new acquaintance and so on. Most importantly, we may have to *infer* what the other person's attitudes are since people do not reveal these immediately and there are considerable individual variations in how much people initially disclose (Nelson-Jones and Strong, 1976). Also, disclosure can be seen as a reciprocal or inter-personal process, in that the amount and type of disclosure made by the other person is influenced by how much we disclose about ourselves and so on (Derlega et al., 1976).

The formation of friendships is evidently more complex than simply being based on similarity. Winch (1958) had suggested that relationships may be seen to be based upon perceived compatibility or complementarity. We may be attracted to someone and seek to pursue a friendship with them in part because they appear to possess some of the qualities that we lack. However, Rodin (1982) emphasizes that although such complementarity of qualities may exist, there is a threshold of disliking so that we would not regard someone as complementary to us if we perceived them to have some critical features that we strongly disliked. She also suggests that a choice between liking and disliking offers too stark a picture of what happens, since some, and possibly many people with whom we interact are disregarded (that is, we do not have any strong feeling about them one way or the other).

Following an initial attraction, people are seen as engaging in various exploratory moves (Goffman, 1971; see also Chapter 2 of this volume), such as suggesting some further joint meeting, engaging in a mutual activity and so on. However, there may be a variety of factors that influence and possibly deter further exploration. These can be seen in terms of the potential costs versus gains that might be involved. Some of these will be practical, for example the person may live at a distance, or have a busy schedule making it hard to meet up and so on. More fundamentally there is the risk of being rebuffed and losing face. There has to be some estimation of the probability that the other person will respond favourably. There are costs or risks associated with the size of the offer that is made, for example suggesting a quick lunchtime drink may be a small move whereas suggesting an evening meal may be larger, because of the greater duration and the expectation that the invited person will have to reciprocate.

Such explorations can be seen as a subtle and complex negotiation process whereby successive offers and counter-offers may be made and care is taken to protect people's feelings, save-face and so on (issues discussed in Chapter 2 of this volume). The nature of this 'dance' may also vary according to cultural norms of politeness or etiquette and a variety of excuses may be employed to protect 'face', for example pressures of work, other commitments or illness.

2.2   Pathways to friendship

The work on liking has suggested that initial impressions give rise to decisions about whether we like or dislike a person, and that once a decision has been made that we like someone then these feelings become the basis for our subsequent decisions along the path to forming a friendship. But what form does this path take? Is it possible to identify stages?

Does it necessarily proceed towards increasing friendship and intimacy? One approach has been to attempt to document the stages that take place as a relationship changes in levels of intimacy. The assumption is that the selection of a close friend or partner proceeds through a sequential set of stages, with each stage focusing on decision-making processes. The work of Levinger (1983) is an example of such an approach. He presented people with lists of relationship activities, such as 'pursuing mutual leisure interests', 'discussing personal matters', 'physical intimacy' and asked them to judge how appropriate each behaviour was for different types of relationships which varied in closeness. He suggested that five distinct stages could be identified: A – Acquaintanceship; B – Build-up – increasing inter-dependence; C – Continuation – development of commitment to the relationship; D – Deterioration – possible down-turn in the relationship, sometimes related to external events/factors; E – Ending – weighing up of the costs and benefits of ending or continuing and possibly starting to contemplate or construct new relationships.

ACTIVITY: 5.6   Think of a friendship that you are currently involved in.

Draw a horizontal line – at the extreme left place the approximate date and setting of where you first met. Note what you remember to be your first impressions of the person and how you got on with each other. Now try to place two or three points or stages along the path to you becoming friends.

Do you feel that your roles in relation to each other have changed, for example from predominantly colleagues to friends? Was there a certain point that you decided that you were friends or did this happen gradually?

Studies such as Levinger's offer a starting point for thinking about the progression of relationships, however they suffer from a variety of shortcomings. One of the key problems is that they suggest a picture of an *active* person who is selecting a relatively *passive* other. In fact, relationships can be seen to involve two people who are *both* active: forming impressions, initiating actions and making decisions. Liking can therefore be seen to emerge as a mutual process, for example the fact that the other person appears to like us may predispose us to like them. We may be less likely to like someone who appears to dislike us. Importantly, Levinger's study also suffers from a serious methodological problem which is that in giving subjects scenarios of people who differed in closeness this *imposes* a structure which pre-empts the question of whether this is or is not a salient feature in how people think about friendships. It is possible that people differ widely in their views of friendship, so that for some people closeness is less important than similarity of interests, or sharing a sense of humour.

Such studies also present people with relatively artificial tasks and reveal little about the complexity and uniqueness of our thinking about relationships. To take a simple example, although there may be some broad agreement about what activities count as 'building intimacy', this may vary between friends and between genders. For some friends activities such as sport may signify intimacy, for others the easy discussion of apparently trivial topics, and for others still they may feel a need to share feelings and discuss intimate details of their lives. We cannot judge this without having a deeper understanding of the individuals and their shared beliefs, for example, their ideas of gender roles. It is also possible that cross-sectional studies which make generalizations about a sample of people obscure the diversity of relationship development, for example, friendships which become intimate but then become less so. People external to the relationship may also exert influence, for example other friends or colleagues (Chapter 6 gives a fuller discussion of the impact of social networks on relationships). Beliefs and values about relationships may shift and a relationship may in some instances transform from one sort of relationship to another, either rapidly or gradually, and even shift back again, for example colleagues to friends and back to colleagues again. Practical or structural factors may also play an important part, for example becoming friends with the neighbours may be largely facilitated by the fact that they are close and because it is a sensible thing to get on and help each other.

Filter theories

One approach that has inspired considerable research is to think of the development of friendships as passing through a series of filters. Kerckhoff and Davis (1962) proposed that people successively 'filter out', or narrow down who they are likely to become involved with more intimately. The development of relationships is seen to involve an exchange of personal information ('disclosures'); about self, views of the other, relationships and each other's general views of the world. These serve progressively to build up a body of knowledge about each other. Kerckhoff and Davis (1962) studied dating couples in the USA over an eight-month period. Each partner of a couple completed a questionnaire (at the start and at the end of this period) which assessed how close they felt to their partner in terms of shared values and complementarity of needs. The findings indicated that for couples who had been seeing each other for less than eighteen months, only similarity in values was predictive of increased commitment. On the other hand, for those who had been dating for over eighteen months, only complementarity of needs was positively predictive.

Consistent with, but extending Byrne's (1961) emphasis on the importance of similarity for liking, Kerckhoff and Davis (1962) argued that similarity of opinions and attitudes was of central importance at the *start* of a relationship. Through the initial exchanges of information couples are seen as weighing up decisions about whether to extend, continue or terminate their relationship. If the person is found to be dissimilar they are 'filtered out' from the group of potential friends. Potential partners are seen as progressively 'filtering out' people who they discover to be unlike them as they find out more about each other.

Duck (1973) offered an important extension of filter theory models by applying Kelly's personal construct theory to suggest that the 'filtering process' proceeds on the basis of the participants making predictions about their *future* interactions. Each person is seen to be conducting a series of experiments, or explorations, by disclosing bits of information about themselves and making enquiries about the other person. From these probes, people are seen as attempting to establish the amount of similarity that there is between them in terms of interests, attitudes and aspirations. This is then employed to predict how they might get on in the future and therefore whether the relationship is worth investing in and continuing with. The nature of the information sought varies as the relationship develops, because we are concerned to derive different types or degrees of validation. At the start of the relationship, the information may be fairly general or apparently superficial, consisting of disclosures about similar tastes in music, leisure interests and friends. However, even 'trivial' incidents such as disagreements or differences of views on, for example, preferences for a particular television programme or food may be employed as indicators of deeper levels of beliefs. As the relationship progresses, the information specifically searched for may move to these more central issues. Miell and Duck (1986) have described a variety of strategies that people employ to gather such information about each other. One of the most obvious is that people ask questions which can lead to mutual question and answer sequences, another is for one partner to 'offer' some self-disclosures in order to encourage the other to do the same. Perhaps a slightly riskier strategy is to provoke some disagreements on a general topic in order to 'cut through' the polite front, to find out about the other person's 'real' feelings.

In these exchanges what is transmitted is not merely concrete information about each other, but also an exchange of constructs or beliefs, which each partner in turn translates and interprets within their own belief system. Based on these exchanges partners may decide to continue a relationship, or to make a decision that it will not work and decide to discontinue it.

Though of value, filter theories have also been found to have short comings, '...filter theories have been extensively criticized, the definition of specific stages and sequences often being so imprecise that a test of their validity is almost impossible except in a very vague way' (Duck, 1988, p. 73). Filter theories appear to assume that validating one's views is central, and yet, as discussed earlier, one other key feature is whether the interactions are in some sense enjoyable, or fulfilling in important ways. What counts as enjoyment or intimacy in one relationship may differ in another, as it might even between partners. In contrast, social constructionist approaches stress that people in relationships jointly create meanings, including what it is to be close, what is 'fun', and so on, through their continual interactions and conversations (Shotter, 1992). Any discussion of relationships as proceeding through stages must take this complexity and negotiation of meanings into account. A related point, again emphasized by Duck (1994), is that the progress of relationships cannot be seen as simply a linear progression to increasing 'intimacy'. It is possible that many relationships achieve a level of intimacy that may not be regarded as particularly high but is felt to be adequate. Also, people may move to a close, intimate relationship and back to a more distant one, due, for example, to external circumstances such as moving away, a change of job or to changes in their other relationships. It is also possible that relationships simultaneously have ups and downs, so that people oscillate between periods of intimacy and distance, for example the same conflicts, rows and disagreements may occur but overall the level of intimacy stays level (Byng-Hall, 1980). 'The problem is that all relationships contain simultaneously both a "bright" side and a "dark" side. Part of the problem of continuing relationships is managing the "dark" side-irritations, squabbles and pains – in the context of the "bright" side' (Duck, 1994, p. 44). Relationships may vary widely in how extreme these ups and downs are and how frequent the shifts between them are.

2.3   Male-female friendships

In many societies there are strict rules regarding the ways in which men and women are allowed to interact. The extent to which sexual feelings are seen to pervade all cross-sex friendships appears to vary. Sex segregation of friendships is still evident in Western European and American societies and possibly more extremely so in, for example, Muslim and Hindu cultures.

A number of studies indicate that friendships between women appear to involve more confiding, intimacy, personal concern, nurturing, and emotional expression than friendships between men (Nardi and Sherrod, 1994; Sapadin 1988). Friendships amongst men in contrast show more aggressive interaction, competition and are more oriented towards discussing practical interests, such as work and sport. Men appear to become close by sharing activities, doing things together and showing enthusiasm for shared activities (Sapadin, 1988). However, these reported differences are usually rather small and there are many similarities in same sex relationships, for example both men and women have been found to place a high value on intimacy, empathy, trust, respect, acceptance, spontaneity and enjoyment of their friendships. It has been argued further that there might be even greater similarity if it were not for structural factors such as work and marital conventions (Allan, 1989 – see also *Reading E*). There is also considerable diversity, for example 'non-conventional' men appear more likely to disclose their feelings than 'conventional' men and single men, possibly in an attempt to make up for the lack of a close female partner with whom to share their feelings, also disclose more to their male friends (Nardi and Sherrod, 1994).

The study of friendships in homosexual relationships is an important area of investigation and sheds some light on same-sex and cross-sex friendships in heterosexual relationships. On the one hand, it has been suggested that gay men and lesbians may not conform to conventional gender roles and thus there may be greater similarities between their friendships than those between heterosexual men and women. On the other hand, it is possible that homosexual friendships may be more complicated by sexual attraction between the partners. A study which attempted to explore some of these issues is described in Box 5.3 below.

BOX 5.3 Gay and lesbian friendship

Nardi and Sherrod (1994) conducted a study by questionnaire of 161 gays and 122 lesbians in Los Angeles (USA). The participants were described as: 'predominantly white, educated, middle and upper-middle class, urban gay men and lesbians in their thirties and forties'. The questionnaire explored three types of friendship with a person of the same sex; casual, close and 'best friend' on the basis of six categories: importance, social support, self-disclosure, activities, conflict and sexual behaviour.

The results suggested that same-sex gay and lesbian friendships were more similar than the same-sex friendships of heterosexual men and women. Both gay men and lesbian women valued, defined and enacted friendships similarly. However, two areas of differences were detected – conflict and sexuality. The levels of conflict reported were similar but lesbian women said that they were more bothered by conflicts and were more likely to express their feelings about these. Gay men were more likely to have been sexually intimate with casual and close friends but not with best friends, whereas lesbian women were twice as likely to say that their best friend was once their lover.

Nardi and Sherrod concluded that their study did not simply support the traditional 'instrumental' versus 'expressive' dichotomy (Nardi and Sherrod, 1994; Sapadin, 1988) which has been found to distinguish friendships between heterosexual men and women, since in some reports homosexual relationships contained both elements.

Overall though, Nardi and Sherrod (1994) point out that conflict and sexuality are precisely those areas where gender differences have been observed in the heterosexual population: 'many gay men persist in behaving in some traditionally masculine ways and many lesbians act in some traditionally feminine ways in specific acts' (p. 197).

ACTIVITY 5.7   Turn to *Reading A* by Hinde and *Reading E* by Allan at the end of this volume. To what extent do they offer contrasting views of differences between the sexes and how may these play a significant role in shaping relationships?

Studies such as that of Nardi and Sherrod (1994) indicate that sexual feelings and gender socialization are important aspects of friendships and may play a significant part in the initiation or otherwise of friendships.

These studies also relate to issues such as whether there are fundamental biologically-based differences between men and women which shape their sexual behaviour, as opposed to these being socially constructed (see Stevens (ed), 1996, for a discussion of this). The studies suggest that both may be important – influences of society, the family, school and the media all appear to play an important part in shaping people's beliefs and actions regarding friendship. However, some fundamental differences between men and women appear to persist despite having alternative sexual orientations. A drawback of the type of questionnaire studies typically employed in this kind of research is that they make generalizations about groups of people and do not allow an examination of the complexity, diversity and subtlety of friendships. There may in fact be considerable variety so that some hetero- and some homo-sexual friendships do not conform to such gender patterning, or at least not on all the points in the friendship's development or maintenance.

Review of section 2

- Choice of friends involves:
  - perceived similarity of partner;
  - validation: sense of support gained for personal views and beliefs;
  - field of eligibles: availability of potential partners.

- Selection of friends can be seen as a dynamic process involving:
  - progressive filtering: making choices about selection of friends based on an active process of seeking out and accumulating information about the person;
  - reconnaissance: trial interactions to test the viability of the friendship.

- Development of friendships may be seen as a dynamic inter-personal process of mutual appraisals and choices to continue or terminate the relationship.

- Development of friendships may be partly based on chance contact and proximity.

- Studies of cross-sex friendships suggest that a variety of social norms and expectations play a significant part in shaping the nature of friendships and the roles partners play.

3   Transition to parenthood

A fundamental change for a couple (dyad) is the transition to becoming a three-some (triad). The most widely discussed example of this is the change caused by the birth of a child, but other cases include an elderly relative joining a couple, one partner in a relationship developing a new intimacy, close work colleagues drawing in a third member and so on. For many couples in long-term relationships there is an eventual change to a triad with the arrival of the first child. In the case of homosexual couples or couples who are unable to give birth to a child there may be a decision to adopt. The processes of moving from a dyad to a triad in different forms of relationships may vary somewhat, but there are also some fundamental similarities, for example the organizational changes involved, the need to include a third person in communications, the increased complexity of emotional attachments and alignments. In addition, this transition involves a variety of specific changes; for a couple with a first child a shift in roles from adults to 'parents', changes in the social network such as a reduction in socializing, contact with health professionals, changes in relationships with parents and other family members, as well as significant economic and physical demands.

3.1   Changing roles

There is considerable diversity in the nature of the transition from couple to parenthood and in the extent to which this transition is planned and deliberate. For some couples, parenthood is an attempt to separate themselves from their own families, and for others it is because one partner has a greater desire than the other to have a child. In other cases the step is taken in the hope of rescuing a deteriorating relationship. In addition, there are an increasing number of cases where the father is predominantly only the provider of the sperm and it is clear that the child will be brought up by the mother alone. Also, there are many cases where parenthood results in the couple separating or splitting-up during the pregnancy or soon after the birth. Whilst acknowledging that there is this diversity, in this section we will be focusing on 'conventional' couples and the potential changes generally precipitated by the transition from dyad to triad and the psychological implications for a relationship following the entrance of a third person.

ACTIVITY 5.8   Read Extract 5.1 'Transition to parenthood' now and note down some of the significant changes in the couple's relationship, the problems facing them, their sense of identity as a couple and potential sources of satisfaction as well as dissatisfaction and conflict.

Extract 5.1   **Transition to parenthood**

Patricia and Steve were in their early thirties and had married two years earlier. In this extract they are discussing the changes the arrival of their baby (4-months-old at the time of this interview) had made to each of them and to their relationship. The following is a series of extracts from an interview with them:

Steve: We both knew that we were not getting any younger, and about the right age to have children ... with Patricia being – turning thirty, it was getting close to the time when we should do it...

Patricia: My parents were keen. I mean, I suppose they're extra happy now because it's a boy because all their other grandchildren are girls...

Patricia: I was quite poorly afterwards really, and – it's just because you're so tired, and everything's so new, and all of a sudden you're completely responsible. Whereas in hospital the auxiliaries will do things for you ... they're [babies] just all-consuming, and just exhausting and you're very emotional anyway...

Steve: Everybody wants to come round ... stream of people ... we haven't been out with friends as much as we would have – mm – and usually it means them coming over here for shorter periods than they would have before.

Patricia: The only time we get with each other is after 9 o' clock when he's gone to bed – by which time I'm usually rushing round trying to do all the things I haven't managed to do during the daytime. And Steve's normally flaked out because he's worked you know. So we don't really get much 'quality time'.

Steve: Mm.

Patricia: And I'm usually so spaced out and exhausted I haven't got anything interesting to say to Steve anyway. I just ask him how his day has been. All I do is – when he first comes in – is hand him Sam and say how awful my day has been. *(Laughs.)* So, the time I think. It's certainly affected our sex life.

Steve: *(Laughs.)*

Patricia: We don't have one! ... I think Steve would have him in the other room, but I don't want to put him in the other room yet. *(Laughs.)* ... It's difficult to know – if we've spoilt him ... He gets very bored. It does get very frustrating for me ... It's bliss just to go shopping sometimes, just to have half an hour on my own without Sam – I can't wait to get back to him then...

Patricia: It's a bonus for me having a little boy I think because it's like an extension of Steve in a way.

> Steve: You might regret that in the future.
>
> Patricia: I don't feel that I have to give any less love to Steven, and give part of that to Sam. It's extra to Sam I think. I worry about Steve being neglected. I mean I know he is on the physical side of things ... I feel very happy with the way I am but I must admit I'm getting to the stage where I would like to do something else as well ... I've considered doing part-time work of some description...
>
> Source: Satchell, M. (1995)

This couple could be described as having prepared themselves perhaps more thoroughly – they were older and more financially secure – than many couples when they become parents. Nevertheless, we can see that many aspects of the transition were unexpected; Patricia did not antici-pate that she would feel so responsible, so tired and so ill. Neither did they anticipate fully how little time they would have left for each other. The extract also illustrates how their experiences are different, partly due to biological factors – the obvious ones being that Patricia suffered the physical stresses of childbirth, *is* tired, her body more dedicated to the baby. Steven, on the other hand, is less tired even though he works out-side the home and tries to 'help' Patricia. This disparity is a cause of some concern, especially in Patricia worrying that Steven may feel sexu-ally deprived, rejected or even displaced by Sam. There is also some indi-cation of concern that Steven may feel peripheral, less close to Sam and possibly excluded from the mother-child dyad.

The couple appear to be continuing to negotiate change, rather than having completed the transition or arrived at some end point. Relationships, it has been argued, are always 'unfinished business' (Duck, 1994; Shotter, 1992) and Steve and Patricia are making some changes without being exactly certain of the eventual outcome, for example whether Patricia will return to work or feel satisfied with remaining at home. The transition involves changes in intimacy and power, with gains and losses occurring simultaneously. As Patricia argues, they may feel closer because they have their own child, but at the same time the baby comes between them, and possibly drives them further apart.

Duck (1994) emphasizes that the excitement and vibrancy of relation-ships is partly the result of the inevitable sense of the 'unknown' about what the future holds. However, what is known and unknown may differ significantly during this transition for each of the two partners. Minuchin (1974) states that men typically 'give birth' about nine months after the child has actually been born, the actual birth and the following period is when things are likely to be perceived as having started to change. In contrast, for women carrying the child inside them, and especially with their awareness of the baby's first movements, the change is a reality for them much earlier (LaRossa, 1986). Their interpret-ations, therefore, are initiated by the fundamental biological differences between men and women and socially constructed in terms of conven-tional cultural ways of delineating changes.

3.2   Change and stress

The transition to parenthood has been widely conceptualized as a period of 'crisis' – a sharp or decisive change in which established patterns were found to be inadequate and new ones demanded immediately (Hill, 1949). Hill further argued that crisis could be a positive or a negative force for change, dependent on three factors (1) the current state of organization or disorganization of the relationship; (2) the resources available to adapt to change; and (3) the interpretations or beliefs regarding the event and the changes. Resulting empirical studies have tended to focus more narrowly, for example on changes in satisfaction as a result of the transition to parenthood. These studies have suggested some decline in satisfaction of the relationship, with a decline in perceived closeness and intimacy and an increase in conflict (Belsky et al., 1983; Cowan and Cowan, 1990 see Box 5.4; LaRossa and LaRossa, 1981). New parents have to deal with unexpected reductions in their autonomy and demands for change in their marital roles. Women also have to cope with the physical symptoms and discomforts of pregnancy and birth and in addition may become insecure about their physical appearance and competence as mothers (Ruble et al., 1990).

However, in spite of this potentially gloomy picture many researchers have found that the changes are manageable. 'Babies do not appear to create severe marital distress where it was not present before, nor do they tend to bring already maritally distressed couples closer together' (Cowan and Cowan, 1988, p. 121)

A problem with studies such as Cowan and Cowan's is that in examining a group of new parents the diversity and uniqueness of the personal experiences of changes may be obscured. In contrast, Smith (1990) conducted a longitudinal case-study examining one woman's experiences of the transition to parenthood employing repertory grids and interviews at intervals of nine, six and three months before the birth of her child and at five months following her pregnancy. This revealed, for example, that the woman's perception of herself became more integrated as pregnancy proceeded, in that she saw herself as being, and having to be, more decisive, but also as less in control of her situation (since she was soon to become dependent on the hospital staff). At the same time she saw herself as becoming closer to her partner as they became a family after the birth of the baby. Interestingly, despite seeing a closeness due to their sharing of the experience of childbirth with her mother she also progressively came to see differences between them, for example seeing her mother as more vulnerable and less resilient than she had previously seen her. The study also revealed that people's retrospective accounts, especially their memories of how they felt at the time, are coloured by how they see things currently. Hence some of the complexity of the changes in perceptions, feelings, identities and roles may be obscured or smoothed over and re-interpreted within the context of current events (see also Miell, 1987).

BOX 5.4   Adaptation to parenthood

Cowan and Cowan (1985, 1988) conducted a longitudinal study of 72 expectant parents. Couples were interviewed and assessed with an extensive set of questionnaire instruments in late pregnancy and again at six and eighteen months after childbirth. A control group of 24 couples who were childless and not becoming parents was employed to provide comparisons.

The results were summarized in terms of five domains:

1   Self and roles – women experienced their self-identity as becoming centred on being a parent more than men and consistent with this, regardless of how egalitarian the relationship originally was, it tended to drift towards a more traditional organization of roles.

2   Marital interaction – in contrast to the childless couples, the new parents perceived an increase in distance between them after the birth, they also reported (90%+) an increase in conflict and disagreement, with the main focus of this being the division of labour and roles. Significantly, this was most closely related to *how* these issues were discussed – neither partner liked to be 'nagged', criticized or to have their efforts go unacknowledged. The new parents also reported positive changes, such as becoming more efficient and effective problem solvers. 'We simply don't have all week to spend on disagreements any more.'

3   The parent-child relationship – a circular relationship was found, so that when things were experienced to be going well between the parents and the child, then the couple's relationship with each other was also felt to benefit. Likewise, when the couple were feeling good about their relationship they felt they had more time, warmth and energy to spend with the child. Partners who described greater differences in ideas about how to raise the child before pregnancy were found to experience greater parenting stress two years later. The influence of the baby's personality was less clear, in that the parent's experience of how difficult the child was may have been related to their level of irritability and marital stress.

4   Three generational perspective – new parents often felt 'sandwiched' between the needs of their own parents and of their baby.

5   Life stress and social support – obvious sources of stress were loss of income if the woman stopped working, physical fatigue and anxiety about the birth and implications of parenthood. For most new parents there was an initial increase and then decrease in support from parents, friends and other family. Overall, however, there were no significant changes reported in the general level of life stress. The negative effects may have been countered by the positive feelings of excitement and closeness at the birth of the child.

In general, the women in this study were less satisfied with themselves and the role arrangements than the men; the women were much more likely to have sacrificed their careers or studies to look after the new baby. The changes were not always in this direction but generally were more variable over the two-year period than for the non-parent group.

In summary it was suggested that the new parents felt their relationship changed more, and more negatively, than the non-parents, but overall the changes in perceived satisfaction were small. However, a variety of external factors do appear to have a significant effect, such as child-care facilities or the 'social pressure' on women to breast feed which means that they are more likely to be tied to the baby.

3.3   Change and patterns of interaction: dyads to triads

Differences in how couples interact, and in particular the level of conflict between them, may be related to their different beliefs and expectations about gender roles and the division of household tasks. In addition, how partners communicate about these issues, and their ideas of what counts as 'good' forms of communication or negotiation may be critical (Fitzpatrick et al., 1994). It is important to see these couples within the context of the transition. As we saw in the case of Steve and Patricia in Extract 5.1, both partners may feel tired at times, distracted by the needs of the baby and unable to offer reassurance to each other. In addition, the transition may reveal differences in beliefs and attitudes that were not apparent previously, for example attitudes to parenting, childcare or what kind of a family they wish to be: 'the transition to first-time parenthood highlights existing differences between spouses and introduces some new ones, in both cases increasing opportunities for disagreement and conflict in their relationship as a couple' (Cowan and Cowan, 1989, p. 139).

In this context of exhaustion, revelation of differences, less time and energy for physical intimacy and increased anxieties, both partners may also be seeking reassurance and support from one another. Set against a background that parenthood 'ought' to be immensely satisfying and fulfilling, partners may feel 'abnormal' about any negative feelings they are having. Such ambiguity of feelings in caregiving relationships are discussed further in Chapter 6.

Autonomy versus interdependence

Arguably, an important task for partners in any relationship is to simultaneously establish intimacy and also claim some independence and 'personal space'. At a practical level, partners may need to separate to fulfil demands of work and maintain involvements with others. However, there is also a need to maintain connections with each other to preserve the sense of intimacy in a relationship. Some writers have referred to this balance between intimacy and separateness as negotiating emotional 'distance'. Each partner may feel a need to satisfy at least some of his or her own needs, hopes and dreams. Yet both must also find ways to coordinate these separate 'life paths' into a mutually satisfying journey. This involves complex and subtle communication if partners are to avoid feeling rejected by attempts at separation or suffocated by excessive 'closeness'.

'The greatest challenge for two excited and usually exhausted spouses making this major life-transition, then, is to work out a way to maintain a sense of individuality and mutuality while becoming a family' (Cowan and Cowan, 1989, p. 139). A critical factor in how effectively this is achieved relates to the beliefs and expectations that each partner holds and also their levels of need for attachment. Experience from clinical work suggests that for some relationships 'symptoms' serve a role of managing distance when partners are unable to negotiate this explicitly (Byng-Hall, 1980).

Couples who hold beliefs which value closeness and sharing of feelings have been found to be more satisfied with their relationship during the transition to parenthood. On the other hand, couples who valued autonomy appeared to become more concerned with dealing with the decreases in their autonomy than in resolving their needs for support (Fitzpatrick et al., 1994). The conceptualizations of autonomy, however, may be more varied and complex, with some couples seeing their close, interdependent relationships as forging them into a 'strong couple' and thereby giving them *more* autonomy to work with in the outside world.

Power and conflict

The general indication in the literature has been that the transition to parenthood does involve some deterioration of the relationship and increased conflict. The recognition of differences as a consequence of the transition have been summarized as partners feeling that they are, 'not on the same side'. However, confronted by a variety of problems that need to be solved, this sense of difference and conflict can aggravate problems. Furthermore, it has been argued that a complicating factor is the possibility of gender differences in communicational styles. Radley (Chapter 2 in this volume) suggests that men and women differ both in their verbal and non-verbal communicational styles and that these differences are related to inequalities of power. Gottman and Levenson (1984) have observed that in situations of conflict, women are more likely to 'open up' emotional issues and try to address and discuss them, whereas men are more likely to try to block or avoid discussions. These gender-based differences in communicational styles may serve to exacerbate rather than relieve the problems and conflict.

A critical aspect of the transition may also be a shift in the balance of power in the relationship. LaRossa and LaRossa (1981) have described changes in 'dual-career' couples, where both partners have continued work after the birth of their child.

Before you read the following extract, consider what aspects of the transition ACTIVITY 5.9 might be similar and different for dual-career couples as opposed to relationships where one partner predominantly takes responsibility for care of the infant.

Extract 5.2   *A dual-career couple – Alex and Amanda*

Amanda: I went back to work when she [the baby] was four months old, and that's the worst part. I'm enjoying my job a whole lot, but I just go crazy because I don't have enough time to do the things I need to do. Don't have time to get the house cleaned and things like that.

Alex : When she doesn't have time to do anything at home, that puts pressure on me to do more things; so that puts pressure on anything that I would do ... I've been involved with some plays, players' group...

Amanda: To be specific *[laughing]* he's off every night of the week until 11.30 ... he still does everything, and I've given up everything.

Alex: That's not true.

Amanda: And that makes me mad ... two or three times people have called me up and asked me to do something, and I just can't do anything ... Probably the best, the number one excuse is that I'm breast-feeding. But I don't think it will change when that stops ... He just gets his way more...

Alex: That's not true ... We're going to have a fight [quarrel] here in a minute ... See what you [the baby] are causing; see?

Amanda: Well, I want to stay with her more. I think he should want to stay with her a little more than he does. But, I mean, I want him to be in the play because he enjoys it so much ... But I still resent a whole lot that he's gone ... I don't even sit down. Come home, like we're putting stuff in the, heating stuff in the oven for supper. We're not eating decent ... he leaves, by the time we finish eating, it's still on the table...

Alex: No, because I clean up the dishes after we get through eating ... I feel guilty about it [leaving] ... For five months I've been home, haven't been doing much at all...

Source: LaRossa and LaRossa 1981, pp. 160–9

Alex and Amanda's account illustrates Gottman and Levenson's point that men appear to be more likely to withdraw when facing stress, but also that shifts in power as a consequence of the transition to parenthood are apparent. When Amanda comments that Alex 'just gets his way more' this implies that she feels she has less freedom, especially in having to have more responsibility for the baby. Amanda indicates that this initially was because of the breast-feeding but at the same time she adds: 'But I don't think it will change when it stops', that is that she expects to continue having less freedom.

ACTIVITY 5.10   Turn to *Reading B:* 'A gender sensitive perspective on personal relationships and therapy' by Arlene Vetere. As you read, note down the different types of power that it is suggested that men and women may possess (see also Chapter 3, section 4.4). In what ways have these sources of power altered during the course of your own or a friend's relationship? How have these alterations in power influenced the relationship?

The two related but distinct components of power: objective and subjective power may both shift significantly as a result of parenthood. Most obviously, the woman may become partly or totally financially dependent on her partner. More specifically, she may also become physically dependent due to the pregnancy, with tiredness, lack of sleep and so on following the birth. Partners may also perhaps hold a belief that women become more emotionally vulnerable after birth, and that men need less emotional support. This profile of beliefs and expectations can serve to increase further feelings of dependency and possibly conflict (Gelles, 1979). Again, the effects of these changes have been found to be related to the beliefs that partners hold. In a relationship which has stressed independence, these shifts to dependency may be perceived with some resentment as stifling and annoying, whereas in relationships which value closeness they may present less of a source of conflict.

On the other hand, it is possible that one or other partner may also gain some power through the baby. It is likely, for example, that the woman will be closer to the child and may be able to exert influence over her partner through the baby, for example by emphasizing what is 'best for the baby' in negotiations or disagreements, or appearing more confident and able in dealing with the baby.

Review of section 3

- The transition to parenthood involves changes in roles and stress. Generally, however, the evidence does not suggest the transition to parenthood is dramatically stressful or traumatic for most parents.

- Structural factors such as social support, childcare and economic circumstances are critical in determining the nature of the experience of the transition. In general, women appear to carry the burden of the changes and responsibilities, even in dual-career couples.

4   Leaving home

Like the transition to parenthood, the 'leaving home' transition has been widely regarded as involving stress for relationships in a family. This transition can be seen as the converse of the transition to parenthood, particularly in that one of the key changes is from triadic relationship back to a dyadic one (or, if there is more than one child, the first child's leaving signals the start of this eventual change). Over the years the relationship between the parents will have incorporated the influence, demands and needs of one or more children. The transition may be gradual, but the point comes where the first child leaves and the family home is no longer their main base. One of the tasks for the parents here is to redefine their relationship, or revisit parts of their earlier relationship and start to contemplate some new roles as a couple with adult children, and possible grandparenthood. In one-parent families sometimes the sense of loss and loneliness can be more extreme, depending on what other support the parent has. For some couples this can be a very difficult time, for example when they discover that they have little in common now or begin to argue over old issues put aside unresolved by the arrival of the children. There is a considerable body of clinical evidence which suggests that the transition can be associated with various forms of pathology, both for parents and for the children (Carter and McGoldrick, 1980; Haley, 1980). However, it is possible that this is an excessively gloomy picture and in this section we will start by examining some of the evidence on this transition from a non-clinical population. This will be followed by a review of transitions where problems are apparent.

The transition can itself be seen as comprising a number of sub-stages or phases; preparation for leaving, 'launching' the young adult and the 'empty nest'. The first may involve a process of gradual separation of the child from its parents, with an increase in autonomy and independence for the young adult. The launching phase involves the actual leaving of the young person along a variety of possible routes, such as to college, independent living or marriage. The 'empty nest' phase occurs when the last child has left, leaving behind the parents or lone parent. There may be considerable variation between families in how these phases occur. Frequently children leave and return for some time, the preparation phase may vary in length for different children and so on. In addition, the nature of the leaving may vary considerably, in some families the child decides to leave against the parents' wishes, and in others there may be pressure applied to the child to leave for a variety of reasons, such as continual conflict with one or both parents or siblings. It is also possible that there are significant gender differences in the way that boys and girls leave home and the effects on the relationship between the parents.

4.1   Changing roles and conflicts

The child launching phase is seen to involve major re-negotiations of family rules, roles and expectations of behaviour. As an example, there may be conflicts or power struggles relating to the young person's attempts to establish his or her own independence and adult status. It is possible that the stresses reportedly associated with the stage are not so much a result of the leaving but of the continuing process of negotiation, insecurity about the child's future, economic stresses and so on (Anderson, 1990). The period has also been seen to be associated with ambivalence on the part of both parents and youngsters. On the one hand the parents have to try to encourage independence and separation, but on the other feel protective and unsure about whether the young person is 'ready' and competent to live on their own. Likewise, the young person may feel insecure about his or her ability to cope, whether they will be lonely and so on, but still want to become independent and resent parental protectiveness as intrusive.

Effect on the parents' relationship

Children's leaving is associated with both positive and negative effects. Some parents experience a sense of loss and confusion about their roles, having become used to being parents they may feel a void or emptiness in their lives. Others have more positive experiences:

> It's a totally new thing. Now there isn't the responsibility for the children. There's more privacy and freedom to be yourself. All of a sudden there are times when we can just sit down and have a conversation. And it was great to go on a vacation alone.

> It's the boredom that has grown up between us but which we didn't face before. With the kids at home, we found something to talk about, but now the buffer is gone. There are just the two of us, face to face…

(Couples quoted in Neugarten and Datan, 1981, p. 277)

However, research suggests that in fact the 'empty nest' stage, when children have gone, is generally found to be the least stressful period. For many parents there may be a sense of relief and satisfaction that they have successfully prepared and launched their children into the adult world. Negative feelings appear to be associated with marriages which were already less satisfactory or where the parents were much older and perceived themselves as more caring and nurturing (Lewis et al., 1979). The position of the young person leaving (in terms of birth order) is also important, such that parents typically experience most stress over the departure of the oldest child (Duvall, 1977). This may be because the first child's leaving symbolizes the onset of this stage, which may evoke memories of the parent's own home-leaving; a sense of loss and change. It may also be that this is the parents' 'first run' at making the changes necessary. By the time the last child leaves it is possible that most parents will have developed the necessary coping resources to adjust more easily to this final departure (Anderson, 1990).

Children's experiences

There are obviously major differences in the circumstances of children in families. In extreme cases the children may have been extremely unhappy, abused, deprived and rejected and hence leaving may, at least temporarily, represent a welcome escape and relief – a chance to live their own lives. However, more broadly, there are other positive findings, such as improved communication and feelings of affection towards the parents following leaving home, especially for boys. Nevertheless, for many young people there may be an initial period of homesickness, grief, depression or loneliness and for some these continue for a considerable time. For more privileged youngsters, for example those leaving home to attend college, research suggests that: 'living away from home at college enabled adolescents to view parents in a more affectionate light and this provided a sense of protection that allowed the adolescent to strive for increased independence, dominance and responsibility' (Anderson, 1990, p. 49).

Anderson (1990) conducted a study of 84 families (in the USA) who each had a child who was about to enter college. In half of the sample the children had decided to live away from home and half would continue living at home, at least during their first year at college. The total sample consisted of 6 per cent only children, 50 per cent first borns, 32 per cent last borns and 12 per cent middle children. The families varied such that 70 per cent of the parents were in their first marriage, over 87 per cent were currently married and had been for an average period of over 20 years. The occupational and educational backgrounds of the families was diverse but the largest grouping was 'lower middle-class' (40 per cent). The aims of the study were to test whether parents whose children left home to attend college experienced a greater level of stress, disruptions of marital communication, parent-adolescent communication, and personal adjustment than parents whose children attended college whilst living at home. It was also hypothesized that the departure of the oldest children and of girls would produce the greatest level of stress, and that mothers would in general be more disturbed by the transition than the father.

The transition is a complex process involving many factors. One significant feature is that of gender differences, both in terms of the children's experiences and that of the parents. The study by Anderson (1990) explored such gender differences. Consider for a few moments what differences you might expect:

ACTIVITY 5.11

1   between the effects on the parents of girls versus boys leaving;

and

2   differences in how mothers and fathers might experience children leaving.

Jot down your responses to compare with what Anderson actually found.

BOX 5.5 A study of parents' experience of children leaving home

Anderson's study employed self-report measures of changes over a period of four months. Parents were sent a set of questionnaires dealing with parental role stress; an assessment of parent-adolescent communication; marital communication; level of adjustment to life changes and measures of general health and emotional well being. (The questionnaire included questions like: 'When you think of your experience as a parent, how [frustrated, tense, worried, bothered or upset] do you feel?'.) These were sent in July prior to the son or daughter going to college, and again in October once they had started. The analysis was in two phases: the first part involved comparing changes for the two groups of parents in relation to birth order of the children. Last born and middle children were combined into one category as compared to first born children (only single children were excluded since they confounded the analysis, being both first and last born). The second phase involved examining the influence of the adolescents' gender on the parents' experience.

The findings offered some broad support for a stress model. Parents reported an increase in negative feelings and less intimate discussion between them as a couple following their children moving away to college. However, a general reduction in stress was reported, especially for fathers, after the child started college. It appeared that parents experienced concern before the child started college, and relief when entrance and starting had been successfully completed.

There were findings of gender differences – in general parents did *not* experience more stress due to a daughter's departure than they did to a son's. However, mothers reported more anxiety about their role as a parent when a daughter started college, irrespective of whether she left home or not. Also, mothers reported that communication with their sons improved when they left home, whereas communication became better with their daughters when they stayed at home. This, Anderson argues, may have been because the greater physical distance reduced sons' fears of losing their independence and helped them to separate. However, daughters appeared to be able to establish their own identity and independence whilst staying at home, staying with significant others in their family.

The communication between the parents was influenced by the child's gender so that the amount of discussion between parents increased when a son left home but decreased when a daughter left. Generally girls were found to sustain a 'higher level of emotional connectedness' and maintain more contact with their parents, especially with their mothers, after leaving home. Since sons tended to cut themselves off more dramatically, this may have left a clearer gap so that parents therefore turned more to each other.

How do these findings on gender compare with the ideas you noted down in Activity 5.8?

Though of interest, such empirical studies have various shortcomings. In attempting to make generalizations across families, the subtle and unique dynamics become obscured. For example, the analysis of the results involves the researcher in making assumptions or speculations about why, for example, couples appeared to communicate with each other more when a son left home than when a daughter left. One solution to these shortcomings would be to interview the families again, or at least a sub-set of them, to provide some insight into their beliefs and the underlying emotions that shape their relationships. Another obvious weakness of the above study is that it did not examine the experiences of the young people themselves. Other siblings may be able to provide yet another interesting, and possibly more detached perspective on the dynamics of the triad made up of the parents and the child about to leave. Cultural and racial differences are also relevant, for example a higher proportion of young adults in the USA go to college, and in the same town as their parents (partly for financial reasons) than is the case in the UK, and hence more regular contact is possible. In some cultures it may be more acceptable for young adults to continue to live with their parents in an extended family household (Dallos and Sapsford, 1995). Such factors will affect whether the transition is perceived as a major break or as a gradual change.

Studies such as Anderson's generally paint a reasonably optimistic picture of the leaving-home transition: 'the findings suggest that the physical departure of a child from home is perceived by most parents as a happy event accompanied by increased feelings of affection toward the adolescent (especially for mothers)' (Anderson, 1990, p. 50). However, cases where the separation is problematic are of psychological interest in revealing more about some of the factors involved in the transition and also to assist the work of clinical psychologists with troubled people and families.

4.2   Experiencing problems with the transition

However the reorganization takes place, a fundamental feature of the leaving home transition is that a reconstruction of meanings, identities and roles must take place so that the young person's status changes from that of a child to that of an adult. Haley (1973, 1980) points out that the human species is the only one where parents and offspring continue to be closely involved after the child has grown to adulthood. There has been much written about the conflicts of this transition, but as we saw in the last section, most families appear to negotiate this in a fairly harmonious and non-problematic manner. At the same time, there is an extensive body of evidence from clinical literature, especially from family therapy, that the leaving home transition *can* be related to the development of serious forms of pathology: 'If the solidification of the marriage has not taken place and re-investment is not possible, the family usually mobilizes itself to hold on to the last child. Prior to that, the family may avoid the conflict around separation by allowing one child to leave and subsequently focusing on the next in line' (Solomon, 1973, p. 186). Children may become drawn in to the parents' concerns and worries in various ways, sometimes this is obvious, such as their responses when parents openly argue or fight (see also the concept of triangulation in Chapter 3, section 4). In other cases it may be more subtle, such as when children become concerned and worried about their parents' problems to the point of sacrificing their own lives.

ACTIVITY 5.12   The extracts below are taken from the accounts of two young women. In the first, Gwyn (14) is a young girl still living at home with her parents. In the second, Claire (19) is a young woman who has left home to attend university.

As you read the accounts consider the following questions:

1   How do the young women's attempts at autonomy appear to be related to their parents' relationship?

2   What issues of autonomy and power appear to be involved in the changes in these two families?

Extract 5.3 *Girls talking about their families*

Gwyn's account (14-year-old)

Mum got ill when I was eight, after she had my brother James. She was taking tablets and they weren't the right ones for her. It was frightening because she used to hallucinate sometimes. She had these feelings that dad didn't want her any more, and that was horrible. Once I rushed down to tell my dad, and she went to me, "Oh, you're taking your dad's side now," It wasn't like her at all ... My mum and dad are a perfect couple; they've got a lot in common and a lot different and they complement each other. ... My sister can't talk to them the way I do, but sometimes I've felt that they didn't confide enough in me when there was a problem. A lot of the time my dad comes home looking really upset and mum and dad go into their room and shut the door and I can hear them crying. I don't know what it's about, but it's always to do with money. They like to be private like that. They never tell me when there are financial problems. There are a lot of secrets they have that I never know about, and I think that's the main problem between me and them. I know they don't want to worry me but I get even more worried when I know something's going on and they won't tell me. Then they ask me what I'm worried about! I can't ask, I feel it's a bit nosy, but now I'm getting older I feel more responsible...

At times I wish I had a bit more freedom, like if my dad's in a mood that he won't let me go out, then I get a bit angry, but usually I'm content with it. Sometimes they don't let me go to places on my own; my dad walks with me and that irritates me because I don't want to be seen with him. He doesn't like the idea of me having a boyfriend, he says boys are all after one thing, he doesn't really want me to grow up. Mum's all right, she had a very strict upbringing and wants me to have more freedom. But I just want to be myself, and not have any expectations made of me.

My place is just home. I'm fed up with trying to conform to people, do what other people want me to do. I'm just with mum and dad now. That's my social circle. They're my real friends, and my sister and my brother. I always know that they'll stick by me whatever. It's something I can't describe, the bond in my family.

Claire 19 – at university reading biology:

I was in my O-level year when it all started. It had been building up for a long time because when I was younger, my family life was very intense. My father's all right really, he's just got a rather volatile temper … I was so scared of him that I wouldn't say anything when he came into the house, then I'd start talking and being normal as soon as he went out.

I'd always been well developed for my age my dad would say 'You're too fat' and make all these cutting comments about it. Perhaps he was just teasing me but I took it very personally … I think getting anorexic was mostly rebelling against him. Most of my eating problems came from my dad being like that himself. When he was being the real fitness freak, we all felt he was getting really cold and self-obsessed, and he used to get into tempers all the time. Subconsciously I thought: I'll show him; and if he stopped eating a certain thing, I'd give it up as well, to show I was on an equal level. I was eating the absolute minimum. I never caused upsets about eating with the family, but I'd pretend I was really full. I managed to lose a pound or two a week … My mum got cross when she cooked things and I wouldn't eat very much, but she was quite good really … The worst time was on holiday this year. I'd got this little bikini on … Mum looked at my ribs and said, 'That's disgusting'. I felt: so what? other people are thin and they don't get into trouble about it…

At that age (18) I wanted to be more independent and they weren't letting me and I didn't know how to express what I felt. But I loved being hungry because I was in control of my own body, it felt great. I'd read about anorexia and thought: no, that can't be me; but I realised it was and I knew why girls go like this, what they were feeling inside. It's just wanting to control something for yourself when you can't. With me it was having very strict parents. Unfortunately it has the opposite effect because it makes parents more protective. They're always making sure you eat up and asking you about your private habits. I had to lie to them quite a lot, which made it worse...

Then I met my first boyfriend, and that changed my whole life. It was like there was a purpose to it and I wasn't worried about eating any more ... After I recovered I began to get much more independent and self-confident. I built myself up to feel: I'm a normal girl and I've got nothing to be ashamed of ... It's brilliant here at university. My parents used to have this image of me as being quiet, conscientious, and very hard-working, and I don't feel like that. When they came to visit, I expected them to be really intrusive and ask me if I was eating properly, but my mum said, 'You seem to be managing all right. I'm glad you're enjoying it so much' ... They seem to accept that I'm living my own life. They're not being possessive any more. I'm really pleased about it, and we get on much better now.

Source: Sharpe, 1990, pp. 21–25, 44–49

These poignant accounts from two young people were generated predominantly as a response to a request for volunteers placed in magazines. Some of the accounts were conducted at the girl's homes with the permission of their parents, but 'most preferred to meet and talk on more neutral territory, like a park or a coffee bar' (Sharpe, 1990). There is always the doubt that accounts such as these may be affected by the young person telling the researcher what they think she/he wants to hear, and censuring parts which they fear might make them, or their parents, appear in a 'bad light'. Nevertheless they do reveal some aspects of the complex web of interconnected relationships that surround the leaving-home transition. The young adult and his/her parents are profoundly interconnected so that decisions (even fundamental ones such as whether or not to eat) are contingent on relationships with others in the family.

Gwyn seems to be very concerned with her parents' worries, adopting a protective (almost parental) position of concern towards them. This appears to have the effect of restricting her own social life, which though she accepts it voluntarily, does pose problems for her. Such ambiguities about roles and hierarchy appear to characterize adolescence and leaving-home. Claire's account illustrates some issues for a young woman at a later stage in the leaving-home transition. Claire sees herself as trying to resist her father. She says less about her relationship with her mother, or the relationship between her parents. It does appear, though, that her parents spent a lot of time being concerned about her anorexia, but not always in a very positive or, for Claire, helpful way. Claire's account also suggests that her mother was generally less critical of her and it may be that Claire became involved in siding with her mother against her father. However, for both the girls, being drawn into their parents' relationship held negative consequences. Gwyn appears to receive little reward for the sacrifices of her time and her concern for her parents. For Claire, siding with her mother does not seem to be rewarded, for example when her mother criticizes her by saying she looks 'disgusting'. Independence is clearly a central issue for both girls.

Clinical work with other young people and their families adds support to the implications of these accounts which suggest that young people may become entangled in and disturbed by their parents' problems. Haley (1973, 1980) suggests that the high incidence of serious psychiatric disturbances in young adults about to leave home may be related to the child becoming entangled in the parents' conflicts. A child who develops 'mental illness' can help to abort the threatened separation of the parents:

> By developing a problem that incapacitates him socially, the child remains within the family system. The parents can continue to share the child as a source of concern and disagreement, and they find it unnecessary to deal with each other without him. The child can continue to participate in a triangular struggle with his parents, while offering himself and them his 'mental illness' as an excuse for all difficulties.
>
> *(Haley, 1973, p.61)*

The task for parents and children, Haley suggests, is for a balance to be struck between such an entanglement and too great a separation if later relationships between the parent and the grown-up child are to be satisfying and successful.

Review of section 4

- The leaving-home transition involves several stages: the preparatory stage; first child(ren) leaving; and the 'empty nest'.
- Stress may be experienced, especially in relation to practical issues and concerns.
- A sense of loss may be experienced but this may be offset by increased feelings of autonomy and independence.
- Relationships may become strained prior to leaving home but frequently these improve some time after the transition is established.
- Transitional difficulties may be related to a young person becoming entangled with unresolved conflicts between the parents.
- Like the previous transitions discussed, leaving home appears to be a complex process that varies between families. Young people's accounts suggest that some have been cast into an adult role prior to leaving home whereas for others it presents a new experience of responsibility and independence.

5   The family life cycle: relationships in context

So far we have examined three phases or periods of change in relationships: development of intimate friendships, first parenthood and children leaving home. These can be seen to imply a developmental sequence – the formation of friendships, becoming a couple, birth of children and children leaving home. In reality, for many people the progression is more complex, the stages may not follow in this order, and in particular many children now do not grow up with both of their parents. On the other hand, there is arguably *some* discernible pattern of development and linkages between generations for which it is necessary to offer an account. Complex and significant connections between family members over generations are obvious in most societies, and it may be helpful to try to understand relationships within a dynamic inter-generational context.

5.1   The family life cycle model

The family life cycle model was developed by family researchers (Carter and McGoldrick, 1980; Duvall, 1977) and clinicians (Burnham, 1986; Haley, 1973). It embraces both the idea of development as driven by a variety of biological forces and the idea that in any given culture there are a set of expectations, beliefs and norms about change and development. For example, in many cultures there are expectations that children leave home at a certain age. These expectations can be seen to be socially constructed in that there are cross-cultural variations, for example in many Asian societies and ethnic minority cultures in the West, the children continue to live with their parents even after marriage and the birth of their own children (Rapaport et al., 1982). There are also local variations and choices – people divorce, decide not to live exclusively with another, live as lone-parents and so on. However, the family life cycle model also draws attention to some potentially universal aspects of relationships and change, for example that certain tasks or demands present themselves, such as the fundamental biological and organizational changes prompted by pregnancy and birth, or the need to readjust roles as 'children' become 'adults'. Given basic realities, such as economic factors, housing, space, changes in health and physical abilities, there may be constraints on the variety of solutions that are possible, for example most societies expect the parents, or at least one of them to take primary care for children. Family life cycle models describe the 'typical' or dominant patterns found in any given society. This does *not* mean that these are necessarily accepted as inevitable or proper, but there can be a danger, as we will discuss later, that the model appears not just descriptive, but *prescriptive*. This is a wider problem for any developmental psychological theory, but is perhaps particularly salient with the family life cycle model in a contemporary social context.

The family life cycle model therefore tries to capture three aspects of change:

1   fundamental biological factors and imperatives;

2   fundamental aspects of change in relationships and roles due to growth and maturation;

3   societal expectations of change and organization of relationships.

Time is a dominant aspect here, for example concerns that may be voiced, such as 'its time we settled down', 'time we started a family' or even 'time to move on and separate' are all influenced by some form of life cycle view of relationships.

You might like to spend a few minutes noting down (1) what you regard to be the 'typical' ages for the following to occur and (2) what some of the key issues are which might affect each of these:

ACTIVITY 5.13

going on a first date	divorce
going steady	first child
co-habiting	children leaving home
marriage	becoming a grandparent

You will probably have included in your notes for this activity some mention of individual factors – that some people mature earlier, take greater risks, enjoy the excitement of new and varied relationships and so on. You may also have mentioned that there are likely to be local variations – perhaps that young people in the cities are likely to start dating earlier and have more partners. Family factors, such as parental attitudes, circumstances, and the role we play in our families may well influence when, and if, we develop an exclusive relationship or marry.

Attempts have been made to integrate these various forces for change into a developmental perspective of relationships. From empirical and clinical studies of relationships, transitions and family life, Carter and McGoldrick (1980) proposed a six-stage model, which argues that though development is continuous it can, nevertheless, be seen as progressing through some key stages which require major adjustments. Initially these have been discussed as transitions, but perhaps more appropriately they can be seen as transformations in the nature of the relationships:

1   the unattached young adult – dating and courtship;

2   the joining of two families through marriage (or cohabitation);

3   the family with very young children;

4   the family with adolescents;

5   launching children and moving on – leaving home;

6   the family in later life – retirement and old age.

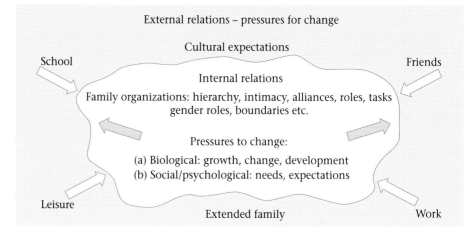

Family life-cycle stages: Transitions

The external and internal demands for change are *continuous,* but become critical at transitional points in a family's life:

- courtship
- early marriage
- birth of children
- middle marriage
- leaving home
- retirement and old age

Tasks: external and internal demands for change
Attempted solutions: ways of meeting the tasks, solving demands for change

Figure 5.1   *The family life cycle*

(Source: Adapted from Dallos, R. *Family Belief Systems, Therapy and Change,* 1991, Buckingham, Open University Press.)

Carter and McGoldrick (1980) emphasize that development is stimulated not only from the current forces for change inside and outside the family (see Figure 5.1), but also forces for change from trans-generational and developmental factors:

> The vertical flow in a system includes patterns of relating and function-ing that are transmitted down the generations in a family … It includes all the family attitudes, taboos, expectations, and loaded issues with which we grow up … these aspects of our lives are like the hand that we are dealt: they are a given. What we do with them is the issue…

> The horizontal flow includes … both the predictable developmental stresses and those unpredictable events, 'the slings and arrows of out-rageous fortune', that may disrupt the life cycle process. [See Figure 5.2.]

(Carter and McGoldrick, 1980, p. 10)

The development of a family and the relationships within it are seen to be influenced both by the external events, such as the financial fortunes of the family, and the biological and social development of its members. In turn these are interpreted within the beliefs, attitudes and traditional ways of coping with problems that have been passed on down the generations.

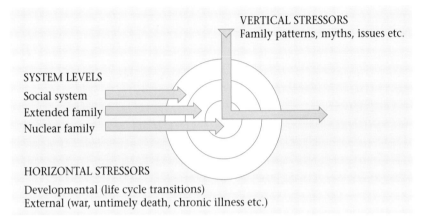

Figure 5.2

(Source: Adapted from Carter, E. and McGoldrick, M, *The Family Life Cycle: A Framework for Family Therapy*, 1980, New York, Gardner.

5.2   Transitions, tasks and attempted solutions

A central concept in the family life cycle model is the suggestion that each transition involves a range of *tasks* – these are a variety of issues or problems that have to be solved at each transitional stage (such as those discussed in sections 2, 3 and 4). Some of these are relatively simple practical tasks, others more clearly psychological – with emotional and cognitive changes. However, even the practical aspects can become suffused with meaning and emotions, for example the absence of a child at the meal table can activate a range of feelings and memories. The tasks involved can be summarized in the following broad categories:

Structural changes. Individuals are involved in re-negotiating the balance of power or hierarchy. The patterns of intimacy may change, for example with the arrival of a baby a couple may have less time for each other and so on. The boundaries may be revised in terms of how exclusive the couple are.

Beliefs and roles. Alongside the structural changes there are important shifts in expectations, self-identity, couple and/or family identity and so on. The arrival of a change adds the identity 'parents' to those of 'individual adult' and 'couple' and the family increases by a generation so that the couple's parents now become grandparents. Accompanying this may be a range of expectations and of beliefs about what these roles should involve, how people should now relate to each other, and what they can expect or be obliged to do.

Skills. Associated with the tasks are a range of skills, for example the move from an unattached young adult to finding a partner involves learning a range of social skills, developing and breaking friendships and sexual relationships. These also involve the rest of the family, for example by them expressing their opinions of a choice of friend or partner in a constructive way, relating to and accommodating new members into the family. Likewise at other stages, such as the arrival of the first child, there are a range of practical and psychological skills – basic care of the child, medical knowledge, and maintaining relationships under conditions of fatigue and stress.

ACTIVITY 5.14   Think back about your own experience of one of the transitions discussed so far in the chapter (or another if you prefer). What do you perceive to be some of the key difficulties and tasks that faced you? How did you resolve them? In retrospect, can you think of other ways that you might have dealt with the changes required?

Couples and families at the transitional stages can be regarded (Carter and McGoldrick, 1980; Duvall, 1977; Haley, 1980) as being presented with a range of 'problems' to be solved, for example the arrival of a child may be dealt with in various ways, depending on the practical and emotional resources available. In some families in-laws may play a key part in assisting the couple practically and emotionally by offering child-minding, financial assistance, advice and information. Another couple may decide to avoid involvement of in-laws and decide to share the childcare or adopt a model where one parent takes the major burden of responsibility. The choices made are *contingent* on the family situation, finances, health, stresses and so on. In some cases a combination of stresses and problems may constrain the 'attempted solutions' perceived to be possible, with the consequence that the couple and the family is unable to carry out the task required. These solutions can be seen as 'emerging' out of the flux of interactions and negotiations rather than simply being made unilaterally by one person or sub-system of the family.

These changes in the family and couple's life cycle involve the establishment of mutually agreed *rules* to guide their actions. In order to know how the other feels, what they want, what they think, the partners need to communicate. All aspects of relationships therefore involve communication and the more accurate and effective this communication is the more likely that positive developments may take place (Mehrabian, 1972; Watzlawick et al., 1974). The styles of communicating may alter along with transitional stages, for example with the arrival of a child a couple may have less time to communicate directly with each other and may start to communicate through the baby. Conflicts between a couple may also be expressed indirectly by disagreements about the baby (Fitzpatrick et al., 1994; Haley, 1976; LaRossa and LaRossa, 1981).

5.2.1   Problems with the family life cycle model

A number of criticisms of the family life cycle model have been voiced: the first centres on diversity and the potentially normative assumptions of life cycle models and the family life cycle in particular. The second, broader criticism is that life cycle models in general tend to assume a linear progression through the stages: 'The family life cycle is not a linear event; it does not begin with a stage, nor does it end with the deaths of members of a particular generation' (Combrinck-Graham, 1985, p. 143).

In addition, there is a danger in naming stages of limiting our attention to only a small sub-grouping of the family. The naming of the 'unattached young adult' as a stage, for example, tends to restrict attention to the individual and draws our attention away from the possible wider (ecological) consequences for the whole family.

> To talk of a marital problem is to create an entity of 'marriage' that overlooks all the forces outside the marriage that have an influence on it. The boundary we draw around a married couple, around a nuclear family, or around a kinship system is an arbitrary one for discussion purposes … It is important to keep always in mind that a family is an on-going group subject to changing external circumstances, with a history and a future together and with stages of development as well as habitual patterns among the members.
>
> *(Haley, 1973, p. 57)*

Many intimate relationships end in separation or divorce with the consequence that at least for some period of time over 10 per cent of children live in lone-parent families (Dallos and Sapsford, 1995). One implication for family life cycle models might be to suggest that the model is flawed because this formation is not formally discussed, or is regarded as a 'deviant' form. However, this misrepresents the aims and contribution of the model. Writers, such as Beal (1980), point out that lone-parent configurations do face some additional problems:

> A major problem for single-parent families is task overload … economic hardship …The major task of raising children is now performed by one parent where previously there were two. Social isolation, increased anxiety, depression, and loneliness may serve to foster decreased functioning … a single-parent (usually the mother) is the focus especially for younger children, around which all task performance occurs and through which all anxiety and stress must be processed…
>
> *(Beal, 1980, p. 258)*

The family life cycle model can draw attention to some of the common tasks that need to be performed and hence make clearer what the special needs of lone-parents are. It is an issue of social policy in any society how these needs are responded to, but to ignore these special needs is to doubly disadvantage such groups. Finally, it should also be borne in mind here that the alterations in roles in a change to a lone-parent family may be to emphasize, rather than reduce 'conventional' roles. For example, mothers in such families often have to adopt an exclusively parental role, since they have little time or resources for any interest outside of their family.

5.3 The family life spiral

Combrinck-Graham (1985) suggests that rather than conceptualizing the family life cycle as a linear process it is more appropriate to consider development as inevitably involving all the generations in the family simultaneously but in different ways. The developmental issues for individuals and relationships in each generation relate and are intertwined with the others.

Individual life cycles

Within any relationship it is also possible to see the individual partners as proceeding through their own personal transitional stages. A number of approaches have attempted to provide a developmental summary of how some key individual issues may coalesce at particular times in our lives. Erikson (1950) argued that as we develop we are faced with various 'crises' or critical issues as a result of societal expectations, biological changes and individual factors, such as personality and beliefs. In adolescence, he argues, youngsters may experience a sense of confusion, an 'identity crisis', of being caught in a difficult transition from being a child to being an adult. How easy or how difficult this transition is may in turn be related to how other family members react and whether they are supportive or pre-occupied with their own problems. Interestingly, in families, the needs of the adolescents and their middle-aged parents may coincide and offer scope for mutual growth or mutual crises. It is possible that the mid-life period is associated with some fundamental and inevitable realizations (about our own mortality, ageing, how to make the best of the rest of our lives and so on) (Levinson, 1978). The following account from a woman elegantly captures some of these themes:

> It is as if there are two mirrors before me, each held at a partial angle. I see part of myself in my mother who is growing old, and part of her in me. In the other mirror, I see part of myself in my daughter. I have some dramatic insights, just from looking in those mirrors ... It is a set of revelations that I suppose can only come when you are in the middle of three generations
>
> *(Neugarten and Datan, 1981, p. 282)*

Individual personal development and experience inevitably involves complex relationships with others. Erikson (1950) expresses this poignantly in his idea of young adulthood as being taken up with the task of developing connections, a sense of closeness, intimacy and sharing of intimate aspects of the self through sharing experiences with others. As a relationship increases in intimacy and commitment, more time might be spent considering joint identity, as well as self identity. Likewise, the mid-life period can be seen to coincide with dramatic changes in families, namely the children reaching adulthood and perhaps leaving home. The children's explorations of their abilities, talents, and the start of sexual intimacies, may remind parents of their own submerged aspirations and needs. Combrick-Graham's (1985) model attempts to integrate the different directions of change in family relationships. She suggests that it is necessary to think of stages as simultaneously involving different changes for the members, for example increased distance and autonomy for some and increased intimacy and closeness for others.

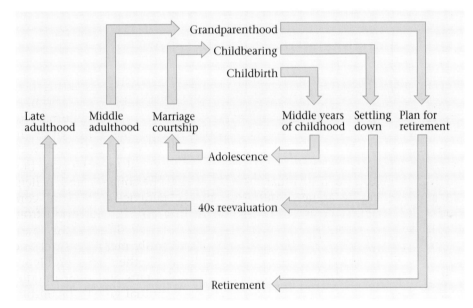

Figure 5.3

In this model (see Figure 5.3), development in the family is seen in terms of oscillating forces which propel people either outward (centrifugal) or inward (centripetal) – between periods of separation and closeness:

Centripetal (close)	*Centrifugal (separating)*
Grandparenthood	children going to school
Childbearing	leaving home
	mid-life crisis
	retirement

The activity of the family around the birth of the baby is seen to epitomize a centripetal period: 'bonding and attachment become preoccupations in relationships with families with infants ... characterized by enmeshment, diffusion of interpersonal boundaries and a high degree of resonance among individuals' (Combrick-Graham, 1985, p. 145).

At adolescence and the leaving home stage, the family may be experiencing a more distant period (centrifugal), where the young adult is spending more time outside the family and preparing to leave to start up his or her independent life. This in turn may allow the parents greater freedom to redirect their own interests and at the same time the grandparents may be embarking on retirement. Each of the three generations may be more absorbed with themselves and therefore distant to the others during this period. This period may then change towards a centripetal one as the young adults start to embark on marriage or co-habitation – a wedding, for example, can start to bring the generations closer together again.

5.4   Changing structures of power

In the examples of transitional stages given in this chapter it has been apparent that shifts in power are inevitable; in terms of the balance between parents and between parents and children, for example. This balance of power is determined by global considerations, such as the general balance of power between men and women – access to jobs, education and so on and also by local conditions – the relative balance of power between partners. One way of conceptualizing power is in terms of the *resources* that each partner possesses (Blood and Wolfe, 1960; Wood, 1993; see also *Reading B* in this volume). The most obvious and objective resources are income, education, physical strength and occupational status. But there are also a range of relative resources, such as physical attractiveness, love, affection, humour, emotional skills and so on. These are more open to negotiation and are to some extent constructed within the relationship. Which resources are dominant and how they are to be employed is to some extent dependent on cultural and subcultural laws and rules or ideologies. For example, partners are 'supposed' to provide for each other financially, emotionally and physically. Failure to provide, to withhold or to abuse these basic resources may be taken as grounds for complaint or ending the relationship.

ACTIVITY 5.15   In what ways do you think the balance of power between men and women generally varies during the course of their 'family life cycle/spiral'? How does this coincide with your own experience?

The power each partner possesses is the range of resources they have available and which can be applied to influence their partner or other members of the family. It is suggested (Carter and McGoldrick, 1980; Haley, 1973; Hesse-Biber and Williamson, 1984) that the distribution of power in any given family is to some extent unique but also shows some general trends in how it alters across the life cycle. It is argued that this occurs because not only do men and women have access to different resources, but this also changes during their lives. Typically men and women have relatively equal power during courtship, and even if there are differences the effects of this may be less marked since they are not yet living together and, therefore, not dependent on each other. With the birth of the first child, and incrementally with the birth of each additional child, a woman's 'internal' power, for example over the children and within the house, may well increase. In contrast, her 'external' power, for example financial and career may well decrease, since it is common for a woman to stop working or reduce her commitment to work. She thus becomes increasingly dependent upon her husband and the more children she has the longer she may need to withdraw from a job or career, losing experience, promotions etc. In contrast, the husband is likely to be based outside the home, he may take on extra work to help with the finances and this may even help his career to develop, thereby exacerbating the power inequalities in the relationship. As the children start school, and when they leave home, the woman's power may increase if she is able to return to work. At the same time the husband's career may be starting to level off. As a couple move towards retirement the balance of power may become more equal but cultural norms may still perpetuate power inequalities.

Changes in education, social norms and sex roles have been proposed as having an influence on how power relations may alter in the future. More women are deciding not to have children, have smaller families or wait until their careers are established before having children. A number of researchers have concluded that the longer the woman stays in the labour market the greater her power in a relationship (Gillespie, 1975; Yogev, 1987). Nevertheless, on average men still earn more and are likely to remain more economically powerful since most women are more likely to gain the unskilled and low paid jobs. Finally, as couples grow older men become a 'rarer commodity' since they die on average eight years before women (Harris, 1978): 'The relative abundance of elderly women relative to men will continue to provide a bargaining chip in the marital relationship' (Hesse-Biber and Williamson, 1984, p. 289).

Throughout the chapter it has been argued that relationships inevitably take place in a wider social context. The family life cycle and spiral models illustrate the importance of the effects of other family members. Particularly through the discussions of gender differences we have also seen that the dominant cultural conceptions: beliefs, stereotypes, and expectations shape what couples perceive to be their relationship options. These wider sources of influence are discussed in Chapter 6.

Review of section 5

- The family life cycle model views relationships as continually changing with major changes demanded at key transitional points.
  - Biological, relational and societal expectations combine to produce significant points of transition.
  - The transitions involve specific tasks or difficulties.
  - Family life cycle models may be excessively normative in assuming that development follows a linear and predictable sequence.
  - However, family life cycle models draw attention to common tasks required, for example in single-parent and nuclear family forms.
- The family life spiral model suggests that development is not necessarily linear and that relationships in families oscillate between periods of closeness and distance.
- Changes in relative power between participants significantly influence their relationship and its development.

6   Discussion and conclusions

This chapter has attempted to illustrate development and change in relationships by exploring three important transitional stages in some detail. Life cycle models have been considered as an attempt to integrate some central themes from these and other transitional stages. However, a major critique of life cycle models is that they are excessively normative and prescriptive – as if it is being suggested that all healthy relationships or family *should* develop through these stages. This may ignore diversity and people's ability and rights to choose alternative life styles, such as lone parent or homosexual couple. A step-family may proceed through the stages in a different order. A 'newly' re-married couple, for example, may find themselves in a 'romantic' courtship phase but at the same time have to deal with adolescent children from the previous marriage(s). They may also have continuing relationships with their ex-inlaws or ex-step-children.

However, the life cycle models need not be regarded as prescriptive but as a scheme for charting the transitional tasks that are likely for whatever variation of family life is under consideration. Also, although there is abundant diversity, the nuclear model of family life tends still to be the dominant image to guide expectations about development, roles and problems in Britain. Many couples and families may attempt to resist, even deliberately try to live in alternative ways, but nevertheless it still shapes our thinking (and that of policy makers). As an example, leaving home may be an important issue in both a step-family and a nuclear family but the nature of the issues and problems may be different. The child in a step-family might already have left home in a sense by moving from one parent to the other, or have established a separate space within the step-family. Nevertheless, the emotions experienced may be guided more by the expectations arising from nuclear families than the realities of their own experiences, that is, feelings of loss at the separation might be experienced because they are 'expected', though in fact the separation had occurred quietly years earlier.

A wider problem with life cycle models can be that they obscure some of the diverse, shifting and unique processes in relationships. Duck (1994) has argued that change in relationships might best be seen not as transitions but as transformations. As new meanings are created, a relationship may alter dramatically. One of the strengths of life cycle theories is that they attempt to combine ideas of the joint construction of meaning in relationships with a recognition of biology, that the processes of growth, maturation and ageing present people with key tasks to solve in relationships. Different cultures, communities and families may define the tasks associated with growth and ageing in various ways, as well as what are appropriate attempted solutions. Nevertheless, it can be suggested that drawing attention to a consideration of critical, transitional or transformational stages has been of some value for both researchers and clinicians. Although there are no simple 'right' or 'wrong' ways to deal with life cycle changes, it is important to explore the variety of solutions that individuals, groups and cultures generate and what the implications of these may be for relationships.

Finally, the analysis of gender differences is essential for the study of change in relationships. As we have seen, the experience of change, expectation of development, deterioration and interventions from others varies for men and women. We might even conclude by suggesting that we should always talk about two life cycles in a heterosexual relationship: the man's and the woman's. However, this might be unfair to many couples who clearly do have insight into each other's experiences and their differences and try to assist each other, especially at critical points. On a positive note, perhaps it is possible that the greater awareness among clinicians and researchers that development and change is not linear but cyclical, that periods of intimacy and distance, harmony and conflict, trust and mistrust may follow each other, may eventually have a beneficial effect. A more 'realistic' model of the 'ups and downs' of relationships may actually lead to *less* conflict and disappointment. However, this view will have to filter into the public domain to have a significant effect.

Further reading

Carter, E. and McGoldrick, M. (1988) *The Changing Family Life-Cycle: A Framework for Family Therapy,* (2nd edn.), New York, Gardner.

Good overview with details of various stages and therapeutic implications.

Perlman, D. and Duck, S. (eds) (1987) *Intimate Relationships: Development, Dynamics and Deterioration,* Sage: Beverley Hills.

Wide-ranging exploration of relationships development with details of a range of different types of studies.

Eron, J.B. and Lund, T.W. (1993) 'How problems evolve and dissolve: integrating narrative and strategic concepts', *Family Process,* vol. 32, pp. 291–309.

Fascinating model with case examples of the ways ordinary difficulties can evolve into problems along with therapeutic implications.

Haley, J. (1980) *Leaving Home,* New York, McGraw-Hill.

Highly readable account of the complexity and potential problems of leaving home with implications for therapy.

LaRossa, R. (1986) *Becoming a Parent,* Sage, Beverley Hills.

A personal overview of the transition to parenthood with details of studies and personal accounts.

Sharpe, S. (1990) *Voices from Home: Girls Talk About their Families,* London, Virago.

Poignant personal accounts from young people about their experiences of leaving home.

References

Allan, G. (1989) *Friendship development: A Sociological Perspective,* Boulder, Co., Westview.

Anderson, S.A. (1990) 'Changes in parental adjustment and communication during the leaving-home transition', *Journal of Social and Personal Relationships,* 7, pp. 47–68.

Baxter, L.A. (1992) 'Root metaphors in accounts of developing romantic relationships', *Journal of Social and Personal Relationships,* 9, pp. 253–75

Beal, E.W. (1980) 'Divorce and single-parent families' in Carter, E. and McGoldrick, M. (eds) *The Family Life-Cycle: A Framework for Family Therapy,* New York, Gardner.

Belsky, J., Spanier, G. and Rovine, M. (1983) 'Stability and change in marriage across the transition to parenthood', *Journal of Marriage and the Family*, 45, pp. 567–77.

Blood, R.V. and Wolfe, D.M. (1979) *Husbands and Wives: The Dynamics of Married Living*, New York, Free Press.

Burleson, B.R. (1994) 'Friendship and similiarities in social-cognition and communication abilities: social skill bases of interpersonal attraction in childhood', *Personal Relationships*, 1, pp. 371–89.

Burnham, J. (1986) *Family Therapy*, London, Tavistock.

Byng-Hall, J. (1980) 'Symptom-bearer as marital distance regulator: clinical implication', *Family Process*, 19, pp. 355–67.

Byrne, D. (1961) 'Interpersonal attraction and attitude similarity', *Journal of Abnormal Social Psychology*, 62, pp. 713–15.

Carter, E. and McGoldrick, M. (1980) *The Family Life-Cycle: A Framework for Family Therapy*, New York, Gardner.

Combrinck-Graham, L. (1985) 'A developmental model for family systems', *Family Process*, vol 24, no. 2. pp. 139–50.

Cowan, C.P. and Cowan, P.A. (1985) 'Transitions to parenthood: his, hers and theirs', *Journal of Family Issues*, 6, pp. 451–82.

Cowan, P.A. and Cowan, C.P. (1988) 'Who does what when the partners become parents?', *Marriage and Family Review*, 12, pp. 105–31.

Cowan, P.A. and Cowan, C.P. (1990) 'Changes in marriage during the transition to parenthood: must we blame the baby?' in Michaels, G.Y. and Goldberg, W. (eds) *The Transition to Parenthood*, Cambridge, Cambridge University Press.

Dallos, R. (1991) *Family Belief Systems, Therapy and Change*, Buckingham, Open University Press.

Dallos, R. and Sapsford, R. (1995) 'Patterns of diversity and lived realities' in Muncie, J., Wetherell, M., Dallos, R. and Cochrane, A. (eds) *Understanding the Family*, London, Sage.

Derlega,V.J., Wilson, M. and Chaikin, A.L. (1976) 'Friendship and disclosure reciprocity', *Journal of Personality and Social Psychology*, 34, pp. 578–82.

Duck, S. (1973) 'Personality similarity and friendship choice: similarity of what, when?', *Journal of Personality*, 41, pp. 80–90.

Duck, S. (ed) (1977) *Theory and Practice in Interpersonal Attraction*, London, Academic Press.

Duck, S.W. (1988) *Relating to Others*, Buckingham, Open University Press.

Duck, S. (1994) *Meaningful Relationships*, London, Sage.

Duvall, E.M. (1977) *Marriage and Family Development*, Philadelphia, J.P. Lippincott and Co.

Erikson, E.H. (1950) *Childhood and Society*, New York, Norton.

Fitzpatrick, M.A., Vangelisti, A.L. and Firman, S. (1994) 'Perceptions of marital interaction and change during pregnancy: a typological approach', *Personal Relationships*, 1, pp. 101–22.

Freud, S. (1940) 'An outline of psycho-analysis' in Strachey, J. (ed) *Standard Edition*, vol 23, London, Hogarth Press.

Gelles, R.J. (1979) *Family Violence*, London, Sage.

Gillespie, D.L. (1975) 'Who has the power? The marital struggle' in Freeman, I.J. (ed) *Women: A Feminist Perspective*, Palo Alto, Calif., Mayfield.

Goffman, E. (1971) *Strategic Interaction*, Oxford, Blackwell.

Gottman, J.M. and Levenson, R.E. (1986) 'Assessing the role of emotions in marriages', *Behavioural Assessment*, 8, pp. 31–48.

Haley, J. (1973) *Uncommon Therapy*, New York, Norton.

Haley, J. (1976) *Problem Solving Therapy*, New York, Harper and Row.

Haley, J. (1980) *Leaving Home*, New York, McGraw-Hill.

Harris, C.S. (1978) *Fact Book on Ageing: A Profile of America's Older Population*, Washington DC, National Council on Ageing.

Hesse-Biber, S. and Williamson, J. (1984) 'Resource theory and power in families: life cycle consideration', *Family Process*, vol. 23, no. 4, pp. 226–78.

Hill, R. (1949) *Families under Stress*, New York, Harper and Row.

Hinde, R.A. (1979) *Towards Understanding Relationships*, London, Academic Press.

Hsu, F. (1981) *Americans and Chinese: Passage to Difference* (3rd. edn.), Honolulu, University Press Hawaii.

Kelly, G.A. (1955) *The Psychology of Personal Constructs*, volumes 1 and 2, New York, W.W. Norton.

Kerchkoff, A.C. and Davis, K.E. (1962) 'Value consensus and need complementarity in mate selection', *American Sociological Review*, 27, pp. 295–303.

LaRossa, R. (1986) *Becoming a Parent*, Beverley Hills, Sage.

LaRossa, R. and LaRossa, M.M. (1981) *Transition to Parenthood: How Infants Change Families*, Beverley Hills, Sage.

Levinger, G. (1983) 'Development and change' in Kelley, H.H., Berscheid, E., Christensen A., Harvey, J.H., Huston, T.L., Levinger, G., McClintock, E., Peplau, L.A. and Peterson, D.R. (eds) *Close Relationships*, New York, W.H. Freeman.

Levinson, D.J. (1978) *The Seasons of a Man's Life*, New York, Knopf.

Lewis, R.A., Franceau, P.J. and Roberts, C.I. (1979) 'Fathers and the post-parental transition', *Family Coordinator*, 28, pp. 514–20.

McCall, G.J. (1982) 'Becoming unrelated' in Duck, S.W. (ed) *Personal Relationships 4: Dissolving Personal Relationships*, London and New York, Academic Press.

Mehrabian, A. (1972) *Nonverbal Communication*, New York, Aldine-Atherton.

Miell, D.E. (1987) 'Remembering relationship development: constructing a context for interaction' in Burnett, R., McGhee, P., Clarke, D. (eds) *Accounting for Relationships*, pp. 60–73, London, Methuen.

Miell, D.E. and Duck, S. (1986) 'Strategies in developing friendships' in Derlega, V.J. and Winstead, B.A. (eds) *Friendships and Social Interaction*, New York, Springer-Verlag.

Minuchin, S. (1974) *Families and Family Therapy*, London, Tavistock.

Murstein, B.I. (1977) 'The stimulus-value-role (SVR) theory of dyadic relation-ships' in Duck, S.W. (ed) *Theory and Practice in Interpersonal Attraction,* London, Academic Press.

Nardi, P.M. and Sherrod, D. (1994) 'Friendship in the lives of gay men and lesbi-ans', *Journal of Social and Personal Relationships,* 11, pp. 185–99.

Neugarten, B.L. and Datan, N. (1981) 'The subjective experience of middle age' in Steinberg, L.D., *The Life Cycle,* New York, Columbia University Press.

Nelson-Jones, R. and Strong, S.R. (1976) 'Rules, risk and self-disclosure', *British Journal of Guidance and Counselling,* vol. 4, no. 2, pp. 201–11.

Piaget, J. (1959) *Language and Thought of the Child,* translated by M. Gabain, London, Routledge (first published in 1923).

Rapaport, R.M., Fogarty, M.P. and Rapaport, R. (1982) *Families in Britain,* London, Routledge and Kegan Paul.

Rodin, M.J. (1982) 'Non-engagement, failure to engage, and disengagement' in Duck, S. (ed) *Personal Relationships 4: Dissolving Personal Relationships,* London, Academic Press.

Ruble, D.N., Fleming, A.S., Strangor, C., Brooks-Gunn, J., Fitzmaurice, G. and Deutsch, F. (1990) 'Transition to motherhood and the self: measurment, stability and change', *Journal of Personality and Social Psychology,* 58, pp. 450–63.

Sapadin, L.A. (1988) 'Friendship and gender: perspectives of professional men and women', *Journal of Social and Personal Relationships,* vol. 5, no. 4, pp. 387–403.

Satchell, M. (1995) *Accounts from Ph.D. Research in Psychology,* Milton Keynes, Open University Department of Psychology.

Sharpe, S. (1990) *Voices from Home: Girls Talk about their Families,* London, Virago.

Shotter, J. (1992) 'What is a "personal" relationship? A rhetorical-responsive account of "unfinished business"' in Harvey, J.H., Orbuch T.L. and Weber, A.L. (eds) *Attributions, Accounts, and Close Relationships,* New York, Springer-Verlag.

Smith, J.A. (1990) 'Transforming identities: a repertory grid case study of the tran-sition to motherhood', *British Journal of Psychology,* 63, pp. 239–53.

Solomon, M. (1973) 'A developmental conceptual premise for family therapy', *Family Process,* 12, 2.

Stevens, R. (ed) (1996) *Understanding The Self,* London, Sage/The Open University. (Book 1 in this series.)

Toates, F. (1996) 'Embodiment' in Stevens R. (ed) *Understanding The Self.*

Watzlawick, P., Weakland, J., and Fisch, R. (1974) *Change: Principles of Problem Formation and Problem Resolution,* New York, W.W. Norton & Co.

Wetherell, M. and Maybin, J. (1996) 'The distributed self' in Stevens, R. (ed).

Winch, R.F. (1958) *Mate Selection: A study in Complementary Needs,* New York, Harper Row.

Wood, J.T. (1993) 'Engendered relations: interaction, caring, power and resposibil-ity in intimacy' in Duck, S.W. (ed) *Social Contexts and Relationships,* Newbury Park, CA., Sage.

Yogev, S. (1987) 'Marital role-satisfaction and sex role perceptions among dual-earner couples', *Journal of Social and Personal Relationships,* 4, pp. 35–45.

CHAPTER 6

EXAMINING THE WIDER CONTEXT OF SOCIAL RELATIONSHIPS

by Dorothy Miell and Rosaleen Croghan

Contents

1 Introduction

In this chapter we will be looking at the world of relationships we have with friends, neighbours, colleagues, acquaintances, professionals and extended family. These relationships can be seen as enmeshing us in a series of overlapping networks, composed of links between all the people we meet and interact with in different ways during our everyday lives. Such networks can be quite extensive, involving relationships (albeit of varying depths and durations) with a large number of very different people which can have an impact on individual relationships within the network.

An underlying theme in this chapter will be the way in which factors external to the relationship itself influence personal interactions and how meanings and discourses within society function to construct and constrain the nature of individual relationships. This level of influence is distinct from the various negotiations conducted at the interpersonal level, which have been the focus of most of the previous chapters in the book.

As was discussed in the introductory chapter, relationships may fulfil many important functions for us, and several reasons for starting and maintaining the range of relationships in which many of us are involved have been suggested over the course of this book. To a certain extent the functions of relationships which are identified will depend on what any particular theoretical perspective identifies as the goal of relating. At a basic biological level, for example, relationships serve the needs of the species and so our sexual relationships can be seen as serving the function of reproduction. A number of theorists have put forward suggestions explaining mate selection from this perspective (for example Buss, 1989; Kenrick and Trost, 1989). Relationships also fulfil deep personal needs for affection, for bonding, and for the expression of identity through interaction with others. There is also evidence that it is through our relationships with others that we constitute ourselves as both autonomous and as connected, as able to reflect and act within the social world in a meaningful and effective way. Chapter 3 showed individuals to be engaged in actively making inferences about others' intentions and motivation. That is, as acting on the basis of the personal meaning they attach to their relationships. But how is the meaning we attach to personal relationships constructed given the essentially *social* nature of our experience, and how free are we to create our own unique experience? We have already seen, in Chapters 3 and 4, evidence of the transactional nature of human relationships in which there is both conflict and transferred meaning. This was extended in the discussions in Chapters 2 and 3 to include an analysis of small group interaction and the social and cultural context, which may define the meaning assigned to particular roles and influence the terms under which the relationship is carried out and the strategies available to participants. In Chapter 5, through looking at change and development, it became apparent that relationships are embedded in wider social networks of family, work and neighbourhood. This chapter will discuss such wider influences on relationships from a range of theoretical and methodological perspectives, reflecting the considerable variation to be found within the field.

Aims of the chapter

1   To consider the extent and means by which factors external to a personal relationship (such as the views or behaviour of other people, and wider societal discourses) can influence that relationship.

2   To explore the nature of the wider social networks in which our personal relationships are located.

3   To problematize the issue of 'support' given by relationships. In particular, to discuss the reports of conflicts and ambiguity to be found in many people's assessments of their personal and professional relationships.

4   To examine critically the notions of 'exchange' and 'fairness' as key considerations in personal relationships and to discuss the role played by individual meanings in defining them.

5   To examine the operation of power within personal and professional relationships.

2   Networks of relationships

In this section we will explore the wide range of relationships in which people are typically involved, looking at how these different networks might influence the relationships within them. Networks can affect individual relationships within them in a number of ways, some very directly (such as relatives intervening in a couple's wedding plans), but also in more subtle ways, interpreting and implementing the values of wider society in defining what is expected and normal for relationships within the network. Later sections of the chapter will take up these more subtle influences.

Personal social networks are typically defined as a collection of individuals who know and interact with a particular target individual or couple. The members of a network all know the target person, albeit to different degrees and with different patterns of interaction, but they do not necessarily know each other (Figure 6.1 shows a single individual's network).

When networks are defined rather broadly like this, to include not only close friends and family but also other friends, colleagues, distant relations and mere acquaintances (indeed, anyone known by name or by their role such as 'John's Mum', or 'the postman') then they can be quite

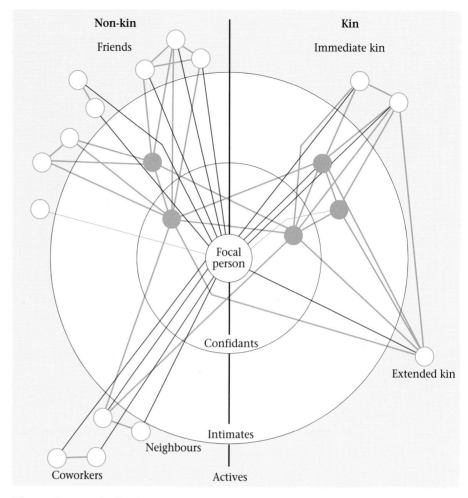

Figure 6.1: An individual's personal network (adapted from Wellman, 1992). Solid lines link members of the network who know each other, dotted lines link the network to the focal person.

large. To try and help people to establish the full range of people known to respondents, a number of methods have had to be developed. Some of these methods are described below and in section 2.1.

ACTIVITY 6.1   You may like to attempt a list (or map, as in Figure 6.1) of your own network, and see how many people you can include. Do you find it helpful to try and use cues such as grouping them in some way (for example 'work colleagues', 'student links', 'family', 'neighbours')? What about looking through your address book? Come back to the list later if you try it – you will no doubt keep thinking of more names to add. You can see that this would be an extremely time consuming process for a researcher to employ when studying the total networks of large numbers of people!

Researchers have long been interested in exploring people's social networks, and in particular in tackling the problem of looking at the structure of the links, between different people in the same network and between those in different networks, and investigations have taken a number of different forms. Whilst mathematical modelling of the possible linkages between people seemed at first to be a promising avenue to explore, the complexities of social structure proved an extremely difficult topic with which to contend. As you may remember from Chapter 5, we tend to meet and mix most with a range of people who are already known to others in our network, such as friends of friends, or those known to our family. There is therefore some degree of 'bias' in the structure of connections between individuals.

Stanley Milgram, a social psychologist working at Harvard University, decided to try and investigate the links between people in a more direct way. He wanted to choose two people randomly from anywhere in the United States and trace the line of acquaintances between them. Box 6.1 gives details of his ingenious study.

BOX 6.1 Milgram's (1977) chain of connections study

Milgram sent a folder of material to a number of 'starting' individuals which gave the name, address, employment, education etc. of a 'target' person, living a considerable distance away in the USA, with instructions on how to try and get the folder to the target – posting it on *only* to another person known to the 'starting' person. This process was then repeated until it was passed to the target person by someone who knew him or her personally. Each person in the chain sent a postcard back to Milgram's laboratory so that he could track the folder and its contents across the country.

In all, 42 of the 160 chains which were started were completed, and the number of intermediary steps in these 42 chains varied between 3 and 10 acquaintances, with a median of 5.5. However, it is likely that some of the chains which were not completed would have required many more steps and that this is why the people gave up on them, and obviously there would also have been practical problems, such as recipients of the folder having changed addresses or just not wishing to take part in the exercise. Not being able to distinguish between these reasons for failure was a major problem for the project.

Examining the chains that *were* completed, Milgram found that most were posted on to a person of the same sex as the sender, with the initial posting to someone on average 600 miles away, and most were sent to friends or acquaintances rather than to relatives. 48 per cent of the chains finally reached one of the targets through three individuals, one of whom worked in the same firm as the target, and the other lived in the target's home town. This suggests that some people in social networks are more likely to channel communications around the network than others.

Milgram (1977) believed that a deeper understanding of the structure of this 'communication net' would illuminate the nature of society more generally. As he put it, 'While many studies in social science show how the individual is alienated and cut off from the rest of society, from the perspective of this study a different view emerges: in some sense, at least, we are all bound together in a tightly knit social fabric' (p. 275).

Other researchers have since established a number of factors which might affect the size of a person's network, including levels of income and occupation, some relatively stable personality dispositions, and stage of the life cycle. They are also concerned with various aspects of the composition of networks (such as the proportion of family, or members of a particular age or social class) and the network's structure (for example how many of the members know each other) and content (for example how supportive of each other the members are). One of the debates within the network literature (referred to in Allan's paper included as *Reading E* at the end of this book) has been whether the trend, particularly in North American culture, towards socializing within the relative privacy of individual homes rather than in local community facilities such as pubs and clubs has changed the composition and nature of our support networks (Wellman and Wellman, 1992).

Does your typical pattern of social life centre on your home, with friends visiting or telephoning, watching television or videos, and perhaps ordering in take-away foods, or are you more likely to visit local cinemas or restaurants, and meet up with neighbours in community centres? Do you feel that the location of such socializing significantly changes its nature?

In the discussion here we will, however, focus on analyses which concern the various network types in which any one person might be involved, and on how these networks might affect the ways we conduct our more personal relationships.

2.1   Types of social networks

Milardo (1992) suggests that there are a number of different social networks which can be identified for any one individual. The first, a network of 'significant others', or intimates, includes those people who are seen as important to the individual such as the spouse or partner, parents, close friends and other family members. 'Exchange networks' refer to those people who provide, or who are thought to provide, material or symbolic support. 'Interactive networks' include those with whom interactions typically occur, the everyday interactions with friends, colleagues and acquaintances who may or may not also be members of other networks. We will look at each of these types of network in a little more detail below. Finally, Milardo suggests that we can also draw up 'global networks', composed of all the people known by an individual and who also know the individual (that is, so as to exclude people such as political figures or other famous personalities), much as you tried to do in Activity 6.1.

Network of significant others

Milardo suggests that what is important here is not the frequency of interaction but the significance attached to it. A parent, for example, remains an important figure in a person's life even when meetings between them are very infrequent. Thus the significant others network can have people linked by both active and passive ties – active ties being based on considerable face-to-face interaction and passive ties based on emotional bonds, perhaps with irregular or infrequent interaction.

To elicit the names of people in this network, individuals are usually asked questions such as, 'Whose opinions of your personal life are important to you?' or, 'With whom can you discuss important matters?' or, 'Who means a lot to you and without whom your life would be difficult?'. Typically, people report about five members in their network of intimates, usually about half of these being family members, and the membership of this network remains relatively constant, probably as a result of the strong blood and legal ties that bind many of the members together.

Exchange networks

The exchange network is made up of the people who 'provide material and emotional assistance' (Fisher, 1982, p. 35). Members of the exchange network might be companions in various leisure pursuits, people providing services such as childminders, or friends and family, but in all cases the intention is to obtain a high proportion of rewarding social exchanges. (In section 4 we will have a more detailed discussion of the principals of fairness which some theorists believe underlie most of our social and personal relationships, not only those with people within the exchange network.)

The exchange network typically has around 20 members, although there is a greater variation in the numbers in this network than in the intimates network. Around 40 per cent of the network is typically composed of family, and because these members tend to know one another, a proportion of this network can be highly interdependent, as compared with the interactive network which is often characterized by relatively loose interconnections between members.

Try and draw up a list of those people who you consider to be part of your exchange network. Who gives you 'material and emotional assistance'? – try and think of a number of different aspects of your life in which you receive such help (for example at work, in your life as a student, at home, with the children, etc.) to widen the range of people you consider. Are your relationships with these people characterized by giving and receiving roughly equal amounts of support, or does one partner appear to get more out of the interactions than the other? We will be considering fairness of exchanges in

ACTIVITY 6.2

section 4. Are the relationships also characterized by conflict? If so, is this more or less the case than with members of your network of significant others? We will return to a consideration of conflict and ambiguity in relationships in section 5.

Interactive networks

The interactive network is made up of those people with whom an individual frequently interacts, and need not have any great overlap with the members of the person's significant or exchange networks. It is difficult to measure people's interactive networks, but a couple of methods have become widely used recently. The first asks people to keep an interaction diary for a number of days or weeks, recording some details of all the interactions lasting more than ten minutes that they have each day, or just keeping a list of names of people with whom they have interacted each day (this latter method is less demanding of time and so can be kept up for longer periods). These types of diary methods require the participants in the research to deliberately monitor and record their own interactions, and this can be a problem for some participants, particularly to maintain it over an extended period of time.

Another method, which does not require the individuals to keep their own records, involves the researcher phoning people on a series of occasions and asking them about the interactions they have had in the last 24 hours. Also, a time-sampling method has been developed by Larson and his co-workers (Larson and Bradney, 1988). In this method, research participants are issued with an electronic pager and are signalled at random times during waking hours over a period of several days or weeks. The participants are asked to log their recent interactions and other data specific to the study, such as their current emotional state, each time they are called. Different studies have identified interactive networks of rather different sizes; ranging widely from about 20 to several hundred.

Does Milardo's classification of network types make sense for you and your relationships? What other types of network might you suggest?

2.2   Network effects on relationships

Researchers have long been interested in the effects which membership of networks can have on particular relationships, especially their effects on a marriage. The first researcher to explore how interactions between couples were affected by their membership of different social networks was Elizabeth Bott, who examined English urban families in the 1950s. Bott identified two distinct types of marriage based on the couple's interactions with other network members. In the first type, both husband and wife were integrated in close-knit kin and friendship networks and received support and help from their respective networks. As a result, Bott suggested, these couples made fewer demands on each other and had lower expectations for support and companionship from their partners. The second type of couple had loose and fragmented social networks (often because of geographical and social mobility, which was often more disruptive in the 1950s than many people find it today) and as a result each spouse relied on the other more than in the first type of couple.

> The first pattern generated less frequent interaction between husband and wife, fewer joint leisure activities, and greater specialization of roles and tasks around the house. The second type of couple shared as many activities and spent as much time together as possible. They stressed that husband and wife should be equals; all major decisions would be made together, and even in minor household matters they should help one another as much as possible.
>
> (Bott, 1957, pp. 52–3)

Bott interpreted her findings as showing that role specialization within the couple was the result of the different types of social network (tightly or more loosely knit). More recent work examining the interaction between types of network and individual relationships has paid greater attention to the influence of cultural norms and values, examining the extent of the interference as well as the support that network members can provide to a couple.

Klein and Milardo (1993) have looked at the various effects of network involvement in personal relationships, or, as they refer to it, 'third party influence'. They argue that this influence has two major components: '...(a) the structure of partners' social networks affects the nature, availability, co-ordination, and timing of influence attempts by network members ... and (b) ... the influence of third parties rests, at least in part, on their ability to define relational competence' (p. 55).

Third parties, Klein and Milardo argue, influence what is seen to be a problem, for example by drawing attention to the fact that the couple 'do not do very much together'. In doing so they give evaluative meaning to certain aspects of the relationship with implications about what should be done about it (in this case, that one or both of the partners should try to find more time for joint activities). The suggestions for action may frequently prescribe 'appropriate' roles for the partners, such as what the third parties believe to be a 'normal' allocation of domestic tasks.

Klein and Milardo examine two ways in which third party influence can affect conflict between couples. They suggest that the conflict in a relationship varies according to the extent to which others point out the possibility of different perspectives on the problem, including the other partner's point of view, as opposed to emphasizing one side of the conflict, such as by taking sides. Third parties may also differ in the extent to which they support conventional, culturally 'approved' rules and behaviour, as opposed to emphasizing the idiosyncratic needs of the couple.

The four quadrants in Figure 6.2 represent types of input according to these two forms of influence.

Upper right – inputs based on the identification of both partners' needs. This involves a 'neutral' position which does not blame either partner and attempts to generate new and mutually acceptable perspectives and solutions. Such input could come from a marital counsellor or someone who is a close friend of both partners.

Lower right – this represents input predominantly geared to one partner's individual needs, as might come from a close friend or relation of one partner.

Lower left – this consists of normative input that serves one partner. This may be an adversarial position, such as deciding who is 'right' or 'wrong' in legal terms or moral strictures presented by the family.

Upper left – this represents normative input where suggestions are based on what are seen as appropriate roles for both partners, or what a 'good' relationship should be.

Influence from third parties is likely to extend over time and to become incorporated into the relationship dynamics. One partner with a close friend who habitually takes his or her side may become an issue for a couple, leading to accusations, jealousy or a sense of desertion by the excluded partner. Klein and Milardo (1993) also suggest that the extent to which others take a mutually supportive as opposed to an adversarial position may relate to the structure of the network. Where there is considerable overlap, such as a couple having shared friendships, the input may be more mutual. It may be in the interests of the tightly knit network to assist and support the relationship. Where each partner

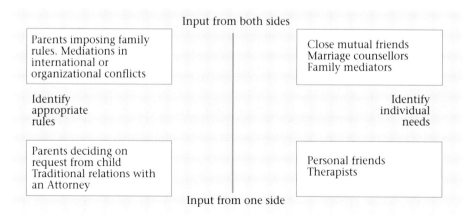

Figure 6.2: Dimensions of third party influence and examples of informal and formal third party rules

Source: Klein, R. and Milardo, R. (1993)

has a separate network it may be that members have difficulty imagining the perspective of the other partner since they have little contact with him or her.

Finally, third party influence appears to vary according to social and cultural norms, among them gender beliefs and values. For example, women may be more likely to be encouraged to accommodate to others and to centre on the needs of their partners rather than themselves, whereas men may be offered more advice about their individual interests such as their careers. In an interesting study of women's friendships, Oliker (1989) found that women were very likely to confide their relationship problems in their friends. Friends often encouraged accommodation to the women's partners in a variety of ways:

> A lot of the time I just looked at the negative. I'd compare Gary to the other husbands. And when you look at someone else's husband, you just see the good side. Jan will point out to me, 'You know, Gary helps with the dishes' or does this or that, 'and Eddie never does'. I'd start to think, 'I really am lucky he does that. He's not all bad.'
>
> *(Woman quoted in Oliker, 1989, p.126)*

At other times the friends encouraged the women to confront their husbands or backed the women up in a conflict, sometimes taking steps to assist a separation.

There have also been several studies of the way in which social networks change in the support they give and the influence they wield over individuals, for example in coping with major life events such as widowhood or the onset of a major illness (Morgan and March, 1992). Some of Morgan and March's respondents commented on how such events led to an increased need for support, a need which was not matched by the response from the social network:

> People don't come by our house anymore. I guess they can't cope with Alzheimer's. It can be so lonely. I get so broken up — torn apart, watching a great guy deteriorate inch by inch, day by day. I also miss communicating with someone who listens
>
> *(Caregiver, quoted in Morgan and March, 1992, p.577)*

Recent widows in the same study found that the practical help they received from their family and married friends also gave them some stress since there was pressure to 'get over' their grief before they felt ready to.

> It's a shock — and I think the worst thing is, by the time you come out of the shock, which for me took 3 or 4 months before I really started realizing, 'Hey, this is real', you know, 'this is forever, this is the way it is.' About that time a lot of your friends and co-workers and whatnot think, 'Well, enough time is past, she should be OK now'.
>
> *(Widow, quoted in Morgan and March, 1992, p. 576)*

Studies such as these have highlighted two issues to which we will be returning. The first is the impact of the 'outside world' on the apparently private world of the couple, in these cases through the expectations, reactions and comments of kin and friends. Later, in section 5, we will extend this to an analysis of the impact of wider cultural norms and values (such as structural differences in power) on the relationship of spouses. The second point to note is the suggestion that network members can provide both support *and* interference to individuals – support is not always provided unequivocally.

Review of section 2

- An individual's total social network may be very extensive and difficult to measure.

- Within the global network, those we know can be divided up into different groups depending on the nature of their relationship with us. Three such sub-networks were discussed here: the network of significant others, the exchange and the interactive networks. These differ in the types and numbers of people likely to be members and the functions of relationships within them.

- Networks of family and friends (third parties) can offer support but can also be perceived as interfering or be characterized as stressful or conflictual in other ways.

3 The positive effects of social involvement

A number of researchers have established a link between the experience of stress and both physical and psychological illness and have attempted to identify factors which might act as buffers between the stress and illness or, more directly, improve a person's well being by reducing stress.

ACTIVITY 6.3   The final section of *Reading C* by Michael Argyle at the end of the book examines some of the effects of relationships on physical and psychological health. You should read this now.

Social network variables, and social support in particular, have received a great deal of attention from these researchers as potential protective factors, and the evidence does seem to suggest that those who have support from their social networks are more able to resist the damaging effects of stressful life events. For example, the stress a person experiences at work (for example urgent deadlines, work interruptions, heavy work load, role ambiguity, many responsibilities) is more closely correlated with indicators of strain (for example high blood pressure, ulcers) for workers with little or no social support than for those with much social support (House, 1980). The rise of self-help groups, particularly within the health field in recent years in Britain, can be seen as an attempt by people in stressful situations to boost the level of mutual aid, cooperation and reciprocity available to support them which mirrors that ideally found in a social network (Vincent, 1992). Such self-help groups, made up of people who have been through the same stressful experiences (whether these be rape, alcohol addiction, cancer diagnosis or miscarriage) give a much needed chance to talk to others who have 'been through it' themselves, rather than to those who are paid to care (a distinction explored further in section 5).

Perhaps one of the most wide ranging studies investigating the link between stress and social support was conducted by Brown and Harris (1978) in Camberwell in London (and since extended to a larger sample in Islington). Their study (described in Box 6.2) investigated the depression experienced by a number of women who were interviewed in depth to investigate the social origins of depression.

The finding in Brown and Harris' study that women's closest relationships sometimes failed them when they most needed support takes up a point made in the previous section that relationships cannot be seen simply as either 'supportive' or 'unsupportive'. There is a considerable amount of ambiguity in relationships and of negotiation between partners about the nature of their relationship, and what they feel they can expect of each other. We have seen in earlier chapters how important these processes of negotiation can be in establishing an agreed definition of a relationship, and in sections 4 and 5 of this chapter we will examine further how partners deal with ambiguity within relationships and establish what they believe to be 'fair' rules about what they can reasonably expect to put into and take out of each relationship.

There have been calls to examine in more detail the everyday negotiation of help and support in interactions precisely because of these ambiguities and subjective definitions of what counts as supportive behaviour. The support that one partner feels he or she has given may bear very little relationship to what the other partner feels he or she has or has not received, let alone what an outsider to the relationship may believe has occurred. Support offered by relationships may take a practical form, such as helping with shopping, or DIY jobs, or it may be more psychological, such as being a 'listening ear' to a friend who needs to share some troubles.

Early attempts to quantify the amount of such help that a person received were calculated simply by counting the number of people in their network and the number of regular interactions with them. However, the frequency of social interaction is not necessarily related to psychological adjustment or to subjective perceptions of help being

BOX 6.2 Stress and relationship support

Brown and Harris selected 71 women at random from the records of general practitioners in Camberwell (the later Islington study included 363 woman followed up for two years after a first interview). All the women were married and aged between 20 and 45 with an eldest child less than 15 years old at the time of being interviewed. The interviewers built up a detailed history of each woman and an account of any ongoing difficulties she was experiencing, and also recorded any incidents of clinical depression amongst the sample. An important difference from several other studies of depression was that Brown and Harris were careful to elicit the *meaning* for each woman of any particular event (such as the birth of a child). Rather than assuming the impact of such an event would be much the same for any woman, they included assessments of other factors which would interact with the life events and affect the way in which such an event would be perceived by the woman (for example her housing circumstances, number of other children, presence of the father).

Brown and Harris' analysis of the interview data suggested that incidences of depression were most likely to be found in interaction with 'provoking agents', the most significant of which were severe events such as important losses or disappointments occurring recently. A second form of provoking agent, which was less influential in the onset of depression, was the presence of ongoing major difficulties such as poor housing or an alcohol-addicted husband. These provoking agents accounted for a large proportion of the incidents of depression picked up in the study, but the researchers also stressed the role of 'vulnerability factors'. Three such factors were identified:

> having three or more children at home under the age of 14;
>
> the loss of a mother before the age of 11;
>
> the lack of an intimate tie with a husband or partner.

The risk of depression was increased if these factors applied, but *only* when they were in the presence of the provoking agents.

Having an intimate tie with a husband or partner (defined by confiding, receiving emotional support and lack of a negative reaction) was confirmed as an important factor in Brown and Harris' later studies, but other close relationships were also shown to be important (usually with another woman friend). Indeed, women who expected to be able to rely on their husbands and then found that they could not do so when a crisis arose were found to be *more* at risk of depression than those women who either did not have a husband present or who did not expect to have support from him, but who did have a close female friend available in whom to confide.

given (Barrera, 1981). Just because I meet and talk to people on a regular basis does not mean that I am actually getting the support I need from them, so just counting up my total number of contacts would not be a good index of the help I receive. Theorists and researchers are now focusing much more on the transactional processes which go on between the partners in a relationship and between individuals and their wider support network. As a result, they are examining features of the people within the network who provide assistance, and also what behaviours are *perceived* as supportive and how individuals decide what support is available for them (Vaux, 1988).

Another problem with measuring the positive benefits offered by relationships is that while family support, especially marital support, is consistently shown to be important, such support can be very contradictory since it may act both as a buffer against stress and yet also as a *source* of stress itself. Section 5 will explore this apparent contradiction further. This recognition that relationships may be unhelpful as well as helpful has shifted the focus of research from the measurement of help given by relationships in terms of network size, towards an understanding of individual *perceptions* of help and also the relational context in which it is given.

The need to take individual perceptions seriously has long been emphasized by humanistic psychologists, who hold that since people are capable of reflecting on and making sense of their experience in a unique way, their perceptions of events are the only true indication of the reality of an interaction.

A discussion of the humanistic approach to relationships is contained in ACTIVITY 6.5
Reading D by Richard Stevens at the end of the book. You should read this now and consider the following questions as you read:

1 What do you believe are the advantages of the humanistic approach?

2 Can you think of any problems in relying solely on the individual's perspective?

3 How, for example, would this approach deal with inconsistency, change or conscious deception in an individual's account given to a researcher?

4 How free are individuals to form their own perceptions, and how easy do you feel it is to assess whether and to what extent they have been coerced or persuaded?

Another approach to the study of relationships, social exchange theory, also stresses the individual's perception of the exchange of mutual rewards and satisfaction in assessing the benefits of relationships. According to this approach (discussed in the following section), what constitutes rewarding behaviour depends on the participants' subjective appraisals of what *they* find helpful and positive.

Review of section 3

- Social support from a network of other relationships has been identified as providing a protective function against stress and other illnesses.

- Defining 'social support' is not straightforward. It cannot be done simply by counting up the number of contacts a person has, or by assuming that close relationships such as with a spouse will necessarily be wholly supportive.

- Research needs to examine how an individual interprets the type and level of support given, perceived, expected and received in a relationship – in other words, to examine the *meaning* of support in a relationship for each person.

4   Principles of exchange, of 'give and take' in relationships

In discussing the notion of relationship networks, and particularly in the outline of exchange networks, we saw how some relationships are based on the partners giving and receiving practical (and emotional) support. An exchange model of relationships, assuming that people assess their relationships on the basis of what they invest in and get out of these relationships, was first proposed by Homans in 1961. This model suggested that people weigh up their past, present and anticipated future rewards and costs in relationships, as well as their partners' outcomes, and consider the relative benefits compared with alternative relationships available to them. Homans suggested that rewards could take almost any form, from concrete gifts to abstract compliments. Indeed, he defined a reward as anything a person receives that he or she defines as valuable. Costs can also take any form, but essentially are defined *by the person* as unpleasant. An important point to note is that most situations do not result in pure benefits or pure costs. Usually each interaction involves trying to achieve the maximum benefits with the least costs.

Having defined these terms broadly, Homans could then talk about the 'outcomes' of interactions. An outcome is the result of rewards less costs and can work out as a profit (rewards high and costs low) or as a loss (costs higher than rewards). According to Homans, people calculate outcomes on the basis of such cost/benefit analyses and seek to secure the best outcome for themselves. As you will see from the discussion below, this rather bald statement has been considerably amended by later researchers and theorists in the exchange tradition, who have questioned a number of points in this argument that profit calculations are the only factors taken into account when assessing relationships.

4.1 Interdependence theory

This theory, proposed by Thibaut and Kelley (1959), suggests that for a relationship to feel satisfactory, the rewards for each participant must outweigh their costs. In discussing how participants assess how satisfactory their relationships are, Thibaut and Kelley suggested that an important consideration is the availability of alternatives to the current relationship. In their theory, they introduced the two notions of 'comparison level' and 'comparison level for alternatives'. Comparison level is 'the level of profit that someone has come to expect in general from the interactions which they experience, that is, it is the rewards and costs of a given relationship in terms of what [he or she] feels [he or she] deserves' (Thibaut and Kelley, 1959, p. 21). This would predict that an individual with a history of highly favourable interaction experiences would be rather more demanding in particular relationships, whilst persons with more modest success in relationships would be content with lesser rewards.

Comparison level for alternatives (often abbreviated to 'CL alt') was defined by Thibaut and Kelley as the lowest level of outcomes in a relationship that a person will accept in the light of available opportunities. If an individual realizes that a number of attractive alternatives exist, he or she will demand reasonably high outcomes from a given relationship. However, if the person does not perceive any available alternatives, or the ones available are relatively unattractive, expectations concerning outcomes will be much more modest.

Duck has argued that the process by which a person comes to perceive the existence of attractive alternatives is in fact one which is a personal reflection on the state of the current relationship:

> The world is always populated with alternative partners in an objective sense. We do not see them as alternatives, nor do we treat them as available, until we become dissatisfied with what we have (i.e. until the meaning of participating in an alternative relationship changes for us). The availability of an alternative is thus a purely subjective thing, not an objective one that can be defined in absolute terms.
>
> (Duck, 1994, p. 163)

Thibaut and Kelley's theory has been extended more recently by Caryl Rusbult whose work suggests that commitment to a relationship is affected not only by outcomes and available alternatives, as Thibaut and Kelley maintained, but also by the *investments* which those involved have put into the relationship. She suggests that the more heavily invested a person is in a relationship, the more he or she will feel committed to that relationship. Rusbult defines investments as resources which are either intrinsic elements, put directly into the relationship (such as time, emotional energy or disclosures about the self) or elements which are extrinsic but are connected to the relationship (such as shared possessions or the existence of mutual friends). Investments are distinguished from ordinary rewards and costs in that investments cannot be taken out of a relationship as easily, and will be lost, or at least greatly decreased in value, if the relationship comes to an end. As a result, the model predicts that investments not only increase the commitment to a relationship but also serve to stabilize it – since to leave the relationship would also mean losing the resources which have been invested in it. A number of questionnaire studies with students and others have given varying but general support to these predictions (for example Rusbult et al., 1986).

So far we have talked about comparing the relative rewards of one relationship with either past relationships or other possible alternative relationships. But it is also possible to compare what you receive from a relationship with what your partner gets out of it. You may be receiving great rewards from the relationship compared with all available alternatives, but may still be put out by the fact that your partner is benefitting even more than you. Other developments of exchange theory have been based on a strong concern over this matter of *fairness* in relationships. It is assumed that individuals will be attracted to relationships where they perceive that the outcomes are relatively fair; or at least to relationships in which they imagine that, although the outcomes are relatively unfair, it is they who will get the better deal.

4.2   Equity theory

Equity theory suggests that we compare our outcomes in a social encounter with our partner's outcomes and that we try to establish equity between the two outcomes in terms of the effort involved in achieving them. So, if two partners receive equal outcomes but one puts in more effort than the other, the exchange is inequitable. However, if one partner receives more outcome for more effort, whilst the other receives less outcome for less effort then the exchange may be an equitable one.

Levels of equity in a relationship have frequently been assessed using the Hatfield Global Measure (Hatfield et al., 1985). This measure asks respondents to rate their relationship by answering the following question: 'Considering what you put into your relationship, compared to what you get out of it and what your partner puts in compared to what (s)he gets out of it, how does your relationship "stack up"?' The Hatfield Global Measure offers options for responses such as 'I am getting a much better deal than my partner', 'My partner is getting a slightly better deal' and, 'We are both getting an equally good or bad deal'. These responses can then be scored to determine how equitably treated the partners feel.

We may feel that it is 'common sense' that in relationships where our partner receives more than we do in relation to the respective amounts of effort we both put in, we will feel angry and annoyed. However, equity theory goes beyond this to suggest that we will also experience some distress if we receive *more* than our fair share – we will feel guilt. In each case we experience dissatisfaction with the relationship, and will try to reduce it, either by demanding that our partner does more, or by doing more ourselves. So equity can be restored either by altering our own inputs or by changing our partner's inputs. This relationship between the reward/cost balance and level of contentment is illustrated in Figure 6.3.

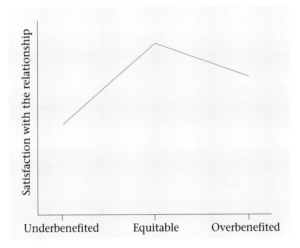

Figure 6.3: Level of benefit from a relationship and contentment with it (equity principle)

Now read Box 2 in *Reading C* by Michael Argyle about a typical study of   ACTIVITY 6.5
equity theory principles, conducted by Van Yperen and Buunk (1990).

Because of the effects of wider social networks on relationships, some researchers have suggested that it is important to study equity principles within the context of the wider social network rather than concentrating entirely on couples, as much research testing equity theory has done (such as Van Yperen and Buunk's study). In her 1987 study, Rook inter-viewed 115 elderly widowed women about the types and amounts of companionship, emotional and instrumental support which they exchanged with the various members of their social network. She found that women who felt either overbenefited or underbenefited reported greater feelings of loneliness than those who felt equitably treated. There were differences in the types and amounts of help received from different members of the social networks, however. The women reported feeling more satisfied receiving instrumental help from their adult children than from their friends, who they felt happiest with when the exchanges were more equitable and reciprocal. This may reflect the fact that the women have 'stored up credits' over their child rearing years that make it easier for them to accept help from their children in later life. Also, accepting help from their children frees the women from asking friends for this, and that in itself may be rewarding. The same act of kindness, such as collecting shopping or painting the house when offered by a friend or an adult child can have very different meanings and relational implications. Again, the subjective interpretation of the help given and received, its legitimacy and the *meaning* the help holds within different relationships, are important factors to explore.

Are equity principles universal?

There have been suggestions that the equity principle is essentially the result of highly individualistic cultures with marketplace economics, and as such is most appropriately applied to capitalist, individualistic cultures, such as that of North America. Some cross-cultural research suggests that in other cultures equity is indeed not the principle strategy used for allocating resources within relationships, or at least not within *all* relationships as the equity theorists suggest. For example, a study by Berman et al. (1985) compared students in the USA and India on their preference for different resource allocation models in a work situation. Respondents had to decide on how to allocate extra pay between two people, an excellent worker and a needy worker. Most American respondents allocated the bonus on the basis of equity (that is, to the better worker), and least on the basis of need (that is, to the needy worker). Among most Indian respondents, however, allocation on the basis of need was the most popular option with the equity allocation being the least popular. The American respondents took more account of need when they were asked how to handle a pay *cut*, but it was still a less popular option amongst the American than the Indian students.

> There are several possible explanations for the differing preferences in these two cultural groups. The first is based on the high visibility and salience of need in the Indian experience. Because need is so obvious in Indian life, Indian culture may be forced to adopt a more need-based norm of justice. In cultures where the minimum needs of the majority of the population are met and where abject need is not widespread, it may be possible to endorse an equity-based norm of justice. The alternative explanation is [that] … in India, the dominant relationships are those of the family and the community, and dependence on one another is seen as positive and necessary. In contrast, in North America, the dominant relationships are more individualistic, and personal independence is stressed. The resources within dependent group-oriented relationships are far more likely to be divided up on the basis of need, even in a North American context (Deutsch, 1975). However, in relationships that are more independent and economic in nature, equity-based distribution is more common.
>
> (Moghaddam, Taylor and Wright, 1993, p. 111)

A further challenge to equity theory comes from critics who suggest that these considerations do not apply in the most intimate relationships. Fairness considerations, it is argued, are unlikely to apply in all relationships, particularly very close ones involving love, since this is commonly perceived as a selfless emotion – in Fromm's terms as 'giving not receiving' (1962). As we will see below, even some theorists who broadly agree with exchange as a principle in personal relationships feel that love relationships transcend this, since these relationships are believed to involve unconditional commitment and a concern for the needs of the partner.

4.3   Communal and exchange relationships

Clark and Mills (1979; Mills and Clark, 1982) have distinguished between two distinct types of relationship – communal and exchange. In communal relationships, the ideal (not unfailingly adhered to) is that partners give to each other out of love and concern for the other's needs, and not out of a desire to keep 'even' with each other, indeed they may positively avoid exchanging on a tit for tat basis. In exchange relationships, on the other hand, participants are very concerned to keep a check on what is given and what is received and to keep these balanced.

Mills and Clark have conducted a series of studies to investigate the implications of this distinction between communal and exchange relationships. They have found, for example, that strangers who are keen to establish an altruistic 'communal' relationship signal this to each other by *not* exchanging information about themselves in a carefully reciprocal manner, unlike those wishing to avoid any such involvement and who are keen to keep the relationship on an 'exchange' basis. They suggest that amongst partners who have known each other longer, communal relationships are characterized by gifts or help being given which are geared solely to the recipient's needs and involve little or no consideration of the giver's past, present or future needs (although there are difficulties here for observers – perhaps including the receiver – since the same behaviour might be evident even if some reciprocity *was* expected – perhaps at a later date or in a different form rather than immediately as in exchange relationships). Mills and Clark believe that people hold the communal basis as an ideal for intimate relationships and that as a result partners actually react negatively when this is violated, for example if they are repaid for doing a favour for a close friend (Clark and Mills, 1979).

As we will see in section 5.2, the suggestion that close communal relationships are governed by the partners fulfilling each other's needs in a relatively selfless way rather ignores the underlying power inequalities between many partners, where what *appears* to be freely given may in fact be given under obligation.

4.4   Social exchange and evolutionary theory

An attempt has been made to integrate exchange principles with an approach which sees successful relationships as adaptive for survival; evolutionary theory. Kenrick and Trost (1989) argue that people are primarily motivated by self-interest, and achieve fairness only as a result of bargaining with another person who is also basically selfish. This is perhaps most clearly seen in the adverts in personal columns where bids are likened to 'the heterosexual stock market', and where 'potential partners seek to strike bargains which maximize their rewards in the exchange of assets' (Cameron et al., 1977, p. 28).

Whilst most social psychologists studying exchange theory have mainly concerned themselves with the process of exchange, Kenrick and Trost argue that, 'the evolutionary perspective assumes that there are important distinctions between the resources exchanged in heterosexual relationships and in other relationships. Exchange of reproductive value is a qualitatively different game, and it is not the same game for females as it is for males' (1989, p. 97). By this they mean that, according to evolutionary theory, in choosing a mate men and women are genetically predisposed to value very different things. The theory suggests that a man is looking for a young woman who will be able to bear children whilst a woman is predisposed to seek out a man who is a proven provider to care for her and her children, and who is therefore likely to be older than her. (In both cases, it is important to stress that a genetic predisposition and *not* a conscious choice is believed to be influencing behaviour.) The types of rewards offered and sought by partners seeking a mate are proposed to be rather different to those in other relationships.

Kenrick and Trost support this claim by examining evidence of sex differences in mate selection such as that gathered by Buss (1989) from people across 37 cultures. In Buss' very extensive study, 10,047 people were asked to complete a questionnaire which asked them to rate a number of factors for their importance in choosing a mate (for example age, character, sociability, intelligence, chastity). Consistent with evolutionary theory, females were found to rate 'resource acquisition' more highly than males, and males valued characteristics indicative of 'reproductive capacity' more than females.

These data provide intriguing insights into the processes which might be involved in exchanges between partners in sexual relationships, going beyond the 'simple rational exchange economics' which Kenrick and Trost (1989, p. 98) argue are presented in some social psychological accounts of social exchange.

You might consider the extent to which you agree with this assessment of social psychological models of exchange processes in relationships. Do you think, for example, that such models assume that people are rational in their judgements of what counts as a fair exchange, weighing up the rewards and costs according to each partner's inputs and outcomes? What of the distinction between communal and exchange relationships?

As Kenrick and Trost suggest, 'Romantic relationships pose a particular problem for theories of people as cool-headed accountants seeking maximal rewards. Those relationships are powerfully laden with emotion from start to finish, from the ecstasies and agonies of early romantic love to their sometimes painful endings' (p. 98). Whilst the evolutionary analysis may well provide us with otherwise hidden insights into what influences romantic relationships, it does not illuminate the processes underlying other relationships such as those with our friends or neighbours. In contrast, the exchange theories discussed in previous sections do attempt to explain the processes which apply more generally to any relationship in which we are involved, albeit by recognizing differences between them, such as that between communal and exchange concerns in relationships of different levels of intimacy.

Review of section 4

- A large body of research has for some time been concerned with examining the exchanges between people in a variety of relationships. Researchers have focused particularly on the rewards and costs associated with relationships and the extent to which partners feel fairly treated.

- Thibaut and Kelley's interdependence theory suggests that partners weigh up the outcomes of a current relationship and compare them with past relationships and alternative ones available to them in deciding whether or not to stay in the relationship.

- Equity theory suggests that partners are most content with a relationship when they are getting a 'fair deal' – that is, putting in about as much as they take out. Questions have been raised about the universality of this theory.

- Mills and Clark suggested a difference between communal and exchange relationships, with fairness considerations only being applied in exchange relationships, whereas the partner's needs were only paramount in communal relationships.

- Evolutionary theory suggests that sexual relationships might be governed by exchange principles operating at a sociobiological level, rather than as conscious choices.

5 Power, conflict and ambiguity in relationships

In this section we will consider the operation of power in relationships. Such power may have a structural basis, in the unequal distribution and control of physical resources, or it may have an ideological basis, that is it may be based on the control of ideas and beliefs. In practice the two often go hand in hand.

As our examination of the social networks available to individuals suggests, structural factors can have important influences on the quality of personal relationships. For example, studies of mothering have pointed out that the quality of the relationship between mother and child is actively influenced by the mother's access to social, economic and relational resources (Longfellow et al., 1982). Similarly, unemployment can have adverse effects on the quality of martial relationships (Fagin, 1981). As a result of such factors relationships, even close relationships, may be characterized by inequalities in power. This power can sometimes be overt, as in situations in which the relationship is of a contractual nature and boundaries are fairly clearly drawn, for example the relationship between employer and employee. However, in most relationships the boundaries are not so clear cut and the way in which power enters the relationship is more veiled and woven into the fabric of the relationship in a way that can make it invisible.

Differences in power arising from the relationships' social context may have a very real effect on the experience of personal relationships. In addition, there may be real conflicts of interest *within* close relationships which reflect the differences in power held by participants and their place in social hierarchies, for example those of class, race and gender. These differences in power which are rooted in structures *outside* the relationship are likely to have effects on the internal dynamics of the relationship. For this reason, a number of authors have argued that it is impossible to understand the meaning of relationships or to begin to understand whether they are beneficial for the individual without also studying the power which partners weald in the relationship and the way in which inequalities in power affect the relationship and the partners' ability to negotiate effectively for what they need (Binney et al., 1981; Brannen and Wilson, 1983). From this point of view it is not enough simply to look at patterns of interaction and to describe individuals in relationships as having different *kinds* of power (for example women having affective power and men having economic and physical power), or of trading off one type of satisfaction for another. It is also necessary to understand how the inequalities in power affect both the nature of the relationship *and* the participants' ability to negotiate effectively for what they need.

Power in relationships may be closely linked to factors like class, race and gender which not only lead people to occupy different social positions but which will also influence the *kinds* of relationships that are available to them and the way those relationships are organized. There is an extensive sociological literature which describes the nature and organization of relationships among different classes and ethnic groups. The work of C. Wright Mills on the demise of the old middle class and the emergence of the new class of white collar workers in western industrial societies provides a classic example of this approach (Mills, 1951). Sociological analyses of relationships, for example Allan's (1989) study of friendship patterns, have emphasized that these not only tend to be class and gender specific but also that the quality of these relationships is influenced by the individual's position in social hierarchies.

ACTIVITY 6.7

This would be a good point at which to read Graham Allan's paper (*Reading E*) on the sociological perspective, in which he looks at the way in which social and economic influences constrain social ties. As you read the paper, you should consider the following questions:

1   In what ways does Allan suggest that personal ties are shaped by wider social constraints?

2   What does such an analysis suggest about our ability to control, direct or change relationships?

Sociological approaches to relationships tend to focus on the way in which the wider social context influences personal interactions. For example Brotz (1962) has shown that social status and stratification are likely to be related to the respect which individuals grant to each other in private life and are embodied not only in differences in access to material resources but also in the interactions between high and low status individuals.

Think back to Goffman's argument in Chapter 2, section 7 of this volume that roles and rules structure relationships and that these are inextricably linked to the wider social context in which they are found.

For Goffman, differences in status and in the ability to control resources were a crucial organizing principle behind social life and relationships, and for this reason he argued that much of social interaction is organized around maintaining and renegotiating social 'selves'. In his article, 'On cooling the mark out' (1962), Goffman gives examples of the way in which con men attempt to adjust the self perceptions of their victims in order to reconcile them to their material loss, and perhaps more importantly, to their loss of face. He makes an analogy between this and the more general process of socializing individuals who have somehow failed to make the grade in their chosen social role into 'more appropriate' subordinate roles, for example in the process of making someone redundant.

Goffman's work shows how formal status and power differences may be mobilized to control ideas.

British cultural studies have provided a wealth of research which looks at the process through which culture, ideology and social stratification are linked in the everyday interactions which people encounter. One example of this is to be found in Willis's (1977) study in which he uses ethnographic methods to focus upon the experiences of working class youths within the middle class culture of the state educational system, and traces the way in which their disadvantage and disaffection is perpetuated through the relationships within that setting.

When we see relationships as framed by inequalities in power, which include the ability to define what is 'normal' and 'natural' in personal relationships, it becomes increasingly difficult to assume that participants in a relationship will have a shared perspective on its meaning, or to see personal perception as free from social constraints.

Assessing individual perceptions of the quality of relationships may also be problematic because of the *contradictory* nature of many relationships, arising from differences in power within them. As has been discussed above, there is considerable evidence that relationships can act in contradictory ways, for example both as a buffer against stress *and* as a source of stress. Even relationships which are built on the idea of intimacy and mutuality may still be full of ambivalence. For example, relationships between parents and children may carry with them aspects of ambivalence and conflict which defy the simple ascription of the labels 'functional' or 'dysfunctional'.

> One day she said to me, 'you make me sick!' And so I said, 'I don't care. You make me sick too'. And her eyes grew big, and so I said, 'You think I like you all the time?' And she couldn't believe it. She said, 'You mean you don't like me?' And I said, 'No. You have ugly ways. You talk ugly. You act ugly. And you think I should like you just because I am your mother?' I said 'You don't like me when I do something you don't want'. So I said, 'It's okay' but she knows underneath, you know, that I love her.
>
> *(quoted in Wodak and Schultz, 1987, p. 186)*

> I had a terrible relationship with my mother, and I was unaware of a lot of why it was terrible until I was older and in therapy and in school … My mother died last June – before she died, within six months of her death, we had worked out things. And oh it was lovely – and I was left with a very good feeling. No guilt. None of the bad feelings I could have been left with.
>
> *(quoted in Wodak and Schultz 1987, p. 176)*

O'Connor (1992) has argued that there has been a tendency in the research on relationships to treat intimate relationships as if they are functional, necessary and unproblematic. However, intimacy can also be associated with destructive relationships. For example, a study by Ratcliff and Bodgan (1988) showed that intimate relationships were unproductive for the women in their study who had lost their jobs, since those closest to them (usually their husbands) had opposed their decision to work in the first place.

The insight that close relationships can be highly ambivalent and full of conflict is well articulated in psychodynamic accounts of personal relationships in which ambivalence and conflict are seen as existing side by side with positive feelings of warmth and attachment (see Chapter 4 of this volume). However it is less well articulated in interpersonal accounts of personal relationships in which the emphasis is on the *joint* construction of meaning and the creation of a shared set of beliefs. Systems theory, for example, has drawn attention to the way in which couples may jointly construct the meaning of their relationship, that is not to say that they will agree about everything but they will agree about the issues which are important and the combination of factors which taken together constitute their relationship. However, as Dallos (Chapter 3 of this volume) has pointed out, it is only recently that the social and cultural context in which these relationships take place has been acknowledged. Thus systems theorists have now acknowledged that it is not possible to treat the family as a closed system. It is also necessary to acknowledge the ways in which the family itself and relationships within it are structured by the social context in which it is located.

Similarly, attributional approaches to relationships (discussed in Chapter 3 of this volume) which have focused on the ways in which individuals make sense of their relationship and their perceptions of others, have also tended to underplay both the ambivalence in relationships and the external constraints on the relationship or the relative distribution of power at anything other than the interpersonal level. Many of these studies have focused on the formation and dissolution of couples' relationships. Victim studies (for example Andrews, 1992), offer an example of the way in which dominant discourses of what is 'normal' and 'acceptable' become deeply enmeshed in the process of making sense of conflict in personal relationships.

If we recognize that relationships are often tied up with feelings of conflict and ambiguity, attempts to assess the quality of relationships by measuring the number of close contacts that people have begins to look too simplistic. For example it might be possible to criticize the Brown and Harris study discussed earlier (section 3) for its implication that a close confiding relationship with a spouse is *necessarily* functional, both because of the ambivalence associated with close relationships and because gender relationships are also likely to reflect wider structural inequalities which may in themselves be a source of stress. O'Connor (1991) points out that the Brown and Harris study did not differentiate between the positive effects of intimate relationships with a spouse and those with close friends, and that although Brown and Harris have revised their work, the study is still seen as evidence of the importance of a close *marital* relationship rather than the importance of *any* close relationship. O'Connor argues that in spite of the difficulties involved in defining relationships it is useful to try to differentiate between a close confiding relationship and one which is close but is primarily character-ized by dependence.

You might like to consider whether identifying the properties of relationships which are 'really' positive solves the problems of ambi-guity and differences in power in relationships. In other words is it ever possible to differentiate between a 'really' positive/functional relationship and one which is not?

While it is very necessary to make some assessment of which situations and which kinds of relationships people experience as positive, in doing so we inevitably encounter problems which are to do with the way in which relationships may act in complex and contradictory ways.

In addition, there are problems in assessing the quality of relationships which centre on the meaning which individuals attach to personal relationships and the way in which their perceptions are formed – not only by individual experience and interpretation (Duck, 1994), but also by the social expectations surrounding relationships. For example, there may be very specific expectations surrounding the contribution which men and women bring to the care of children. These expectations are likely to vary between and within cultures but they are none the less meaningful to participants, who are likely to interpret their personal experience in the light of the more general expectations which define the nature and extent of their contribution and which therefore define when duty ends and support begins.

Studies which look at the way in which individuals make sense of their relationships have found that the expectations surrounding social roles may have a powerful influence on account making. For example, Bograd (1988) and Sculley (1990) studied the accounts given by violent offenders, in which they found that the justifications which men con-victed of 'domestic violence' offences and of rape gave for their abuse of women were strongly rooted in the social expectations surrounding gen-der roles. Sculley argued on the basis of her findings that many of the rapists she interviewed had high and unrealistic expectations of women based on their stereo-typical understanding of women's roles. They therefore placed women on a pedestal and justified their rape in terms of their victim's failure to live up to the high standards they expected in the women's behaviour. So, for example, if women drank, told dirty jokes or were sexually promiscuous they were seen as legitimate targets for rape since, Sculley suggests, they had violated social expectations sur-rounding women's roles. Similarly Bograd (1988) has argued that men who abuse their wives justified this in terms of their wives' failure to live up to the husband's rigid social expectations surrounding their role as wife or mother. This kind of justification is vividly illustrated in the newspaper account of a rape trial in Extract 6.1.

Extract 6.1 *Woman talls of double rape ordeal*

A WOMAN was raped in her bedroom after being threatened with a knife, a court heard.

The 33-year-old mother-of-two from Oxfordshire told the jury at Oxford Crown Court how her attacker produced the knife, told her to undress, pinned her to the bed and cut her underwear off with the five-inch blade.

She said he raped her. When she put on some fresh underwear he repeated the attack.

Mr Simon Draycott, prosecuting, said [the defendant] knew the alleged victim.

On the night of the alleged rape, he visited her while she was getting ready to go out and quizzed her about where she was going.

Later he turned up in the night-club where she was dancing with friends.

He followed her home and an argument broke out during which he asked her to take her clothes off.

Mr Draycott said: 'He pushed her on the bed and sat astride her, slapped her across the face calling her a slut and not a good mother.'

The case continues.

(The Oxford Mail, 1994)

It is worth noting here that personal accounts both reflect *and* create cultural expectations. Thus, in the example above, the rape defendant is creating a version of events which in turn contributes to the expectations surrounding male/female relationships.

A number of researchers have also examined the way in which an individual's position in social hierarchies affects the meaning they attach to personal relationships. Pleck (1985), for example, has shown that there are important differences in what men and women *mean* when they use the term 'friendship' and has described men as seeing friendships in terms of opportunities to socialize around given tasks, while women see friendship in terms of intimacy (Chapter 5 had a further discussion of these differences). Similarly, anthropological and historical studies of relationships (for example those of Mort, 1987 and Aries, 1962) have shown that subjective definitions of relationships are likely to be highly historically and culturally specific. Mort has traced the changing meaning attached to marriage and sexual relationships since the early nineteenth century in Britain. Similarly, Aries has traced changing historical patterns in the relationships between parents and children. Both have argued that the meaning of such relationships can only be understood with reference to the social and historical context in which they occur. Wetherell and Maybin (1996), discussing the complex relationship between personal identity and culture, suggest that our emotional lives and relationships are socially constructed and that because of this, in spite of individual differences, it is possible to detect distinctive patterns which distinguish the emotional life and relationships of participants in, for example, Japanese and North American cultures. The way in which personal identity and relationships are shaped by culture was illustrated by Wetherell and Maybin with an extract from anthropologist Dorinne Kondo's account of her attempts to integrate her Japanese-American self into traditional Japanese culture.

> Can you think of any situations in which you have had to make the transition from one culture to another? This might not be as extreme as the example of moving from one physical location to another, it might involve a transition between, for example, home and work cultures or between status groups (for example working class background to middle class occupation) or between different generations. What kinds of adjustments did you have to make? What strategies did you have to adopt to be accepted? What questions do such transitions raise about personal identity? Is it necessary, or possible, to be the same person all the time?

If we adopt this view of relationships as socially constructed, it becomes difficult to unravel personal meaning from the social context, or to feel able to predict with confidence that what people say and how they act is somehow indicative of an 'inner self' which is untainted by external reality. When we look closely at relationships what we seem to see are partners striving to *create* meaning in a situation in which, because of their different positions in cultures and social hierarchies, they are likely to have different though overlapping versions of what the relationship means. Such a view implies that there may be a dysjunction between *representations* of relationships and the way they are *experienced* by participants, especially those who weald relatively little social and economic power. Reality may be presented in a way which serves the interests of some social groups at the expense of others.

However this is not to argue that individuals and their relationship are passively moulded by their culture or by more powerful social groups. It is also important to look at the differences in perspectives of participants in a relationship and at the way in which the ideas of the more dominant group may be both assimilated *and* resisted by those who are engaged in a relationship. It may be useful to recall Goffman's concept of 'role distance' described in Chapter 2, section 7 of this volume, and his argument that socialization into any role is never complete and that individuals are not necessarily immersed in the roles they take on. They are in a sense acting out a variety of roles and are capable of questioning their identity and as Goffman puts it, of 'Going out of play'.

In the following sections we will look at a number of relationships in which there is an expectation that the needs of participants will be met, in order to show how such relationships embody aspects of power and inequality. We will also focus on the ambivalence in such relationships which may simultaneously provide a source of satisfaction *and* an acute source of stress. In doing this we will need to begin to consider the nature of power itself and how it is manifested in personal relationships. We will also consider the question of autonomy and determinism, and ask in what sense and to what extent individuals are free to construct their identity and relationships. Our previous discussion has implied that power is somehow embodied in social structures and involves the ability of the powerful to impose their definitions and will upon others. But if we accept this view how can we account for both resistance to this attempted imposition and change in relative power? These are some of the questions which you will need to begin considering here.

5.1 Professional relationships

As Clarke (1992) points out, 'in the late twentieth century, it is taken for granted that some of our needs for care and personal support will be met by strangers, people whose job of work it is to respond to and deal with intimate aspects of our lives and personalities' (p. 5). These relationships are often designed to fill in gaps in an individual's informal social network or to provide specialist care which would otherwise be unavailable. Professional 'caring' relationships are unusual in that in theory at least the professional carer is in a position to provide expert help and guidance to a client who is not able to reciprocate in kind. There is therefore a formal imbalance in the resources available to the care giver and to the recipient.

The 'caring' professions are founded on humanist principals of self actualization which emphasize the need for the individual to become whole with the professional's help. Thus the professional ethos of such professions defines professional intervention as value free, as simply a matter of fulfilling basic human needs for compassion, respect, dignity and trust, and therefore as unproblematically helpful. However, such relationships are unequal not only because of the dependency of those who are in receipt of the care and the lack of reciprocity in such relationships, but also because of the professional's status as 'an expert'. To be a professional implies the appropriation of specialist knowledge and skills and the establishment of a monopoly of these skills, and of a process of internal assessment whereby professionals may be judged only by a body of their peers. As Edleman has argued, 'this assumption of expert knowledge implies that the professional has ways to ascertain who are dangerous, sick or inadequate, that he or she knows how to render them harmless, rehabilitate them or both; and that the procedures for diagnosis and treatment are too specialized for the lay person to understand or judge them' (1977, p. 60). The 'caring' professions thus have a crucial role in defining the nature of, and the solution to their clients' problems and also ultimately possess the ability to enforce their definitions through legal sanctions.

Feminist and Marxist critiques of professional 'caring' relationships highlight the way in which experts are empowered to impose their own definitions of clients' needs, and trace this power not only to their professional expertise but to the relatively privileged positions of professionals in class, race and gender hierarchies. For example, Oakley (1981) has described the way that the medical profession actively defines appropriate 'normal' behaviour in pregnancy and childbirth.

According to this argument, professionals may ultimately have the power to impose punitive sanctions on their clients, and to control their relationship by more subtle means. Recent approaches to professional social work relationships have focused on the process through which clients are defined by professional practice. For example, Ahmed (1986) has examined the way in which racist assumptions operate to define and control Asian women in their interactions with social workers.

This kind of approach, in which power is linked to the ability to define what is normal and to implement this through professional practice, owes much to Michel Foucault's analysis of the way in which apparently objective and natural structures in society (for example science or sexuality) are linked to historical and social processes. Foucault argued that through these processes concepts like the body, madness and sexuality become defined and are understood in a way which makes other forms of representation unthinkable, and through this they are able to create a situation in which professional definitions of social problems come to be seen as natural and unchallengable (Foucault, 1979, 1980).

This implies a distinction between structural power (which implies the ability to actively coerce someone into doing what you want) and ideological power (the ability to control the ideas that are available to individuals and their acceptance of them). Ideological power can be seen as a form of 'top down' coercion through which ideas are imposed on the powerless. However Foucault was also interested in the *process* through which individuals, contexts and groups *become* powerful and in the ways in which new ideas and structures are generated. For this reason, Foucault was particularly interested in the resistance which arises at the point at which power is applied. Thus, for Foucault, repression and resistance were interlinked – 'there are no relations of power without resistances, the latter are all the more real and effective because they are formed right at the point where relations of power are exercised' (1980, p. 142).

There is ample evidence of resistance in clients' responses to professional intervention. For example, studies of the views of social work clients found that they made clear distinctions between their own and social worker's versions of events (for example Barford, 1993). The self-advocacy groups set up amongst young people who have been in care, people with disabilities, and women dissatisfied with medical intervention show that those on the receiving end of professional intervention can not only define their own needs but they can also actively resist attempts to impose definitions upon them (Cook, 1987; Taylor, 1993).

In entering into a relationship with a professional body, individuals appear to be negotiating from a position of disadvantage and they are to some extent obliged to comply with professional definitions of their needs. This is illustrated by a discussion of the way in which the relationships of social workers and their clients operate. This is a relationship in which social workers are operating from a professional knowledge base which was traditionally founded on social learning and psychodynamic models of human behaviour and which has played down structural disadvantage and inequalities of class, race and gender. Thus, social work intervention has traditionally focused on *psychological* methods of intervention, rather than on addressing in practical ways the social conditions in which their clients live. In addition to the earlier distinction made between practical help and emotional support, more recently social work has been severely short staffed and underfunded and has been forced to rely on methods of crisis intervention rather than providing the long term resources needed to support families. Social workers, whatever their personal views on the role of structural disadvantage in social problems, have been obliged to operate within these parameters. However, social work clients tend to be characterized by their low social status and relative deprivation. They are thus likely to be acutely in need of practical help. It is therefore possible to interpret the giving and receiving of aid in such relationships as an unequal struggle in which each party tries to put their own definitions of the problem on the agenda.

Read the account in Extract 6.2 below which was given by a young woman recalling her experience of professional intervention, and see if you can detect: (1) the ways in which Leonie's definitions of her support needs appear to differ from those of the professionals she is dealing with; (2) her attempts to resist unwelcome intervention; and (3) the extent to which she had absorbed professional definitions of her problem.

ACTIVITY 6.7

Extract 6.2   *The professional caring relationship*

Leonie: ...I was in the process of moving flats. I was moving from the top flat down to a middle flat which was bigger and roomier, and as you stayed there longer at Grove House you got a better flat, and the flat I moved into had fleas. The cooker was uncookable in, so for 2 to 3..., for about a week I was cooking upstairs and living downstairs, and none of this was took into consideration whatsoever, and in the end when they did take Jason [son] they took him for a week they said, 'You can take him back at the end of the week because you need the time to sort this new flat out to get it up to standard'. Come the end of the week when Jason should have come back I said, 'What about him coming back' they said, 'No, sorry, we're going for an adoption, you are just unfit'. They took me to a meeting a couple of weeks later, decided they were having him adopted and I was asked to find myself alternative accommodation.

Interviewer: And that all happened very quickly?

Leonie: Yeah, extremely quickly, I mean they had been going up to wherever Steve [Jason's father] was on the fair on the fairground, and having words with Steve, seeing what he felt of me as a mother. It was his word against mine because he was older.

Interviewer: And he was no help because he was gone anyway? And do you think they told you enough about what was going on, did you understand what was happening?

Leonie: No, not really, well when they took him, they promised to give him back in a week, it was the only reason that I let him go out that door. Alright yeah they had the care order on him they could take him any time they wanted...

Interviewer: They weren't prepared to let you live on your own with him ?

Leonie: No.

Interviewer: Why was that? Did they think he was at risk or something?

Leonie: Quite possibly, yeah. Because I had some bad times when he was little. I actually went to them for help to ask them to help me to teach me to look after him before something happens. But that didn't come into consideration either, the fact that I'd gone to them and said, 'Look I'm not coping, help', and that should have come into consideration, or I think it should have done. I mean looking back on it yeah, they had reason to think he was at risk. [pause] I mean if I was doing summat and they tried to explain to me the proper way of doing to, I would say, 'What's wrong with the way I'm doing it?' and I wouldn't listen to people.

...If you haven't been brought up properly you can't bring a child up properly yourself can you?

Leonie's account suggests that power in a relationship acts in very subtle ways. It is not simply a question of the more powerful participant imposing their definitions of reality on others. Those at the 'receiving end' of unequal relationships may both resist *and* assimilate the definitions of their experience which are being presented to them. However it is important to remember that relationships are located in a wider network of systems and structures. Thus the apparently more powerful party in the relationship may *themselves* be constrained by their relatively powerless position in social hierarchies and by their own inability to control the agenda and to fix the rules of the encounter. For example the social workers dealing with Leonie were likely to be constrained by their own relatively low status within the professional hierarchy. Similarly it is important to note that social work as a profession is often under siege and constrained by inadequate levels of funding and staffing. Had these material resources been available the social workers involved might have been able then to offer a more 'labour intensive' approach which might have enabled Leonie to keep her child.

> You might consider the extent to which, given their statutory responsibilities towards child protection, their lack of material resources and the common media hostility towards social work as a profession, the social workers involved with Leonie were free to adopt an alternative course of action.

It would also be wrong to assume that social workers do not question and attempt to re-define their position. One of the most interesting aspects of the radical critique of social work practice and its coercive effects on clients already outlined is the way in which it has emerged very largely from within social work itself. There is a long history of radical (Marxist, feminist and liberal) dissent within social work which has attempted to take up the cudgels on behalf of clients and to shape social work into an empowering rather than a repressive service for clients in which social workers have aligned themselves with clients and adopted the clients' perspective (see, for example, Boushel, 1994; Saraga, 1993)

What this suggests is that both clients and professionals participating in formal caring relationships are subject to constraints, and that these constraints may reflect the wider structures of power within society and the ability to control and ration scarce resources. Thus while some features of dependency and inequality may be embodied in formal structures which dictate an imbalance in the relationship, participants are also enmeshed in wider social networks and systems which constrain and empower them in different ways. Therefore when we look at any interaction we need to understand to what extent and in what meaningful ways individuals have control over the relationship and freedom to act within it.

5.2 Caring in close relationships

Inequality in relationships may arise not only from formal differences which distinguish those with professional power and status from those who are the recipients of care, but also in less formal relationships in which there are differences in personal power arising from physical, economic or emotional dependency. In these intimate relationships, subjective interpretations of the quality of the relationship are closely tied up with the participants' sense of personal identity and the meaning they attach to the relationship. Thus it becomes even more problematic to tell where external definitions of the relationship end and internal interpretations begin. Many 'caring' relationships are likely to be informal and organized on a voluntary basis. For example, the majority of the care provided for the elderly or for those with disabilities is carried out by relatives (usually women) in the home (Finch and Groves, 1980). These relationships may be freely entered into and based on personal feeling of care and commitment and yet at the same time may carry with them elements of stress and ambiguity which arise from the unequal nature of a close personal relationship in which one party is more or less totally dependent on another.

The imbalance created by extreme dependence can permeate the whole relationship. In the following account Lillian describes her relationship with her elderly mother for whom she cares. In this account it is possible to observe the way in which the physical and emotional work of caring and the consequent stress and frustration become inextricably linked with the quality of the relationship.

> Lillian: 'Following one of the falls mother became incontinent. Her bedding and clothing had to be changed frequently. I found the soiling difficult to cope with. I heaved and retched. That upset my mother no end … It gradually dawned on me that my life had become more and more centred around my mother. I realized with horror that I was a clock watcher. Whatever I might want to do had to be disregarded to meet her needs. I looked for support and found none. My mother relied solely on myself, as mother's health improved mine deteriorated. My nerves and body were crying out for a rest. I tried to tell my mother and the family I needed a break, this was met with the stinging remarks I had brought her here and regretted doing so. I will never regret giving my mother a new lease of life but the process is very wearying. She says she cannot do without me'.
>
> *(quoted in Briggs and Oliver, 1985, p. 102)*

However, informal caring relationships may also bring problems for those who are forced to be dependent. As the following account from a young woman paralysed by an accident illustrates, dependency may bring its own problems, since to receive support is often neither comfortable nor easy.

> Pam: 'He [her father] imposed on me the obligation to fight my disability, to take on the standards of others which he was totally governed by. Basically he was trying to compensate for what were his losses not mine. Being financially dependent on your parents at an age when you've never had an opportunity to establish a life apart from them tends to ensure that your relationship remains locked in a time warp. You remain a perpetual teenager in their eyes. No concession is made to the fact that you are an adult and in the normal course of events would have left home'.
>
> *(quoted in Morris, 1993, pp 144–5)*

Thus caring in close relationships may be complicated by the intimate personal history which participants share. The personal aspects of such informal relationships may obscure some of the differences in power between participants and make it doubly difficult for those who are in receipt of care to resist the definitions which are imposed on them. It may also, as we have seen, make it difficult for carers to voice their dissatisfaction and frustration with the caring role without seeming to deny the strength of their relationship with those they care for.

As with the professional carers in our first example, it is important to remember that informal carers can only be said to be powerful in very limited ways in relation to their dependent relatives. They themselves may have very limited access to material resources and effective help. (There is an extensive literature on the plight of overworked and under resourced carers, see for example Finch and Groves, 1980; Qureshi and Walker, 1989.) These conditions of relative deprivation which originate *outside* the interaction provide the framework within which the relationship is carried out and are likely to restrict the extent to which carers can control their environment or obtain adequate respite from it or provide the kind of care they feel their relative may need – the carers may not be able to set the agenda for the interaction themselves. We also need to bear in mind that carers are bound to those they care for by complex ties of love and duty which may be perceived as inescapable, and which may feel just as constraining as the need for physical assistance. The meaning which a relationship has for the individual and the extent to which they have been socialized into accepting a particular role may thus be a powerful constraint on the freedom and autonomy of individuals within relationships.

In this sense individuals in personal relationships are drawing on dominant discourses of what is 'normal' and 'natural' in their situation. The professionals in the first example may have a prior identification with professional norms and will have been trained to define social problems and to structure their relationships with clients in a particular way. Similarly, a daughter may find it unthinkable that she should not care for her elderly mother, not only because of her affective ties but because of her acceptance of a view of the mother-daughter relationship which implies lifelong care and inter-dependency. This again raises the question of how free and autonomous participants in a relationship, even those who are apparently operating from a position of power, 'really' are.

Similarly, the problems we have discussed suggest that it is difficult to separate power from dependency or to conceive of a dependent relationship which is not also an unequal one. In contrast to the work of many exchange theorists (discussed in section 4) which emphasizes the reciprocal nature of relationships, even if the balance is only repaid at a later date or in some other way, this analysis of relationships in terms of power underlines the unequal and non-reciprocal nature of many relationships and suggests that care, even if it *appears* to be freely given, has a price for which the recipient must pay.

In the next section we will look at close relationships in which there is an expectation of *mutuality* and of *interdependence* rather than dependence. Again we will focus on how differences in power affect the benefits which can be gained from such relationships. However the particular focus here will be on the way in which social representations influence the subjective construction of the quality of the relationship and the ability of participants to negotiate successfully for the help they need.

5.3   Expectations of mutuality in intimate relationships

As we have seen elsewhere, love and intimacy are among the primary needs and motivations governing human experiences. Intimate sexual relationships are experienced as intensely personal and uniquely meaningful, however such relationships are also located in a social context which defines the way in which they are expressed (Wood, 1993). Thus the expression of sexual intimacy within relationships is not a given but is, as Rosalie Brunt (1982) has argued, 'a highly mediated cultural phenomenon, directly experienced only by immediate participants, consigned to secrecy and privacy and not (usually, regularly) directly available to witness by others' (p. 147). There are therefore tensions in such relationships, not only between interdependence and personal autonomy, but also between social expectations and personal experience, which are likely to manifest themselves in the day to day contacts with intimate partners.

There are a range of social norms and expectations surrounding the expression of intimacy and the meaning of close relationships which provide a framework through which our experience of such relationships will be mediated. Firstly and perhaps most importantly there is 'the heterosexual assumption'. Feminists, and particularly radical feminists (for example Rich, 1980), have drawn attention to the way in which this assumption – that heterosexuality is the norm and that other forms of sexuality are deviant – permeates our culture and finds expression in legal practice, in medical and welfare discourses and in media representations of sexuality. For example, Smart (1984) has shown how this assumption operates against the interests of lesbian mothers in child custody cases. An adjunct to this, as a number of writers (for example Appleby, 1993) have pointed out, is the 'able bodied assumption'; that is, that heterosexual relationships find their true expression in relationships between able bodied men and women and that those with disabilities are somehow a-sexual. As Kennedy (1989) has argued, this assumption of a-sexuality can have serious consequences for young people with disabilities whose experience of sexual abuse is often dismissed as unthinkable.

The heterosexual assumption can act in contradictory ways. On the one hand such an assumption designates heterosexual relationships as normal and therefore they are offered a privileged place in society in which they are socially sanctioned and encouraged, while on the other hand such social sanctioning carries with it a high price in terms of the specific expectations which surround heterosexual relationships. In this way it can be argued that in spite of the prejudice and discrimination which they experience, those whose sexuality is characterized as 'abnormal' may be more free to explore and construct their own sexual identity untrammelled by the narrow social definitions which govern intimate sexual relationships. For example, Appleby (1993) reports that many of the women with disabilities she interviewed felt more free to construct their own sexual identity since they were assumed to be a-sexual and no model of sexuality was pushed at them.

As Wetherell (1990) has pointed out, heterosexual relationships have become closely identified with a romantic discourse which plays an important role in identifying, labelling and constructing the meaning which individuals ascribe to their relationship – 'The woman and the man, the heterosexual couple, recognize their experience and determine its quality through the words which are available' (p 5). In other words, the meaning which partners ascribe to their relationship is derived from specific social representations of what it is to be a couple and to be in love. Thus when couples enter romantic relationships they know to a certain extent what to expect, and in labelling themselves 'a couple' and their experience as being 'in love' or in a 'romantic' relationship, they are in some sense taking on socially derived meanings of their experience. The way in which particular representations of experience are made available, adopted and negotiated in everyday life is a complex question taken up in more detail in Wetherell (1996).

A further assumption connected with the romantic discourse of heterosexual relationships is that of mutuality, that such relationships are based on the *giving and receiving* of affection and support. Thus the heterosexual relationship carries heavy expectations of mutual support and fulfilment. As Stivens (1978) has observed, the male-female bond is accorded special status in much of modern Western society, and considered to be the relationship through which men and women fulfil their deepest support needs. This construction of the heterosexual relationship as the primary support relationship tends to undermine and devalue the support which might be derived from other relationships, for example from family and friendship ties. Furthermore, as feminists have argued, the heterosexual relationship is profoundly *unequal* and is based on very real differences in physical, economic and ideological power between men and women.

In spite of suggestions that a more equal division of labour is emerging in families with more overlap between gender roles, studies have generally found that there have been only marginal increases in the male partner's participation in child care and domestic work overall in recent years and that inequalities in the contributions of men and women persist even in dual-earner families (Pleck, 1985).

In spite of these differences in power, the unspoken expectations arising from the representation of heterosexual relationships as both private and mutually fulfilling is that the heterosexual couple will somehow create a private place in which such differences do not matter. However, when we look more closely at the day to day interaction engaged in by heterosexual couples and particularly when we look at how such relationships are defined and negotiated (as Dallos did in Chapter 5 of this volume), it becomes clear that such differences are not so easily banished and that they enter into the fabric of the relationship itself.

One example of this is to be found in the way in which women in heterosexual relationships attempt to negotiate with their male partners for help with child care and domestic work. It is impossible to understand this process without understanding wider ideological constructions of men's and women's roles in marriage which define their roles *vis-à-vis* child care and domestic work. Thus the negotiation of assistance is closely tied up with the meaning which men and women give to their relationships and their roles within them. There are powerful social expectations around parenting and family life which ascribe to women the lion's share of child care and domestic work, assigning to the male partner a tangential role. Because child care and domestic work are seen as in essence 'woman's work', the man's contribution is seen as optional and women must negotiate for assistance with these tasks. Thus research into the negotiation of the division of labour in heterosexual relationships has shown that women are at a disadvantage in these negotiations and that men are able to select not only the extent of their involvement but also the kinds of task they are willing to undertake (Graham, 1983; Schilling, 1985).

The way in which differences in power may enter into the negotiations is illustrated by the following extract in which a heterosexual couple discuss the division of labour following their first child's birth:

> Fred: I play with [the baby] and hold her and mess around with her, you know. But as far as you know doing all this other stuff, man, I ain't got, I don't feel like it right?
>
> Flo: Right.
>
> Interviewer: Does it surprise you, his attitude, or were you expecting this before the child was born?
>
> Flo: I expected it. That's why I was thinking I wouldn't go back to work for a while.
>
> Fred: She knows me by now, she knows me by now [laughing].
>
> *(Heterosexual couple quoted in LaRossa and LaRossa, 1981, pp. 74–5)*

However, what we see here are not only differences in power within the relationship which enable Fred to withhold his support and prevent Flo from forcing him to contribute more, but an apparent internalization by both parties of the social expectations surrounding men's and women's roles within the family. As Arendt (1970) has argued, control in heterosexual relationships can be exercised not only through economic or emotional sanctions, but also through the legitimization of power through consent. This process of legitimization, as Bell and Newby (1976) have noted, is primarily based upon the 'affective identification' of the wife with her husband – that is, on the woman's belief in the importance and the quality of her romantic relationship with her male sexual partner. However the construction of heterosexual relationships as both mutually supportive and as existing on a level at which structural inequality cannot impinge, makes the woman's argument that the relationship *feels* unequal useless. Thus social representations of relationships can have very real effects on the support which is offered and also on the meaning which participants ascribe to support.

This is not to argue that such definitions are meekly accepted by either party in a relationship. If we return to Fred and Flo's negotiations we can see that Flo is actively resisting Fred's characterization of child care as 'non work', and trying to get child care put on the agenda as equally demanding and thus as deserving of support:

Fred: Well, 'cause, I've just been working longer and been tired and I didn't feel like it. That's right. Now maybe when I start working less and coming home earlier, I'll feel better right? That's right, it has a lot to do with your mental status, that's what it is, you gotta give your mind a break. That's right. See, yours is in neutral all the time.

Flo: Ha! Ha! Ha!

Fred: You're just going around here at the house when, you know, I got, – how much brains does it take to wash the dishes?

Flo: You think I wash dishes all day?

Fred: Vacuum, change diapers, do all that stuff. See, you don't have pressures not to think and that's why you can go.

Flo: Oh [laughing]. You don't think a kid gives you any trouble in the day time, huh?

Fred: Not that much, no.

Flo: They have their good days and their bad days, just like you do.

Fred: I know that, I already said that earlier, but I'm just saying.

Flo: So then it has pressure on me. Right?

Fred: Yeh, but it's not the same kind, Flo.

Flo: It's still pressure.

Fred: You are just talking about that...

Flo: It's just a different type...

Fred: Yelling and screaming and whining and crying: that's easy to put up with...

Flo: But you don't want to put up with it, okay?

Fred: Not in conjunction with what else I have to put up with, no. See, it's different...

Flo: Even on weekends, right?

Fred: On the weekends I'm resting.

Flo: Housewives don't get a rest.

(Heterosexual couple quoted in LaRossa and LaRossa, 1981, pp. 74–5)

Flo and Fred's negotiations can be understood not simply in terms of the imposition of externally derived definitions on the relationship, either through coercion or through the internalization of social expectations, but as evidence of the couples' *active* engagement in making sense of their experience within the framework of social meaning accorded to the relationship (as discussed in Chapter 3). There are parallels here with the way in which the welfare clients discussed earlier both resisted and assimilated professional definitions of their experience. In both situations there is a contradiction between the *representation* of the relationship as positive, and the *experience* of inequality within it. In both situations there is a struggle to set the agenda and to define the terms of the relationship. In addition, Flo's responses show that she is not without some sources of power within the relationship, for example her relationship with her child. From this it might be possible to argue that she is not powerless but simply possesses different *kinds* of power. However, we cannot infer that because participants may possess different sources of power that their ability to set the agenda or to gain their objectives will be *equivalent*.

While it may be relatively easy for clients in professional relationships to distance themselves from the relationship and to see professional definitions of support as imposed from the outside, resistance for women in heterosexual relationships is likely to be complicated by the value which they attach to their relationships. Their prior identification with a romantic discourse – which dictates that the heterosexual relationship is inherently supportive and mutually beneficial – places them in a double bind such that to challenge the inequality in the relationship is also to call the relationship as a whole into question. Because of this, there is evidence that women in these situations try to reinterpret their experience of inequality in ways which allow them to retain a positive view of the relationship, for example by de-emphasizing the importance of their contribution or by re-framing the problems they encounter in terms of their personal inadequacy. Brannen and Moss (1991), for example, have shown that women in unequal relationships consistently tried to play down their spouse's lack of practical support, and emphasized instead their emotional support. As Brannen and Moss observe, 'paying homage to emotional support deflects attention from the underlying inequalities in men's and women's material situations and serves to bridge their very different experiences' (p. 213). Similarly, Croghan and Miell (1992) have shown that the mothers in their study were inclined to justify their spouse's unequal contribution to child care and domestic work in terms of the men's other work commitments or their lack of expertise, or to play down the work involved in child care and their own need for support, castigating themselves for their inability to cope un-aided.

These intimate relationships illustrate the difficulties in assessing the quality of the relationship and the extent to which social and cultural expectations are embodied in personal relationships. When faced with a 'lack of fit' between their expectations of equality and their experience of inequality, individuals are likely to try to create a personal account which accommodates both their personal experience and the powerful social representations which set the boundaries of what constitutes a 'normal' relationship. Thus to understand the meaning of a relationship it is necessary, as we have stressed throughout this chapter, to understand the connections between personal meaning and social representations.

It is also important to understand that this interaction takes place within a wider social context which may place constraints on Fred's access to both material and emotional resources. Thus, although Fred may appear to be powerful in this encounter he may be relatively powerless in terms of other social hierarchies, for example those of race or class. He may also have embraced a traditional male role which, while enabling him to resist his domestic responsibilities, leaves him with fewer emotional resources. An individual's ability to effect change is likely to be dependent on the value attached to the resources at his or her disposal, both within the context of the relationship *and* within the social context in which the relationship is embedded. This value is itself likely to be constructed in response to wider social processes and structures. Personal interactions, even in intimate relationships, therefore need to be understood within the context of wider social structures which may empower or disempower participants, either by granting them unequal access to material resources or by privileging one participant's view of reality.

Review of section 5

- Relationships cannot be treated simply as measurable objects, we also need to understand the meanings which individuals ascribe to them. Such meanings are likely to be contradictory, ambivalent and transitory rather than having one definitive meaning.

- Relationships are constituted at a number of different levels. Even those relationships which appear to be intensely personal and private are influenced by the wider society in which they occur. It is impossible to unravel individual perception (subjectivity) from social expectations.

- Differences in power which are rooted in structures outside the relationship are likely to have effects on the internal dynamics of the relationship, and the meaning which participants give to those relationships.

- Relationships and the events occurring within them may be presented in a way which serves the interests of some social groups or individuals at the expense of others. Participants in relationships both assimilate and resist these definitions of their experience. However, their ability to effect change and to challenge these definitions is related to the relational, discursive and economic resources at their disposal.

6   Discussion

In the preceding discussion we have found that in attempting to assess the benefits and functions of a relationship we have encountered a number of problems which we will summarize here. Firstly, perceptions of the quality of relationships are subjective – relationships cannot be assessed as if they had a constant, unchanging reality. It is not therefore possible to measure them without having access to the perceptions of the individual. Looking at behaviour 'from the outside', or counting up the members of an individual's social network will not necessarily help us to understand the *meaning* which individuals ascribe to their relationships. This brings us back to the problem of subjectivity and of studying subjective experience raised in Wetherell and Maybin (1996) and to the idea that the meanings which constitute a person's experience of the world *emerge* from their interactions with their social world. They are *not* fixed but are always open to interpretation and renegotiation.

Secondly, subjectivity is in itself highly complex and is constituted at the personal *and* at the societal level. As we have seen from the discussion of the meaning of intimate relationships, it is very difficult to unravel personal meaning from the social expectations which surround the relationship. These social representations are likely to affect the way in which participants define the relationship and thus the way they relate to others and the demands which they think they have a right to make in terms of nurturance and support. Subjective meaning is not therefore *either* internally derived *or* externally imposed, but is a complex amalgam of both.

Thirdly, relationships are not consistent. They change over time, but they are also fraught with inconsistencies and ambiguity which make it difficult to know whether in measuring what people say or do at any one time we can have access to the 'real' meaning of the relationship. A focus on relationships as both changing and ambiguous leads us to question whether we can ever be certain that we can be in a position to assess what someone 'really' thinks of a relationship. It may be more useful to see the individual as actively constituted by the social context in which she or he operates, and as holding a number of contradictory versions of reality at one and the same time. This is a point taken up by McGhee (1987) who argues that personal relationship researchers tend to assume a view in their theoretical models of an active self-monitoring self who responds to the changing demands of the interactional situation, but then suspend that insight in order to measure individuals' responses, treating their accounts as once-and-for-all statements which somehow capture what they *really* think about a relationship.

In assessing the functions of relationships we have also encountered problems associated with power and conflict and have shown that these may reflect formal and informal balances in the relationship, and tend to be closely related to the ability to define the agenda and to control scarce resources. However, in discussing power in relationships we have tried to avoid problems of categoricalism, that is of seeing one category of people (for example, professionals, men, or carers) as *necessarily* more powerful. As we look closely at the operation of power in personal relationships it becomes clear that power cannot be seen as a *property* of individuals or groups but instead is the *product* of inter-subjective processes and interactions amongst individuals and will vary according to the context and conditions in which the interaction occurs. Power needs to be seen as a fluid, variable and contingently produced *outcome* of interactions We cannot assume that power will always reside in certain sites or with certain individuals. Power *emerges* in social interactions. It is helpful to think of power in relationships as an effect rather than a cause of strategic success achieved by actors during their interactions with other actors in particular situations. As Sue Lees (1986) has argued, 'There is no hidden reality of power. Rather there are the material practices, the discourses of power and the myriad of conversations and actions which daily constitute it'.

Wetherell and Maybin (1996) take a social constructionist view of relationships and discuss the concept of the emergent self in which identity is seen not as a separate internal territory but as constantly emerging and created through our responses and interactions with others. If we adopt this view of relationships as both changing and contradictory, and as actively constituted in day-to-day interaction, the question of what constitutes a 'positive' or a 'fair' relationship then becomes a question not of discovering the 'real' nature of a relationship, but of accepting that relationships are changing, conflicted and ambiguous and that what we are seeing in relationships is the active construction of meaning which is always evolving and which is constituted at a number of levels.

In this chapter we have problematized an apparently simple question about the benefits of relationships and you may be left with the impression that we have led you into deeper and deeper water and then just left you there! You may also have been left with a rather gloomy and negative view of the chances of experiencing an unequivocally positive relationship because of the inherent imbalances in power in personal relationships.

However, to end, we will look at an example which illustrates the ways in which an understanding of the problems associated with power, inequality and ambiguity in relationships, coupled with a willingness to listen to the voices of those who are in need of assistance and are therefore in a relationship of dependency, can be used to re-define such relationships in a way that the recipients themselves would describe as helpful.

One example of an attempt to set up relationships in which the negative aspects of care which can arise from stress and from power differences can be minimized is to be found in the buddying relationships which are set up to befriend people with Aids or Aids related illnesses. This kind of help is offered by strangers, partly because Aids is a highly stigmatizing illness and this stigma has meant that many people who are ill have not been able to call on informal social networks such as neighbours and families, but also because there may be a need for recipients to enter into a relationship with someone who is *not* intimate and who does not carry the complex history of emotional attachment and ambivalence which, as we have seen, characterizes many intimate relationships. Although buddies are initially strangers, they often form close relationships with those whom they befriend. This is a relationship which is deliberately set up to be non-hierarchical and as far as possible to mitigate the adverse effects of dependence by placing decisions in the hands of the recipient. In these relationships, formal power is minimized and the receiver of help is in a position to define the terms of the relationship as far as possible. Thus some buddies provide practical help or advice, while others provide a close relationship which continues throughout the lifetime of the person they have befriended (Bould and Peacock, 1989).

We are not suggesting that this relationship overcomes the problems of power and ambivalence outlined earlier. However, it does suggest that relationships which acknowledge and address differences in power and the feelings of ambiguity which arise from these differences stand a better chance of fulfilling individual needs. We would suggest that acknowledging that relationships are located in the wider social context is an important prerequisite to understanding them. Without that insight there is a danger that we will overestimate personal autonomy, and see relationships as existing in a social and cultural vacuum in which each participant is faced with an infinite range of possibilities and each is equally free to determine the quality and the nature of the interaction.

Further Reading

Duck, S. (ed.) (1993) *Social Context and Relationships,* Volume 3 of *Understanding Relationship Processes Series,* Newbury Park, CA, Sage.

This book contains a number of accessible chapters which consider the wider social context of relationships.

Duck, S. (ed.) with Silver, R.C. (1990) *Personal Relationships and Social Support,* Newbury Park, CA, Sage.

This book has a series of chapters concerned with the support provided by personal relationships, many of them reporting empirical work. Some of the chapters deal explicitly with the effects of networks of others in providing social support.

O'Connor, P. (1992) *Women's Friendships* New York, Guilford, and Nice, V. (1992) *Mothers and Daughters, the Distortion of a Relationship,* London, Macmillan.

Both of these feminist analyses focus on the ways in which close relationships are structured by wider social expectations.

The *Journal of Social and Personal Relationships* is an extremely useful source of articles covering research in this area. It is also worth looking at the *Journal of Marriage and the Family* and at the journal *Personal Relationships.*

References

Ahmed, A. (1986) 'Cultural racism in work with Asian women' in Ahmed, S., Cheetham, J. and Small, J. (eds) *Social Work with Black Children and their Families,* London, Batsford B.A.F.F.

Allan, G. (1989) *Friendship. Developing a Sociological Perspective,* Brighton, Harvester Wheatsheaf.

Andrews, B. (1992) 'Attribution processes in victims of marital violence: who do women blame and why?' in Harvey, J., Orbuch, T., and Weber, A. (eds) *Attributions, Accounts and Close Relationships,* New York, Springer Verlag.

Appleby, Y. (1993) 'Disability and compulsory heterosexuality' in Wilkinson, S. and Kitzinger, C. (eds) *Heterosexuality: a Feminism and Psychology Reader,* London, Sage.

Arendt, H. (1970) *On Violence,* New York, Harcourt, Brace and World.

Aries, P. (1962) *Centuries of Childhood: A Social History of Family Life* (translated from the French by R. Baldick), London, Jonathan Cape.

Barford, R (1993) *Children's Views of Child Protection in Social Work,* Norwich, Social work monographs.

Barrera, M. (1981) 'Social support in the adjustment of pregnant adolescents: assessment issues' in Gotttlieb, B (ed.) *Social Networks and Social Support,* California, Sage.

Bell, C. and Newby, H. (1976) 'Husbands and wives, the dynamics of the deferential dialect' in Leonard Barker, D. and Allen, S. (eds) *Dependence and Exploitation in Work and Marriage,* London, Longman.

Berman, J.J., Murphy-Berman, V., and Singh, P. (1985) 'Cross-cultural similarities and differences in perceptions of fairness', *Journal of Cross-Cultural Psychology*, 16, pp. 55–67.

Binney, V., Harknell, G., and Nixon, J. (1981) *Leaving Violent Men,* London, Women's Aid Federation.

Bograd, M. (1988) 'How battered women and abusive men account for domestic violence: excuses, justifications, or explanations?' in Hotaling, G.T., Finklehor, D., Kirkpatrick, J. T. and Straus, M. A. (eds) *Coping with Family Violence: Research and Policy Perspectives,* Newbury Park, CA, Sage.

Bott, E. (1957) *Family and Social Networks,* London, Tavistock.

Bould, M. and Peacock, G. (1989) *Aids. Models Of Care,* London, The Kings Fund Centre, The Terence Higgins Trust.

Boushel M (1994) 'The protective environment of children. Towards a framework for anti-oppressive, cross cultural and cross national understanding', *British Journal of Social Work*, 24, pp. 173–90.

Brannen, J. and Moss, P. (1991) *Managing Mothers. Dual Earner Households after Maternity Leave, London,* Unwin Hyman.

Brannen, J. and Wilson, G. (eds) (1983) *Give and Take In Families,* London, Allen and Unwin.

Briggs, A. and Oliver, J. (1985) *Caring Experiences of Looking after Disabled Relatives*, London, Routledge & Kegan Paul.

Brotz H. (1962) 'Social stratification and the political order' in Rose, Arnold (ed.) *Human Behaviour and Social Processes an Interactionist Approach,* London, Routledge & Kegan Paul.

Brown, G.W. and Harris, T. (1978) *Social Origins of Depression,* London, Tavistock.

Brunt, R. (1982) 'An immense verbosity: permissive sexual advice in the 1970s' in Brunt, R. and Rowan, C. (eds) *Feminism, Culture and Politics,* London, Lawrence and Wishart.

Buss, D. (1989) 'Sex differences in human mate preferences: evolutionary hypotheses tested in 37 cultures', *Behavioural and Brain Sciences,* 12, pp. 1–49.

Cameron, C., Oskamp, S. and Sparks, W. (1977) 'Courtship American style: newspaper ads', *Family Co-ordinator*, 26, pp. 27–30.

Clark, M.S. and Mills, J. (1979) 'Interpersonal attraction in exchange and communal relationships', *Journal of Personality and Social Psychology*, vol. 37, No. 1, pp. 12–24.

Clarke, J. (1992) 'A crisis in care-challenges to social work' in Clarke, J. (ed.) *The Comfort of Strangers: Social Work in Context,* London, Sage.

Cook, J. (1987) *Whose Health is it Anyway? The Community and the National Health Service,* London, New England Library.

Croghan, R. (1992) *The Experience of Stress and Support Amongst First Time Mothers*, Unpublished PhD Thesis, The Open University.

Croghan, R. and Miell, D. (1992) 'Accounts of intimate support relationships in the early months of mothering' in Harvey, J., Orbuch, T., and Weber A. (eds) *Attributions, Accounts, and Close Relationships*, New York, Springer-Verlag.

Deutsch, M. (1975) 'Equity, equality, and need: what determines which value will be used as the basis of distributive justice?', *Journal of Social Issues*, 31, pp. 137–49.

Duck, S. (1994) *Meaningful Relationships: Talking, Sense and Relating*, Thousand Oaks, CA, Sage.

Durkheim, E. (1897/1951) *Suicide*, New York, Free Press.

Elleman, M. (1977) *Political Language: Words that Succeed and Policies that Fail*, New York, Academic Press.

Fagin, L. (1981) *Unemployment and Health and Families*, London, D.H.S.S.

Finch, J. and Groves, D. (1980) 'Community care and the family: a case for equal opportunities', *Journal of Social Policy*, 9 (4).

Fisher, C. S. (1982) *To Dwell Among Friends*, Chicago, Il., University of Chicago Press.

Foucault, M. (1979) *The History of Sexuality*, London, Allen Lane.

Foucault, M. (1980) *Power and Knowledge* (edited by C. Gordon), Harvester, Brighton.

Fromm, E. (1962) *The Art of Loving*, London, George Allen & Unwin.

Goffman, E (1962) 'On cooling the mark out' in Rose, A. (ed.) *Human Behaviour and Social Processess an Interactionist Approach*, London, Routledge & Kegan Paul.

Graham, H. (1983) 'A labour of love' in Finch, J. and Groves, D. (eds) *A Labour of Love*, London, Routledge & Kegan Paul.

Hatfield, E., Traupman, J., Sprecher, S., Utne, M. and Hay, J. (1985) 'Equity and intimate relations: recent research' in Ickes, W. (ed.) *Compatible and Incompatible Relationships*, New York, Springer-Verlag.

Homans, G.C. (1961) *Social Behaviour: Its Elementary Forms*, New York, Harcourt, Brace and World.

House, J.S. (1980) *Occupational Stress and the Mental and Physical Health of Factory Workers*, Ann Arbor, MI, University of Michigan Institute for Social Research, Survey Research Centre.

Kennedy M. (1989) 'The abuse of deaf children', *Child Abuse Review*, vol. 3, pp. 3–7.

Kenrick, D.T. and Trost, M.R. (1989) 'A reproductive exchange model of heterosexual relationships' in Hendrick, C. (ed.) *Close Relationships* (Review of Personality and Social Psychology 10) Newbury Park, CA, Sage.

Klein, R. and Milardo, R. (1993) 'Third-party influence on the management of personal relationships' in Duck, S. (ed.) *Social Context and Relationships,* Newbury Park, CA, Sage.

LaRossa, R., and LaRossa, M. (1981) *Transition to Parenthood. How Children Change Families,* Beverley Hills, Sage.

Larson, R. and Bradney, N. (1988) 'Precious moments with family members and friends' in Milardo, R. (ed.) *Families and Social Networks,* Newbury Park, CA, Sage.

Lees, S (1986) *Losing Out. Sexuality and Adolescent Girls*, London, Hutchinson Education Ltd.

Longfellow, C., Zelkowitz, P., Saunders, E. (1982) 'The quality of the mother child relationship' in Belle, D. (ed.) *Lives in Stress,* Newbury Park, CA., Sage.

McGhee, P. (1987) 'From self reports to narrative discourse: reconstructing the voice of experience in personal research' in Burnett, R., McGhee, P. and Clarke, D. (eds) *Accounting for Relationships: Explanation, Representation and Knowledge,* London, Methuen.

Milardo, R. (1991) 'Linking social networks and marital relationships', paper presented at the *Third International Network Conference on Personal Relationships,* Bloomington, Illinois.

Milardo, R. (1992) 'Comparative methods for delineating social networks', *Journal of Social and Personal Relationships,* 9, pp. 447–61.

Milgram, S. (1977) *The Individual in a Social World,* New York, McGraw-Hill.

Mills, C.W. (1951) *White Collar,* New York, Oxford University Press.

Mills, J. and Clark, M.S. (1982) 'Communal and exchange relationships' in Wheeler, L. (ed.) *Review of Personality and Social Psychology* (Vol 3), Beverley Hills, CA, Sage.

Moghaddam, F.M., Taylor, D.M. and Wright, S.C. (1993) *Social Psychology in Cross-Cutural Perspective,* New York, W H Freeman and Co.

Morgan, D. and March, S. (1992) 'The impact of life events on networks of personal relationships: a comparison of widowhood and caring for a spouse with Alzheimer's disease', *Journal of Social and Personal Relationships,* 9, pp. 563–84.

Morris, J. (1993) *Pride Against Prejudice: Transforming Attitudes to Disability,* London, Women's Press.

Mort, F. (1987) *Dangerous Sexuality. Medico-moral Politics in England since 1830*, London, Routledge and Kegan Paul.

O'Connor. P. (1991) 'A woman's confidants outside marriage: shared or competing sources of intimacy?', *Sociology,* 25, 2, pp. 241–54.

O'Connor. P. (1992) *Women's Friendships,* New York, Guilford.

Oakley, A. (1981) 'Normal motherhood an exercise in self control' in Hutter, B. and Williams, G. (eds) *Controlling Women. The Normal and The Deviant,* London, Croom Helm.

Oliker, S. (1989) *Best Friends and Marriage*, Berkeley, CA, University of California Press.

Pleck, J. (1985) *Working Wives, Working Husbands,* Beverly Hills, Sage.

Qureshi, H. and Walker, A. (1989) *The Caring Relationship,* London, MacMillan.

Ratcliff, K. and Bodgan, J. (1988) 'Unemployed women. When social support is not supportive', *Social Problems,* 35, pp. 54–63.

Rich, A. (1980) 'Compulsory heterosexuality and lesbian existence', *Signs,* 5 (4) pp. 631–60.

Rook, K. (1987) 'Reciprocity of social exchange and social satisfaction among older women', *Journal of Personality and Social Psychology,* 52, pp. 145–54.

Rusbult, C.E., Johnson, D.J., and Morrow, G. (1986) 'Predicting satisfaction and commitment in adult romantic involvements: an assessment of the generalizbility of the Investment Model', *Social Psychological Quarterly,* 49, pp. 81–89.

Saraga, E. (1993) 'The abuse of children' in Dallos, R. and Mclaughlin, E. (eds) *Social problems and the Family,* London, Sage/The Open University.

Schilling, R. F. (1985) 'Coping with a handicapped child. Differences between mothers and fathers', *Social Science and Medicine,* 21, 8, pp. 857–74.

Sculley, S. (1990) *Understanding Sexual Violence. A Study of Convicted Rapists,* Boston, Unwin Hyman.

Smart, C. (1984) *The Ties that Bind. Law, Marriage and the Reproduction of Patriarchal Relations*, London, Routledge and Kegan Paul.

Stivens, M. (1978) 'Women and their kin' in Caplan, P. and Bujra, J.M. (eds) *Women United, Women Divided*, London, Tavistock.

Taylor, G. (1993) 'Challenges from the margins' in Clarke, J. (ed.) *A Crisis in Care? Challenges in Social Work,* London, Sage/The Open University.

Thibaut, J.W. and Kelley, H.H. (1959) *The Social Psychology of Groups,* New York, Wiley.

Van Yperen, N.W. and Buunk, B. (1990) 'A longitudinal study of equity and satisfaction in intimate relationships', *European Journal of Social Psychology,* 20, pp. 287–309.

Vaux, A. (1988) *Social Support: Theory, Research and Intervention,* New York, Praeger.

Vincent, J. (1992) 'Self-help groups and health care in contemporary Britain' in Saks, M. (ed.) *Alternative Medicine in Britain,* Oxford, Clarendon Press.

Wellman, B. and Wellman, B. (1992) 'Domestic affairs and network relations' *Journal of Social and Personal Relationships,* 9, pp. 385–410

Wetherell, M. (1990) 'Romantic discourse: analysing investment, power and desire', paper presented at the *Discourse and Gender Workshop, Psychology of Women Section of the B.P.S,* London, Birkbeck College.

Wetherell, M. and Maybin, J. (1996) 'The distributed self: a social constructionist perspective' in Stevens, R. (ed.) *Understanding the Self,* London, Sage/The Open University (Volume 1 in this series).

Willis, P. (1977) *Learning to Labour. How Working Class Kids get Working Class Jobs,* London, Saxon House.

Wodak, R. and Schulz, M. (1987) *The Language of Love and Guilt,* Amsterdam/Philadelphia, John Benjamins Publishing Company.

Wood, J.T. (1993) 'Engendered relations: interaction, caring, power, and responsibility in intimacy' in Duck, S. (ed.) *Social Context and Relationships,* Volume 3 of *Understanding Relationship Processes Series,* Newbury Park, CA, Sage.

Conclusions

by Rudi Dallos and Dorothy Miell

Keypoints and themes

Having now read through the first six chapters of this volume, we hope that you have been stimulated by them and have gained a 'feel' for the theories and research in the study of social interactions and personal relationships. The extracts given in the Introduction to the volume, and in places throughout the following chapters have perhaps helped to portray and capture for you some of the variety, fascinating complexity and poignancy of 'ordinary' human relationships.

We hope that a key point that has emerged for you is that the study of relationships is an exciting and rapidly expanding field for social psychology. There has been a tremendous growth in social psychological research of various types in the area, and there have been significant contributions and cross-fertilization of ideas emanating from applied and clinical work with relationships, such as therapy with couples and families. As with any relatively new field, there is a trade off between the vibrancy of new ideas and approaches, and the consequent difficulties in tracing any coherent or dominant story of what has been happening. In covering (not all of) the field, the six chapters of this book have ranged over a wide spectrum of research methods, inputs from different disciplines and philosophical and epistemological orientations. Though the chapters do, to some extent, emphasize different theoretical perspectives, they are based around aspects of relationships rather than predominantly focused on any given perspective. An important reason for adopting this approach is that research on relationships is a relatively new field for psychology and the perspectives, methods and epistemologies are not, and possibly cannot be, entirely clearly and neatly delineated.

Early attempts to study relationships by isolating certain components were found to be inadequate, offering only partial, narrow and incomplete accounts of relationships, and it has been argued that this field requires a broader approach which frequently needs to combine perspectives. This is perhaps unusual for psychology at the moment. Many of the fields of psychology have adopted clear, though arguably excessively polarized perspectives. As an example, many social psychologists have shown a tendency to adopt either cognitive/experimental positions or constructionist/qualitative ones. In some cases the two approaches hardly appear to have any dialogue with each other. The field of relationships is rather different to this. As you have seen, some studies employ a number of methodological and epistemological perspectives simultaneously, with some studies of friendship involving in-depth interviews, rating scales *and* experimental manipulation of variables. On one level this can be described as naive or confused, but on another as a necessarily pragmatic and useful approach given the complexity of the nature of relationships. What we have done therefore in this book is to present the chapters as representing the field, by embracing themes of relationships, such as emotional aspects, cognitions, patterns and processes, functions, change and development and so on. These do broadly fall within or focus on particular perspectives more than others, but there is also considerable overlap. Below, we summarize some of the key points about the study of relationships which have been made in this volume:

1   Multi-disciplinary: the chapters have drawn upon material from a variety of disciplines, including psychology, sociology, psychoanalysis, biology, therapy and cybernetics.

2   Range of methods and epistemologies: these have ranged from experimental studies involving manipulations of variables, to observational studies, surveys employing questionnaires, interview studies attempting to ascertain the meanings individuals ascribe to relationships, clinical studies and action research, longitudinal studies employing observation, diaries and ratings.

3   Range of domains of analysis: the studies have ranged from analyses of individuals in relationships, to the local dynamics of relationships and patterns of interactions and shared beliefs, to analyses of the position of relationships in the wider societal framework. This latter is an ecological approach looking at how relationships are embedded in a wider network of relationships and within the structures and ideologies of their society and culture.

The following dominant themes have occurred in various combinations in the chapters in this volume, sometimes one has been the dominant focus of a chapter and in others the themes have been presented in a more inter-connected way:

1   *The active person* – people as potentially active in shaping their lives, their sense of self and identity and their relationships. Such a view regards relationships as constructed from a continual process of negotiation involving each person's beliefs, emotional needs and actions.

2   *The construction of meanings* – relationships as centrally concerned with evolving definitions of the meanings of the relationships, and of each partner's actions. Also, this has explained how the local or internal definitions of relationships are influenced by the wider ideologies present in society, transmitted through language and commonly held beliefs.

3   *Biological factors* – biological models which view relationships as evolving organisms and regard the development and deterioration of abilities as promoting necessary changes. These are also seen to shape the motivations people have and the cycles of changes and transformations that relationships proceed through.

4   *Power* – the centrality of issues of power, control and influence, especially in relation to gender differences.

5   *Change* – the idea that within both the interpersonal and the societal domains, ideas about relationships are evolving, shifting and contested.

6   *Cognitive perspectives* – the view of relationships as composed of individuals who are actively trying to understand, predict and explain their own and each other's actions.

7   *Emotionality and unconscious dynamics* – at various points in earlier chapters relationships have been explored from the perspective of the role of emotional attachments, needs and the influence of unconscious factors, including transferences from earlier relationships.

Introducing the Readings

The remainder of this volume consists of five Readings specially commissioned for this book. These are written from within different traditions and orientations to the study of relationships. You should already have read them at least once, as you were referred to them in your work on the earlier chapters of this volume, but you may now want to re-read them and consider the ways in which they interrelate, including trying to identify any points of disagreement between them.

We asked each of the authors when writing these papers to attempt to outline their 'personal' view of the importance, relevance and particular contributions of their tradition. One of our intentions was to convey how some of the dominant traditions and influences of thought in social psychology (experimental psychology, biology, humanism, sociology, feminism and interactionism) currently influence the work and thinking of psychologists. We have not attempted to cover all the influential perspectives, partly since some (for example the social constructionist and the psychodyamic) are discussed in some detail elsewhere in the book. Instead, we took a range of perspectives which are influential to varying degrees within the study of relationships and interactions and offer you a rather more detailed 'insider's view' of the contributions of these perspectives. By presenting them as the personal views of people committed to these perspectives, we have tried to give you a flavour of the central concerns and priorities of each perspective in a way that is not possible in the body of the chapters, where we have attempted to relate the findings of a range of perspectives to particular topics.

A core theme that runs through the earlier chapters in this volume and figures strongly in the Readings is that of autonomy and choice. Throughout our life each of us has to contemplate and attempt to make many decisions or choices about our relationships. As you may remember from Chapter 1, people describe making various choices in their accounts of their relationships; how they came to be friends, how close they feel they should be to someone, in what ways it seems legitimate to act in a relationship, what actions 'broke the rules' and so on. In the

Readings, questions about the range and limitations of such choices can be traced as a central theme. Robert Hinde discusses how biological factors may be responsible for the apparent differences between men and women in their relating and how these differences (such as women as more nurtrurant and men as more aggressive) define the nature of relationships between men and women and the choices about what roles they can play. Graham Allan also explores how relationships are constrained by differences between the genders, but in contrast to Hinde he argues, from a sociological perspective, that our choices are shaped by ideological and structural aspects of our culture. Gender identities and material circumstances are intertwined through access to work, education and skills, he argues, and these operate so that women are more likely to play a dependent role in relationships and men a more powerful one. Continuing this theme, Arlene Vetere discusses how such cultural factors shape the moment-to-moment interpersonal nature of relationships. Most importantly, she argues that the problems that emerge need to be seen as not predominantly a failure on the part of the individual participants, but as a function of the limited choices that they are materially and conceptually able to make in their dealings with each other. In contrast, the experimental (Michael Argyle) and the humanistic (Richard Stevens) perspectives argue, from quite different theoretical positions, that it is possible to enhance the choices that people have available in their relationships either by educating them with knowledge derived from the careful experimental study of the skills and mechanisms involved, or by a commitment to openness, authenticity and growth.

We can also see a dilemma regarding choice emerging in our study of relationships: on the one hand people can feel that relationships offer them more options, cater for their needs in various ways, open up submerged aspects of themselves and so on. On the other hand, relationships can be seen as constraining, for example in the simple reality of having to consult one's partner or friend about a course of action, such as choosing a holiday or going out for a drink, and generally in being concerned about how another may think or feel about an issue. Furthermore, many of our 'choices' may not be conscious or overt. Psychodynamic theories have suggested that feelings from our past relationships may sometimes determine our choices without us having any conscious awareness of this. Also, systemic perspectives suggest that each person's actions, feelings and thoughts are contingent on the actions of the other participants. Each person may not be aware of how they are responding to, and *at the same time* also shaping or constraining the other's choices. These inter-locking webs of mutual anticipations and influences may produce a powerful and fixed relationship pattern which shapes the repertoire of perceived options.

There are other major themes running through the Readings as you will see, but we suggest that this question of choice is a significant and important one that will help you to compare, contrast and relate the Readings back to the material in the earlier chapters.

READINGS

Contents

Reading A
Gender differences in close relationships

by Robert Hinde

1   Introduction

Not a few academic disputes arise because the question under discussion has been inadequately formulated. Nowhere is this more true than in discussions of gender differences in close relationships, which have, in the past, been bedevilled by attempts to explain them either in terms of culture or in terms of biology. It is now recognized that such a simple dichotomy can never be useful, and that to think in terms of *either* a biological perspective *or* a cultural one is naive. The much disputed issues of nature or nurture, malleable or immutable, fade away if we pose the problems sufficiently precisely. This essay, therefore, attempts to focus discussion by distinguishing five questions. The questions are: What are the differences in behaviour between men and women in close personal relationships? How do the differences develop? Why are the differences in the direction in which they are? Why are the differences as large as they are and patterned in the way that they are? Why do the extent and patterning of the differences vary amongst cultures? It will be argued that the answer to the first is psychological, the second both biological and psychological, the third biological, the fourth psychological and the fifth anthropological.

2   What are the differences in behaviour between men and women in close personal relationships?

A considerable literature has documented the differences in behaviour and personality between men and women. None of these differences are absolute, overlap between the sexes being the rule. Nor can individuals be arranged along a unidimensional scale of masculinity-femininity — the characteristics on which men and women tend to differ have some independence from each other. Nor are the differences independent of cultural influences: cultural variation in the extent and patterning of gender differences is enormous. Nevertheless in any one culture there are statistical differences between the behaviour of men and women in close relationships, and some of these have a cross-cultural generality greater than can be accounted for by chance. Thus it is generally the case that men are more physically aggressive and more assertive than women, less conforming and susceptible to persuasion, more likely to initiate sex, more likely to seek out erotic or pornographic material, and so on (Block, 1976; Deaux, 1984; Fisher, 1983; Maccoby and Jacklin, 1974). In choosing a sexual partner, there is some evidence that men place more importance on physical appearance than do women (Berscheid and Walster, 1978) and in choosing a long-term mate, women place more emphasis on status and dependability (for example, Hendrick et al., 1984).

Furthermore, girls tend to play imaginative games based on relationships (mother-child, husband-wife) more than boys, who play games involving a wider range of often adventurous roles (Brooks-Gunn and Matthews, 1979).

A number of sources of evidence are in harmony with the view that relationships are more important to women than to men. Thus in the primary and middle school years, and even earlier, girls tend to form one-to-one relationships, while boys play in groups, often with an emphasis on dominance and/or status (Hartup, 1983). When adolescents were asked about their anxieties, the boys tended to concentrate on changes to or consequences of their assertiveness, the girls on changes to their relationships (Magnusson and Olah, 1981). Girls tend to show more prosocial behaviour than boys, and to be more verbal. Later adolescent and early adult females place more emphasis on affection and less on physical intimacy than males (McCabe, 1982). Gender stereotypes indicate that in conversation adult men are more likely to assert, challenge, make statements or ignore than are women, while women tend to use conversation constructively to negotiate or maintain relationships. Although the actual gender differences in conversational style are in practice often small and context dependent (Canary and Hause, 1993), the stereotypes are important because the behaviour of the individuals is evaluated against the more extreme social stereotypes. For example, assertiveness in women calls for more comment than assertiveness in men.

While many of these differences are in the direction of the gender stereotypes generally held in western societies, the stereotypes generally greatly magnify the differences. We shall return to this issue later.

3   How do the differences develop?

There are two extreme views here. One is that the sexes differ 'naturally' in their behavioural propensities, often with the implication that the differences are a direct consequence of the genetic difference. The other is that they are solely a consequence of differences in experience. Both of these are incorrect: the truth is more complex than either and still not fully understood. The first, nativist, view ignores the undoubted effects of socialization practices and the cultural differences in the extent and patterning of gender differences. The second ignores the evidence that there are some constraints on and predispositions for learning which may differ between the sexes, that the *direction* of the gender differences in close relationships is virtually culturally ubiquitous, and that differences in brain structure appear very early on. Detailed summaries are given by Huston (1985): discussion here is directed solely towards integrating the two extreme views indicated above.

There is considerable evidence that the organization of the brain differs slightly between men and women (Gorski, in press; McGlone, 1980; Wada et al., 1975). These differences probably occur quite early on and could be the direct consequence of the genetic difference between men and women, of hormonal influences, or of differences in experience. Most attention has focused on the second of these possibilities. There is strong evidence that pre- or perinatal hormones can affect behavioural propensities in animals: a female monkey foetus exposed to male hormones at a certain stage in development will tend to show more male-like behaviour subsequently (Goy, 1970; Phoenix, 1974). The evidence on this issue is conclusive for rodents and monkeys, though there are of course differences between species and the effects of early social experience may influence the role of hormones later. Thus it can reasonably be concluded that the early (prenatal in primates) hormonal environment of the embryo could produce slight differences in brain organization between males and females. Direct experimental evidence for humans is, of course, not available. However, masculine tendencies shown by females who have been exposed to androgenic hormones in foetal life, either because of medical interventions or because of abnormal adrenal activity, strongly suggest that similar principles apply (Erhardt and Meyer-Bahlberg, 1981). Hormones are, or course, important also at and after puberty.

However, differences in experience play a critical role. In rhesus monkeys, differences in early social experience can affect the incidence of gender-typical behaviour (Goldfoot and Wallen, 1978), and it is clear that girls and boys tend to have different socialization experiences. The psychological processes through which these differences in experience produce their effects are often seen as theoretical alternatives, but several different processes certainly operate. The first thing most parents want to know when a baby is born is whether it is a boy or a girl. Thereafter, parents tend to treat girls and boys differently. In an experimental situation parents tend to behave towards young children they do not know according to the sex they believe them to be, rather than their actual sex (Smith and Lloyd, 1978). Indeed some authorities believe that gender assigned at birth is the crucial determinant of later gender role behaviour (Money and Ehrhardt, 1972). Parents not only reinforce behaviour that they see as appropriate for the child's sex, but they also provide toys that are deemed to be appropriate — in western cultures dolls for girls and cars for boys, for instance (Maccoby and Jacklin, 1974; Rheingold and Cook, 1975). (Of course this could be because they perceive or know that boys are more likely to play with some toys, and girls with others.) At an early age a child comes to see itself as a boy or a girl, recognizes that the appropriate ways to behave differ between boys and girls, and attempts to behave in a gender appropriate way (Kohlberg, 1966). There is, however, some evidence that preference for sex-typical toys may precede knowledge of gender stereotypes, at any rate for boys (Perry et al., 1984). Behaving appropriately may include identifying with and modelling themselves on the parent of the same sex (Bandura, 1973). Later, it is suggested, individuals may come to process much of the incoming information in accordance with cognitive schemata involving sex-linked associations (Bem 1981a and b; Spence and Helmreich, 1981).

It cannot be too strongly emphasized that all these processes are guided by the stereotypes current in the culture. The parents acquire from the culture views about how boys and girls *ought* to be treated and how girls and boys *ought* to behave. Although they may have some ideas of their own, those views, and those of other individuals, determine their behaviour. These stereotypes are, of course, created by the individuals in the society in question and in general reflect their behaviour. Often, however, they distort the pattern and exaggerate the extent of the differences between the behaviour actually shown by men and women (Hinde, 1991; Nicholson, 1984).

4   Why are the differences in the direction in which they are?

Gender differences in behaviour differ dramatically between cultures in both degree and in patterning. Nevertheless, the direction of the differences is surprisingly uniform. Thus in nearly all cultures men are more likely to initiate sex than women, men are more aggressive than women, and so on. Whether or not there are occasional exceptions does not affect the present argument, the nearly ubiquitous trend demands explanation. It is thus not enough to ascribe the differences in behaviour to the stereotypes, for the direction of the differences portrayed by the stereotypes must be explained.

The argument used here is a biological one and depends on the view, true for all species, that natural selection operates to produce behaviour that will maximize the reproductive success of individuals. Since the physiological requirements to maximize reproductive success differ between the sexes, natural selection results in the evolution of sexually differentiated reproductive strategies. This is not to say that the socio-sexual strategies used by men and women, or the differences between them, are fixed and unmodifiable. Natural selection may have operated to produce predispositions to acquire particular types or styles of behaviour (Hinde and Stevenson-Hinde, 1973; Seligman and Hager, 1972).

What are the differing reproductive requirements for males and females? The issues here are general for nearly all mammals and indeed other species, and stem from the differing reproductive requirements of the two sexes. Males produce many sex cells, females relatively few. To stand a chance of parenthood, a male has merely to inseminate a female, whereas a female mammal must nurture the embryo, foetus and infant through pregnancy and lactation. Thus competition between males for females tends to be more severe than competition between females for males, and the variance in male reproductive success is greater than that of females. Natural selection has therefore operated to augment the competitiveness of males, so they tend to be physically stronger, larger and/or more aggressive than females according to the breeding system of the species. The more females each male attempts to acquire, the greater the differences. And because females produce fewer sex cells, because of the demands of pregnancy and lactation, and because a female mammal 'knows' that her infant is her own whereas a male can be cuckolded, each infant is more important to the female than to the male. In the short term, therefore, males will tend to guard females to ensure they are not inseminated by other males. In the longer term, if male protection or assistance in the rearing of the young is required, the long-term male-female relationship will be more important to the female than to the male. While there are wide species differences in the relations between

---

BOX I   Sex ratios

In most mammals, males are about as common as females. This is a necessary consequence of natural selection. Suppose first that the costs incurred by a parent in rearing male and female offspring are equal. If there are too many females in the population, it will pay parents to produce males because competition between males to fertilize females will be reduced, and their breeding success increased. If there are more males than females, the reverse will be the case. The population will thus stabilize round a 50:50 sex ratio.

However if one sex is more expensive to produce than the other, it will pay a parent to produce fewer of that sex, because natural selection will operate to provide maximum return (in terms of subsequent descendants) per unit investment.

If offspring of one sex are likely to produce more descendants in the long run than offspring of the other sex, parents are more likely to put more resources into the former. However the issues are complicated by the nature of the social system. Thus red deer hinds of low rank tend to produce more females than males because their daughters are likely to have a higher breeding success and because daughters cost less to rear than sons. For some non-human primates the reverse is the case, low ranking females tending to produce more males, because in their case sons are likely to be more successful than daughters. However there is little evidence that mammalian parents actively discriminate between male and female offspring (Clutton-Brock, 1991).

In humans, living in hierarchically arranged societies, females tend to marry upwards. Thus a tendency for parents to value sons more than daughters is most marked in the upper social strata (Dickemann, 1981).

the sexes (and the occasional occurrence of polyandry raises slightly different issues) these generalizations must hold for virtually all mammals because they stem from basic physiological differences (Clutton-Brock, 1991). We can be sure they were true for evolving hominids.

We can have no direct knowledge of the socio-sexual arrangements that obtained when humans were evolving, but there is an indirect source of evidence. In every species anatomy, physiology and behaviour are coadapted: as a trivial example, birds have wings, they have a respiratory and circulatory system suitable for flight, and they fly. In the same way the anatomy and physiology of the genitalia are coadapted to the socio-sexual behaviour of the species in question. For example, chimpanzee females sometimes mate with a number of males in succession. In such circumstances, competition for paternity takes the form of sperm competition inside the female genital ducts. Thus, male chimpanzees have large penises and enormous testes and accessory glands. By contrast the male gorilla, who has more or less undisputed access to a harem of females, has a relatively tiny penis and testes. How does this apply to humans? Men are larger and more physically aggressive than women. They have (relative to other apes) exceptionally large penises, and can copulate more often than they can fertilize an ovum, for the sperm count drops temporarily after each ejaculation. Women, unlike female apes, are sexually receptive almost throughout the cycle, and conceal (even from themselves) when copulation would lead to conception. Unlike other primates, they also have sexually attractive breasts (Short, 1979).

These facts can be reconciled as follows. The sex size difference suggests that early humans were mildly polygynous (simultaneously or successively). The other features are in harmony with the view that sex had a bonding function as well as a reproductive one, the concealed ovulation serving the female's interest to keep the male near her as there was no way for him to know when copulation would lead to conception, and if he left her he could be cuckolded. This in turn suggests that male assistance in the rearing of the young was valuable or essential. While it would have been primarily in the female's interest to maintain the bond with the male because the female had more interest in the current infant, the male would incur few costs and might increase his reproductive success by inseminating other females (Alexander, 1977; Hinde, 1984).

It could be suggested, of course, that this argument has involved selecting facts to fit a theory, but there seems to be no other theory which integrates so many facts about the *direction* (not the amount or patterning) of sex differences in behaviour. The argument is not affected by the fact that in many cultures marriages are arranged, because it will be in the biological interest of parents to optimize the reproductive success of their grandchildren. While this biological approach takes account of the greater strength of males, it sees its significance as lying primarily in competition between males.

5   Why are the differences as large as they are and patterned in the way that they are?

Behavioural differences in infancy are small. Young rhesus monkeys show some clear sex differences — males tend to be somewhat more aggressive, show more rough and tumble play, and more often take up the male copulatory position. Baby boys tend to be larger, stronger and more vigorous than baby girls (Maccoby and Jacklin, 1974), though not all studies agree in this. While such differences may provide a basis for differential parental behaviour, the gender differences seen in adulthood, and the differences between cultures in the ways they are patterned, demand explanation.

Here we return to the perspective of developmental psychology. A number of processes in the interactions of children tend to exaggerate the differences. As we have seen, young children tend to play in same-sex groups, and to choose different games and toys. These differences are markedly influenced by differential treatment by adults, which in turn probably depend in large measure on sex differences in the children's behavioural propensities. Children soon come to see themselves as either boys or girls. Maleness or femaleness becomes an important part of the individual's identity, each sees him or herself as belonging to the group of 'boys' or 'girls'. Members of groups in general tend to look more favourably on members of their own group than on members of an out-group, and to exaggerate the differences between them. Similar processes may operate in children, so that they come to exaggerate the differences between boys and girls. Certainly, in middle childhood, they tend to denigrate the out-group with such phrases as 'boys are dirty' or 'girls are sissy' and to play games in which the differences are emphasized.

Around puberty a different process operates — each tends to exaggerate in themselves those characteristics that they deem to be attractive to the opposite sex, in order to obtain a desired partner of the opposite sex, as well as the approval of their own sex. The role of the stereotype here is clear. Furthermore, individuals are reinforced for behaving in a stereotypical gender-appropriate way. The media present males and females in exaggeratedly sex-stereotypic ways, and individuals may use media images to confirm and extend their biases (Hinde, 1991). Stereotypic views of domestic responsibilities have repercussions in constraints on careers and on leisure activities. Stereotypes about the sorts of employment appropriate for men and women bias career choices, and confirm individuals in sex stereotypic fashions (Colley, 1986; Harnett and Bradley, 1986).

Thus a wide variety of processes tend to confirm and extend gender stereotypes and their impacts on individuals.

6   Why do the extent and patterning of the differences vary amongst cultures?

Here we can identify at least two groups of factors. First, amongst pre-industrial societies, the pattern of gender differences in the society must, at least in relation to overall characteristics, fit the way of life. Child-rearing, at any rate with very young children, is inevitably part of the female role, and we have seen that aggressiveness has been selected for part of the male role. Beyond that, sex role differentiation tends to be stronger in fishing/hunting communities than in those based on agriculture or husbandry, and smaller in families with nuclear family groupings which are relatively independent of each other (Barry et al., 1957). The modern nuclear family has reinforced the role of the woman in child care and the man in the external world (Shorter, 1975).

Second, the different aspects of the sociocultural structure must more or less fit one with another. Not only must different requirements not clash, but we strive for some degree of coherence in our view of the world. In one study (see Box 2 below), Williams and Best (1982) studied the extent to which adjectives were seen as male-typical or female-typical in 25 different societies.

BOX 2   Sexual stereotypes in relation to other cultural values

Williams and Best (1982) arranged for 52–100 university students, with more or less equal numbers of men and women, to be interviewed in each of 25 countries. Each subject was given 300 items from an adjective check list and asked to say whether, for each one, the word was more frequently associated with men or with women. The number of items associated with either men or women by more than 67 per cent of the respondents was assessed. 49 items were associated with males in at least 19 of the countries, 25 with females. The adjectives were also rated for favourability by panels of judges: it was thus possible to calculate a favourability score for the male- and female- associated adjectives in each country. The degree of differentiation of the stereotypes in different countries was also calculated. Predominantly Catholic countries were then compared with Protestant ones, and Hindu with Muslim. Female stereotypes had a higher favourability score in those countries where there were female deities or a near-deity (Hindu and Catholic) than in those with an exclusively male pantheon. This suggests a link between religious and everyday activities, with an influence of the former on gender stereotypes.

---

7 Conclusion

That women and men have different attitudes towards, and behave differently in close relationships is undeniable, though those differences are exaggerated in the gender stereotypes held in most societies. The differences cannot be accounted for in terms solely of biology or solely of experience. Rather we must seek to tease apart a complex interplay between the two. Biological differences in basic propensities are acted upon by socialization processes, and the differences are further exaggerated by a variety of psychological and sociological processes. In these processes the culture-specific gender stereotypes, themselves created and maintained by the behaviour of individuals and exaggerating the actual differences between men and women, play a crucial role.

Further reading

Alexander, R. D. (1980) *Darwinism and Human Affairs*, London, Pitman.
A socio-biological perspective.

Ashmore, R. D. and Del Boca, F. K. (eds) (1986) *The Social Psychology of Female-Male Relations*, London, Academic Press.
A multi-author volume reviewing sex role development and sex roles.

Clutton-Brock, T. (1991) *The Evolution of Parental Care*, Princeton, Princeton University Press.
A biologist's view, mostly concerned with animal data.

Deaux, K. (1985) 'Sex and Gender', *Annual Review of Psychology*, vol. 36, pp. 49–81.
A general review article.

Hargreaves, D. J. and Colley, A. M. (eds) (1986) *The Psychology of Sex Roles*, London, Harper and Row.
A multi-author volume reviewing sex role development and sex roles in childhood and adulthood.

Huston, A. C. (1983) 'Sex-typing' in Mussen, P. H. and Hetherington, E. M. (eds), *Handbook of Child Psychology*, vol. 4, pp. 388–464, New York, Wiley.
An important review chapter of developmental issues.

MacCormack, C. and Strathern, M. (eds) (1980) *Nature, Culture and Gender*, Cambridge, Cambridge University Press.
An anthropological perspective.

Rhode, D. L. (ed.) (1990) *Theoretical Perspectives on Sexual Difference*, New Haven, Yale University Press.
A predominantly feminist perspective.

References

Alexander, R. D. (1977) 'Natural selection and the analysis of human sociality' in Goulden, C. E. (ed.) *Changing Scenes in the Natural Sciences, 1776–1976*, pp. 283–338, Philadelphia, National Academy of Sciences.

Bandura, A. (1973) *Aggression: a Social Learning Analysis*, Englewood Cliffs, New Jersey, Prentice Hall.

Barry, H., Bacon, M. K. and Child, I. L. (1957) 'A cross-cultural survey of some sex differences in socialization', *Journal of Abnormal and Social Psychology*, vol. 55, pp. 327–32.

Bem, S. L. (1981a) 'Gender schema theory: a cognitive account of sex typing', *Psychological Review*, vol. 88, pp. 354–64.

Bem, S. L. (1981b) 'The BSRI and gender schema theory: a reply to Spence and Helmreich', *Psychological Review*, vol. 88, pp. 369–71.

Berscheid, E. and Walster, E. H. (1978) *Interpersonal Attraction*, 2nd ed., Reading, Mass., Addison-Wesley.

Block, J. H. (1976) 'Issues, problems, and pitfalls in assessing sex differences: a critical review of *The Psychology of Sex Differences*', *Merrill-Palmer Quarterly*, vol. 22, pp. 283–308.

Block, J. H. (1984) *Sex Role Identity and Ego Development*, San Francisco, Jossey-Bass.

Brooks-Gunn, J. and Matthews, W. J. (1979) *He and She: How Children Develop their Sex-role Identity*, Englewood Cliffs, New Jersey, Prentice-Hall.

Canary, D. L. and Hause, K. S. (1993) 'Is there any reason to research sex differences in communication?', *Communication Quarterly*, vol. 41, pp. 129–44.

Colley, A. (1986) 'Sex roles in leisure and sport' in Hargreaves, D. J. and Colley, A. M. (eds) *The Psychology of Sex Roles*, London, Harper and Row.

Deaux, K. (1984) 'From individual differences to social categories: analysis of a decade's research on gender', *American Psychologist*, vol. 39, pp. 105–16.

Erhardt, A. A. and Meyer-Bahlberg, H. F. L. (1981) 'Effects of prenatal sex hormones on gender-related behaviour', *Science*, vol. 221, pp. 1312–18.

Fisher, W. A. (1983) 'Gender, gender role differentiation, and response to erotica' in Algeier, F. R. and McCormick, N. B. (eds) *Changing Boundaries: Gender Roles and Sexual Behaviour*, Palo Alto, Mayfield.

Goldfoot, D. A. and Wallen, K. (1978) 'Development of gender role behaviours in heterosexual and isosexual groups of infant rhesus monkeys' in Chivers, D. and Herbert, J. (eds) *Recent Advances in Primatology*, London, Academic Press.

Gorski, R.A. (in press) 'Individual development over the life-span' (ed. D. Magnusson), Cambridge, Cambridge University Press.

Goy, R. W. (1970) 'Early hormonal influence in the development of sexual and sex-related behaviour' in Quarton, G. C., Melanchuk, T. and Schmidt, F. O. (eds) *Neurosciences: a Study Program*, New York, Rockefeller University Press.

Harnett, O. and Bradley, J. (1986) 'Sex roles and work' in Hargreaves, D. J. and Colley, A. M. (eds) *The Psychology of Sex Roles*, London, Harper and Row.

Hartup, W. P. (1983) 'Peer relationships' in Mussen, P. H. and Hetherington, E. M. (eds) *Handbook of Child Psychology, vol. 4, Socialization, Personality and Social Development,* New York, Wiley.

Hendrick, C., Hendrick, S., Foote, F. H. and Slapion-Foote, M. J. (1984) 'Do men and women love differently?', *Journal of Social and Personal Relationships*, vol. 1, pp. 177–95.

Hinde, R. A. (1984) 'Why do the sexes behave differently in close relationships?', *Journal of Social and Personal Relationships*, vol. 1, pp. 471–501.

Hinde, R. A. (1991) 'A biologist looks at anthropology', *Man*, vol. 26, pp. 583–608.

Hinde, R. A. and Stevenson-Hinde, J. (eds) (1973) *Constraints on Learning: Limitations and Predispositions*, London, Academic Press.

Huston, A. C. (1983) 'Sex-typing' in Mussen, P. H. and Hetherington, E. M. (eds) *Handbook of Child Psychology, vol. 4, Socialization, Personality and Social Development*, New York, Wiley.

Kohlberg, L. (1966) 'A cognitive development analysis of children's sex role concepts and attitudes' in Maccoby, E. E. (ed.) *The Development of Sex Differences'*, Stanford, Stanford University Press.

Maccoby, E. E. and Jacklin, C. N. (1974) *The Psychology of Sex Differences*, Palo Alto, Stanford University Press.

Magnusson, D. and Olah, A. (1981) 'Situation-outcome contingencies', *Reports from the Department of Psychology, Stockholm*, Stockholm, University of Stockholm.

McCabe, M. P. (1982) 'The influence of sex and sex role on the dating attitudes and behaviours of Australian youth', *Journal of Adolescent Health Care*, vol. 3, pp. 29–36.

McGlone, J. (1980) 'Sex differences in human brain symmetry', *Brain and Behavioural Sciences*, vol. 3, pp. 215–64.

Money, J. W. and Ehrhardt, A. A. (1972) *Man and Woman, Boy and Girl*, Baltimore, Johns Hopkins University Press.

Nicholson, J. (1984) *Men and Women: How Different are they?*, Oxford, Oxford University Press.

Perry, D. G., White, A. J. and Perry, L. L. (1984) 'Does early sex typing result from children's attempts to match their behaviour to sex role stereotypes?, *Child Development*, vol. 55, pp. 2114–21.

Phoenix, C. H. (1974) 'Sexual behaviour of laboratory and wild-born rhesus monkeys', *Hormones and Behaviour*, vol. 10, pp. 178–92.

Rheingold, H. and Cook, K. (1975) 'The content of boys' and girls' rooms and as index of parents' behaviour', *Child Development*, vol. 46, pp. 459–63.

Seligman, M. E. P. and Hager, J. L. (eds) (1972) *Biological Boundaries of Learning*, New York, Appleton Century Crofts.

Short, R. (1979) 'Sexual selection and its component parts, somatic and genital selection, as illustrated by man and the great apes', *Advances in the Study of Behaviour*, vol. 9 pp. 131–58.

Shorter, E. (1975) *The Makings of the Modern Family*, New York, Basic Books.

Smith, C. and Lloyd, B. (1978) 'Maternal behaviour and perceived sex of infants', *Child Development*, vol. 49, pp. 1263–5.

Spence, J. T. and Helmreich, R. L. (1981) 'Androgeny versus gender schema: a comment on Bem's gender schema theory', *Psychological Review*, vol. 88, pp. 365–68.

Wada, J. A., Clarke, R. and Human, A. (1975) 'Cerebral hemisphere asymmetry in humans', *Archives of Neurology*, vol. 32, pp. 239–46.

Williams, J. E. and Best, D. L. (1982) *Measuring Sex Stereotypes*, Beverly Hills, Sage.

Reading B
A gender sensitive perspective on personal relationships and therapy

by Arlene Vetere

I trained as a clinical psychologist in the early 1980s. At that time I would meet families whose interpersonal struggles and difficulties often seemed to be related to their gendered role relations and their perceptions of choices, control and opportunities that arose within that context. A familiar example on my child placement was the triangle of a highly cohesive mother-and-child relationship with a peripheral father, which appeared to compromise aspects of the child's psychological and social development. It always seemed to me that any attempt to reinvolve the father both as a co-parent with his spouse and as a more involved father to his child to help resolve the dilemmas about the child's progress, always left the woman and mother at a disadvantage, if not at a loss! She was being asked both to share her power as a parent and to develop quite quickly alternative interests and sources of satisfaction and self esteem outside of parenting. Something, we might speculate, for which many women are not well socialized.

It was a source of disappointment and puzzlement to me that my clinical psychology training had not prepared me for these eventualities, and that it offered nothing by way of explanatory frameworks or models of intervention. Nor was it likely to, given the continuing neglect of family life as the emotional and developmental context for children and adults by mainstream academic psychologists (Vetere and Gale, 1987).

My experiences as a family process researcher were similar. Not only did I have to contend with this somewhat puzzling neglect of the psychological significance of family life, but also with the gender blind nature of existing family interaction theories. Thus it was with recognition and relief that I turned to feminist scholarship on family theory and intervention. As a clinical and academic psychologist, this brought me into a close, highly charged and potentially creative encounter with the feminist critiques of family process theory, family therapy and family therapy theory. In addition, this encounter shed a different light on the gender bound nature of my academic and clinical trainings and the training institutions.

Williams and Watson (1994) point out that clinical psychologists and clinical researchers, amongst others, have been slow to appreciate the links between social inequalities, such as gender inequality, and psychological distress. By ignoring these links, we serve, albeit inadvertently, the interests of privileged social groups. However most people work with individuals and families to help them improve the quality of their lives and not to support unjust social divisions. They suggest we can begin to resolve this dilemma:

- by acknowledging gender and other social inequalities in interpersonal distress in both our therapy and research questions;

- by developing our knowledge, based on talking to men and women in families abut their different experiences of family life and learning from the research on men, women and children's experiences of therapy;

- by understanding our own experiences of power and powerlessness.

In my view, feminist scholars have made important contributions that inform our conduct when working both as researchers and as therapists with family members. Such contributions include the recognition that men and women have different experiences of self, of others and of life; that men's experience in general has been more widely articulated and women's has been under-represented; the recognition that women do not as yet have equality of opportunity in the workplace; placing the family in historical context and challenging our view of family life as 'given'; and calling for a re-examination of family life, such as redistributing household and childcare responsibilities, validating non-traditional sexual and living arrangements, ending women's economic dependence on men, and fighting for reproductive rights.

In my view, two of the unfortunate and unforeseen consequences of some of the more radical critiques has led, in some circles (1) to a devaluation of men's emotional experiences and modes of expression and (2) to an appraisal of women's heterosexuality as an eroticized form of subordination (Kitzinger, 1994). We do not generalize about women within the radical critique, but it seems that men are all treated as men. Spellman (1990) discusses an example of this problem of essentialism using Iris Murdoch's paradox of the pebbles on a beach. The pebbles are all different, yet all instances of a single thing, 'pebblehood'. And men are all packaged as male, often within a predatory male discourse (see Thomas, 1993). Hunter (1992) draws our attention to the difficult and limited gender positions available to men. For example, the identity of 'sissy' is available to men who speak about their emotional experiences, who often both need to qualify them first and give up something in the eyes of other men. Is this therefore an emasculating process within current definitions of masculinity and, if so, overlooked by radical critiques?

Many feminist scholars have argued that the issue of asserting authority and power and having it acknowledged and respected is more difficult for women. Whilst not ignoring the diversity of women's experiences, women are seen to be relatively inexperienced with leadership roles and the overt use of power, and many have been socialized in a non-verbal way of interacting that communicates submission, indecision and weakness in certain interactional contexts. Herein lies a paradox: competent and knowledgeable women perform certain roles as teacher, parent and so on; and yet live in a context, it is argued, that privileges men.

Embedded in this is a further paradox; an individual man's experience of daily powerlessness. Arguments to the effect that he is advantaged by living in a patriarchal culture are not likely to speak to his experience. It is interesting to note that some family researchers have suggested that part of an explanation for a man's violence to a known woman is based on his perception of powerlessness in their interpersonal relationship and his resort to physical violence to maintain control and exert influence (see Goldner et al., 1990, and Minuchin, 1984).

Williams and Watson (1988) provide an analysis of interpersonal power bases that is helpful in understanding some of these paradoxes. In addition, they provide pointers to understanding both the psychological and interactional consequences for couples who accept patriarchal explanations for sexual inequality, and the consequences for family life of differential access to power bases by men and women, such as, the needs of both partners are not mutually satisfied, unacknowledged conflict arising out of unmet needs could act as a source of resentment and distress, and the couple would not have the means to resolve these issues directly. (See Foreman and Dallos (1992) for a worked example of a couple with sexual difficulties.)

Traditionally, men and women have had differential access to sources of power and the means of access are determined largely by gender role stereotypes and expectations. Power in family process theories is defined as the relative influence of one person over another. Women are believed to influence others more indirectly and to rely on their own personal resources, such as perceived attractiveness, empathy, kindness and close interpersonal relationships for the exercise of power. Whereas it is believed men have access to, and are therefore able to utilize, a different set of resources, such as strength, skill and competence in the public domain and tend to be less likely to rely on interpersonal and intimate relations for the exercise of power. Thus men are subject to normative expectations that centre on intelligence, competence, strength and instrumentality, and thereby rely on an *expert* base of social power. Women are said to be subject to normative expectations that centre on nurturance, empathy, warmth and sensitivity and thereby rely on a *referent* base of social power. According to this analysis, gender inequality is to be found within private and public worlds, perpetuated by unequal access to differentially valued power bases.

The specific power bases identified by Williams and Watson are domestic, affective, relational, reproductive, sexual, economic, ascribed, physical, contractual, informational and language. Women are said to have greater access to the first five, and men to have greater access to the last six. Domestic power comes from the provision or threat of withdrawal of domestic services. Affective power is often assigned to women when they are believed to be the nurturers of family relationships, taking responsibility for family members' emotional well-being. Relational power is based on connectedness between people, within and outside the family. Reproductive power may be a diminishing resource for women as the value of children as an economic resource declines. Some men are said to consider it their right to have a sexual relationship with women, so sexual power may be exercised by withholding sexual relations.

Economic power is arguably the major power base in Western societies. Women's work within the home is largely unwaged and women constitute the bulk of the part-time workforce in lower paid service industries (*Social Trends,* 1990). Ascribed power is given to people by society on the basis of some characteristic or attribute, such as race, class, sex. Physical power, or the threat of its use, is largely available to men because of their greater physical size. Contractual power is the ability to leave the relational field, most often noted by family therapists with their difficulties in convening and engaging men. Informational power values knowledge and skills as resources and varies according to the value system of the social group, for example, men's knowledge about the public world versus women's knowledge about the more private world of the family. Finally the power of language refers to a power base that commonly names and describes experience and reality.

So, what for me is a gender sensitive approach to family theorizing, family therapy and family therapy research? Every family therapy session I am involved with as therapist, trainer and/or supervisor is about both the politics and meaning of growing up and the politics and meaning of gender. Political because our family work has consequences for the expression and distribution of power. We need to be as clear as possible about what prevailing gender values and beliefs, amongst others, we are reinforcing or challenging. Gender sensitive family therapy, for me, is not a set of prescriptions or techniques, rather it is a process between the therapist and the family by which all family members negotiate their individual and relationship needs. Thus a gender sensitive approach to therapy and research examines how gender roles and stereotyping affect each individual in the family, relationships between individuals in the family, relationships between the family and other social institutions, and relationships between family members and the therapist/researcher. Such an examination emphasizes the social context as an important systemic determinant of behaviour and recognizes that men and women face unique problems as a result of their socialization. These issues are equally important for clinical audit when I talk with families about their experiences of being in therapy as part of our attempts to evaluate family members' satisfaction with our service.

A gender sensitive approach to family therapy and its evaluation can incorporate many factors, some of which include the following:

1 Family therapists and researchers can examine their own values regarding gender as they are expressed in therapy, supervision and therapy training and research. To what extent are our ideas about differences between men and women based on sexist stereotypes? For example, Wheeler and colleagues (1989) challenge the prevailing nuclear family/middle class conceptualization of family life cycle theory; it needs to broaden to include other choices available to men and women, such as remaining single and establishing an intimate

social network, marrying and choosing not to have children, choosing to be a single parent, choosing homosexual/heterosexual cohabitation with or without children, and so on. This reconceptualization releases us from discussion of family life in terms of stereotypic roles, such as courtship, marriage, birth of first child, and so on. Currently I am interviewing family members about the inter-personal consequences for family life and individuals within the household of living with and raising a child with a diagnosis of autism. The interviews are semi-structured and do not assume nuclear family composition, neither do they assume gendered role divisions.

2   Family therapists approach the issue of self-reflexivity in therapy by using their 'gendered selves', for example, by modelling alternatives to traditional roles. Working in mixed co-therapy pairs provides opportunities for exploring different styles of communication and negotiation between men and women; similarly when working with a team of therapists observing from behind a one-way screen, interventions can be gendered rather than delivered in a gender 'neutral' manner. Both men and women therapists can exercise authority, show competence and draw and underline interpersonal boundaries whilst at the same time offering respect, empathy and careful listening.

The implications of self-reflexivity for family researchers are equally important, such as, recognizing how the different perceptions of a female interviewer might influence a male or female family member respondent when describing the quality of family and marital relationships, role divisions, conflict resolution, and so on.

3. Until recently, gender sensitive therapy has been women centred. Much less has been written about men's experience in family therapy. We know that men are both less likely to seek help with their emotional concerns and more likely to wait to a later stage of psychological distress before seeking help than are women, which in a family context could lead to therapists relying on women to initiate therapeutic contact and to take major responsibility for inter-personal and lifestyle changes. The reliance on women informants extends to the field of family and developmental research, where it is largely women who are interviewed about the effects on family life of diverse circumstances, such as rearing a child with developmental disabilities, post-divorce effects on children, and so on.

The questions thus arise as to the difficulties in engaging men and fathers in therapy and the implications for men and women in families of *not* engaging men. Bennun (1989) offers some important pointers from his research into the relative effectiveness of two types of family therapy. He found that men in family therapy preferred a therapist style that was active, competent and goal setting. In addition, they were more likely to stay in therapy when the therapist was optimistic about the outcome and showed a positive liking for the family. It could be said that the use of active methods in family therapy help to integrate the father back into the parental subsystem and enhance feelings of self-esteem as a father, thus reducing feelings of inadequacy and helplessness believed to be associated with peripherality as a father (Minuchin, 1974).

The psychological costs for men of living in a gender stereotype bound culture, such as pressure to conform to the dominant image of masculinity and fears of being thought to be like a woman have been researched less extensively, but have important implications for family research and family therapy and should not be overlooked in our zeal to emancipate women.

4   Family therapists and family researchers can ask questions that make explicit the beliefs, decisions and behaviours that illustrate to what degree equality and reciprocity exist between men and women in the family. For example, we might ask a couple how they decided who would work in paid employment; how they distribute caretaking responsibility for their children; how much flexibility they think they have in these arrangements; how satisfied they are with these arrangements; who benefits and who carries most cost.

Family therapists can facilitate consideration of a wider range of perspectives, behaviour and solutions, that may be less constrained by more traditional definitions of gender roles and personal identity. For example, when discussing parental teamwork and shared childrearing responsibilities, paying careful attention to the implications for both partners by ensuring that the woman is willing to share parental responsibility and has other ways of expressing her competence, and that the man is willing to bear the cost in the workplace of being more involved with his family. It is assumed that the allocation of roles solely on the basis of gender is to be questioned.

Acknowledgement of the positive motives and personal costs to men and women in their present living arrangements may well help in the initial joining process.

5   Family therapists can use methods of positive reframing and relabelling to challenge and shift the conceptual and emotional perspective on an individual or a relationship; so, what may have been thought of as personal inadequacy can be reinterpreted as socially prescribed. Thus we can explore with women what they have been taught about being women in comparison to their actual competencies, interests and needs; and with men what they have been taught about being men, or what they have been taught about women, and so on.

6   Family therapists and family researchers explore differentials in power between men and women. Williams' and Watson's analysis of interpersonal power bases is helpful in formulating questions about how the presence or withdrawal of these sources of power affect everyday processes, such as decision making, negotiation and conflict resolution.

It is imperative that we do not marginalize the needs of either women or men in our research and therapy. When working with men and women in families we need to be aware of how the issues discussed above influence what we do, say, ask and explore *and why*.

Finally, I wish to discuss the training of clinical psychologists, clinical researchers and family therapists. Such training takes place in a gender bound culture, influenced by the context of training, the curriculum and the relational processes between trainer and trainee. This brings me back to where I started with my training experience. For example, as far as I am aware clinical psychology training courses do not scrutinize their institutional hierarchies and their training programmes for the potential impact of gender differences and gender inequalities on the training process and training relationships. The discussion of gender issues and gender sensitive work with families still appears to be sidelined to one-off workshops, without any consideration of the burgeoning field of family research.

In conclusion, I do not believe that clinical psychologists, family theorists and family therapists have deliberately promoted sexist beliefs and practices, but by failing to take account of differences in status and power between men and women in our society they have allowed gender to remain a hidden dimension in both family life and professional training. A gender sensitive approach to research and therapy training helps to address and reverse this far-reaching oversight. In my own experience, feminist ideas have been incorporated only slowly into training and practice. So it is exciting to see psychologists more involved in this work and more prepared to see families as they are, to explore all living arrangements for their creativity, potential and competence, and to support each family member's needs, rather than trying to preserve one particular form of family life.

References

Bennun, I. (1989) 'Perceptions of the therapist in family therapy', *Journal of Family Therapy*, 11, pp. 243–55

Foreman, S. and Dallos, R. (1992) 'Inequalities of power and sexual problems', *Journal of Family Therapy*, vol. 4, no. 4, pp. 349–71.

Goldner, V., Penn, P., Schneinberg, M. and Walker, G. (1990) 'Love and violence: gender paradoxes in volatile attachments', *Family Process*, 29, pp. 343–64.

Hunter, A. (1992) 'Same door, different closet: a heterosexual sissy's coming-out party.' *Feminism and Psychology*, 2, pp. 367–85.

Kitzinger, C. (1994) 'Problematizing pleasure: radical feminist deconstructions of sexuality and power' in Radtke, H.L. and Stam, H.J. (eds) *Power/Gender: Social relations in theory and practice*, London, Sage.

Minuchin, S. (1974) *Families and Family Therapy*, London, Tavistock.

Minuchin, S. (1984) *Family Kaleidoscope*, New York, Harvard.

Social Trends (1990) London, HMSO.

Spellman, E. (1990) *Inessential Woman: Problems of Exclusion in Feminist Thought*, Aylesbury, The Women's Press.

Thomas, A. (1993) '"Masculinity" as misogyny: an exploration of the cultural context of sexual harassment', *Paper presented to the Women and Psychology Conference*, University of Sussex, July.

Vetere, A. and Gale, A. (1987) *Ecological Studies of Family Life*, Chichester, Wiley.

Wheeler, D., Avis, J.M., Miller, L. and Chaney, S. (1989) 'Rethinking family therapy training and supervision: a feminist model' in McGoldrick, M., Anderson, C. and Walsh, F. (eds), *Women in Families: A Framework for Family Therapy*, New York, Norton.

Williams, J. and Watson, G. (1988) Sexual inequality, family life and family therapy in Street, E. and Dryden, W. (eds) *Family Therapy in Britain*, Buckingham, Open University Press.

Williams, J. and Watson, G. (1994) *Clinical Psychology Forum*, vol. 64, pp. 6–12.

Reading C:
The experimental study of relationships

by Michael Argyle

1 Introduction

Relationships have been studied in many different ways and from many different perspectives, but in this Reading I shall focus on an exploration of the contribution of experimental and related methods. There has been much criticism of experiments in social psychology as being artificial and unrealistic, but it can be argued that they may be the best, sometimes the only way to test hypotheses and show causal influences. It is particularly difficult to do experiments on relationships, but in this Reading I shall explore what can be done.

2 Methods

Laboratory experiments have not been much used for the study of relationships. Their traditional advantage is that it is clear that variable A has probably caused B rather than vice versa, and possible alternative explanations in terms of variables C and D can be eliminated by holding them constant by means of ingenious control groups. In the best experiments many other variables really are held constant; for example we shall look later at physical attractiveness as an experimental variable; this can be manipulated by producing more or less attractive confederates, or other subjects, but attractive individuals may also differ in personality so it is better to alter the appearance of confederates, making them more attractive with cosmetics, or less attractive by using a wig. The main disadvantage is that the experimental task and situation may be artificial and unlike real life, so there is low external validity. There may also be ethical problems over deception; a solution to this is to present video tapes which are judged by subjects, as in the experiments comparing verbal and non-verbal signals referred to later (p.347). Another solution is to do role-play experiments in which subjects are asked to suppose that they are carrying out a real interview, or sitting on a real jury. The debate over the artificiality of laboratory experiments was at the heart of the 'crisis in social psychology' of the early 1970s.

Other experiments are carried out in the laboratory, in order to use special measures or tests, but do not involve manipulation of variables.

A good example is the experiment by Noller (1984) in which married couples were asked to communicate ambiguous verbal utterances (for example 'I'm feeling cold, aren't you?') in different non-verbal styles (for example 'Please come and warm me with your body'). Unhappy married couples did less well because the husbands were poor senders of different non-verbal signals.

It is a matter of opinion and judgement which kinds of experiment have an acceptable degree of external validity. A debatable example is the experiment carried out by Clark (1986) which showed that in 'communal' (that is, affectionate) as opposed to 'exchange' (more business-like) relationships, the subjects did not keep track of their own inputs but were more concerned with the needs of the other while doing a laboratory task, even when the other would not be able to reciprocate later. 'Communal' was operationalized by leading the subject to believe there was the possibility of a romantic relationship with the other person, though no actual long term relationship was involved.

There are other kinds of laboratory experiment, in which for example the subjects sit in booths, press buttons and think they are giving each other electric shocks, etc. There are different views about experiments such as these; my own view is that since they remove verbal and non-verbal communication, have no rules, no recognizable situation, and no relationship with the other subjects involved, these experiments can tell us nothing about social behaviour in the real world.

Some use has also been made of field experiments, that is experiments carried out in field situations, in which the subjects are unaware of the experimental manipulation. A good example is the famous 'computer dance' experiment by Walster et al. (1966) which showed the effect of physical attractiveness on choice of partner, and is described in Box 1.

Quasi-experimental studies involve the collection of longitudinal data, in a design which makes it possible to make some causal inference. Van Yperen and Buunk (1990) found that measures of perceived equity predicted satisfaction with marriage one year later, better than marital satisfaction predicted equity — the 'cross-lagged correlation' design. This is described later in Box 2. These quasi-experimental designs have become widely used in the relationships field. Multiple regression is used to tease out the strength of the effects of different possible causal variables, and a series of such regressions leads to 'path analysis' of the causal process involved. A simple example is our finding that extraversion affects happiness via its effect on assertiveness, and this is reported in Box 3.

BOX 1   Attractiveness and partner choice

Walster and her co-workers invited 376 male and 376 female college first years to a dance, at which they were assigned a partner at random (except that the male was always taller) and were asked to fill in some questionnaires. The physical attractiveness of each of the students was rated on an 8-point scale by four 'administrators' (actually researchers) as they collected their tickets.

The main finding was that the individuals rated more attractive by the researchers were liked more by their partners, and were more likely to be asked out again, and in fact this did happen. The effect was greater for attractiveness in the eyes of the partner (rather than of the researchers), and the effect was nearly as strong for males as for females. The correlations were as follows:

Table 1   Correlation between rated attractiveness of subjects and ratings by their partners

	Females	Males
liking by partner	.44	.36
partner wanted to date again	.39	.31
liking and physical attractiveness as judged by partner	.78	.69

A number of other variables were assessed, such as examination grades, but physical attractiveness was by far the strongest predictor.

It was predicted that subjects would like their partners more if they were of similar attractiveness to themselves, but this was not found to be the case.

This is an impressively realistic study, with very clear results. However it only studied the very first stage of courtship, and other research has found that physical attractiveness is less important at later stages.

3   The origins and development of relationships

The three key variables in friendship are proximity (or frequency of meeting), similarity (in interests and values, not personality) and rewardingness. All three variables have been shown to be important in a variety of well-designed studies. Laboratory experiments in which amount of gaze, percentage of smiling, or proximity have been manipulated have shown that such non-verbal signals are seen as friendly and lead to the sender being liked more (Argyle, 1988). In an early quasi-experimental field study by Newcomb (1961) two groups of 17 students were accommodated in free halls of residence; after 15 weeks 58 per cent of those with initially similar attitudes chose each other as friends, compared with only 25 per cent of those with dissimilar attitudes. There are some interesting complications about the causes of liking, for example proximity works for students, who have a great deal in common, but not for many neighbours, since they do not. And although we have found that non-verbal signals have more impact on liking than initially equated verbal ones (Argyle, 1988), Ellis and Beattie (1986) argued that more effective verbal moves like compliments and self-disclosure might alter this finding. The implication of a lot of this research is that potential friends, who are similar, available, and often rewarding, may be found at work, but if this is no good they may be found by 'joining a club in your neighbourhood'. A study by Willmott (1987) showed that clubs are indeed important, especially for middle class individuals (Table 2).

Table 2   Where friends come from

	Average number of friends		
	Middle class	White collar	Working class
Work friends	4.72	3.15	2.51
Childhood or school friends	3.10	1.56	1.34
Friends met through clubs, churches, leisure etc	2.68	0.66	1.08
Neighbours who became friends	1.99	1.59	1.80
Ex-university or polytechnic	1.76	-	-

Source: Willmott, 1987

I have recently found that in some kinds of clubs the relationships reported are very close and supportive; for example, 37 per cent of church members said that their friendships at church were closer than their other friendships, a finding yet to be accounted for (Argyle, 1996).

Self-disclosure is important in forming a close relationship; it is a sign that the other is trusted. It has been found that people who say that they are 'lonely' often spend a lot of time with their friends, but do not talk about sufficiently intimate things. Love, which sometimes leads to marriage, has similar origins. Walster et al. explored the role of physical attractiveness, as shown in Box 1 above.

4   Theories of relationships

There are several important theories about relationships, and all have been tested by rigorous methods, though all have their problems — sociobiology, attachment theory and attribution theory for example. Here we will look at experimental tests of theories based on reinforcement. It is well established that we like others who are rewarding, verbally, non-verbally or by being helpful; the most popular individuals are the most rewarding in these ways (Jennings, 1951). Many experiments have shown that subjects like other people who reward them, or who are present when they are rewarded by someone else, or even if they meet in a pleasant room! Reinforcement was once believed to be the key factor in all interpersonal attraction (for example Clore, 1977). This principle has been widely used in marital therapy and other social skills training. However there are some relationships where reinforcement seems less important. As we saw above, 'communal' relationships like romantic love have a strong altruistic component, and those involved attend to the other's needs rather than their own rewards. Another apparent exception is kinship, which seems to survive for decades with little reinforcement.

Exchange theory is an elaboration of reinforcement: the main hypotheses are that people try to maximize their gains and minimize their costs in relationships, that partners will reciprocate the rewards delivered, and that they will stay in a relationship if the balance of rewards over costs is thought to be above that likely to be obtained in any alternative relations available, taking into account the costs of the transfer. While this theory has been widely used as a framework for thinking and research about relationships, it has proved very difficult to test satisfactorily. And the issue of the costs of friendship may be a problem for this theory. Hays (1985) carried out a longitudinal study of college friendships and found that although rewards increased, ratings of friendship were also positively correlated with the costs incurred, and that this correlation increased as the friendships progressed. Friendship closeness correlated with rewards *plus* costs, not rewards *minus* costs. And there is the problem of the altruistic aspect of close relationships, as we have seen.

Another derivative of reinforcement thinking is equity theory, which says that we will be satisfied by and remain in a relationship if we see it as fair, in the sense that we are receiving the same ratio of rewards in relation to inputs as the other; an input might be properties or behaviour such as income, beauty, housework, etc. The problem here is that contra-dictory findings have been obtained in different studies. However in Box 2 we show the results of one of the most carefully conducted ones, which obtained the predicted results for women but not for men.

BOX 2   Equity and relationship satisfaction

Van Yperen and Buunk (1990) carried out a longitudinal study of 736 individuals, including 259 couples who had been married for some time; their average age was 39 and 70 per cent had children. A single global measure of equity was obtained from one question answered on a 7-point scale, relationship satisfaction from an 8-item scale. As Figure 1 shows, there was some correlation between the two at the same points in time, especially for women. As predicted, satisfaction was greater for the equitably treated than for those who thought they were over- or under-benefiting, though the effect of over-benefiting was only found for women. A cross-lagged correlation analysis found that equity at time 1 predicted satisfaction at time 2 more than the reverse, though this was only significant for women.

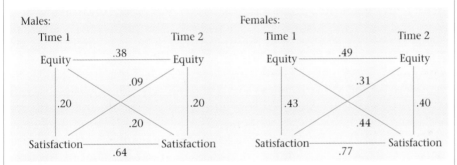

Figure 1   *Model for the effect of equity, assessed by the Hatfield Global Measure, on relationship satisfaction, for males (n = 148) and females (n = 155)*

It was predicted that equity would increase with time, but it did not. It was expected that the global equity score would correlate with the sum of perceived equity over 24 different areas, but there was little relationship: equity was not assessed by counting rewards and costs. The main contributors to feelings of global equity were assessment of relative commitment to the relationship, sociability, inattentiveness, and unfaithfulness. Twice as many women as men felt underbenefited, and more men than women felt overbenefited. And as we showed above, equity does more for women's satisfaction than men's.

This is one of the best studies of equity theory, and it confirms some of the main ideas. However the theory seems to work better for women, and there are some problems about the measurement of equity.

5   The components of relationships

I and my co-workers have found it useful to look at relationships as social systems, rather like games, with their special rules, skills and moves (Argyle and Henderson, 1985). This could be looked at as another 'theory' of relationships, though it is not a rival to the others, rather it deals with other aspects of relationships. It has proved very useful when training people for relationships, since these are the features which they need to understand. Normally we are not consciously aware of these things, but in order to train people it is necessary to raise their awareness, at least for the time being, though they usually cease to think about them once they have learnt how to cope successfully. When we look at the components of different relationships it becomes clear that they are not all the same. For example the rules for close relationships like love and marriage are the opposite of some of those for work relationships, which prevent rather than encourage closeness.

Activities, like the moves in a game, go a long way to describing relationships. We know that neighbours for example speak to each other frequently, give each other a lot of minor help, but rarely visit one another for a meal or drink. Kin on the other hand meet more rarely, especially middle class ones who tend to live at a distance, but are prepared to give really serious help. These studies consist of statistical comparisons of individuals in different relationships, who live at different distances, for example, and fall short of being experimental. We did however compare the activities of work mates of four degrees of closeness and found that the closer ones helped and cooperated more over the work, and talked about it, but they also engaged in a lot of joking, games, gossip and fooling about (Argyle and Henderson, 1985). In marriage, one of the most common and characteristic activities is watching television (Argyle and Henderson, 1985), and watching television in the family sitting room has become a central part of family life, certainly one that takes up a great deal of time. Another very common marital activity we found was having arguments, and indeed conflict is another feature of marriage. We discuss the activities shared by friends later; these turn out to be very enjoyable.

Rules are behaviours which it is generally agreed should be followed, in a game or in a relationship; sometimes there are sanctions for not following them. They normally develop in order to solve problems; the rule of the road was devised to prevent collisions. We have found that every relationship has a set of informal rules, which are widely accepted in the culture, reflecting the nature and problems of each one; for neighbours there are rules about privacy, noisy pets and children, and boundaries. Work relations need rules about cooperation. There are even rules of apparently unruly situations such as fighting among women (Campbell, 1981). And the rules for the same relationship are rather different in Japan and Hong Kong. What happens when the rules are broken? Here we can collect stronger data, though not quite experimental, to find out whether the rules are of any real importance. We studied a sample of lost friendships and asked whether this had been because one of the friends broke one of our friendship rules. The results are shown in Table 3.

Table 3 Friendship rules and reasons for break-up of friendships

	Moderately or very important in breaking up friendship Percentages	Slightly important in breaking up friendship Percentages
Being jealous or critical of your other relationships	57	22
Discussing with others what was said in confidence with him/her	56	19
Not volunteering help in time of need	44	23
Not trusting or confiding in you	44	22
Criticizing you in public	44	21
Not showing positive regard for you	42	34
Not standing up for you in your absence	39	28
Not being tolerant of your other friends	38	30
Not showing emotional support	37	25
Nagging you	30	25

It can be seen that 'third party rules' were particularly important, for example being jealous or not keeping confidences (Argyle and Henderson, 1984). This is because friends come not one at a time but in whole networks, and networks have to be handled with skill.

Skills. To make friends, to attract a partner, or to stay married, needs social skill, and this involves more than knowledge or understanding, it requires the capacity to perform them, just as driving a car or sports skills do. Indeed the analogy with such motor skills has been very illuminating: both require the delivery of skilled actions, perception of the effects produced, the capacity to take corrective action, and both kinds of skill can be trained in a similar way. These skills can be discovered by comparing those who are successful and those who are not. Those who are socially isolated and have no friends are found to be very unrewarding, have poor non-verbal communication, and little conversational power. Some of the social skills of marriage are being rewarding, being good at negotiating and being prepared to compromise when there is disagreement. There are some more intricate skills about sequencing — not engaging in 'negative reciprocity' and avoiding cycles of interaction which regularly end in rows. The skills thus located can be included in training courses, and if these work this is further evidence that the right skills have been found.

An example of research on social skills is provided by Argyle and Lu's finding (Box 3) that extraverts have good assertiveness skills, and this is part of the explanation of their happiness.

BOX 3   The role of social skills in relationships

Argyle and Lu (1990) had already confirmed that there is a strong relationship between happiness and extraversion; the study reported here was designed to find out why. It was predicted that it might be because extraverts possess some social skills which enable them to manage their relationships better.

The subjects were 63 adults, average age 38. A measure of happiness and several self-report measures of social skills were given at time 1 and again 4 months later. Multiple regressions were calculated to see whether happiness at time 2 could be predicted from happiness and various social skills at time 1. As is shown in Figure 2, extraversion taken alone predicted happiness at time 2 (r = .39), but if assertiveness was taken into account this fell to r = .28. Extraversion also predicted assertiveness (r = .49) and this in turn predicted happiness. It was concluded that the effect of extraversion on happiness is partly due to the assertiveness of extraverts.

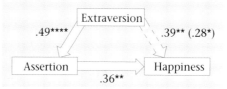

Figure 2 Assertion as a mediator of the extraversion — happiness relation. (Note that the figure in the parenthesis is the reduced coefficient when the mediator is present.)

This study is given as an example of a popular design — longitudinal with multiple regression, and a simple example of path analysis, showing the chain of causation.

Ideas and beliefs. People do not fall in love unless they have learnt about love, from Hollywood films or Mills and Boon novels. And the nature of love and marriage in Europe now is quite different from what it was in the last century, or is today in India and Japan. Marriage in the West now involves more equality, companionship, shared friends and leisure, more conversation, than before. People cannot make friends unless they know what friendship is. La Gaipa and Wood (1981) found that a group of disturbed adolescent girls who had no friends had not understood that friendship involved loyalty, commitment and concern for the other. 'Mateship' in Australia requires further degrees of all these. There is a lot to understand about relationships; we have seen some examples, that friends come in networks, that marriage involves a lot of conflict, for example.

6   The effects of relationships

Happiness. All relationships produce happiness, but especially marriage, as many studies have shown. There are shorter term benefits too. In a study by Larson (1990), subjects were paged electronically on many random occasions, cueing them to fill in self-report scales. They were most happy when with friends, followed by being with family and least happy when alone. There are various explanations for this. Friends often engage in enjoyable leisure activities when together, and they smile a lot and exchange other positive non-verbal signals.

Mental health. Close relationships are particularly important for mental health; social support has a 'buffering' effect on stress. This was shown in a classic study, often replicated, by Brown and Harris (1978) in South London. Those women who had experienced stressful life events were much less likely to be depressed if they had a partner with whom they could discuss their problems (Table 4).

Table 4   Depression, stress and social support (% depressed)

	Support		
	high	mid	low
Percentage women who had stressful event	10	26	41
Percentage women with no such events	1	3	4

Source: Brown and Harris, 1978

This study illustrates the process of 'buffering', whereby social support comes into operation when there is stress to be dealt with.

Health. A number of large-scale longitudinal studies have been carried out, of which the one by Berkman and Syme (Box 4) is one of the best.

BOX 4 The effect of relationships on mortality

Berkman and Syme (1979) carried out a celebrated study of the effects of relationships on health. The data here are for 4,725 adults in Alameda County, USA, all married and aged between 30 and 69. At Time 1 their health was assessed, together with ratings of satisfaction in four areas of social support — marriage, close friends and kin, church and other groups and organizations. Nine years later only one variable was assessed — how many had died.

Mortality was less for those with all four kinds of social support, but especially from marriage and from close friends and kin. A single index of network support was constructed, giving more weight to these more intimate relationships. The figure shows the effects of greater or lesser degrees of network support on mortality.

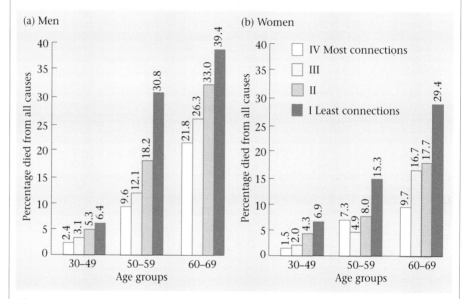

Figure 3 *Social networks and mortality*

(Source: Berkman and Syme, 1979)

Further analysis found that the effect of networks was greater for women. And networks affected death from several main causes — heart disease, strokes, cancer and others. The apparent effect of social relationships could not be explained by class differences, or by differences in health practices such as use of alcohol, smoking, obesity or exercise, nor by differences in initial health, which were all controlled for.

This study has been replicated many times, not always with such strong effects. One criticism was that the initial health assessment was based on self-report; however other studies with objective measures have found much the same.

Conflict. As well as benefits there can also be a lot of conflict and distress in relationships. There is a lot of conflict in marriage, in parent-child relationships — particularly with adolescents, between superiors and subordinates, and between siblings. Although marriage is the greatest source of satisfaction it is also the greatest source of conflict (Argyle and Furnham, 1983). The reason is that there are so many things that need to be decided when people live in close proximity. About one marriage in three breaks up, and 28 per cent of couples have hit each other. We found that arguing and disagreeing were among the most characteristic marital activities. The solution to these conflicts has been indicated already — keep to the rules and acquire the necessary skills.

Social skills training is widely used to train lonely people to make friends, for marital therapy, for training supervisors, and for training parents. This is done by role-playing, with video-playback, modelling from films, and by educational methods. The results on the whole have been very successful; the main problem is finding which are the best skills to teach in the first place. This will vary with culture, class and history, so that there needs to be continuing experimental research to find out (Argyle and Henderson, 1985).

References

Argyle, M. (1988) *Bodily Communication*, London, Methuen (2nd edition).

Argyle, M. (1996) *The Psychology of Leisure*, London, Routledge.

Argyle, M. and Furnham, A. (1983) 'Sources of satisfaction and conflict in long-term relationships', *Journal of Marriage and the Family*, 45, pp. 481–93.

Argyle, M. and Henderson, M. (1984) 'The rules of friendship', *Journal of Social and Personal Relationships,* 1, pp. 481–93.

Argyle, M. and Henderson, M. (1985) *The Anatomy of Relationships*, London, Penguin.

Argyle, M. and Lu, L. (1990) 'Happiness and social skills', *Personality and Individual Differences,* 11, pp. 1255–61.

Berkman, L. S. and Syme, S. L. (1979) 'Social networks, host resistance, and mortality', *American Journal of Epidemiology,* 109, pp. 186–204.

Brown, G. W. and Harris, T. (1978) *Social Origins of Depression,* London, Tavistock.

Campbell, A. (1981) *Girl Delinquents,* Oxford, Blackwell.

Clark, M. S. (1986) 'Evidence for the effectiveness of manipulation of communal and exchange relationships', *Personality and Social Psychology Bulletin,* 12, pp. 414–25.

Clore, G. L. (1977) 'Reinforcement and affect in attraction' in Duck, S. (ed.) *Theory and Practice in Interpersonal Attraction,* London, Academic Press.

Ellis, A. and Beattie, G. (1986) *The Psychology of Language and Communication,* London, Weidenfeld and Nicholson.

Hays, R. B. (1985) 'A longitudinal study of friendship development', *Journal of Personality and Social Psychology,* 48, pp. 909–24.

Jennings, H. H. (1951) *Leadership and Isolation,* New York, Longmans Green.

La Gaipa, J. J. and Wood, H. D. (1981) 'Friendship in disturbed adolescents' in Duck, S. and Gilmour, R. (eds) *Personal Relationships, vol. 3 Personal Relationships in Disorder*, London, Academic Press.

Larson, R. W. (1990) 'The solitary side of life: an examination of the time people spend alone from childhood to old age', *Development Review,* 10, pp. 155–83.

Newcomb, T. M. (1961) *The Acquaintance Process,* New York: Holt, Reinhart and Winston.

Noller, P. (1984) *Nonverbal Communication and Marital Interaction,* Oxford, Pergamon.

Van Yperen, N. W. and Buunk, J. P. (1990) 'A longitudinal study of equity and satisfaction in intimate relationships', *European Journal of Social Psychology,* 20, pp. 287–309.

Walster, E., Aronson, V., Abrams, D, and Rottman, L. (1966) 'Importance of physical attractiveness in dating behaviour', *Journal of Personality and Social Psychology,* 4, pp. 508–16.

Willmott, P. (1987) *Friendship Networks and Social Support*, London, Policy Studies Institute.

Reading D
A humanistic approach to relationships

by Richard Stevens

1 A psychology for living

I have always been interested in psychology for the insights it might offer into the experience of life and for the potential it might have for providing some guidance in the ways in which we live. This interest naturally led me to humanistic psychology for it has been the only psychological perspective to make such concerns a central feature of its approach. The psychologists who founded the movement in the late 1950s did so because they believed that the prevailing approaches of the time, behaviourism and psychoanalysis, were abstract and remote from real-life experience. They wanted to make psychology more relevant to the experience of being – to feelings of love and sadness, of fear and desire, of being creative and spontaneous, of excitement and anxiety, affection and responsibility; in short to make it relevant to the emotions and awareness of living.

There was much excitement in those early days at the prospect of exploring the actuality of experience in a disciplined way. Although it might be argued that the impact of humanistic psychology on mainstream psychology has been more limited than its founders would have hoped, there is little question that its ideas and values have radically influenced the practice of psychotherapy and counselling and have changed the ways more generally in which we think both about ourselves and relationships. It still has much to offer, I believe, today. Unlike experimental psychology, it has not filled journals with reports of research, for the vagaries and the subtleties of real-life experience do not readily lend themselves to investigation by the methods of science. While humanistic psychologists have produced excellent research studies (Carl Rogers is perhaps the prime example), the importance of their contribution is more to do with providing ideas to stimulate us to become more aware of and think about ourselves and others, and techniques to help us to change and live more fulfilling lives. This is in line with a fundamental assumption of humanistic psychology, that people are not fixed by the situation of their birth or the style of their upbringing or surrounding culture but that any one of us is potentially capable of self-directed *personal growth*. A central focus of these ideas and techniques for awareness, change and personal growth has been on the ways in which we relate to each other. Relationships have always been at the heart of the humanistic approach. Most humanistic techniques for growth involve sharing and relating either in a group context or one to one with another member of the group or with a counsellor, or a friend. It is through the deep experience of relating with others that we become more aware of ourselves and more open to growth.

I experienced the humanistic style of relating at first hand when I went to Montreal in the 1970s. The initial purpose of my visit had been to attend the conference of the American Psychological Association (APA). I discovered that immediately following this was 'Consciousness 2000', the annual convention of the Association for Humanistic Psychology (AHP) and I stayed on for it. The difference could not have been more striking. In place of the several thousand, busy, self-contained and aloof participants at the APA conference were people who were far more open to each other, prepared to connect and to be direct about their feelings and thoughts. The humanists appeared to live their psychology whereas the APA participants could have been from any professional background or discipline, biologists or engineers. It seemed to me at the time, and still does to me now, that if psychology has understanding of relevance to the human condition then it must surely affect the ways we experience and conduct our lives.

In addition to the concept of personal growth, there are two other fundamental ideas which underpin the humanistic psychologist's model of the person. One is the importance of *subjective experience*. To understand another person, you have to understand how they experience themselves and their world, however difficult this may be. The other is that each person is *unique*. Each of us has a particular biological endowment, a particular personal history and social network which have helped to make us uniquely what we are. I have found these humanistic principles (that is, the emphasis on the actuality of personal experience, the assumption that we are capable of personal growth, and the acknowledgement of our uniqueness) to be of great value in life and for relationships in particular. In the next section, I will show how they can be applied in one-to-one personal relationships like close friendship or love. Subsequently, I will extend this discussion to the value of applying the humanistic approach to relationships more generally.

2 Intimate relationships

A key feature of being a person is subjective experience. If we meet, I experience you and you experience me. In a relationship, we are both aware of the other as an experiencing person. I know that you perceive and have feelings about me and, what is more, I know that you know that I do; and of course the same is true for you. This complex interaction between two experiencing persons in a relationship is what we call *intersubjectivity*. This makes it clear that a relationship (even a brief interaction) is not just a simple, two-way communication flow. At the very least, a relationship is potentially unpredictable for each of the participants because it is a function of them both. This can make it exciting (or scary): at the very best it can be wonderful.

One problem with our awareness of the fact that we live in an essentially private personal consciousness is that it can generate a sense of aloneness or separateness from others. This is what is sometimes referred to as *existential isolation*. This is not the loneliness which comes from the need to be with people, but awareness of, as Yalom has expressed it, the 'unbridgeable gulf between oneself and any other being' (Yalom, 1980, p. 355). Erich Fromm (1957) has suggested that the experience of existential isolation generates profound anxiety from which we seek to escape. One important potential of relationships is that, because they offer the possibility of connecting with another person's world of experience, they offer us a means to do so. However, as most of us have experienced, problems in achieving intimate connection can arise precisely because a relationship involves inter-relating two unique subjective worlds. One problem is understanding the other. Laing (1972) has written some elegant poems on the knots which people can get into because of their misplaced interpretations about what their partner is feeling. Our very uniqueness means we have our particular interpretative biases related to our cultural background, personal history, personality or cognitive style. We may, for example, too easily see rejection or criticism, even in cases where none is intended, for human beings have an extraordinary and imaginative facility for re-interpreting the world to fit what they expect to find.

For a relationship with its intersubjectivity to work well, *good communication* is essential. For the humanistic psychologist this means that the partners need to be capable of sharing what each other feels and thinks about what is going on. How can this be achieved? This is where humanistic psychologists such as Carl Rogers (1951) have provided such useful guidelines. Although I shall illustrate these in the context of intimate relationships as this is where they can be seen to good effect, the broad principles can be applied more generally.

One problem that can arise in attempts to resolve conflict in a relationship is that there is a joint attempt to define 'reality' or what 'actually happened'. (For example, a couple might argue over a quarrel they had the previous night; 'It's the fact you don't care which upset me!' 'But I do care!' Perhaps you know the kind of thing.) The humanistic approach is to acknowledge that the only reality here is *the feelings of both the participants*. Even though these may not have coincided, this is really 'what went on'. Any attempt to establish who is 'right' is merely an exercise in power rather than a clarification of what happened. It is also counterproductive in that it is quite likely to leave one partner resentful at having their reality defined for them, and therefore potentially corrosive to the relationship.

Strategies for effective communication between partners can be derived from Rogers' work in psychotherapy. Here he has developed (Rogers, 1951) the widely-used technique of non-directive counselling. This works on the principle that what is critical in psychotherapeutic counselling is to provide a way for clients to feel comfortable and free enough psychologically to say what they really think and feel about themselves and their situation. Then by talking about and so becoming more aware of their own feelings, clients may come to a greater understanding of their situation and of how to develop and move on.

The same basic principles can be applied to relationships. The humanistic position on relationships is that each person is the expert on his or her own feelings. The important goal here is for each to share his or her subjective experience with the other and to really understand how their partner feels and thinks about what is going on. In this way their relationship can grow in a genuinely fulfilling way for both. The best strategy for achieving this is for each partner in turn to allow the other to express how he or she sees and feels about the situation, and simply try to understand and appreciate this, without immediately commenting, criticizing or attempting to correct. (Though of course the one listening can come back afterwards and express what he or she felt on hearing their partner's account.) The partner who listened first then in turn tries to express in similar style what he or she is thinking and feeling. To encourage the sharing of feelings it is necessary to suspend judgement to avoid evaluation, to create a psychological climate of what Rogers has called 'non-evaluative warmth'. Usually if this can be achieved, differences dissolve or feelings change because these often rest on a failure to appreciate how one's partner sees and feels about the situation. Even where they do not (for, of course, there may be a genuine difference of view) then even here, the result is that each person gets to know their partner better. There will be less scope for projecting unrealistic images onto each other.

Although this can sound simple on paper, it is not of course so easy in practice. If emotions run high, it can be difficult to offer non-evaluative warmth. A cooling-off period may be called for before real communication can begin. It not only requires commitment to the relationship but also the agreement and cooperation of both partners to see the value of and to go along with this approach. It may take courage to listen to and appreciate aspects of your partner which you may find disturbing. Courage will also be needed to take the risk to be honest and authentic about what you feel and who you are, particularly when this may not be to your partner's taste. And genuine care and love are vital if you are to accept your partner for what she or he is, and not for what you would like him or her to be.

One suggestion here is not only to try this kind of communication in response to a conflict, but to set a particular time say each week for each of you to take turns at expressing to the other, in the ways indicated above, what you are currently feeling 'here and now' about the relationship between you.

As we noted earlier, the humanistic approach asserts the possibility of personal growth. This idea rests on a model of the person as agent. In other words, people are regarded as being capable of acting on their world. They can change aspects of it and initiate things. They have, to some degree at least, the ability to choose what they do. A relationship is about two (or more) agents in interaction. Both can make choices and through their actions and words influence what happens between them and their partner. So the relationship between them is not fixed but is open to change. Nor is it the product of either partner but of them both. Although each person may bring to it particular needs, hopes and expectations, the humanist position is that a relationship is a dynamic, ongoing process of *mutual creation*. For a fulfilling relationship both partners need to participate in this process. This requires that both of them try to communicate their feelings and acknowledge the reality of the feelings of their partner; it involves being open to and exploring together different forms which the relationship may take; even experimenting with different styles of being and living together and monitoring together the feelings these evoke.

The third aspect of the humanistic approach to intimate relationships is to acknowledge the uniqueness of oneself and one's partner. In his book *The Art of Loving*, Fromm argues that a relationship is only of real value if it does not seek to deny the existential reality of our separateness in the ultimate individuality and uniqueness of the partners involved. For him, the solution to human separateness lies in what he calls 'productive love' where 'the paradox occurs that two beings become one and yet remain two' (Fromm, 1957, p. 21). For Fromm then, love consists in the union of two people without the loss of their individuality or 'integrity as persons'. This implies the responsibility to try to be aware of your own style and needs, and to be alert to how these may influence your way of relating to your partner. It means taking responsibility for your own actions and the effect that these may have on the relationship: not, however, trying to take responsibility for your partner (this, although it may often appear in the guise of care, is too often a strategy for control, and a failure to pay due respect for the agency of the other). Fromm summarizes the basic elements of love as 'care, responsibility, respect and knowledge' (1957, p. 25).

As partners are unique, so each relationship is also unique. There are no set prescriptions for the form a relationship should take. What I have described here is the humanist ideal. But the humanistic perspective recognizes that relationships can take different forms. An important assumption, as we have seen, is to accept the reality of people's feelings (while acknowledging that these may be able to change). There may be good reasons for sustaining a relationship in which the approach described here would not be possible or appropriate. An open style of relating requires that both partners want and are able to participate. It may be that this is not true of one or other of the two people in a relationship yet it may be necessary for them to stay together because they are still caring for their children, for example, or because, if they part, they fear they might always remain alone. In such cases, collusion (that is, where both partners tacitly agree to avoid potentially conflictful or painful areas) may be the best way to keep their relationship going.

Good relationships can take different forms but the humanist view is that the most fulfilling ones come through effective communication, through awareness and acceptance of the uniqueness of the other and the reality of what you both feel, and through the idea of a relationship as a mutual creation. And even where the potential for connecting in such ways seems very limited, it may well be worth a try.

3 Other kinds of relationship

The preceding discussion has been about intimate relationships between close friends and lovers. In effect, such principles are usually more easily applied between friends than between lovers. Because friends are less likely than partners to be living together, there is less potential for needs coming into conflict. Expectations in relation to friends are likely to be lower than those in respect of partners. And because the sexual link is absent (or is in less intense form) jealousy is less likely to occur. If your friend has met up with a new and exciting potential sexual partner, you are more likely to be overjoyed than upset. Intimate friendship is an arena where needs and feelings can be expressed freely and without inhibition. The measure of close friendship is the degree to which the friends can be open and themselves – the essence of the humanistic prescription.

Within *families* it may be harder to apply the humanistic approach. Relationships are embedded in the emotional patterns of the past and children may be unwilling to take the requisite responsibility and interest. But even here some degree of application of the principles is usually possible and beneficial.

With *strangers*, the humanistic style of relating can also apply. For it represents an attitude, an approach to being with the other: being prepared to be open when this is appropriate, being responsive to the other as a person (acknowledging their own way of experiencing and capacity for agency), and with an interest in establishing authentic communication to whatever extent the situation makes this appropriate and desirable. This was my experience at the AHP conference in Montreal with people I had never met before.

Because of the power differences and hierarchical and manipulative structures which are often in place, *work* may seem a more difficult arena to apply humanistic ideals, but even here they have an important place. Developing effective sharing techniques can often help with the problems that occur between colleagues because of a failure to understand what the other is thinking and feeling about a particular situation. It can also help reduce the alienation that can come when communication is blocked or has broken down. The humanistic psychologist called into an organization as a consultant is likely to place priority on the objective of developing more authentic communication (see, for example, Rogers, 1970). Although situations where an employee knows they are being evaluated are likely to limit the ability to be open (one reason why counselling and appraisal do not make good bed-fellows), it can be helpful even here for a manager to be open at least about the content and context of his or her assessment. The humanistic approach, however, would be to acknowledge the distortions produced by hierarchical structures, and to try to move towards more open and democratic ones in which open relating is more possible and where the potentials and feelings of individuals have more scope for productive expression (Maslow, 1965; Rogers, 1970). An example of this applied to the development of professional skills is the peer assessment groups designed by Heron (1979) where colleagues get together to set personal goals and share feedback and assessments.

4 Techniques and research

Much research in psychology rests on the assumption that behaviour is determined and the researcher aims to discover what the determinants are. While, humanistic psychologists do not deny the influence of biology, early development and social context on the ways in which we relate to each other, their emphasis, as we have seen is on human agency, choice and the capacity for self-directed change. A lot of their effort has been directed at developing techniques to facilitate this. We noted Rogers' approach of non-directive counselling. He was also instrumental in developing encounter group work where participants come together, often for many days, to share experiences in as open a way as possible (see Rogers, 1970). This kind of approach has also been tried in the development of multiracial communities and in facilitating communication between groups from different cultures. Thus Rogers set up a workshop designed to reduce international tension in which policymakers and opinion leaders from different countries were encouraged to relate to each other in a person-centred and humanistic way (Rogers, 1987). So the thrust of humanistic psychology has been to provide methods, concepts and principles based on analysis of the nature of the human condition to help people (and groups) to develop their capacity to relate to others.

Humanistic psychologists have also pursued more orthodox research. Some of this has been directed to assessing the effects of the techniques they have employed. Thus Rogers and his colleagues have made numerous carefully designed studies of the effects of counselling and the processes underlying it. Lieberman et al. (1973) carried out an intensive study of the effects of different kinds of encounter group, using a variety of measurements and assessments by both observers and the participants themselves. Another approach has been the phenomenological analysis of aspects of relating. So Register and Henley (1992) collected accounts from 20 volunteers of their experience of intimacy. They carefully analysed these, producing a narrative digest of each one and noting significant themes and statements. The final analysis yielded a set of themes which seemed to be integral to the experience of intimacy. These included an intensified sense of presence, the removal of interpersonal boundaries, the creation of something new through merging, and the paradoxical sense that intimate connection was both a surprise and yet destined.

Perhaps the most interesting work has been the exploration of alternatives. Rogers, in his book *Becoming Partners* for example, has presented a fascinating study of marriage and alternatives to it (Rogers, 1973). This study was based on direct accounts of being in different kinds of relationship taken from counselling sessions as well as from interviews and written submissions. These constitute, as he puts it, 'a series of slices, pictures, perceptions – of relationships, breakdowns, restructurings – in a wide variety of partnerships ... highly intimate and meaningful accounts of the man-woman relationship as it is actually lived – with all its tragedies, dull plateaux, ecstatic moments or periods, and instance after instance of exciting growth' (ibid, p. 14). Such research essentially provides people with the material to use themselves in the process of their own learning and self-development. The understanding and insights yielded by the intimate pictures of different relationships in themselves constitute the 'data for learning'.

> To see all the vicissitudes of such unions from the perspective of the person who is living the experience achieves what are for me several important ends. Such material does not push itself on the reader, saying 'This is the way you must be; it does not point with alarm saying, 'Don't go down this path'; it does not come to clear conclusions; it is very simply a person or a couple saying to the reader, 'Here is the way it is and was for *me* or *us* – and perhaps you can learn from this some things which will help you in making your own changing, risky choices'.
>
> (ibid, 1973, p. 12)

5   In conclusion

I value the humanistic approach to relationships because I think that its model of the person with its emphasis on subjective experience, agency and uniqueness makes sense in terms of my experience. To understand relationships, we do need to take into account the importance of lived experience and the meanings people attribute to their partners and themselves. And we need to acknowledge that we can only get at this by encouraging people to share with us what they think and feel. I have seen how people undergoing humanistic growth work have changed in their attitudes and the way they approach relationships: how they become less demanding in their expectations, more aware of and able to articulate their own feelings, more accepting of the other and open to the different forms relationships might take. (For a personal account of such changes see Extract 1.)

I believe also that it is important for psychology to acknowledge the human capacity for agency and therefore the relative 'openness' of the human condition: that people and relationships are not just pre-ordained but are capable of self-directed change. I applaud the goal of humanistic psychology here – not just to seek understanding but to provide the material and techniques to stimulate and support people in the skills and process of relating to others.

Extract 1

This is an extract from a woman's account of personal change stimulated by humanistic ideas, counselling and group-work.

I lived 29 years following everybody else's rules and norms in all the structures of my life: family, peers, social circles, education, work and love relationships. My whole sense of being was through someone else: how I was seen, accepted and loved by my parents, my friends, teachers, co-workers, lovers. Of course I functioned and appeared to be a whole, integrated person to the outside world but my real self was rarely expressed, primarily for lack of reflexive awareness and ultimately for fear of rejection.

These structures were reassuring in a way but a growing sense of frustration and absence of identity was invading me. When I came out of an important eight-year relationship (based on non-met expectations, non-communication and emotional dependency often resulting in sterile conflicts), the first feeling I faced was that of utter panic at the prospect of being 'on my own', without any parameters enabling me to define my self within this new dark infinite-like stretch of life. Loss and void.

Therapy and group encounters helped me to slowly re-discover and re-create my own parameters and fill this vacuum I was experiencing. A new sense of self awareness was being built. A new acceptance of who I was developed, bringing along in the open a sense of self worth not through others for the first time, nor through the therapist, but a genuine ME, far too long neglected and under-estimated, who was longing to express itself and be heard! And also a definite sense of responsibility for my own life which was quite new, exciting and still frightening at times.

Basically, this therapeutic work helped me to envisage relationships in a totally different way. To start with, I don't exist through them any longer. I don't lose myself in the process of developing a relationship. I have learnt to be myself, respect myself, my own experience of situations and at the same time the other's point of view, which is unlikely to be the same. I expect and assume less, that is, I try to communicate how I feel and seek feedback, however hard it is to take sometimes. I also practise giving feedback to others, in a sensitive but truthful way. Communication has become a key word for me. Another key word mentioned before is respect. Respect for yourself and the other. Nobody else is going to feel like I do and I won't feel anybody else's feelings. It is a fact of life, to be mutually acknowledged. Feeling differently about something should not imply being rejected. My 'personal growth' work has also led me to look at my boundaries. How NOT to say 'yes' when I actually want to say 'no' and not to build unnecessary resentment, blaming the other for the consequences. This has been helpful and rewarding, although not easy!

M.H.

References

Fromm, E. (1957) *The Art of Loving*, London, Allen and Unwin.

Heron, J. (1979) *Peer Review Audit,* London, British Postgraduate Medical Foundation.

Laing R. (1972) *Knots*, Harmondsworth, Penguin.

Lieberman, M.A., Yalom, I.D. and Miles, B. (1973) *Encounter Groups: First Facts*, New York, Basic Books.

Maslow, A.H. (1965) *Eupsychian Management – a Journal*, Homewood, Ill., Irwin.

Register, L.M. and Henley, T.B. (1992) 'The phenomenology of intimacy', *Journal of Social and Personal Relationships,* vol. 9, pp. 467–81

Rogers C.R. (1951) *Client-centered Therapy*, New York, Houghton.

Rogers C.R. (1970) *Encounter Groups*, Harmondsworth, Penguin.

Rogers C.R. (1973) *Becoming Partners: Marriage and its Alternatives,* London, Constable.

Rogers, C.R. (1987) 'The Rust workshop', *Journal of Humanistic Psychology*, vol. 26, no. 3, pp. 23–45.

Yalom, I. (1980) *Existential Psychotherapy*, New York, Basic Books.

Reading E
A sociological perspective

by Graham Allan

1   Introduction

The point of engaging in any branch of the social sciences is to generate a better understanding of the basis of social action. At times this is linked to resolving a particular social issue which is causing public concern; at other times the focus is more strictly academic, in the proper sense of this term. Either way, the aim of the social scientist is to explain why social action and relationships are as they are. In researching personal relationships, no matter what the background discipline, the social scientist typically asks such questions as: 'Why are personal ties patterned in the way they are?' 'What shapes them?' 'What holds them together and gives them their order?' 'How, and under what circumstances, does this order change?' Behind these questions lie others. 'To what extent are we free to choose our relationships, not just in terms of personnel, but also in the way we organize and arrange them?' 'Can we shape them as we please? And if so, what factors affect what does please us?' 'Why are we more at ease in some relationships than others?' 'Why do some people attract us while others hold little interest for us?'

Often in our everyday life, the uncritical assumption we make is that we are each active in creating our own personal relationships and are in consequence freely responsible for them. From all the people we meet, we choose which ties are worth giving our energy to, which we want to develop further and which we want to let go. And generally we also assume that how we develop these ties as personal relationships is largely a matter of individual volition and control. Unlike relationships which are rooted in the harsh world of economic and professional life, we construct our personal worlds – our worlds of family and friendship in particular – according to implicit and mutually agreed criteria over which few others have any right of direction. Thus we feel active in constructing our own marriages; we develop relationships with our children which are special to us; we give more attention to some friendships than others.

Yet as soon as such claims are made, we can recognize that their truth is only partial. Yes, we are active in these processes, but there are limits in the extent to which we feel fully in control of them. To paraphrase Karl Marx's famous injunction that men make history, but not in ways of their own choosing, so we all make personal relationships, but not just in ways of our own choosing. We do not generate our ties in a social, economic or, for that matter, psychological vacuum. The ways we do so – the 'choices' we make – are patterned by a wide range of structural constraints over which we as individuals and as dyads are able to exercise only limited control, even if the ideologies we construct about our relationships claim differently. At one level, the way our different relationships are patterned and structured may be 'internal', consequent, say, upon our relational experiences at earlier times – the mode of attachment in infancy or the levels of trust in others we were able to establish in adolescence. Equally though, how we develop relationships will also be influenced by 'external' factors. Thus the social conventions or norms which have been collectively established about appropriate ways of managing relationships will play a part in how we as individuals or dyads 'choose' to develop our personal ties, as will the social and material conditions under which those ties are activated and the competing claims which are made of our diverse personal resources.

It is these concerns which have always interested me and which I want to discuss here: how apparently 'free-floating' personal relationships are not just personal, are not just a matter of preference or choice, are not simply individual constructions. I want to focus on the ways these ties are constrained and consequently patterned by social and economic influences over which those involved have less rather than more control. What is particularly interesting is the ways in which order is imposed on the development of our varied personal relationships without our being conscious that this is happening. Thus from this perspective, the 'choices' we make about our personal relationships are not choices in a simplistic, conventional sense. Rather they are choices which are constrained, 'boxed in', by underlying elements of our social experience and our social circumstances. I take unravelling these processes and showing how the individual is heavily rooted in the social to be the essence of a sociological perspective on personal relationships and as essential to a proper understanding of how such ties develop.

2   Constructing marriages

Let me give a simple example of the type of analysis for which I am arguing, an example that at one and the same time clearly embodies the highly personal and the structural. In contemporary western society, the organization of marriage (and other long-term sexual partnerships) is increasingly seen as an individual matter, becoming less institutionalized over time and more a consequence of private negotiations between the couple involved (Cancian, 1987; Giddens, 1992). While not necessarily the case in other cultures or historical periods, this is certainly the ideology of marriage – the socially legitimated set of beliefs and ideals about how marriage should be, the dominant 'marital blueprint', to use Cancian's (1987) term – which is given most currency by many younger cohorts currently constructing their sexual partnerships. Yet when one examines the outcome of all the negotiations and dialogues which occur, it is evident that most marriages continue to be structured similarly (see for example Mansfield and Collard, 1988). This is not to argue that marriage partners' beliefs about their role in actively constructing their own union are entirely unfounded, nor that marriage is unaltered from previous eras. Couples certainly appear to be more reflexive than in the past about their relationships, they spend more time debating how they would like it to develop. Indeed such reflexive talk is increasingly seen as an inherent element of what sucessful 'coupledom' should be. Yet it is equally evident that many of these individually constructed marriages end up having much in common, with similar 'decisions' being made by each couple about their most appropriate organization and content.

To put this simply, despite the differences that exist, the social and economic contexts within which most marriages are grounded tend to result in their being patterned in broadly similar ways. Thus, while in the earlier phases of couplehood an emphasis is often placed on equality, this appears to give way to a quite marked division of labour once the marriage is established, especially after the birth of any children. Here, differential gender socialization and the assumptions made about the partners' relative nurturing proclivities combine with the realities of a labour market which itself is highly stratified in terms of gender. Despite proclamations to the contrary, the result is generally that husbands and wives contribute differently to the domestic economy and find that the roles they play within their marriage are marked by difference. Notwithstanding changes in the demography of employment, wives continue to carry principal responsibility for domestic organization and routine child care, increasingly combining this with some level of paid work, while husbands have the major responsibility for financial provision (Mansfield and Collard, 1988; Morris, 1990; Brannen and Moss, 1991).

Within this there are, of course, important variations. Some couples strive harder than others to share a wider range of tasks; through being in highly paid jobs some wives are able to make alternative domestic arrangements and protect their careers; unemployment can have a bearing on domestic organization (though see McKee and Bell, 1987 as well as Wheelock, 1990); and so forth. However, what emerges overall is a common pattern of domestic and marital organization which in many respects tends to be set in the early phases of marriage. Decisions – though in many ways the term 'non-decision' seems more appropriate as these issues are so rooted in common-sense understandings and taken for granted perceptions of what is natural and/or inevitable – are made which once set in motion become increasingly difficult to challenge or change. So while wives do become more involved in paid work as children grow older, these changes appear not to undermine in any radical fashion the essential division of labour and responsibilities established earlier in the household.

There may now be fuller discussion and comment on these arrangements than in previous times. Indeed, as noted earlier, it appears that increasingly a reflexive element within coupledom is normatively prescribed. That is, one of the emerging 'rules' of intimacy within marriage and other established relationships is that the couple should share their feelings and debate their relationship. Conventionally, it is wives more than husbands who are more skilled in these forms of intimacy, more willing to engage in such intimate talk and more concerned about the significance of emotional expression within their relationships (see, for example, Duncombe and Marsden, 1993). In this, sharing, emotional support and 'togetherness' have over time taken on different meanings within the context of what counts as a successful 'partnership' – a word whose popularity itself says something about the shifts there have been in the construction of long-term sexual and romantic relationships. The issue to emphasize here is that these emerging ways of constructing intimacy, however imperfectly realized, have a social and cultural impact and not just an individual one. We are each active in constructing our own 'special' relationships, yet we do so in broadly similar forms, each within the confines of our social and economic location, influenced by the currently dominant beliefs and ideologies of romantic love.

3 The social organization of friendship

Although not always so apparent, other forms of personal relationship are also patterned by social, cultural and economic factors, including those which appear to be entirely voluntary and not at all institutionalized. As a classic example, consider friendships, ties which on the surface appear to be freely chosen and of little social consequence or concern. How we manage our friendships, what activities we engage in, who our friends are, all seem to be matters which are individually determined and best understood as the consequence of the interaction developing between those involved. Yet when these relationships are analysed a little more fully, it becomes apparent that, just like marriage, they are shaped in broadly similar ways with different people apparently choosing to develop them along similar lines. With aspects of social location – gender and class, for instance – playing their part, these bonds are just as much social, just as much patterned, as other seemingly 'personal' relationships.

I first became interested in analysing the social patterning of ties like friendship in the early 1970s (see Allan, 1979). At that time, friendship had received rather little attention from social researchers of any background. Psychologists were focusing on attraction, often between strangers in laboratory settings (see Duck and Gilmour, 1981); sociologists occasionally reported the levels of friendship found in occupational or community studies. Even those sociologists concerned with patterns of social integration and/or the breakdown of social solidarity had relatively little to say about friendship. Undoubtedly the most interesting research into friendship then was conducted by anthropologists, generally concerned with demonstrating the significance of informal relationships within a society's broader structural framework. In particular, the work of

Robert Paine (1969) on middle class friendship in industrialized society stood out as especially valuable for its substantive insights and for its theoretical approach.

Paine emphasized the importance of what he termed 'rules of relevancy' and 'standards of equivalency' for analysing the effective boundaries of different types of relationship. 'Rules of relevancy' refer to what is considered permissible within a particular relationship, while 'standards of equivalency' concern the nature of the exchanges which occur within the tie. While exchange patterns within relationships have generated much theoretical and empirical work in psychology especially, it was the notion of rules of relevancy that I found most useful in making comparisons between the social character of friend and kin ties (Allan, 1979). The concept of 'rules' is an obvious one to apply to personal relationships precisely because it does emphasize the routine and regular way in which these ties are organized and patterned, whether the rules are seen as socially or personally framed. Yet, of course, the analogy of rule itself generates difficulties as the rules in question are not fully rules in the normal sense. They are not like the rules of football or chess, for example, where there are either referees to ensure compliance or where the game breaks down as soon as the rules are broken.

Rather, the rules of relevancy within relationships often remain implicit. Forms of social control operate in sustaining them but these are not always recognized as such. Moreover, the rules are emergent rather than fixed or codified with the players themselves playing a part in their creation. Yet the message behind Paine's argument is that friendships, like other relationships, *do* have an order, a form or a shape, which is part of the cultural package of how these relationships are 'done'. As the term 'rules of relevancy' implies, he was especially interested in the boundaries that were constructed around friendships (and by implication other forms of personal relationship); in other words what was included in their remit and what was excluded. Analytically, this allows different types of relationships to be compared and provides a way of looking at the location of relationships within what we might term 'social space'. While these rules of relevancy are generally implicit in any relationship and liable to be modified over time, they are not just constructions about individual ties. They are rooted more widely than this, being based on the general knowledge and common understandings we have about the ways the relationships in question are routinely framed. The individuals involved weave their own pattern, but the character of the cloth on which they do so is socially prescribed.

Thus, for example, one characteristic of middle class friendship is that the relationship is given precedence over any activity it involves. The friendship is defined as being about the solidarity of the people who are friends rather than solely about engaging in common pursuits. Some relationships are bound more clearly by an activity – working together, being members of the same sports club, or whatever – but these relationships are unlikely to be defined as friendships. Relationships which are recognized as friendships are far less likely to be context-specific; they involve a recognition that a range of social activities are relevant to the friendship, even if in practice the tie tends to be restricted to a small number of standard settings. The use of the home is particularly important in 'de-contextualizing' these ties and developing them as friendships. By socializing with others in the home rather than a given external leisure arena, the boundaries of the relationship are extended and the private world opened up. In contrast, working class ties often appear to be developed differently, typically being far more context-specific. Getting to know someone well in one setting does not necessarily lead to activity elsewhere. The tie remains framed by the activity, thereby giving those involved greater control over it. (For a full discussion of these issues, see Allan, 1979; 1989.)

The main point here is that different patterns of friendship emerge in different social and economic circumstances. There is no single model of informal personal relationships, but equally how such relationships are framed is more than an individual matter. But if resources affect the organization of friendship in this way, so too are other aspects of people's lives going to influence the informal ties they develop with others. Here I think it is useful to go back to a concept that was first introduced into the social science literature by Elizabeth Bott in 1957 in her discussion of social networks, but to use it in a somewhat different way. This is the concept of 'immediate social environment'. What I want to suggest is that no one factor influences the way in which an individual's personal relationships are shaped. Rather what matters is the overall context of people's lives, the opportunities they have to develop and service ties like friendships, the resources they have available, the other constraints there are on their time. It is within this overall context, which I think can usefully be termed their immediate social environment, that the patterns of sociability and association emerge. Yes, they make choices about these, but they do so within the contours of the immediate social environment in which they are embedded (Allan, 1989; Allan and Adams, 1989).

So, as discussed above, class position is important in patterning friendships, but it does not act alone. Other structural features, like gender, marital status, phase in the life course, domestic and caring responsibilities, employment patterns, financial circumstances, and the like, also influence the room for manoeuvre individuals have over the construction and maintenance of their friendships. Again simple illustrations will suffice to make the point. Wellman (1985), for example, develops the argument that in Toronto (and by implication elsewhere in the modern world) communities are no longer geographically-bound. Rather each individual is involved in their own 'personal community', their own set of more and less significant relationships which are consequent upon the position of the individual within the social division of labour. However some individuals are far more dependent on the local area for their relationships than others. Their lives are lived at a more local level and their opportunities for developing ties in other spheres are restricted. For example, full-time housewives are tied in to locality and develop their friendships within this context rather more than others. People in employment, on the other hand, are likely to have more dispersed networks and be less dependent on any one context for their sociable ties. Yet still the actual pattern of ties they develop will be influenced by the character of their work and the extent to which it provides a framework for developing particular bonds.

4   Conclusion

In conclusion, what I have tried to show in this Reading is that understanding personal relationships involves more than exploring the dyadic encounters which any relationship entails. Personal relationships are essentially social. They take place within social arenas; they occupy social space; they are framed by social conventions and common understandings. As a result, these relationships are structured by factors which lie outside the dyad. Analysing how these factors impinge on the decisions (and non-decisions) individuals make about their involvement in and their ordering of different relationships is important if they are to be understood fully.

References

Allan, G. (1979) *A Sociology of Friendship and Kinship*, London, Allen & Unwin.

Allan, G. (1989) *Friendship: Developing a Sociological Perspective,* Hemel Hempstead, Harvester-Wheatsheaf.

Allan, G. and Adams, R. G. (1989) 'Aging and the structure of friendship' in Adams, R. G. and Blieszner, R. (eds) *Older Adult Friendship*, Newbury Park, Sage.

Bott, E. (1957) *Family and Social Network,* Tavistock, London.

Brannen, J. and Moss, P. (1991) *Managing Mothers: Dual Earner Households After Maternity Leave,* London, Unwin Hyman.

Cancian, F. (1987) *Love in America,* Cambridge, Cambridge University Press.

Duck, S. and Gilmour, R. (eds) (1981) *Personal Relationships,* London, Academic Press.

Duncombe, J. and Marsden, D. (1993) 'Love and intimacy: the gender division of emotion and "emotion work"', *Sociology,* 27, pp. 221-41.

Giddens, A. (1992) *The Transformation of Intimacy,* Oxford, Polity Press.

McKee, L. and Bell, C. (1987) 'His unemployment, her problem: the domestic and marital consequences of male unemployment' in Allen, S., Waton, A., Purcell, K. and Wood, S. (eds) *The Experience of Unemployment,* Basingstoke, Macmillan.

Mansfield, P. and Collard, J. (1988) *The Beginning of the Rest of Your Life?,* Macmillan, London.

Morris, L. (1990) *The Workings of the Household,* Oxford, Polity Press.

Paine, R. (1969) 'In search of friendship', *Man,* 4, pp. 505-24.

Wellman, B. (1985) 'Domestic work, paid work and net work' in Duck, S. and Perlman, D. (eds) *Understanding Personal Relationships,* London, Sage.

Wheelock, J. (1990) *Husbands at Home,* London, Routledge.

Index

Acknowledgements

Grateful acknowledgement is made to the following sources for permission to reproduce material in this book:

CHAPTER 1: Holland, C. Unpublished Ph.D. Thesis, Open University, © C. Holland.

CHAPTER 2: *Text:* Edelsky, C. (1981) 'Who's got the floor?' *Language in Society,* 10, Cambridge University Press; Shotter, J. (1987) 'The social construction of an "us": problems of accountability and narratology' in Burnett, R., McGhee, P. and Clarke, D. (eds) *Accounting for Relationships: Explanation, Representation and Knowledge,* Methuen & Co; Goffman, E. (1972) *Interaction Ritual: Essays on Face-to-Face Behaviour,* Penguin Books Ltd. *Figures:* Figure 2.1: Scheflen, A. (1964) 'The significance of posture in communication systems, *Psychiatry,* 27, pp. 316-31, Washington School of Psychiatry; Box 2.5: Knapp, M. L. and Hall, J. A. (1992) *Non-Verbal Communication in Human Interaction*, 3rd ed, Copyright © 1992, 1978, 1972 by Holt, Rinehart and Winston, Inc. All rights reserved. *Table:* Table 2.1: Coates, J. and Cameron, D. (1988) *Women in Their Speech Communities: New Perspectives on Language and Sex,* Longman Group UK Ltd.

CHAPTER 3: *Figures:* Figures 3.1 & 3.2: Reprinted from CIBA Foundation Symposium, 33, Brazelton, T. B., Tronick, E., Adamson, L., Als, H. and Wise, S. 'Early mother-infant reciprocity', pp 50-53, copyright 1975 with kind permission from Elsevier Science NL Sara Burgerhartstraat 25, 1055 KV Amsterdam, The Netherlands. *Photographs:* p 7 & p15: From Trevarthen, C. (1980) 'The foundations of inter-subjectivity: development of interpersonal and cooperative understanding' in Olson, D. R. (ed) *The Social Foundations of Language; Essays in Honor of Jerome S. Bruner,* W. W. Norton and Co, courtesy of Professor Colwyn Trevarthen.

CHAPTER 4: Bollas, C. (1987) *The Shadow of the Object: Psychoanalysis of the Unthought Known,* Free Association Books, © Christopher Bollas 1987.

CHAPTER 5: *Text:* Satchell, M. (1995) *Accounts from Ph.D. Research in Psychology,* © M. Satchell; Sharpe, S. (1990) *Voices from Home: Girls Talk About Their Families,* Virago Press. *Figure:* Figure 5.1: Dallos, R. (1990) *Family Belief Systems, Therapy and Change,* Open University Press; Figure 5.2: Carter, E. and McGoldrick, M. (1980) *The Family Life-Cycle: A Framework for Family Therapy,* Gardner Press, Inc; Figure 5.3: Combrink-Graham, L. (1985) 'A developmental model for family systems', *Family Process,* 24, (2).

CHAPTER 6: *Text:* 'Woman tells of double rape ordeal', *The Oxford Mail,* August 1994, Oxford and County Newspapers. *Figures:* Figure 6.1: Klein, R. and Milardo, R. (1993) 'Third party influence on the management of personal relationships' in Duck, S. (ed) *Social Context and Relationships,* p. 67, copyright © 1993 by Sage Publications Inc. Reprinted by permission of Sage Publications Inc; Figure 6.2: Wellman, B. (1992) 'Men in networks, private communities, domestic friendships' in Nardi, P. (ed) *Men's Friendships,* p. 75, copyright © 1992 by Sage Publications Inc. Reprinted by permission of Sage Publications Inc.

CONCLUSION: *Figure:* Figure 3: Berkmam, L. S. and Syme, S. L. (1979) 'Social networks, host resistances and mortality', *American Journal of Epidemiology,* 109, pp. 186-204, Johns Hopkins University; *Tables:* Table 2: Willmott, P. (1987) *Friendship Networks and Social Support,* Policy Studies Institute; Table 4: Brown, G. W. and Harris, T. (1978) *Social Origins of Depression,* Tavistock.

COVER ILLUSTRATION: Kasimir Malevich, Sportsmen, c. 1928–32, oil on canvas, 142 x 164 cm., State Russian Museum, St. Petersburg.